This path-breaking study of Egyptian popular culture provides fresh and vital insights into the long struggle of modern Egypt to define its identity. Dr. Armbrust examines Egyptian television, recorded music, the press, and the cinema. These popular media have broken radically with cultural icons of Egypt's past, while offering ordinary people a way of coming to terms with the clashing values of nationalism, modernity, and Arab classicism. However, since the 1970s, popular culture has also become a site of contestation. The delicate balance between conservative nationalist imagery and a modernist ethic has been increasingly put in question by producers and consumers of the media, reflecting a sense that the representations of modernity do not reflect the experience of Egyptians.

Cambridge Studies in Social and Cultural Anthropology

102

MASS CULTURE AND MODERNISM IN EGYPT

Cambridge Studies in Social and Cultural Anthropology

The monograph series Cambridge Studies in Social and Cultural Anthropology publishes analytical ethnographies, comparative works and contributions to theory. All combine an expert and critical command of ethnography and a sophisticated engagement with current theoretical debates.

A list of books in the series will be found at the end of the volume.

MASS CULTURE AND MODERNISM IN EGYPT

WALTER ARMBRUST

CAMBRIDGE
UNIVERSITY PRESS

Published by the Press Syndicate of the University of Cambridge
The Pitt Building, Trumpington Street, Cambridge CB2 1RP
40 West 20th Street, New York, NY 10011-4211, USA
10 Stamford Road, Oakleigh, Melbourne 3166, Australia

First published 1996

Printed in Great Britain at the University Press, Cambridge

A catalogue record for this book is available from the British Library

Library of Congress cataloguing in publication data

Armbrust, Walter.
Mass culture and modernism in Egypt / Walter Armbrust.
p. cm. – (Cambridge studies in social and cultural anthropology ; 102)
Includes bibliographical references.
ISBN 0 521 48147 3. – ISBN 0 521 48492 8 (pbk.)
1. Egypt–Civilization–1798– 2. Popular culture–Egypt. 3. Mass media–Egypt–History–20th century. I. Title. II. Series.
DT107.826.A76 1996
962′.03–dc20 95-39632 CIP

ISBN 0 521 48147 3 hardback
ISBN 0 521 48492 8 paperback

Transferred to digital reprinting 2001
Printed in the United States of America

SE

Contents

Illustrations

Plates

Figures

Acknowledgements

This book is about the relationship of popular culture to modernism and national culture in Egypt. The research is based on films, television serials, songs, various types of writing, and approximately four-and-a-half years of living in Egypt as a student (1985–86), researcher (1989–90; 1993), and employee (1990–91).

A number of individuals deserve mention for the roles they played in various stages of this book. Paul Dresch offered superb intellectual guidance throughout my graduate education in anthropology. Al Phillips inspired me to write about popular culture and provided a comparative perspective by broadening my appreciation of American popular culture. Roberta Dougherty, my wife since 1991, was with me when I first experienced much of the material discussed in the book, and always offered useful perspectives on my subject matter and writing. John Shoup, my first Arabic teacher, was also present through much of the research and offered valuable commentary on Egyptian popular culture. Andrew Shryock and Michael Fahy read and influenced my work at various stages. The following individuals also read the book in manuscript form and influenced my thinking in various ways: Juan Cole, Nicholas Dirks, Jane Gaffney, Joel Gordon, Brinkley Messick, Everett Rowson, Brian Spooner, Ted Swedenburg, David Wilmsen, Kate Zirbel.

Many Egyptians contributed to my perceptions and knowledge. In particular Nādiya Muḥammad, Jehan Muḥammad, Amānī Muḥammad, ʿAbd al-Raḥmān al-Sharqāwī, Muḥammad al-Sharqāwī, and Khālid al-Sharqāwī taught me about life in Egypt, gave me valuable perspectives on the Egyptian educational system, and patiently helped me with my often imperfect Arabic. All were generous with their time, forgiving of my mistakes, and amazingly willing to include me in various activities that brought me in contact with their wide circles of friends and relatives. Louis Greiss, Hānī Shenūda, and Muḥammad Zādah offered valued perspectives on Egyptian popular culture and contacts with others in the culture industries.

Thanks to the following individuals for helping arrange permission to publish the various materials reproduced in the book: Ragaa Nakkash, editor-in-chief of the Dār al-Hilāl publishing company for the materials used in chapter 4; Moneib Shafie, chairman of the Egyptian Chamber of Cinema, for photographs (all of which the Chamber of Cinema generously provided) from *Pay Attention to Zuzu*, *Resolution*, *Ragab on a Hot Tin Roof*, *Shaban below Zero*, and *Crabs*; Muhammad Mustafa Saad, general manager of the Rūz al-Yūsuf publishing company, for the Salah Jahin cartoons originally published in *Ṣabāḥ al-khayr*; Salah Inani for his poster *A Hundred Years of Enlightenment*, and for permission to use the poster on the dust jacket; Hussein al-Imam for permission to translate the lyrics of the theme song to *Crabs*, and for his help in the translation.

Naturally any remaining mistakes and misconceptions in the book are my own responsibility and do not reflect on the efforts of any of the individuals named above.

Institutional support for my fieldwork came from a Fulbright-Hays dissertation grant, and later an American Research Center in Egypt postdoctoral fellowship. In the United States most of my support came through the University of Michigan's Center for Middle Eastern and North African Studies and, in the most crucial year of writing, the Michigan Institute for the Humanities.

Note on transliteration

The text follows the *International Journal of Middle East Studies* transliteration standard for words in literary Arabic. Dipthongs are written "au," or "ay" where appropriate. The "l" in the definite article "al-" is always retained, but the "a" is elided when the definite article is preceded by the prepositions "bi-," "fī," "li-" and "ʿalā," as well as "wa-" (and).

Transliterations of colloquial text follow *A Dictionary of Egyptian Arabic* (Badawi and Hinds 1986) with some modifications: consonants that conform to literary pronunciation are rendered according to *IJMES* guidelines; long vowels in colloquial texts are marked with a macron as in *IJMES* rather than the doubled letter used in Badawi and Hinds.

Names are only fully transliterated the first time they appear in the text; in later citations long vowels and emphatic consonants are dropped. Names of Egyptians have been rendered as they are pronounced in Egypt, e.g. "Gamāl" rather than "Jamāl." Names regularly cited in English are written according to common usage (e.g. Abdel Nasser and Naguib Mahfouz).

1

Introduction

In November of 1993 I attended a swearing-in ceremony at the Egyptian Bar Association. A friend's daughter was to be inducted, and I was asked to join her and her mother at the Bar Association's headquarters in downtown Cairo to photograph the event. They were not a wealthy family, and a ceremony to commemorate their daughter having made it both through college and into the Bar was for them a momentous occasion. Unfortunately, in the view of the legal establishment it was just another first Tuesday of the month – the day when the swearing-in routine takes place and another group of unemployable lawyers is turned out into an unimpressed labor market.

Almost no pomp and circumstance were invested in the event – it was an absence of ritual where one was expected to take place. No attempt was made to tell the proud new lawyers what they should do, or when. Instead, the entrance to the swearing-in chamber was forcibly barred, and prospective lawyers and their families pressed against the door in a frantic mob. The guards were letting small groups trickle in, but no attempt was made to convey information about how the ceremony was to be organized. It was survival of the fittest, and my friends were simply not willing enough to engage in physical combat to be among the first into the room. Finally we gave up and had a cup of tea while waiting for the crowd to thin down.

The young woman who was to have celebrated her professional triumph lashed out in irritation: "This is like trying to get on the bus – they treat us like a bunch of peasants. Before you know it they'll be taking off their belts and whipping us. I thought this was a respectable place, and what do I find? Chaos." While we were having our tea the girl murmured to her mother: "*Zaḥma ya dunyā zaḥma / Zaḥma wi-tāhū al-ḥabāyib*" (how crowded is the world; crowded and friends lose their way). Her mother smiled, and replied: "*Zaḥma wi-la-ʿad-shⁱ raḥma*" (crowded and merciless). I knew the next line, so I added: "*Mūlid wi-ṣaḥb-u ghāyib*" (a saint's festival without the saint [the point being that everything was utterly chaotic]).

These lines were quoted formulaically, as one might a proverb. But "how crowded is the world" was no proverbial wisdom, or at least not the kind that comes from an imagined pristine folk culture. Rather, it was a line from a popular song – the sort spread by modern technology such as cassette tapes or a microphone in a nightclub. Reciting a verse from "How Crowded Is the World" was an ironic way of commenting on a frustrating predicament. Part of the irony lay not just in the words to the song, but in the singer, Aḥmad ʿAdawīya, who is scorned by the official media as hopelessly vulgar. The song first became popular in the late 1970s or early 1980s. The mother and her daughter in the Bar Association probably knew it from pirated cassette tapes sold in places such as al-ʿAtaba al-Khaḍrā, a neighborhood located in a transitional zone between European-built downtown Cairo and more traditional areas. My friends at the swearing-in ceremony frequently recommended al-ʿAtaba as a place to buy things cheap; the media often denounces it as a wild place where stolen goods are fenced and bad taste runs rampant.

Adawiya is rarely given air time on the radio or television. I knew him and the song quoted at the Bar Association not from a pirated cassette sold in al-ʿAtaba, but from a film called *Shaʿbān taḥt al-ṣifr* (Shaban below zero, 1980). My friends probably hadn't seen the film because women go to the cinema less often than men, and they could not afford a VCR to watch it at home. *Shaban below Zero* starred a popular comedian named ʿĀdil Imām, who is similar to Adawiya and the neighborhood of al-ʿAtaba in that most of his *oeuvre* is cited in establishment media as a symbol of vulgarity. The film was in fact a remake of a 1942 movie called *Lau kuntⁱ ghanī* (If I were rich). The original film from the 1940s was a light comedy which ended with the triumph of a new middle class. The 1980 remake of the film in which Adawiya sang "How Crowded Is the World" ended with the problems of its beleaguered characters unresolved.

This was the context of a brief invocation of a popular song: middle-class people feeling humiliated at the hands of an institution that is supposed to enable their upward mobility. They respond by reciting words from a song that the sort of people who control institutions such as the Bar Association, not to mention the establishment media, denounce. The song itself was bought and sold in a particular popular-culture context which included a range of potential associations of place and person also considered unsavory by the media. "How Crowded Is the World" occurred in a film that reverberated with connotations of class; and finally, the film resonated with historical significance – comparative snapshots of the middle class separated by almost forty years.

Popular culture features in the lives of most Egyptians and, to some extent, in all of the Arabic-speaking Middle East.[1] Academic disinterest in mass-mediated popular culture of the region is therefore puzzling. Something like a "postmodern condition" in which reality and images blur into each other, perhaps even define each other, has come into being under our noses. This cannot be the same postmodern condition as pertains to the West. Or can it? So far academics have made only the most minimal attempt to analyze the phenomenon or even to comment on it.

The chief barrier to studying Egyptian popular culture is that it is commercial and oriented toward an Arabic-speaking market. Commercial culture is sometimes depicted as erasing authentic non-Western cultures, and in Egypt the dilution of local culture by Western influence is, in fact, a common element in both artistic performance and critical opinion on the part of layman and expert alike. But to interpret Egyptian popular culture either as a straightforward imitation of the West or, conversely, as cryptic resistance to hegemonic power, would as often as not lead one to misunderstand the character of the art. A concern with Egypt's relationship to the West is one of the defining characteristics of Egyptian popular culture, yet blind adoption of Western culture has never been an unambiguous or uncontested feature of modern Egypt.[2] At the very least, as Appadurai and Breckenridge note, "every society appears to bring to these [popular] forms its own special history and traditions, its own cultural stamp, its own quirks and idiosyncracies" (Appadurai and Breckenridge 1988, 5).

The commercial nature of Egyptian popular culture automatically excludes it from the incipient canon of "Third World" cultural productions which is defined by Western scholars in metropolitan institutions, and tends to include only works that make sense to monolingual audiences in that context (Ahmad 1992, 78–81). Many of the works slotted into the Third World canon are postcolonial, critical of the West, and endorse nationalism as the only effective strategy of potential resistance (Jameson 1986).[3] This implies either that the only difference between works selected and those not selected is aesthetic sophistication – as if attributions of sophistication or naiveté were unproblematic – or that works not selected are rejected on some unspecified ground (Ahmad 1992, 107).

Critics who point out the metropolitan character of the "Third World literature" category, however, offer no satisfactory alternative. For example, Aijaz Ahmad's alternative bypasses texts produced and consumed by people in non-Western cities but ignored by academics. What he has in mind, instead, are "genres which are essentially oral and performative, sites of production located at a great remove from the great cities, entire linguistic complexes as yet unassimilated into grids of print and translation" (*ibid.*, 80–81). Ahmad's non-metropolitan text, in other words, is folklore, which in an Egyptian context is a nonstarter as an unclassified site of resistance to either colonial or postcolonial nationalist hegemony. Since the 1950s such "oral and performative sites of production" have been part of the Cairo University curriculum. The process of classifying Egyptian folklore – whatever the character of the folk texts themselves – fits comfortably within a nationalist discourse. To search for uncontaminated texts "located at a great remove from the cities" would be pointless; an archive for such material exists already.

In Egypt the texts that have received the least academic scrutiny are not the primordial utterances of the noncolonized, but those produced and disseminated in the new media: cinema, television, radio, cassette tapes, lowbrow magazines. Much of this material is implicated in nationalist and modernist discourses, but both the arbiters of metropolitan Third World canons and their critics consider it unworthy of comment.[4] Consequently only a tiny fraction of Egyptian films, for example, are shown in the West, and usually those selected are least representative of what most Egyptians like to watch. If these films are shown they are usually classified with other "Third World films," many of which are made under radically different conditions.[5]

The issue is not whether the texts selected – electronic or otherwise – are good or bad. Much of what is read and taught as Third World literature written in English by Indians and Africans, for example, deserves to be read; many of the North African films with which Egyptian cinema is often unfavorably compared are excellent. The distinction between what we experience as Third World culture and non-Western texts excluded from the canon is not always strictly a differentiation between "works of art" and "vulgar commerce"; there is also a differentiation between non-Western artists with privileged access to more lucrative markets (not to mention the capital and training that permit access) and those without such access. The distinction between works produced with an eye on metropolitan audiences or markets and works made to be consumed outside the metropole is important, at least for anthropologists, who generally claim to have some interest in how others interpret and interact with the world.

Yet until fairly recently even anthropologists resisted analyzing material outside the incipient metropolitan canon on methodological grounds. Mass media fit poorly with a discipline that saw its main contribution coming from participant observation of people considered primitive. Fortunately these methodological prejudices have been questioned, although not abandoned outright. As Talal Asad notes, anthropology is still largely concerned with "nonmodern" peoples – a tendency which has somewhat marginalized the discipline (Asad 1993, 19–24). By implicitly assuming the premodernity of their subjects anthropologists are left with a methodological bias toward orality. Consequently a recent review of the state of the art in anthropological approaches to mass media began with a disclaimer: "There is as yet no 'anthropology of mass media'" (Spitulnik 1993, 293), and later noted that "recent developments [in the anthropology of mass media] have been criticized for being still too theory-driven, biased by populist agendas, and merely unknowing rediscoveries of earlier approaches in communication research" (*ibid.*, 299).[6] It is common for anthropological analyses of media to carry a heavy theoretical superstructure, but no references to non-Western literature or bodies of popular culture (mediated or not), no sense of what dialogue or lyrics are like, and no attempt to convey any sense of the conditions under which popular culture is made or consumed. "*Mūlid wi-ṣaḥb-u ghāyib*" as Ahmad Adawiya would say – a saint's festival without the saint, or in this case textual analysis without the text.

A problem in writing about Egyptian popular culture is that the audience does not discuss it as an academic might. Its social significance is masked by the mention of names: names of entertainers and the performances associated with them, of lines from films or songs, or titles of well-known works, which are used in everyday life as a kind of shorthand for the narrative or text in which they occur. Invocation of such texts may occur in oral contexts, but cannot be understood strictly in terms of orality, nor in purely local terms.

This does not mean that talk of popular culture is reducible to a code language of textual fragments – people quoting Ahmad Adawiya in the Bar Association, for example. People also engage in direct conversation about a given film or television show. But even direct conversation about popular culture assumes familiarity with key texts. When I engaged Egyptians in conversations about popular culture such interaction was "synthetic" in the sense that I, an outsider, initiated them. But such conversations could only make sense after I had learned something of the names that dominate any exchange on popular culture, and something of the structured rhetoric that informs both the texts behind the names and the way the names are deployed in social interaction.

But to focus entirely on such discussions would give the impression that the social context of popular culture is circumscribed – that popular culture is like a ritual that somehow recapitulates the social order in certain well-defined situations. The names of entertainers can be mentioned in almost any context to make a point. My friends and acquaintances in Egypt did this by drawing upon an enormous corpus of works with which they grew up: Egyptian films, Egyptian films originally written for the theater, Egyptian films based on Egyptian novels, Egyptian films based on foreign novels, foreign films, Egyptian films based on foreign films, Egyptian films based on Shakespeare, Egyptian versions of contemporary Western films, Egyptian remakes of Egyptian films, Egyptian films that laced references to earlier Egyptian films into their narratives, actors whose screen personae were based on an accumulated corpus of stage, film, and television performances, songs that adapted Western genres to Egyptian tastes, songs that took a Western soundtrack and replaced the words with Arabic lyrics – the permutations of influences and transformations are endless. To approach anything remotely like a "native" ability to understand how Egyptians deploy their common stock of imagery and personalities requires a familiarity with popular texts that is more like what Orientalists do with medieval texts – relating them to each other, comparing them with other textual traditions, juxtaposing them, classifying them – than like the anthropologist's fantasy of spending a year with "informants," "picking up the language in the field," and relying on "theory" to do the rest.

Egyptian popular culture has no up, no down, no beginning or end. We can start with Adil Imam and eventually find ourselves in al-ʿAtaba; we can start with *If I Were Rich* and end up with Adawiya. With minimal effort we can even wend our way to the Bar Association, which suggests that the hypertextuality of popular culture implicates what is conventionally known as high culture, as well as the officially (and academically) despised categories of non-metropolitan low culture. This does not, however, mean that the mad hypertextuality of popular culture is without structure. *If I Were Rich* and *Shaban below Zero* implicate each other – are variations on the theme of modernity gone wrong. In the earlier film it is put right again, but not in the later version. Both films imply an ideology of modernity inherent in their own narratives and constructed through numerous other narratives and an increasingly pervasive institutional structure. Together the films exemplify a broad distinction between two periods in modern Egyptian history. They are, on one hand, from around the turn of the century (when modernity began to be a pressing concern in Egypt) until 1967, and on the other hand, after 1973.

The transitional years between 1967 and 1973 were tumultuous. At the earlier date, 1967, Egypt experienced a confidence-shattering defeat at the hands of a foreign power (Israel), which caused Egypt and the Arab world to reexamine, although not necessarily to abandon, the cultural assumptions through which their modernity was constructed. At the end of this transitional period, in 1973, Egypt reestablished its honor on the battlefield, but military respectability coincided ironically with the twin shocks of regional power shifting away from Egypt toward the oil-producing Arab Gulf countries, and what many saw (and still see) as economic surrender to the West – forced adoption of a market economy known in Egypt as the *infitāḥ*, or Open Door. Before 1967 Egypt, in its own estimation and in the opinion of many outsiders, seemed to be on an inexorable path to modernity; after 1973 the pace of change has, if anything, accelerated, and yet it has become more difficult to discern a unifying logic beneath the transformations.[7]

Modernity, apparently inevitable before 1967 and beleaguered after 1973, is the key to mediated popular culture. What is modernity in Egypt? In the West modernity emphasized discontinuity as a means of clearing the ground for more rational forms of society – what Harvey (1989, 16) calls "creative destruction." Egyptian modernity is also avowedly rationalist, but puts a greater emphasis on maintaining continuity with the past. In the twentieth century, mass media has been an important means for disseminating modernist ideology in Egypt. One reason for this is the organic association of modernity and nationalism. As Benedict Anderson put it, "the growth of what might be called 'comparative history' led in time to the hitherto unheard-of conception of a 'modernity' explicitly juxtaposed to 'antiquity,' and by no means necessarily to the advantage of the latter" (Anderson 1991, 68). But it is precisely the invention of modernity that makes it possible to imagine a history separate from cosmology – a necessity if people are to start thinking in terms of what Anderson calls an "imagined community" sharing a defined space through human history. In all societies the radical changes of modernity are to some extent balanced with the conservative, backward-looking character (or fabrication) of nationalism. This has been recognized for some time, as we can see from the following statement made by Joshua Fishman in 1972:

It is quite apparent . . . that there is a built-in dialectic within nationalism, a quite inevitable tension between its major components. Most obvious is the tension between the requirements of modernization and those of authentification. The one emphasizes the instrumental uniformities required by modern politico-operational integration and is constantly straining toward newer, more rational, more efficient solutions to the problems of today and tomorrow. The other emphasizes the sentimental uniformities required by continuity-based sociocultural integration and is constantly straining toward purer, more genuine expressions of the heritage of yesterday and of long ago.[8] *(Fishman 1972, 20–21)*

More recent writers retain Fishman's basic formulation of nationalism, but with somewhat different emphases.[9] Consequently, when an Oxford-based Egyptian literary critic – an immigrant to the West – writes about the "modern Arab litterateur" outside the metropole in an Arabic-language journal published in Cairo, he does so in distinctly nationalist terms:

[The litterateur] represents on the one hand – in his capacity as an educated man – a point of departure in the path of change, indeed, a point in which is crystallized the desire for renewal and modernization and for a change in the life of the community. On the other hand, however, the litterateur – in his capacity as the faithful guardian who preserves his literary and linguistic heritage – represents the desire for stability and conservatism . . . and it is possible for us to say in a very general way that the development of modern Arabic literature is the development, or transformation, of the position of the litterateur generally from the extreme of continuity and conservatism to the extreme of transmutation, change and renewal. *(M. M. Badawi 1984, 100)*

Modernity's close relationship to nationalism makes the "conservative radical" to some extent a generic feature of all contemporary societies. But of course modernities of different societies also have unique features. In the case of Egypt and the Arabic-speaking world this unique relationship between modernity and nationalism appears most clearly in language.

Popular culture has been linguistically important in Egypt because it has historically been a qualitatively different vehicle for establishing national identity than official discourse. The two – popular and official discourse – have always been conceptually distinct. In both Egypt and the West modernity began with a rediscovery or reinvigoration of classical languages. Europeans tried to write classical Latin rather than "vulgate Latin" or the local dialects they spoke, but eventually discarded classical languages in favor of more practical (and more easily learned) standardized vernaculars. Using vernaculars greatly amplified the effect of print technology and became a powerful force for European nationalism. But in the case of Egypt and the Arabic-speaking world the classical language is intrinsic to the practice of religion, and cannot be consciously and publicly discarded. Theoretically the national vernacular of all Arab nations is translocal: classical Arabic, albeit a somewhat "modernized" (grammatically streamlined) variant of it. Europeans tried to write like Cicero; Arabs tried to emulate the Qur'ān (with the understanding that attaining full qur'ānic eloquence was beyond human capability). But unlike Europeans, who discarded their classical model of linguistic eloquence in the wake of the Reformation, Arab writers continued to insist on classicism as a literary ideal, although in practice modern "classical" style varies considerably from region to region and continues to evolve. Parallel to the ideologically and culturally justified adherence to "classical vernacular" a standardized and locally referenced spoken vernacular developed. Mass media were important in establishing this shadow vernacular, precisely because of their imported character: there are no clear conventions to adhere to in the new media as there are in writing. Hence in modern Egypt we are dealing with two "national vernaculars," one rooted in classicism and deeply valued, but hard to learn and territorially ambiguous; the other colloquial, easily understood and highly practical, but a hard sell in terms of prestige. In practice styles of expression are much more complex than this binary model suggests, but ideologically the distinction remains.

After the early 1970s the carefully constructed balance of modernist transformation through a classicist vehicle, and nationalist imagination in a local vernacular, began to come undone in Egypt. The contrast between the 1980s vintage film *Shaban below Zero*, in which a popular but officially disapproved performer sang the lines my friends at the Bar Association quoted in a moment of frustration, and its 1942 predecessor, *If I Were Rich*, illustrates the distinction between pre-1970s modernist popular culture and more ambiguous later productions. In the original film the problems of modernity were neatly solved through the intervention of an educated aristocrat who not only had money, but also the know-how to run modern institutions. *If I Were Rich* ended with everybody returning to their rightful places: happy workers dance in the streets, and the educated aristocrat marries an educated girl from a poor and traditional Egyptian neighborhood – the perfect merger of high and low culture in the service of modernity.

The more recent *Shaban below Zero*, like its 1942 predecessor, throws its characters into a whirlwind of problems typical of modern life. But this time there is no educated aristocrat to appear as *deus ex machina*. There is no image of a successful middle class. The erasure of the middle class – the focal point of modernist and nationalist ideology – is in fact the most striking theme in *Shaban below Zero*. The 1942 film ends with everyone living happily ever after; the 1980 film ends with the protagonist – a bureaucrat and the educated heir to the modernist tradition – taken to prison in manacles.

Putting films such as *Shaban below Zero*, and singers such as Adawiya, in a wider social and artistic context makes an invocation of "How Crowded Is the World" in the Bar Association comprehensible. The film and the singer are emblematic of a time when the old formulas of popular culture no longer seem as meaningful because the institutions and ideology they sought to buttress no longer seem entirely plausible.

Popular culture, properly contextualized, reveals much about the state of contemporary Egypt. In this case the hiccup of disgust expressed by my friends' quotation of a vulgar song at a polite occasion gone sour was prescient. In May 1994, a few months after the swearing-in ceremony at which my friend's daughter was inducted, the Bar started agitating for a general strike when ʿAbd al-Ḥarith Madanī, one of their members, was tortured to death for defending Islamists in court. The state responded to the threat of a strike with mass incarceration of lawyers. Tear-gassing and imprisoning lawyers might well be a popular move in postmodern America, but one should keep in mind that it is very nearly the last thing we should expect to see. In Egypt it actually happened, and the event was far from popular. The crushing of the Bar Association was, however, an indicator of the growing irrelevance of the ideology and institutions associated with Egyptian modernity. So, for that matter, is the rise of the nonsynthesizing popular culture of Ahmad Adawiya and Adil Imam. "How Crowded Is the World" has a definite appeal, at least when one's symbolic entry into the middle class resembles nothing so much as trying to get onto a crowded bus.

2

"The White Flag"

Walah Ḥammooo! Al-timsāḥa, yalla!
(Muḥammad, bring the car!)

Faḍḍa al-Maʿdāwī in the opening
scene of "Al-Rāya al-Bayḍā"

It starts with an idyllic scene framed on everyone's television: peaceful seagulls wheeling in a blue sky, the Alexandria shoreline with beautiful apartment blocks clustered on a Mediterranean bay, a windswept corniche, boats bobbing lazily on gentle swells. Then comes a crash, startling like a cannon shot, followed a split second later by a harmless wave pounding the corniche. Momentary anxiety recedes, then returns when images of a cannon bombardment, buildings falling, and planes bombing helpless cities flash briefly between more images of waves. Gradually the noisy mayhem replaces the noisy waves. Then the cannons, too, gradually give way to a looming bulldozer, almost unrecognizable because it appears mainly as a large steel blade about to swallow up the screen. Suddenly the bulldozer freezes. A businesslike female voice intones, "Excuse me. This isn't a new world war. It's Fadda." We see the face of a heavily made-up woman, about sixty years old, wearing a garish rhinestone-encrusted headscarf. Her mouth is wide open because she is yelling: "*Walah Ḥammooo! Al-timsāḥa, yalla!*" (Ḥammo, boy! The crocodile, let's go!), the "crocodile" being her new Mercedes.

The theme song begins – traditional lute backed by synthesizer. City streets in Alexandria and a bearded man taking a photograph of a villa on the corniche replace the vulgar woman as the narrator gives voice to words flashed on the screen:

For the love of beautiful Alexandria, and for everything that is beautiful and authentic, Usāma Anwar ʿUkāsha and Muḥammad Fāḍil present their new story "The White Flag," a battle mapped out by Usama Anwar Ukasha. The events of this *musalsal* are realistic; they have happened and continue to happen. But the names, places and persons are not real, and any resemblance or correspondence between these events and reality is coincidental, or the result of artistic necessity. Still, we confirm that the resemblance to real events is intentional, because these things have happened, and continue to happen.

The volume of the music rises. On the screen we now see the villa in an oval frame. The bulldozer blade moves forward in square "windows" that flash across the screen behind the oval while two sets of names, presented as "teams," are rolled as credits. The whole cacophony of images dissolves into another shot of the shore as a gong sounds, like the opening round of a boxing match. The final words of the opening sequence flash on the screen: "Round one."

By this time the attention of many viewers was riveted on what was happening. The date was December 5, 1989, approximately 7:00 P.M., and though it looked like an experiment in the theory of montage, it was actually the character Fadda al-Madawi firing the opening salvo of an Egyptian serial, "The White Flag." The transformation from peaceful seagull to threatening bulldozer was broadcast for the next fifteen nights to a progressively larger and more interested audience, which could be judged by the emptying of streets at broadcast time (there is no Egyptian "Nielson" rating to gauge viewing figures) and by the entry of "White Flag" lore into daily conversation.

The line about the crocodile became famous. "Crocodile" is slang for a Mercedes Benz 300 – a long, low model costing, if one were to buy it legally with taxes paid, around a quarter of a million Egyptian pounds at the time the serial was broadcast.[1] An older 200 or 230 model, boxier and less expensive, is called *khanzīra* (pig), and the newer aerodynamically rounded model with low front and raised trunk is *zalamukka* (a "parson's nose" – the backside of a chicken). These nicknames for cars were reckoned "low slang," even underworld slang. Indeed, everything in the appearance and behavior of Fadda al-Madawi, the character who yelled for her "crocodile" in the opening sequence, and once in the course of the show, was intended to scream "vulgarity" to the program's audience. By all accounts, this depiction of colorful vileness was a smashing success. Fadda's rhinestone-covered headscarf was a parody of a neo-Islamic *ḥijāb*, worn to convey *ḥishma* (modesty) in public. Her speech, much more generally than her reference to the "crocodile," was unmistakably low class: "*Walah Ḥammō*" (Hammo boy) instead of a less slangy "*Yā walad Muḥammad*," or a simple "*Yā Muḥammad.*" Fadda's call for her "crocodile" constituted a kind of Dirty Harry phenomenon; just as the renegade cop's icy "Make my day" entered the American vernacular, so Fadda al-Madawi's "*Walah Ḥammō* . . ." entered the Egyptian.

Fadda's call for her car became a catchphrase because the serial in which she appeared captivated the public. The story, in brief, was about a fishmonger by the name of Fadda al-Madawi. Fadda was a *muʿallima* (a small independent merchant; usually a male role – *muʿallim*) who had become a millionaire real-estate developer. That her rise was due to dirty dealings became clear as the serial unfolded. In the course of "White Flag"'s fifteen episodes Fadda tries, by means mostly foul, to acquire a villa owned by Dr. Mufīd Abū-l-Ghār, a retired diplomat recently returned to Egypt after a thirty-year absence. The villa, built by a European in the nineteenth century but then used by Egyptian nationalist heroes, symbolizes the Arab cultural renaissance. Its owner, Dr. Mufid, is a man who preserves what is best in his culture, and takes from other cultures what is beneficial. In doing so he typifies a vision of modern Egypt. On its most basic level, the fifteen-part battle for the villa depicts a struggle between good and evil. On a more concrete level, it is about an Egyptian struggle to preserve local identity but, as the anonymous tanks, planes, and bulldozer suggest, it is also a battle for civilization itself.

The use of the "crocodile" catchphrase was largely a joke. A young male friend living in a poor quarter of Cairo left the house calling to his brother Muḥammad, "*Walah Ḥammō! Al-shanṭa, yalla*" (Hammo, boy – the bag, let's go!). There would have been no point in him or thousands of others impersonating Fadda if the joke had not touched on something real – the knowledge that someone who talked like Fadda al-Madawi could never legally acquire the means to buy a *timsāḥa* – but a joke implies ambiguity. Many people who were accustomed to living on a few hundred Egyptian pounds per month said, with very little prompting, that a person who could afford a LE 250,000 car had to be a criminal, yet such cars are not uncommon in modern Cairo. One young man related that he had counted twenty-five luxury-model Mercedes Benzes in the three minutes it took him to walk across a bridge from one side of the Nile to the other. The traffic, he said, was unusually heavy, but he only counted cars from one direction. The basis of the joke is real.

The character of Fadda al-Madawi became, for a time, synonymous with greed and vulgarity. I heard other stories about Fadda. Someone on a crowded bus accused a young man who transgressed the bounds of politeness of "being a Fadda." In the course of an argument in a departmental meeting over whether or not to offer extra classes for students, a university professor accused his adversaries of "promulgating the spirit of Fadda al-Madawi." A mechanic who had not seen the program instantly knew what I was talking about when someone prompted him, "The show with '*walah Ḥammō*.'" When reminded of the phrase he launched into a lament about the misuse of money and the futility of education in the face of brute greed.

The press also made reference to "White Flag," usually in the context of stories about injustice inflicted on the poor or defenseless by the rich. On March 17, 1990, an article appeared in *Akhbār al-yaum* entitled "Fadda al-Madawi's Bulldozer Appears in al-Darrāsa" (a poor neighborhood of Cairo). The article described an attempt to bulldoze a dyehouse that had been inherited by rapacious relatives who wanted to tear it down, along with the surrounding buildings, so as to sell the vacant land at a much higher price to developers. The owners did this by sending a bulldozer and a group of thugs at 4:00 A.M. The manager of the dyehouse was in the building at the time and would have been buried under the rubble but for a group of his neighbors who confronted the bulldozer, and were themselves confronted by ten heavies armed "with pistols, bayonets and swords." The building's destruction was forestalled for a time. But the new landlords were eventually able to carry out their plan. In the end the neighbors sat down in front of the bulldozer, which was preparing to finish the destruction of the remaining walls. One of their number went to file a police report while the landlords stood and poured abuse on them. The only result was that the bulldozer driver was arrested, leaving the owners free.

Another article appeared on March 3, 1990, in the same newspaper, entitled "The *Muʿallima* Fadda Appears on Gabal Muqaṭṭam." This time the victim was Muṣṭafā Ḥasan, an aging ex-gymnastics champion of Egypt, who was beaten up defending his home from bullies sent by a fruit seller who had bought the land occupied by Hasan's villa. Like the residents of al-Darrāsa, Hasan had refused to surrender. But resistance proved futile. In the end Hasan's wife was attacked and he himself was beaten and stabbed by the thugs, then left for dead. The article showed Hasan, a white-haired elderly man, displaying his bruises and broken feet from a hospital bed.

Many people characterized the serial as a polemic against "the power of money." A common lament heard in the context of "White Flag" was "*baʕēna balad filūs*" (we have become a nation of money). Some refused to accept the idea that there could be fundamental conflicts among powerful people (such as Fadda and the owner of the villa), no matter how different their levels of education – a taxi driver claimed: "There are men of power [*sulṭa*] and men of money, they are never in conflict." More often, however, "the power of money" was not equated uncritically with class conflict. Many were astonished that an ex-ambassador could be threatened by a low-class person such as Fadda al-Madawi, and claimed this possibility was something new. As an auto mechanic said: "'White Flag' shows how much ignorance there is in this country. It didn't used to be like this in the old days. A lawyer and a *muʿallima*? In the past an important man like that would have taken his rightful place. Things would have been run the way they should."

Any suspicion that "White Flag" simply stirred up class resentment, or conversely, rallied people to the side of the authorities, was dispelled by the complexity of its reception. Large crowds flocked to public meetings in which the director, and sometimes writers or actors, discussed the program with interested viewers.[2] The crowds were well heeled, predominantly middle class, and divided equally between men and women. Although the newspaper articles and the angry denunciations of "the power of money" suggested people were "madder than hell and not going to take it any more," the prevailing atmosphere at these meetings was one of polite civic concern. One of the questions addressed to "White Flag"'s director Muhammad Fadil in an Alexandria meeting was: "Why did you choose to make Fadda al-Madawi a woman and Dr. Mufid a man? I had envisioned it the other way around." Fadil's answer was: "To achieve maximum separation between the two types – to heighten the sense of good versus evil." He consciously set out to create a story structured around a stark, essentially caricatured, opposition between good and evil. But why does a program that clothes good and evil in obvious reference to opposed social classes appeal so strongly to a middle-class audience that need not identify with either of the classes represented? To understand the specificity of an Egyptian serial such as "White Flag," which drew an audience of millions, we need to take a detailed look at both the work and its context.

The sharp opposition of good and evil, at first glance, appears typical of melodrama, a genre usually assumed to be antithetical to a "realist" perspective.[3] But events and characters in reality and drama alike may actually be marked by sharp differentiation, exactly as melodrama suggests. Cairo is, after all, a city in which twenty-five LE 250,000 cars pass by multitudes of LE 100–per-month workers in the three minutes it takes a man to cross a bridge. Not to address such a remarkable disparity would perhaps be more unreal than making it a basic condition for the narrative. In any case, "White Flag" does not neatly resolve its oppositions, as one might expect in melodrama. The opposing sides may be clearly marked, but the relations between them are ambiguous, as are many things in modern Egypt.

An all-star cast

The creators of "White Flag" were considered among the best in Egyptian television. The director, Muhammad Fadil, had already made a long string of *musalsalāt* (dramatic serials, pl. of *musalsal*), the most important of which was probably "*Al-Qāhira wa-l-nās*" (Cairo and the people). "Cairo," broadcast in the late 1960s and early 1970s, was unusual in that it resembled an American sitcom more than a soap opera. The characters remained constant, but the narrative was broken into largely unrelated half-hour segments that repeated certain major themes – modernity and cultural authenticity, sometimes in conflict, usually resolved harmoniously. "Cairo" was a comedy.

"White Flag" was written by Usama Anwar Ukasha who, like Muhammad Fadil, is widely recognized as a leading Egyptian writer of television serials. Some go so far as to identify Ukasha as the founder of Egyptian "television literature" (*al-adab al-tilifizyōnī*). Samīr al-Gamal, author of a book on Ukasha, asserts that the writer of "White Flag" "reintroduces us to television drama in a novelistic form which has the flavor of Naguib Mahfouz, the ability of Yūsuf Idrīs and the depth of Yaḥyā Ḥaqqī" (al-Gamal 1991, 9).[4] Ukasha wrote the scripts of many notable television successes, including "*Layālī al-Ḥilmīya*" (Ḥilmīya nights) – a historical drama set in the Ḥilmīya quarter of Cairo and broadcast during the Ramaḍān holiday from 1988 to 1992 – and "*Al-Shahd wa-l-dumū'*" (Honey and tears), which was a 1984 hit still remembered fondly in 1990 by those of college age.[5] "Honey and Tears" is said to have been the first serial to have inspired the idea of holding public meetings to discuss the work (*ibid.*, 17).

The fans of Ukasha's drama insist that his works have a dual character: on the one hand his stories are *adab* – literature – and on the other hand they appeal to the masses. As al-Gamal says, Ukasha's dramas "have broken through the impediments of colloquial Egyptian language to enter the Arab heart and mind" (*ibid.*, 17–18). Such carefully phrased endorsements of vernacular expression's capacity to engage ordinary people in art appear occasionally in establishment discourse. More often such discourse holds literature and colloquial expression to be mutually exclusive – a feature of modernist ideology that will be touched on later. For now it is sufficient to note the eagerness of critics to praise artists they see as capable of "elevated" vernacular expression:

> Usama Anwar Ukasha has made the writer into a star. When he reaches his pinnacle, we reach it with him. Whereas [we ordinary writers] are just obscure names known only in literary circles, he is a star known in the streets. [Characters such as] "ʿAmm Sayyid al-ʿagalātī" and "il-wād Qalāōẓ al-qahwagī" ["uncle Sayyid the bicycle repairman" and "young Qalāōẓ the café waiter" – names evocative of traditional quarters] are known by students in schools and universities in exactly the same way as Naguib Mahfouz, holder of the Nobel prize – and exactly the same as soccer captains, cinema stars, and [popular singers] ʿAbd al-Ḥalīm Ḥāfiẓ, Muḥammed ʿAbd al-Wahhāb, Farīd al-Aṭrash and Umm Kulthum.
>
> *(Muḥsin Zāyid in ibid., 18–19)*

Allowing for hyperbole, Usama Anwar Ukasha was indeed a well-known name beyond the confines of the entertainment industry. I met nobody who actually put him in the same class as Abd al-Wahhab and Umm Kulthum, who are music stars of the order of a Frank Sinatra or a Louis Armstrong, but I did meet many people who instantly recognized the name and identified him readily with "Honey and Tears" and "White Flag." Since Egyptians (much like Americans) tend to associate films and television shows with actors more than with directors or writers, the association of Usama Anwar Ukasha's name with his works is an indication of unusual street-level popularity.

But if actors, more than directors or writers, are the important element of both familiarity and popularity for the audience, then "White Flag" was still in good hands. None of the megastars of the Egyptian screen was cast in either of the two main parts – Fadda al-Madawi or Dr. Mufid. This may have been largely because both parts called for older actors – one a bachelor who had supposedly spent thirty years of adult life abroad, the other of lower-class background and with three adult children. The character of Dr. Mufid had to be educated, sophisticated, worldly, and at the same time clearly tied to the local symbolism of cultural authenticity. One actor, Gamīl Rātib, fitted the cosmopolitan role beautifully. In fact, he had spent much of his life abroad. While he was a young man his aristocratic family stood to lose much from the nationalizations of the Abdel Nasser period. They fled to France in the 1950s, where Ratib pursued a theatrical career. He made one film in Egypt, an obscure work called *Anā al-Sharq* (I am the East, 1958), which he himself described as a disaster produced largely as a vehicle for the lover of one of the film's financiers. Ratib returned to Egypt for good in 1975, to launch an active film and television career.

A handsome, somewhat European-looking man with a deep, mellow voice, slightly accented in his Arabic (so Cairenes told me), Ratib is almost always cast in the role of a rich man, although often with a moral resonance quite different from that of the relentlessly upright Dr. Mufid in "White Flag." In the film *Shaban below Zero* (1980), for example, he plays the aristocratic role for laughs, appearing as a decadent character eagerly taking advantage of the liberal "open-door" economic policies of the post-Nasser era.[6] No matter what the moral resonance of his roles, however, when an Egyptian audience sees Gamil Ratib, the association is with money and privilege.

The real casting coup in "White Flag" came in the selection of the villain, Fadda al-Madawi. As director Muhammad Fadil said, he wanted maximum contrast between the hero and the villain. Making one male and the other female was part of this, but much of the contrast was suggested also through social opposition in terms of something akin to class, and certainly to education. Fadda al-Madawi was as ignorant, cloddish, and venal as Dr. Mufid was educated, worldly, and incorruptible. The director's brilliance in casting lay in realizing that the contrast could be depicted more effectively by finding an actress who could play the role as comedy. He did not want Fadda al-Madawi to be a character people hated, but rather a character people loved to hate – an Egyptian J. R. Ewing, the villain on the American serial "Dallas" who made the show into something more than melodrama. He found his J. R. in the person of Sanā' Gamīl, who took the role of Fadda and stole the show. It was her performance, more than any other element in "White Flag," that emptied the streets while the episodes were being aired.

Sana Gamil's life in no way approximated her role in "White Flag," as Gamil Ratib's did his. Although she was born in the Upper Egyptian town of Asyūṭ she comes from a well-off family, and is educated.[7] Many people, particularly if they were young, said they thought of her mainly in aristocratic roles. Gamil has indeed played the aristocrat, particularly in a number of recent television serials with which the younger generation may associate her.[8] But in the course of her long career (starting in the 1950s) she also had extensive experience playing both low-class and *baladī* (rustic) roles. For example, in the film version of Naguib Mahfouz's *Bidāya wa-nihāya* (A beginning and an end, 1960) she played the part of Nafīsa, a poor urban girl forced into prostitution. Another of her notable *baladī* roles was in *Al-Zauja al-thāniya* (The second wife, 1967), in which she played the wife of a corrupt village headman who, in contravention of Islamic law, forced a poor man to divorce his pretty young wife so he could marry her himself.

Many of Sana Gamil's roles were comic, a fact well appreciated by director Muhammad Fadil. Wisely he let her natural vivaciousness bubble out. Indeed, her performance so engrossed the audience that some felt she was too successful, and drew attention away from what they thought should have been the morally edifying message of the serial. This was made clear to me by one young man, a stern Islamist and little given to irony, when I suggested that Fadda may have been more loved than Dr. Mufid. "Do you think we like the things that Fadda al-Madawi did?" he replied. "You think we like to see our heritage trampled? Rich people exploiting the poor?" He left little doubt that for some (or in some contexts – particularly in conversation with a foreigner who might misunderstand the events in the serial) "White Flag" produced a clear vision of the moral implications of the events portrayed. Yet the serial also made people laugh, and this was accomplished through ambiguities in the relations between characters.

"Moral edification" is a didactic strategy, its appeal limited to certain contexts. For many people the difference between the corrupt Fadda and the "morally edifying" character of Dr. Mufid was marked most strongly in their different mannerisms of speech. Dr. Mufid did not necessarily get the best of such a comparison. Fadda, according to many, "spoke a language we could understand," whereas Dr. Mufid sounded stilted, and perhaps a bit too good, both morally and grammatically, to be really interesting. Some suggested that people actually admired Fadda al-Madawi. Dr. Mufid's proper but stuffy Arabic (even French accented according to many), compared to the colorful language spoken by Fadda, was supposed to be the repository of historical value for all Egyptians, but his position was bound to appear compromised to some. How compromised the aristocratic Dr. Mufid appeared was largely a matter of scale: in the larger context, facing the European world, he looked fine; Egyptians of all sorts might feel he represented Egypt favorably to the world at large. *Vis-à-vis* the average person trying to make ends meet on LE 100 a month, he was potentially problematic, for certainly he was not one of them. The character was respected for his moral worth more than taken to viewers' hearts.

Although the cast of "White Flag" was large and featured established stage and screen names as well as new talent, only one other figure in the show was really crucial. This was the character of Nūnū, one of Fadda's henchmen. Nunu was played by Sayyid Ziyān, a successful comedian, readily recognizable to an Egyptian audience, but not a major box-office name. The character serves Fadda al-Madawi loyally through most of

"White Flag." He dreams of amassing fortunes as huge as Fadda's, and deludes himself into thinking she treats him as a colleague – a *muʿallim* – when in fact he is nothing but a "go-fer."

Nunu usually dresses with neither the gross parody of style characteristic of his boss, nor with any of the sophistication displayed by Dr. Mufid. Rather, he is a barrel-chested, pot-bellied ruffian from the docks who has fallen in with a bad crowd. That his heart is in the right place becomes apparent in later episodes when he makes an awkward but honorable attempt to wed Fadda's daughter, a lewdly luscious and morally deformed young woman. Fadda rejects his proposal humiliatingly. Hurt, he asks her help once more, this time to make a cassette tape of him singing his own compositions. She tells him in no uncertain terms that he is a servant, not an equal, and finally he begins to look at Fadda and her actions more closely. We see him singing his pitiful little song to Hammo – the driver of Fadda al-Madawi's "crocodile" Mercedes:

it-timsāḥa, it-timsāḥa	The crocodile, the crocodile
il-mōza rakba wi-mirtāḥa	The chick is in it, on easy street
ʕultilha ya ḥilwa khudī-ni gānb-ik	I said, "Hey babe, let me in!"
ʕālit-li malaksh^{i} misāḥa	She said, "Ain't no room for you."

Nunu hangs suspended between the bright shining modernity of Dr. Mufid and the rank corruption of Fadda, ill-equipped to see either clearly. The character of Nunu embodies the ambiguities of class, heritage, and education, the last of which is consistently sold to the public by official media as a healthy bridge between the salutary aspects of tradition and a well-merited enhancement of class. Nunu, more than any other character in the serial, articulates the central concern of the production, namely that something in the machinery of cultural transformation has gone drastically wrong.

Nunu is conspicuously the only character in the entire show who truly believes in Fadda al-Madawi, as opposed to the many hangers-on who merely recognize her potential as a source of wealth. The battle between Fadda and Dr. Mufid is really over a symbol: a villa, a building which represents a particular version of Egypt's cultural heritage, but in the end just a thing which stands for values. Nunu, although he is on Fadda's side throughout most of the story, in the end gives flesh and blood to the abstract values implied by the villa. His symbolic importance, for reasons we shall see later, derives from the fact that his formal education, of which he had at least some, was interrupted at an early age. His arrested education leaves him in limbo between the ignorant Fadda al-Madawi and the worldly Dr. Mufid. We see him occasionally reading to Fadda – but reading tortuously and ungrammatically.

Throughout the *musalsal* Nunu is bothered by some unexplained malaise. Normally a zealous henchman of the charismatic Fadda, he is constantly assailed with doubts both about his boss's attitude towards him and about the morality of her actions. Nunu's trademark phrase, said usually when he is depressed over his growing realization that Fadda has been taking advantage of him, is *rūḥ-i maʿdaniyya* (my spirit is metallic), a malapropistic garbling of *rūḥ maʿnawiyya* – "morale," or "spirit."[9] What the phrase does is aptly symbolize the assumed effect of formal schooling – assumed by the producers of the show and readily perceived by the audience – which is to draw the person out of one world and transport him or her to another world. Nunu has been drawn out, but not fully transported; he is in limbo and can be easily taken advantage of by the unscrupulous, such as Fadda al-Madawi. Language is the marker of education, and education mediates several of the serial's key oppositions.

Choosing sides

The other characters in "White Flag" all cluster around either Dr. Mufid or Fadda al-Madawi. Indeed, they are presented in the credits as members of one or the other "team." The first member of Dr. Mufid's team is Amal, a talented female journalist who, like Nunu, suffers from a crisis of confidence. Amal's father, a physician, teaches in Alexandria University's medical school. Dr. Mufid's lawyer Anīs is a humble widower who has raised his son, Hishām, by himself. Hisham, for his part, is an aspiring artist, and an employee in one of Alexandria's "Palaces of Culture" (one of the venues at which Muhammad Fadil held his public meetings on "White Flag"). He falls in love with Amal but, like her, suffers from a crisis of confidence in his professional life, which impinges on his personal life. Another of Dr. Mufid's team is ʿArabī, who is the fully educated son of one of Fadda's associates, a fishmonger named Ḥanafī. Arabi is what Nunu could have been had he completed his schooling; he worked as a high-school teacher in the provinces until he lost his job for protesting against inaccuracies in the government history textbooks. Arabi is in love with Fāṭima, Fadda's niece who managed somehow to become well educated (she is a college student). We are made aware of Fatima's serious approach to culture and learning (as opposed to Fadda's own children, who have obtained college degrees through bribery and privilege) in a scene in which she and Fadda's daughter Simḥa are watching a videocassette of the film *Fahrenheit 451*. Simha gets irritated and wants to watch something crass.

Fatima, however, is obviously interested in this eminently didactic, and foreign, film. Fatima's quality is also made apparent through her modest clothing, which clashes with the gaudy apparel of Simha. So much for the respectable, good-hearted figures around Dr. Mufid.

Fadda's opposing team begins with Nunu and Hammo, the two hired men who sometimes do Fadda's dirty work. Her closest business associate is fellow fishmonger Hanafi (father of the heroic Arabi), whose youngest son, pudgy teenager ʿImād, is sometimes seen reading the papers to the illiterate Fadda. Hanafi is generally a passive accomplice of Fadda, but is not often involved in her more dastardly deeds. Fadda's lawyer, Abū Ṭālib, however, is more than willing to help carry out the most egregious offenses against Fadda's enemies. He is the evil alter ego of Dr. Mufid: educated but only so that he can better manipulate the system to his own benefit.

Fadda's three children – the bratty daughter Simha, and the tank-like sons Fikrī and Khayrī – are in the same mold. Fikri and Khayri, through bribes, cheating, and private lessons,[10] have become professionals – one a doctor and the other an engineer. The daughter, Simha, is a moral disaster. She is petulant, arrogant, and pointedly educated in what Nunu calls *khawāgāti* (foreign) schools, which in Egyptian serials are invariably equated with cultural ruin. In the course of the program she falls in love – in her case rather like a vulture claiming a piece of carrion – with the tortured artist Hisham, the son of Dr. Mufid's lawyer. She communicates her desire first by trying to buy his affections, then through such means as phoning him from her hilariously vulgar room, decorated childishly with cartoon-animal wallpaper, and saying nothing – merely holding the phone to a stereo speaker blasting a 1988 pop song by female vocalist Samīra Saʿīd, who throatily croons, "*mish ḥ-atnāzil ʿannak ʿabadan mahma ykūn*" (I won't give you up no matter what).

Fadda's brood completes the cast. Relations between characters in "White Flag" knit social oppositions into an intricate structure composed of purely local distinctions. But these distinctions nonetheless define Egyptian society within the modern world. The "modern man" is understood by the audience to be educated, Westernized, and yet imbued with *aṣāla* (authenticity) – all elements of an ideal personality spelled out in terms familiar to the viewer. Attempts to pair images of locally recognizable authenticity with Western cosmopolitanism occur frequently in all establishment-controlled media. For example, a high-school science text:

> We must search for the roots of our authenticity and its distinguishing marks, and combine what is authentic with what is new in a way that leads us finally to the creation of *the authentic Egyptian type* – a type derived from the new to an extent

> that makes it "contemporary" but gives it authenticity to an extent that makes it "Egyptian." . . . Although there is nothing to prevent the present borrowing from the past so that the current of life becomes one, inevitably some basic aspects of the past must be "modernized" so as to make those currents grow. But if the present clings to the past, then it makes itself a handed-down and mummified imitation, unaffected by the florescence of life. If authenticity means there is no present without a past, then the continuation and advancement of life means there is no past without a present.
>
> *('Abd al-Gawwād and 'Āmir 1988, 9 [authors' emphasis])*

The science text perfectly describes Dr. Mufid's part. All the traits that combine in an individual to form the "authenticized" modern man come to the viewer via the idiom of education. It is this idiom that makes the program's central concern – the *failure* of education – comprehensible. Dr. Mufid's "team" of educated individuals ripe for middle-class success are, in fact, depressed and constantly threatened with defeat. But their failure is still articulated through the old, imperiled language of mature adaptation to the West through adherence to authentic Egyptian values.

In Egyptian teledrama good and evil, the "white hats and the black hats" of American pop culture, are cast in different terms than those Americans are used to. Aside from the occasional depraved thug, plainly telegraphed to the audience through such means as a leather jacket, facial scar, or simple filth, the distinction tends to be made in terms of taste. "White Flag," like many contemporary soaps and films, communicates bad taste and its attendant moral flaws through clothes.[11] The practice of associating blind imitation of Western fashion with decadence is a tradition dating at least to the late nineteenth century,[12] and the convention persists in "White Flag," where Khayri, Fikri, and Abu Talib often appear wearing enormous, riotously colored neckties, sometimes covered by bright green or yellow sweaters. Nunu, a neophyte to the *nouveau riche* world of Fadda, is at his most ridiculous when he attempts to dress up. Poor Nunu, in a sweat to propose to Fadda's daughter Simha, not only cannot get the tie right, he can't even get his hair right; despite his earnest attempts to flatten it down with grease or water, it sticks up in odd points, signalling his discomfort. The corrupted women, of course, indicate their badness by dressing immodestly. Curvaceous Simha, as fond of mismatched colors as her obese brothers, is also not shy about displaying her body in tight or revealing clothes, a point emphasized in her first appearance in the *musalsal*, gyrating to an ear-splitting disco record as her mother tries to speak to her. Fadda, being an older woman, uses a different strategy. Rather than flout modesty, she clasps it to her in grotesque forms, appearing almost always in a jewel-encrusted headscarf –

something between the *ḥijāb* of neo-Islamic style (see Macleod 1991 for more on the social milieu of the *ḥijāb*) and the conservative dress of uneducated traditional women. Her office decor carries parody still further: the wall behind her desk sports a gaudily decorated qur'ānic verse around a gold-framed portrait of herself in rhinestone *ḥijāb*. The portrait completes the joke: surrounded by false protestations of piety, she is smoking a water pipe, in a pose typical of a *muʿallima* – a small businesswoman, usually a butcher or coffeehouse keeper (or fishmonger [see el-Messiri 1978b, 527]) – whose virtues traditionally are not those of Islamic learning.[13] But of course Fadda, in her "crocodile" and high-rise apartment, is no typical *muʿallima*.

The "good guys" appear in well-tailored suits of muted color, their taste juxtaposed in several parallel ways to the vulgarity of the Fadda team. Fadda watches bellydancers on television, grunting hearty approval; Dr. Mufid relaxes by reading his evening paper while listening to Stravinsky, and sheds a tear when Fadda's hooligans destroy a priceless antique Chinese vase in his home. Hisham, the young artist on Dr. Mufid's team, lives in a room that is more like a studio, surrounded by his own soulful artworks. Where Simha listens to disco music, Amal, the journalist and would-be lover of Hisham, deals with her depression by reading Ṣalāḥ Jahīn – the "poet of Abdel Nasser" who wrote wise and sensitive colloquial quatrains in addition to his widely respected nationalistic poetry. Fadda first appears leaving her high-rise in the "crocodile" to the tune of "Yankee Doodle," played grandiosely on a synthesizer. Her "crocodile" makes a stark contrast to Dr. Mufid's well-worn Fiat compact, which Fadda's hooligans burn in the guerrilla war to obtain the villa. Dr. Mufid's lawyer Anis (Hisham's father) appears at the breakfast table with his son, wearing a traditional *gallabiyya*, peeling an orange or a banana while he dispenses fatherly wisdom; Fadda's evil lawyer Abu Talib, by contrast, coyly bribes officials and pathetically attempts to impress Dr. Mufid by offering to show him karate films or *Rambo*.

"White Flag" consistently seeks to communicate the gulf between the two sides through juxtaposition of cultural markers. Plot functions mainly to set up ever-sharper contradictions between the two "teams," continually raising the stakes, but not introducing any fundamental change to the opposition outlined by the end of the first episode. Class plays an important role in constructing this opposition, but what drew the audience in was not simply the presence of class – this has been a part of television and film representation since the beginning – but the way class is now problematized.

Terms of identity

In "White Flag" everything revolves around the idea of a middle class, which, in ideological terms, is more than a statistical mean somewhere between rich and poor. Egyptian middle-class identity is tied to Egyptian nationalism and rests on an ideology of transformation from "traditionalism" to "modernity." The process of transformation is complex, encompassing parallel versions of *aṣāla* (authenticity), one classicist and the other "folkloric," which never sit together comfortably. Heritage is not simply there but must constantly be sifted and reworked in the cause of progress. Again our high-school science text:

> [We must make] an objective study of the Egyptian heritage and all the sources and tributaries connected with it, extracting general principles which lead to a clarification of all of the positive and negative aspects of our heritage . . . Clearly to catch up with the [modern] age we must begin from where others left off; [the imperative of] authenticity does not allow us to follow this path [to modernity] from where our ancestors left off . . . After we renew what is authentic in our culture and tie it to what is useful from our modern lives, we must disseminate this civilization among the people . . . cultural elements are diffused in society from above to below . . . Thereby our civilization will come to have an Egyptian face, and the phenomenon of occidentalism, which makes our heads walk on the ground while our feet are hanging in the air, will be eliminated. *('Abd al-Gawwād and 'Āmir 1988, 10–11)*

The depressed and endangered state of all the "good guys" in "White Flag" indicates that this modernist ideology has become problematized for some, and perhaps endangered for all. But the message that culture and progress spread "from above to below" can still be delivered in the context of television drama without losing a broad audience. Who, then, is below?

At several points in "White Flag" Dr. Mufid or his allies emphasize the importance of enlisting the aid of the common people, to whom they refer as *awlād al-balad*. *Ibn al-balad* (the singular of *awlād al-balad*) can be glossed as "son of the town," or "son of the place/region" – a real Egyptian, and a regular guy; sometimes the salt of the earth, in other contexts a rough diamond. Arabi is *ibn al-balad* smoothed and polished by high culture. By contrast Nunu, with his broken education (marked by his broken Arabic), remains unpolished, coarse, and misdirected, though decent at heart if only he would accept the guidance of his cultural betters.

Ibn al-balad is sometimes described as a sociological type – someone who lives in a *ḥāra* (a traditional quarter), works at certain occupations (usually independent trades) and wears a *gallabiyya* (traditional robe).[14] But the term is also said to apply to "behavioral characteristics and norms" as well as "a specific group of Egyptians" (el-Messiri 1978a; Booth 1990, 143–44). The adjectival version of *ibn al-balad* is *baladī*, which "tends more to be a label applied by those who consider themselves not *baladī*; while the noun [*ibn al-balad*] incorporates a strong sense of self-identity" (Booth 1990, 144).

The adjectival sense of *baladī* does indeed occur in expressions of denigration. For example, I once heard a newspaper editor attempt to allay the fears of new employees, nervous at the erratic disbursement of pay, by saying that the new paper "would not be run in a *baladī* way."[15] He elaborated by saying the operations of the paper would be straightforward, not convoluted or slapdash. Or in a discussion of clothes the European-style fashions advertised on television might be denigrated as *baladī*, not the "real thing," but a crass local imitation that nobody of taste would wear.[16] In such situations *baladī* means not just "local," but "unsophisticated," "crude," and invariably "premodern." True taste, by contrast, is described in slang terms such as *hayh ʾistandard* (high standard), *shīk ʿawi* (very chic), or *fāshun ʿawi* (very fashionable). Those terms can, of course, be turned against one, used in parody of the *infitāḥi* – the *nouveau riche* brought to tacky prominence by the policies of a free market.

But while the term *ibn al-balad* and its adjectival derivative *baladī* can be used derogatorily, in other contexts the terms can invoke tradition in a positive sense, and can have nationalistic overtones. A much-loved food such as *maḥshi* (stuffed vegetables) or *mishsh* (a kind of fermented cheese) might be described approvingly as *baladī*. When I asked for three teaspoons of sugar in my tea Egyptian friends, whose image of the stereotypical foreigner was of someone who took little or no sugar, frequently remarked approvingly that this was *baladī* (or sometimes simply as "Egyptian" with the comment *itmaṣṣart* – you have become Egyptian).

Booth and el-Messiri both characterize the sociological connotations of *ibn al-balad* as relatively recent – probably dating no earlier than the nineteenth century when the old social division between a Turco-Circassian ruling elite and the Egyptian masses broke down (Booth 1990, 144–45; el-Messiri 1978a, 30). In the old social structure all native Egyptians could have been referred to as relatively undifferentiated *awlād al-balad*.[17] By at least the 1920s a new situation prevailed: below the level of foreign rule (British and French), which never achieved wide legitimacy in Egypt, elites of different sorts were all "Egyptian." *Ibn al-balad* began to take on its modern connotations of the *ḥāra*, or traditional quarter, of the small merchant, the adherent to a traditional code of honor (for men) known as *shahāma* (meaning both "gallantry" and "astuteness" [el-Messiri 1978a, 80–83]) – in short an Egyptian who depended less obviously, if at all, on the modernizing foreign order than did functionaries of the bourgeoisie.

The point of media constructions such as "White Flag" is to bring the salutary image of *ibn al-balad* – a diamond in the rough – together with his cultural betters, thereby uniting Egypt's vernacular past with its modernized future. One of the means for accomplishing this operation is an implied comparison of taste and learning with the other view of *ibn al-balad* – that of the laughably out-of-date rube or bumpkin.

As a term of self-definition, rather than a sociological signifier, *ibn al-balad* became semantically opposed to *ibn al-zawāt* (classical *ibn al-dhawāt*: "son of the nobility," i.e. the ariṣtocracy).[18] Today the term *ibn al-zawāt* can be used in some contexts with more or less positive connotations; it can have the cachet of old money and perhaps even a certain nobility of character. In the 1920s, however, the term had many of the connotations of "*nouveau riche*": frivolity, effeminacy (in men), immodesty (primarily in women), greed, sloth. The term was associated with a crashing sense of cultural inauthenticity, invariably linked to the adoption of Western style in comportment and material life. In contemporary linguistic practice many of the negative connotations of *ibn al-zawāt* have been transferred to other terms, such as *bitūʿ l-infitāḥ*, "those of the Open Door [post-Nasserist economic policy]" – sometimes simply *infitāḥi* – the people who have made fortunes and drive Mercedes.[19] These are the terms that readily apply to Fadda and her cronies, just as the *ibn al-balad* label applies to Arabi and, more problematically, Nunu. The opposition between an authentic *ibn al-balad* and an inauthentic imitation foreigner, renamed somewhat since the 1920s, remains salient in the television drama of the 1990s.

Along with appeals to an imagined folk identity, the producers of the serial went to great lengths to weave around Dr. Mufid a heavy symbolic web of *turāth*, or "heritage." Various characters in "White Flag" embellish the history of the villa at length, sometimes with reference to history, other times fancifully: it was used by nationalists fighting the British; it contains a secret chamber holding priceless documents that illuminate Egyptian history; Dr. Mufid has stuffed it full of priceless works of art from both East and West. Another scene embroiders the heritage theme by showing Dr. Mufid musing over a book on the artists of Alexandria. He contemplates his artistic and intellectual *isnād*,[20] turning the pages slowly, starting with a photograph of Sayyid Darwīsh, singer of the 1919 Egyptian revolution and a founder of modern Egyptian music; another photograph of painter Maḥmūd Saʿīd (1897–1964), who employed European technique acquired in Alexandria and Paris to create stylized images of Egyptian folk life; then a study by painter Muḥammad Nāgī (1888–1956), who worked with Monet;[21] of literary giant Taufīq al-Ḥakīm; a photograph of Sayf Wanlī (1906–76), who augmented his painting talent with theater set design, including sets for European productions of *Carmen* and *I Pagliacci*; finally a Sayf Wanli portrait of nationalist icon Gamal Abdel Nasser. These are all figures from the pantheon of Egyptian modernity – artistic, intellectual, and political pioneers in an ongoing synthesis of European technique with Egyptian subject matter. The portraits scene ends with Dr. Mufid's dreamy countenance as he contemplates the burdens placed on the cultural vanguard that he represents.

The character of Dr. Mufid is not intended as a distanced ivory-tower intellectual, too elite to involve himself in the everyday affairs of the world around him. He continually offers encouragement and support to the star-crossed lovers, Amal and Hisham. He treats his servants – one a sophisticated man forced into difficult circumstances by his opposition to corruption, the other a simple but honorable Nubian – with the kind of dignity and respect that can only be meted out by a man who is secure in his position. Dr. Mufid is in every way the Egyptian renaissance man: worldly, conversant with European technique, but deeply committed to the finest his culture offers.

Given the elaborate attempts to link the members of Dr. Mufid's team to a kind of highbrow authenticity, it was surprising so many people associated the series not with "threats to our priceless heritage," but with "the power of money" or "the dangers of materialism." No doubt part of this was due to Sana Gamil having stolen the show as Fadda. But the serial represented the bearers of high culture as essentially dysfunctional. Both Hisham and Amal live in frustration, she tormented by an emotional blackmail effected by the subject of one of her journalistic exposés, he racked by doubts about his worth as an artist. The impossibility of self-fulfillment in professional life renders their would-be love affair an endless round of mistrust and bickering. Dr. Mufid had devoted his life to serving his country, but now he seems powerless in the face of Fadda's aggression. One is never quite sure whether his weak opposition to Fadda derives from principle, or whether he simply lacks the guts to fight back. Arabi, the teacher, has been fired. His sweetheart, Fatima (Fadda's niece), wants to get out from under her aunt's thumb, but can't unless Arabi, her one hope for escape, can achieve enough prosperity to offer marriage. All of the characters in Dr. Mufid's "team" are in some sense thwarted. Quality cannot succeed in a world dominated by the likes of Fadda. The character of Dr. Mufid himself inspired distant respect rather than ardent love.

If the audience of "White Flag" was moved by the attack on Dr. Mufid – as many were – without identifying passionately with the victim, then what was it that raised the serial from success to phenomenon? To begin with, many people identified with Fadda's class, if not with her morals. "We understand Fadda – she talks like us." A few, in cynical moments, asserted that the masses coveted Fadda's riches, that the whole country was as infected with greed as she. But the program, in fact, had a built-in appeal to Fadda's class, distinct from her person. This lay in the repeated appeals made by Dr. Mufid himself to "*awlād al-balad*" – the "salt of the earth" or the raw clay with which cultural elites like himself could mold an image of the modern Egyptian. Simply put, he wants them to take sides with either the crass or the moral and cultural.

The battle is joined

Throughout the serial characters address the masses with increasing frequency and greater insistence. We see this early on when Arabi, son of Fadda's henchman Hanafi, is presented to Dr. Mufid as *ibn al-balad* made good, and the older man is impressed. He tells Arabi how surprised he is to find that a person from a lower-class background could become truly educated. Their ensuing conversation is a straightforward appeal to the masses:

ARABI You would have thought that [people from the popular quarters are vulgar] if not for me?

DR. MUFID Of course. Because you are the son of the *muʿallim* Hanafi, and of this popular [*shaʿbī*][22] environment. And this means that the matter [i.e. Fadda's attempts to take over the villa] has no relation to class or to social position; it is connected only with circumstances – circumstances which concentrate the power of money in the hands of the ignorant and encourage them to scorn beauty, to destroy authenticity and to leave no value sacred.

ARABI I understand, Doctor. This vulgarity isn't a characteristic of most people; on the contrary, there are many people from the Baḥrī quarter, and Kōm Shaʕaafa and Muḥarram Bēh – a thousand quarters from all over Egypt which are downtrodden. And yet the people from these quarters sense beauty, understand it and believe in it. The attack on you from those who want to take the villa and destroy it isn't from them; those who attack you are a boil which is nurtured by defects which afflict society and upset its balance.

This is a familiar appeal, made by intellectuals who occasionally venture afield from the confines of classicism: their concern with the people is not with the sort of debased *baladī* culture typical of Fadda, but with the salt of the earth, who only need enlightenment to be Egypt's backbone. The rhetoric is widespread. We see a nearly identical statement, for example, in an issue of a 1986 mass-circulation weekly devoted to the work of Bayram al-Tūnsī, a *sha'bi* (popular) poet of the mid-twentieth century:

> *Ibn al-balad* . . . is a man who, despite his poverty, is intelligent, aware, of ready insight, light-hearted, cheerful by nature, a joker [*ibn nukta*], brave, and gallant in his boldness. But social circumstances impose upon him ignorance and poverty, so he flees from reality in drugs and participates – unknowingly – in cultural backwardness through which his country drags him. If someone would stand ready to work for his treatment, and for his revival, his awakening would be magnificent.
> *(al-'Azab 1986, 36)*

Although not everyone in Egypt accepts this discourse of "improvement," such rhetoric nonetheless occurs in all media – so often that it passes unremarked. In context the condescension of calls to art and culture is muted by sheer repetition.

Dr. Mufid is just the person to oversee the "awakening of *ibn al-balad*," and Nunu is the perfect "ignoramus by social circumstances." What leads finally to Nunu's awakening is the progressive widening of the battle between Fadda and Dr. Mufid. Their struggle eventually goes beyond their respective "teams"; Dr. Mufid attempts to enlist the support of artists and intellectuals so as to publicize the issue of the villa. Fadda counters by bribing the officials of all the cultural institutions in Alexandria to withdraw their support for Dr. Mufid. She makes large, well-publicized donations to the arts, and the officials begin to publish pro-Fadda articles. The more spineless members of the art world give a celebration in honor of "Fadda al-Madawi, patroness of the arts." We see banners being raised at the Palace of Culture on the Alexandria corniche, Hisham's workplace. One says, "The Palace of Culture welcomes the honored guest Fadda al-Madawi, number-one intellectual." Fadda's trademark "Yankee Doodle" on a synthesizer plays in the background.

Dr. Mufid's counterstrategy is to let Fadda disgrace herself, then hijack the proceedings to make an appeal for public sympathy. After the banner scene we see Fadda practicing her speech before her moment in the spotlight. Fadda's team has appealed to Hanafi's son Arabi – the only educated person they know – to write the speech. Arabi, however, is on Dr. Mufid's side and writes a parody of a speech, which Fadda turns into an even more laughable debacle.

The event at which Fadda speaks is a war of symbolic appeal to the people. Fadda both displays her ignorance, symbolizing the sort of "cultural backwardness" that intellectuals regularly decry, and attempts to present herself as a *bint al-balad*. The partially educated Nunu acts as her adviser. We see him in an "*ismōking*" ("smoking jacket" – an absurdly outmoded symbol of elegance), teaching Fadda the words of her speech and getting them hopelessly tangled. The scene fades into the real speech before a large crowd of *awlād al-balad*, some of whom were paid by Fadda to cheer her on, others of whom came spontaneously to support Dr. Mufid. Dr. Mufid and his supporters are in the audience, as are members of Fadda's "team." Much of the fun derives from the use of language:

FADDA (speaking a ponderous grammatically incorrect classical Arabic): Ladies and gentlemen, I face you with thanks and gratitude.

HAMMO (standing in the crowd of paid supporters): Seven, seven (the crowd yells "fourteen"), seven, seven (crowd yells "moon of fourteen" [This is one of Fadda's attempts to invoke the vernacular tradition; they are comparing Fadda to the full moon fourteen days into the lunar month, saying that she is beautiful]).

FADDA (slaughtering the classical Arabic language): The truth is, what I did is an expression of a deep belief in art and in the serious role which it plays in the life of the people.

HAMMO (standing again in the crowd): Life of the people! Life of the people! (The crowd responds.)

FADDA Some people ask, "What is the relationship of culture to fish?" (The bribed arts official sitting next to her starts to look nervous.) The truth is that the connection was established a long time ago – since the time of Alexander of the two horns [Alexander the Great].[23]

HAMMO Long live Alexander of the two horns! Two horns! Two horns! (The crowd responds.)

FADDA Alexander, father of Alexandria – is this sweet? ("Sweet!" the crowd replies.) – loved fish very much, and built Alexandria on the coast just for the sake of fish.

NUNU (standing behind her on the podium): Wrong, *ya ḥagga*! [A *ḥajja* is literally someone who has gone on the pilgrimage to Mecca, but in Egypt also a term of respect given to elders. Nunu begins to panic as Fadda departs from the text.]

FADDA (pushes Nunu aside and continues without a text, now speaking in low colloquial): And who was the teacher of that Alexander? He was a very very very *very* famous *khōga* ["teacher": she uses an obsolete, deeply colloquial and etymologically Persian word].

NUNU Aristotle, *ya ḥagga*, Aristotle.

FADDA That's right, Aristotle. He knew that if he ate a bowl of stewed fish [*ṣayyadiyya*, another *baladī* reference that clashes with her allegedly high purpose] his brain would open up and he would become cultured (the crowd becomes restless, some in shock, others in support).

HANAFI (in the crowd, proudly to the person seated next to him): My son Professor Arabi wrote this speech.

FADDA (to Nunu): What's going on? Did I do something wrong?

NUNU No, that's right. Aristotle.

THE BRIBED OFFICIAL (in a growing panic): Finish up, finish up!

DR. MUFID (standing in the audience): I want to say something.

BRIBED OFFICIAL Excuse me, sir, but your name isn't in the program of the party.

DR. MUFID What party? This is a farce (he rushes to the microphone before anyone can stop him). I don't want to make a speech, or to say very much, I just want to bring to your attention the reality which appears before you. The "honorable" Madam Fadda al-Madawi, who stands before you delivering this precious speech on the relation of fish to culture, wants to apply these words to the house of Abu al-Ghar: she wants to turn history and art into a bowl of fish stew!

At this point the meeting threatens to dissolve into chaos. Hammo tries to whip up the crowd in favor of Fadda, but many people – inhabitants of the popular quarters, the true *awlād al-balad* – rally spontaneously to Dr. Mufid. It looks as if a fight will break out, but Hanafi gets Fadda's people under control, giving the lawyer Abu Talib a chance to launch a counterattack.

ABU TALIB (grabbing the microphone): In answer to the doubters and the rumor-mongers, I am compelled to announce a huge new project – the big surprise of the night: a gift from Madam Fadda al-Madawi to all of Alexandria! (He pulls out an architectural drawing.) The "Simha City for the Arts"! [Simha, we remember, is Fadda's vulgar, spoiled daughter.] A completely finished city of 30,000 square feet. Including the following: two movie studios which will return the center for film production to Alexandria, which long ago had the first studio in Egypt (we see Dr. Mufid looking disgusted); two studios for television production, a lab for printing and developing film, a center for recording with computerized equipment (we see Nunu's eyes light up), a high-rise apartment for the administration of the city for the arts (the bribed official looks pleased with himself and straightens his tie), a supermarket with "*restaurān*" [he appeals to class snobbery, inserting a foreign word], three hamburger restaurants, three video outlets, three shoe stores – all together, four outlets selling elegant and modest clothes (the camera turns to Fadda in her gaudy Islamic parody). And I want to use this occasion to reply to Dr. Mufid Abu al-Ghar that Fadda al-Madawi wasn't going to buy his villa just to destroy it, but to make it a part of the city for the arts to which she has given the dearest name she could – that of her daughter, that mistress of chastity and virtue, Simha Shāṭir (he slurs the name in his excitement, spraying spittle on the crowd).

Fadda's speech and the ensuing imbroglio set the stage for the final confrontation. Although she has silenced officialdom with her bribes to the artistic community, Fadda cannot stop Amal from publishing revelations on the sleazy way she built her empire. Outraged, she has Amal and Hisham kidnapped, drugged, and then picked up in a police raid in one of Alexandria's seamier quarters. Dr. Mufid capitulates; it is the villa in exchange for Amal and Hisham, whom Fadda can free through her influence with the authorities.

We see a stony-faced Dr. Mufid boarding a taxi, a rough stick beside him in the car. The taxi proceeds down the corniche – figuratively down because he descends into progressively rougher neighborhoods. He disembarks in a very rough area indeed, and proceeds down an alley festooned, ironically, with a banner reading "Alexandria is beautiful – keep it clean." He passes Hanafi and Hammo, who stare in astonishment. Even they seem to feel the tragedy of the moment. Upon the stick hangs a white shirt, which precedes Dr. Mufid into Fadda's office, the door held open by an amazed Hammo. A deal is struck: the villa at the market price, plus an extra LE 100,000 thrown in by Fadda in a grotesque parody of generosity, in exchange for the release of Amal and Hisham from prison. Fadda and Dr. Mufid then proceed to a realtor's office to sign the documents. Fadda stands, her arms raised, a smile on her face, screaming for her "crocodile," her fancy Mercedes: "*Ḥammo! At-timsāḥa yalla*!" In her moment of triumph she ties the images together, and the audience become aware that the victory of barbarism over civilization was encoded in the introduction. But the end of the serial realigns the elements of class and culture to suggest the fight goes on elsewhere.

The members of Dr. Mufid's team gather to console the dejected man. They insist on a last-ditch defense of the villa and the heritage it represents. Dr. Mufid, weary, defeated, tries to tell them the game is over, but his loyal followers refuse to surrender. The final confrontation begins with the same juxtaposition of elements presented in the introduction: the villa, then the approaching bulldozer.[24] But from the villa now come three lines of people: first the intellectuals, led by Hisham, then the *awlād al-balad*, with Arabi at their head, and finally a group of students led by Fadda's niece Fatima. On the other side a much smaller group of people arrives to support the bulldozer: first Fadda in the "crocodile," driven by her lackey Hammo, then Abu Talib. On the villa side Dr. Mufid pushes his way to the front of the intellectuals. Nunu comes to the front of the *awlād al-balad*; he has finally understood the depth of his former boss's corruption, and formed a new alliance with the upholders of Egypt's modernist heritage.

Fadda rants at the defenders of the villa to no avail. "Let her bulldoze us," says Hisham. "We're no better than the people you bulldoze every day," screams Amal. "You've bulldozed me for a long time," says Nunu, "but not today." Beside herself with rage, Fadda screams that the bulldozer will advance whether or not people are in its way. Dr. Mufid, heartened by his followers' defiance, finally recovers his nerve. He meets Fadda's threat in Gandhian style by sitting on the pavement. His followers sit beside him. They link hands, raising them above their heads in an unmistakable show of unity. The bulldozer advances. Just before it makes contact with the first line of people the image freezes. The sound of a printing press, audible as the scene builds to its climax, becomes louder, then the voice of the narrator intones, "An appeal: those sitting on the pavement around the villa of Abu al-Ghar in Alexandria call upon you to sit with them so that Dr. Mufid and company are not forced to raise the white flag." The theme song plays as stills of the defiant faces of Dr. Mufid's supporters flash on the screen. End of "White Flag."

Texts and the "real world"

The problem of what a "text" means to its author and its audience is one of the thornier issues in anthropology, or for that matter, any discipline (Harvey 1989, 49–51; Thompson 1990, 133–135; Clifford and Marcus 1986). The world constructed in "White Flag" appears to have the possibility of multiple interpretation built into it. For one thing, the viewer could identify with the classical heritage represented by Dr. Mufid, or with the "folk" heritage embodied in Arabi and the *awlād al-balad* who stood by Dr. Mufid in his time of need, or, for that matter, with the corrupt Fadda and her cronies. Both Dr. Mufid and Arabi also represented modernity – a point driven home repeatedly by references to the value of true education, improvement, and taste. Yet the drama was sufficiently complex to be seen and enjoyed as a whole by people of different backgrounds. It was plausible enough to hold a general audience. The episodes were knitted together by the image of modernity that centered on Dr. Mufid and Arabi – an ideal plainly threatened by the crass and vulgar. The idea of such a juxtaposition was not thought absurd by the show's viewers. Dr. Mufid's position relative to Fadda's vulgarity is what the drama turns on.

These elements of plot and character were not articulated by most people. They were unremarked. What was articulated clearly, though, was a truth people thought the show revealed. In the words of a mechanic and occasional taxi driver (who was, when he said the following, passing by some particularly ostentatious villas in his car): "Money dominates everything too much. It has become too easy for one to sell his conscience to get money, especially young people who want to get an apartment. They will lower themselves considerably to get money. They can't get what they want through education." A university student said: "The serial shows that everything works through money. One doesn't need education to get what he wants." Some even explicitly denied that an ideological message would reach the masses, as if they themselves were among the few who grasped the point of a serial watched by millions. For example, another student: "The show consisted of symbols, I mean good and evil were represented by Fadda al-Madawi and Gamil Ratib. But not all the viewers are at the same level in terms of education and awareness. They can't understand what the program is trying to say." But the same person said: "I like ["White Flag"] because it says the truth. Everything here works through influence and bribes."

A certain measure of disillusion was to be expected from the state of Egypt's economy. But the blockages shown in the careers of Dr. Mufid's associates are real. The whole modernist project, of which Mufid himself is the product and champion, faces severe obstacles and the intellectuals who stand with him before the bulldozer are marginalized in the economy of the free market.

The state, we recall, was the employer of "White Flag"'s young artist, Hisham, who worked in the Palace of Culture in Alexandria. Hisham may have enjoyed organizing art exhibits at the Palace of Culture, but the serial never directly alludes to the likelihood that his pay was very poor. The lowest rung on the government pay scale in 1978 was $20 per month (Leila, Palmer, and Yassin 1988, 8). Given that the serial was produced in the late 1980s, and that Hisham was a college graduate, we may assume that his pay was higher – perhaps in the neighborhood of $75 per month. It is an understatement to say that Hisham would need some time to save for a spacious apartment such as the one his father Anis (Dr. Mufid's lawyer) lived in.[25] Without parental help he would never get it.

The fate of Arabi, Dr. Mufid's *ibn al-balad*-turned-intellectual, may have been somewhat better. A typical schoolteacher in 1978 could expect to make in the neighborhood of $40 per month (*ibid.*). Again, allowing for inflation one can assume that by the late 1980s he would have been earning slightly more. Teachers, however, can augment their salaries by offering private lessons. By 1990 the practice had been made legal under certain circumscribed conditions (small groups where the family of each student paid a government-controlled sum for extra tutoring). Many people, however, did not believe that students had much chance for success in the educational system unless they paid far more than the legally permitted sums to private teachers.[26] This often resulted in bad feelings between teachers and students or their families. The teachers felt that they were being underpaid, and the students that they were being cheated.[27] Arabi, of course, was portrayed as an exceptional teacher laboring selflessly in an Upper Egyptian provincial town. But he would have to be very selfless indeed to live on his official salary.

Fadda is a caricature, but a caricature with a point. Mercedes "crocodiles," "pigs," and "chicken's backsides" do indeed roll through the streets of Cairo and Alexandria carrying people whose material success has little to do with official imagery of culture and education. Their wealth, in the eyes of many, can only have come from theft. Fadda is no more literal an image of the real world than are the selfless idealists she opposes; but the clash of values each represents was felt as real by viewers. Were it not real, Fadda herself would not have touched the nerve she did.

The secret to its success lay in its portrayal of social deadlock – rare in an Egyptian television serial, and more arresting to the audience than the obligatory *musalsal* didacticism. A portrayal of deadlock was as effective in selling the serial to the audience as a high-budget, hyper-realistic production rubbing everyone's nose in the often grim realities in which they live, because the opposed images defined a field of contestation for national identity and brought social problems to light with unusual clarity. If the structure of double deadlock so prominent in the serial's climax – modernity face-to-face with backwardness and *ibn al-balad* staring down *ibn al-zawāt* – contributed to the program's popularity, how are such oppositions played out in other social arenas? How long has the deadlock been there?

3

The split vernacular

The classical language was very strange and very far from the minds of the fellahin, from their concerns and imaginations. And when I started to write in the classically correct, formal style and language, I felt that a barrier had gone up between me and my friends. I felt alienated, as if I were some kind of snob.

Poet ʿAbd al-Raḥmān al-Abnūdī (Tresilian 1991, 14)

As a subject of analysis "popular culture" in the Egyptian context mirrors the ambiguities inherent in the images of "White Flag." There is no satisfactory gloss in Arabic for "popular culture." *Al-thaqāfa al-shaʿbiyya* is one obvious possibility, but the phrase conjures images of saints' festivals, healing rituals, mannerisms of speech, and certain types of clothing thought to be typical of traditional people – "folklore," in other words. Indeed, some intellectuals lament the fact – or really the assumption – that films and televised serials such as "White Flag" have replaced traditional folklore with a stock of nonlocal images divorced from "their" reality. For example, film critic Samīr Farīd says: "Because the cinema is the art of the educated person and the illiterate alike, it has taken the place of folklore for the illiterate just as it has become a new art for the educated" (Farīd 1988, 6). Such commentary typically assumes a separation of masses and intellectuals, from which the distinction between folklore and art derives. No term stands for their eventual synthesis. "Mass culture," in this view, would be that of the nonintellectuals, merely folklore of the modern age.

Others consider "folklore" an evil to be stamped out by a benevolently modern state, and encourage the substitution of almost any cultural model that is not the traditional "backward" one (see, for example, L. ʿAwaḍ

1969a). But both views of "folklore" and the people who practice it leave ambiguous the relationship between "them" (the "folk") and the mass-culture fantasies that intellectuals themselves produce. "Popular culture" then becomes a convenient scapegoat for the failure of modernity: either the "folk" can't understand it because they are still premodern, or television and films have corrupted them so that they no longer retain a firm grasp on the fundamentals of their own culture. Yet as "White Flag" suggests, popular culture can also provide a means to articulate contradictions felt in the lives of the very people viewed by many producers – and certainly many intellectuals – as either backward "folk" or unformed clay to be molded by the influence of modernity.

The didactic strain in commentary on culture is often striking, not least when a nonelite cultural strain is accorded value. As Dr. ʿAbd al-Ḥamīd Yūnis, a prominent Egyptian folklorist, put it:

> The first rule by which the folklorist is obliged to work is to "sift the folk heritage" so as to select samples characterized by authenticity [*aṣāla*], refinement [*raqī*] and the potential for inspiration [*ilhām*] and which are among the aspects of cultural history, or the reflections of artistic and literary expression. The first principle to which those who collect, catalog and display [folk culture] must adhere is to differentiate between true folk material and material wrongly ascribed to the people, using scientific methods of collection and classification, constructing a detailed archive, and then selecting what is representative of a given trait or quality so that it can then be displayed to the public. *(Yūnis 1970)*

Heritage is not simply there, but something to be properly organized. Vulgarity should be struck from the record and the folk be admitted to Egypt's heritage on condition of "authenticity." "Scientific" methods sort the crass and regrettable from the sources of refinement and of inspiration, and modernist language defines the residue of this operation by equating the lowly and peripheral, wherever they are found, with the backward. This used also to mean the rural. For example, Gabriel Baer summarizes the views on the peasantry from the perspective of the urban *ʿulamāʾ* as reported by the seventeenth-century Egyptian writer ʿAbd al-Gawwād Khaḍr al-Shirbīnī:

> Steady immersion in dung and mud makes the fellah contemptible . . . Instead of praying or reading the Qur'an they think about their flocks . . . They meet in the mosque in order to do business . . . and while praying they occupy themselves with all kinds of profane matters . . . Even worse, the fellahs are thieves . . . It is quite usual for fellahs to steal shoes of other fellahs during prayer in the mosque . . . He is also importunate and pertinacious . . . In addition, he does not escape a kind of vilification which is common in various branches of Arabic literature, namely the accusation of sodomy (with animals). *(Baer 1982, 16–18)*

Although the causes for the alleged backwardness of the peasantry have been reexamined in modern times – particularly in the postindependence Nasser era (*ibid.*, 22–36) – the lack of esteem for peasants by contemporary urban writers remains consistent with al-Shirbini's seventeenth-century diatribe. A passage by Luis Awad, a prominent literary critic and journalist, illustrates the low regard intellectuals have for culture of "the folk":

> The question which must be asked frankly and realistically is this: is the culture of the Egyptian countryside truly suitable today to be raw material for the civilization of the twentieth century? I say [the question must be asked] realistically because a certain degree of romanticism has entered our outlook on the peasants and simple people since we have adopted the principle of glorifying the masses. Personally – although I am civilized to the marrow – my mind is with the city and my heart with the countryside; I am not innocent of this romanticized view of the people.
>
> But the enormity of the gap between city and countryside, which makes even the dregs of the bureaucrats refuse to return to the countryside from which they have come because of its severe poverty and the harshness of its life, makes me doubt frankly that our folk culture and all that goes under the heading "folklore" is suitable material for life in the twentieth century after all these centuries of isolation from the civilized world . . . The bourgeoisie of Cairo is trying to save the bourgeoisie of the provinces from the coarse hell of the countryside lurking all about them like a ghoul waiting to ambush them and swallow them up. Some of us have mistakenly seen these efforts as a means of organizing folk culture in service of the arts and what is called "mass culture" [*al-thaqāfa al-jamāhīriyya*].
>
> *(L. Awad 1969b, 6)*[1]

Awad's rejection of everything associated with peasants is more vehement than is usual. Abdel Nasser's government, from 1952 on, had glorified "the peasant," though the peasant was of course to be drawn to modernity by revolution. Even during the Nasserist period, however, "peasant culture" was something to be transcended.

Awad's condemnations of the countryside's "coarse hell" are easily transferred to the "urban peasants" in Cairo whose proximity to the centers of high culture makes them even more of an affront to modernity. The ambiguities surrounding *ibn al-balad*, the "son of the town," can easily be swept aside by intellectuals in a reformist mood. But the countryside, be it rural idyll or rural hell, is no longer a place where the "folk" can be located plausibly as separate from intellectuals. In the twentieth century, Egypt has been turned inside out.

To begin with, mass education, the orthodox route to modernity in official culture from Luis Awad to "White Flag," swims against an inexorable tide of rising population: from around 10 million at the turn of the century to over 40 million by 1981.[2] As in many "developing countries" much of the increase has been absorbed by urban areas,[3] and there has been no net increase in Egypt's inhabited area.[4] Furthermore, there is no question of reversing the population shift to the cities, as the amount of available land in the countryside has drastically declined over the past century.[5] And if the situation in the country as a whole is sobering, that of the cities is even more so. Cairo, with a population conservatively estimated at 12 to 13 million, already contains nearly a quarter of Egypt's population, and may double in size in the next twelve years. The infrastructure of Cairo was never planned for more than a population of 1.5 million.

The state's best efforts to promote education have barely kept pace with population increase. Primary-school enrollment rates rose from 1960 to 1979, but not by much – from 80 to 89 percent for boys, 52 to 63 percent for girls (Richards and Waterbury 1990, 112). Despite the high priority assigned to education in official rhetoric, government spending on education actually fell from 1970 to 1981.[6] The overall number of people passing through schools has increased, as have all demographic numbers. The number of people with access to significant educational resources remains tiny even though the sheer number of students passing through the system continues to increase.

State rhetoric touts education as a mighty engine of refinement and progress on one hand, while on the other hand state-sponsored television broadcasts sensationalistic programs that turn on the failure of modernity. One such program, "*Zaḥma*" (Crowdedness), links crime and overpopulation, tacitly acknowledging the irrelevance of learning. "*Zaḥma*" is a "scared straight" program that begins with scenes of crowded streets as an electronically reverberated voice intones "*zaḥma . . . zaḥma . . . ZAḤMA!*" The teeming crowds of the program's introduction then give way to allegedly true stories of lurid crime, augmented by interviews with prisoners.

The pessimism of "*Zaḥma*" is too prevalent a feature of the free-market policies since 1974 for the state to ignore.[7] The appearance of new money in the midst of such impoverishment is what the image of Fadda al-Madawi, the venal fishwife and Mercedes owner of "White Flag," so compellingly captures. Her opposite, Dr. Mufid the cultured modernist, was the product of an earlier generation – that of Luis Awad, and the last in which prosperity accompanied educational progress.[8]

The paradox, then, is that modernist rhetoric, an imagery of breaking with the past and of cumulative progress, has flourished in commentary on culture high and low, while the world to be reformed by these efforts remains sluggishly unresponsive. The fixity of modernism itself is a further paradox. Not just in Egypt but anywhere such language is prominent, one is always running, always progressing, and never quite catching up. This language of modernist reform has changed little, at least since the Khedive Ismail's time (1863–79). This rhetoric articulates with further terms that also remain fixed and claim to describe at least as much – primarily terms having to do with language.

Egyptian linguistic ideology

It is widely accepted that constructs of cultural identity are immanent in linguistic practice. In Egypt metalinguistic discourse centers around the idea that language is highly polarized – that "proper language," both spoken and written, is classical, and all else degenerate. Under certain circumstances this polarity can be reversed so that nonclassicist ideals are valued in opposition to those of foreigners, but in either case Egyptian writers usually talk about language in terms of dichotomy. Linguistic practice does not conform to these idealized notions. However, a practice-oriented account of the situation would seem dubious to most Egyptians; the entire matter of language can hardly be discussed in an Egyptian context in any terms other than abstracted structure. If we are to find a link between language and society that is not a construction only of our own theory, we should focus on this claim, made by many Egyptians both within and outside the academy.

Linguistic ideology is an integral part of Egyptian perceptions of the *nahḍa* (renaissance) – the cultural transformation of the Arabic-speaking peoples that has taken place since the mid-nineteenth century. A central element of the *nahḍa* was a shift towards rationalism, the "modernization" of the Middle East. Egyptian intellectuals readily acknowledge a movement toward Western-influenced modes of thinking in such seminal works of the twentieth century as Ṭāhā Ḥusayn's autobiography, Naguib Mahfouz's novels, and Taufiq al-Hakim's dramas, all of which explore a transformation from tradition to modernity that is fully cognizant of European thought (e.g., Ḥusayn 1935; Maḥfūẓ 1956, 1957a, 1957b; al-Hakim 1973). But while intellectuals allow for European influence on their modernism, they also insist strongly that the roots of their transition to modernity lie in their own culture, and that the essence of Egyptian modernism is to maintain an unbroken link with their own tradition. This is true for all genres in all media. For example, in his autobiography author Taufiq al-Hakim describes his rationale for wanting to write an Egyptian novel:

> Laying the foundation of an Egyptian narrative literature is something that can be undertaken only by its own man, by a native son . . . Each generation is responsible for itself and for preparing the ground for the next. It would not have been right to

leave it to the future, for its future would not come about except on the basis of the present. The novel that is written today is no more than a link in the chain of the natural growth of tomorrow's novel. Any delay in the forging of this link creates a gap, protracts a stage, and forms an obstacle to the momentum of growth.

(al-Hakim 1964, 113)

"White Flag's" Dr. Mufid could not have put it better; indeed "forging links of authenticity" was precisely the point, for example, of the scene in "White Flag" in which the learned Mufid gazes at the faces of his cultural antecedents, including Taufiq al-Hakim, in the pages of *Artists of Alexandria* (see chapter 2). These ubiquitous references to unbroken linkages and images of authenticity – an un-Western way to convey a sense of modernity – suggest that our problem is to explain not just how European systems of order and rationality were imposed on Egypt from outside (as in, for example, Mitchell 1988), but also how they were incorporated from within. In Egypt's long struggle to assimilate parts of European culture and reject others, language has been a key battleground.

Contact with Europe imposed a social system on Egypt that facilitated the growth of a printed vernacular, giving what Benedict Anderson, in a wider context, describes as "a new fixity to language, which in the long run helped to build that image of antiquity so central to the subjective idea of a nation" (Anderson 1991, 44). However, Egypt's particular "image of antiquity" strongly influenced what happened. The mode of expression chosen for print media was a "classicist vernacular" – an oxymoron in Europe, where national languages were defined against antiquity, but natural in Egypt, where there was a long tradition of preserving the written language against the spoken, and a belief that spoken language was a degenerate variant of that written.[9] Adopting a national vernacular in Egypt, therefore, required more than the standardization of an unstable language. Linguistic reformers had also to be wary of "unfixing" a written language (classical Arabic) that was already believed to be not only stable, but imbued with divine perfection.[10]

To complicate matters, very little time elapsed between the introduction of print technology – the natural domain of classical culture – and the appearance of other technologies and conventions of representation to mass audiences, such as the theater, gramophone, radio, and cinema. These media have done much the same work as print technology in fixing a vernacular, but it was the colloquial Arabic of Cairo that was standardized by nonprint media, not classical Arabic. This means that the vernacular identity of Egypt has a split personality: classicist (with its tradition of high-culture transmission) and oral colloquial (with no accepted role to play in the arts or sciences). Although the practice of "nationalizing" the colloquial was made possible by the new technologies, the new media did not eradicate previous attitudes to language. Indeed, the *de facto* elevation of colloquial Arabic to an artistic medium (in the theater, cinema, and recorded music) may have even made previous assumptions about the nature of language, and the superiority of the classical, more salient in defiance of a complex reality.

Modernists, no matter what their reputations or opinions regarding classical Arabic, were still eager to declare their allegiance to it and, by implication, their hostility to using the vernacular out of what they felt was its proper sphere. Taha Husayn, a pioneer in developing modern Arabic prose style and a minister of education (1950–52), went on record as being

> unalterably opposed to those who regard the colloquial as a suitable instrument for mutual understanding and a method for realizing the various goals of our intellectual life . . . It might disappear, as it were, into the classical if we devoted the necessary effort on the one hand to elevate the cultural level of the people and on the other to simplify and reform the classical so that the two meet at a common point.
>
> *(Ḥusayn 1954, 86)*

Husayn's hostility to writing in the colloquial was shared by many other intellectuals, as well as the state, which rarely recognizes or rewards writers who use colloquial.[11] As recently as 1990 Ibrāhīm Madkūr, president of the Arabic Language Academy in Cairo, reiterated Husayn's optimism that elevated classical language would eventually displace colloquial as the everyday language of Egypt:

> Language is human and cultural behavior – an identity given to its owner and an address for the personality and the nation. I ask each mother, father and school to put these [classical] meanings into the child's character, and to deal with him accordingly . . . If the home and the schools are improved, and cooperate in creating a sound educational and linguistic environment, it follows that society will be free from the abnormal social phenomena which have arisen among us.
>
> *(Madkūr 1990, 47)*

As with the language of folklore touched on earlier, the idea that colloquial Arabic can and should be replaced by a modernized classical standard may be traced back toward the nineteenth century and forward to our own time, but it had particular force under Abdel Nasser (1952–70), when mass education – the only means through which classical literacy could be inculcated in large numbers of people – became a reality in Egypt for the first time. A representative work on the issue of using the colloquial in literature is Nafūsa Zakariyyā Saʿīd's *The History of the Call for Colloquial and Its*

Influence on Egypt (N. Saʿīd 1964). The book was published when Gamal Abdel Nasser's socialist-tinged nationalism was in full swing; it was as secular and progress-oriented a period as any in modern Egyptian history. Nonetheless, Said affirms the assumptions of functional differentiation into parallel language types, as well as the superiority of the classical in a modern setting. She does, however, question the uniqueness of the situation:

> *Fuṣḥā* [classical Arabic] is the language used to write poetry and prose, and for intellectual production generally. The language of speech, *ʿāmmīya* [colloquial], is the language used in daily matters and in which everyday speech is conducted. The former follows rules which govern its expression, whereas the latter does not follow such rules because it changes spontaneously with each generation and according to the circumstances surrounding it . . . The existence of a colloquial side-by-side with a classical language is a natural phenomenon in all languages. The existence of the phenomenon in Arabic, then, is not an aberration; if we follow the history of Arabic we would find that it persists throughout the ages. *(ibid., 3)*

If the difference between colloquial and classical Arabic is little more than normal variation in register found in all languages, why, then, should there be a "call for colloquial" in Arab society, and why should it cause concern? Qur'ānic Arabic, says Said, represents the perfection of the Qurayshi dialect, adopted by all the other tribes before the rise of Islam. The distance between writing and speech was not as great as in modern times, she asserts, and the wide divergence between colloquial and classical styles stems from *alḥān* (sg. *laḥn*) – grammatical errors – made by newly converted non-Arab Muslims (N. Saʿīd 1964, 4–5; Makdisi 1990, 125–29). The point of early writing on colloquials, therefore, was not "the study of the colloquial for its own sake, as the Orientalists and their followers have done, but to serve classical Arabic by correcting the mistakes made by the masses" (N. Saʿīd 1964, 7). This is the same position taken by modern authors who want to incorporate some features of the colloquial by strictly defining the contexts in which it can be used, especially in genres new to Arab society such as theater or the novel (Cachia 1967, 18–21).

The precolonial situation, as Said describes it, was one in which "classical Arabic lived beside the colloquial . . . without there being any rivalry. Each specialized in its own field: colloquial took the arena of interaction in life and the expression of material and temporal needs, and had no ambition to be the language of high literature" (N. Saʿīd 1964, 7). Consequently, in Said's view, the "call for colloquial" in late nineteenth- and early twentieth-century Egypt was an attempt to promote an unnatural situation in which "everyday language" would take the place of proper literary language. Said sees this colonization of language as a plot to force Egyptians to unify spoken and written language at the level of the colloquial, which would separate them from their past by promoting the teaching of colloquial as a written language and separate them from their fellow Arabs. European studies of the colloquial, such as Seldon Wilmore's *The Spoken Arabic of Egypt* were an attempt

> to deceive Egyptians into believing that their opposition to adopting the colloquial would expose them to greater danger than they realized, namely the extinction of both the modern and the ancient [written] languages, in favor of a foreign language as a result of their increased contact with the European nations. This was to make them accept the colloquial for writing – because it was the lesser of two evils.
>
> *(ibid., 27)*

An interest in the linguistic and everyday practices of "ordinary people" – a conspicuous concern of contemporary Western writers (e.g. Ortner 1984, 149–150; Bourdieu 1991; de Certeau 1988) – can have a distinctly imperialist cast to Egyptians.

The idea that linguistic register is fundamentally linked to the classical heritage, and the classical heritage in turn is predominantly religious, was always a key assumption of the nineteenth-century "renaissance." The idea continues to hold sway, although it can be emphasized differently, depending on the audience. For example, M. M. Badawi, an Oxford-based Egyptian scholar, begins an article on literary modernism in an Egyptian journal by emphasizing qur'ānic Arabic as a modern literary model:

> The Arabic language has an enormous antiquity . . . [which] is not provided to many of the societies of the Third World . . . The prevalent feeling of the Arabs throughout the long centuries was that their language was the most exalted and the best of languages. Naturally, various factors strengthened this feeling and generally rooted it in the mind of Arab civilization. Among these factors, without a doubt, was the status of Arabic as the language of the Holy Qur'ān and the concepts that were derived from it and which were associated with the wonders of the Qur'ān and all that is in it. Thus literature was connected with religion by way of the relationship which existed between the Arabic language and the Islamic religion, and the development of the concept of literature occurred such that it was not devoid of religious content, or of religious connotations and associations and inferences. *(M. M. Badawi 1984, 98)*

When writing on modern Arabic literature for an English-speaking audience he also insists on continuity with classical models, particularly in regard to premodern literature, but also in later writing. However, the association of classical heritage and religion is comparatively muted:

> Compared with earlier periods of Arabic literature the Modern period, often referred to in Arabic as *al-Nahḍa* (= renaissance), requires an approach that is at

> once simpler and more complicated. While Classical Arabic literatures can safely be regarded as fundamentally a continuum, Modern literature constitutes in certain important respects an entirely new departure, even though its break with the Classical has sometimes been exaggerated, for despite its borrowing of European forms such as drama and the novel, Modern literature never really completely severed its link with its past. The *Nahḍa* was in fact a product of a fruitful meeting of two forces: the indigenous tradition, and the imported western forms.
>
> *(M. M. Badawi 1992, 1)*[12]

Whether the relation between religion and classical heritage is highlighted or subdued, in scholarly depictions of Arab modernity the emphasis is always on the continuity between the present and the classical past. The vernacular past embodied in (or derived from) colloquial language never enters into the picture.

When Egyptians did take up the "call for colloquial," says Said, it was, at first, for purely limited purposes: "entertaining the masses sometimes, or for their education or refinement occasionally" (N. Saʿīd 1964, 75).[13] Early attempts to write "serious" colloquial poetry, she says, were failures: "These examples show us how humor and satire were often written in the *zajal* at the expense of language, exposing the Arabic language to those of the foreigners with whom we had relations" (*ibid.*, 325). She quotes a poem by Yaʿqūb Ṣanūʿ, a nineteenth-century writer best known as a pioneer in the Egyptian theater (see Grendzier 1966), as an example of early colloquial literature that had recourse to entire English phrases, ostensibly because the language was too impoverished to make the point in its own terms:

Ya m-aḥlā l-inglīziyya	*ummi ʿayn zarqā wi-shaʿr aṣfar*
Ya khasāra di ṣ-ṣabiyya	*fīh gōz-ha l-ʿaskari l-aḥmar*
Shuftᵃ ha imbāriḥ ya asyād-i	*ma-kan-sh ḥawālē-ha inglīz*
Fa-ʕult-il-ha "ya mīlaydī	gīf mī akīs īfyūblīz"
How sweet the Englishwoman	blue eyes and blond hair
What a shame, this girl,	whose husband is the red [English] soldier
I saw her yesterday, fellows	no Englishmen around her
And said "*My lady*	*give me a kiss if you please*"

(N. Saʿīd 1964, 325)

Explaining Sanu's use of English in the above passage as "satire at the expense of language" is a purely ideological maneuver. The passage actually derives both its humor and its nationalist content from juxtaposing familiar Arabic expression with a ridiculous English phrase, highlighting the coarseness of the situation and shifting the blame to the libertine foreigner. Sanu's humor comes at the expense of the English, not at the expense of the language.[14]

In the first decades of the twentieth century, Said says, colloquial poets experimented with a variety of styles and regional dialects, yet by the 1930s the regional variation had decreased.[15] Colloquial poets of the period were, in her view, categorized by one of two tendencies: those who wanted to develop a purer colloquial, and those who wanted to move colloquial closer to classical style. The second group, she thought, had won. This was unlikely and empirically unsupportable – a case of ideology writing the history rather than a fair estimate of what sort of vernacular culture was actually being produced and consumed either in public venues or in private life.

The purist camp, she asserts, were opportunists who wanted nothing but fame, and wrote in colloquial simply because they had not mastered the classical (*ibid.*, 336–38). Vulgarity becomes the main issue. As evidence she offers a poem by Muḥammad ʿAbd al-Minʿam, known as Abū Buthayna, which describes a man wasting his life drinking in a bar, leaving his wife no recourse but to beg from the neighbors. The poem ends on a haranguing note: "*Ya rāgil iʿʕal ya minayyil / ya kharāb-i minnak ya kharābi*" (Hey man, wise up, you wretch / what a mess you are, what a mess) (*ibid.*, 338). It is the depiction of a low-class situation that Said finds objectionable.

The approved current in colloquial poetry was more openly didactic. Said quotes Ḥusayn Maẓlūm Riyāḍ to the effect that "the capable *zajal* writer should insert easily pronounced and heard [classical] Arabic into the poem so that it can raise colloquial to a higher level than that of the street and narrow the distance between the classical and the dialect" (*ibid.*, 338–39).[16] Riyad consequently translated the quatrains of Omar Khayyam into colloquial, which Said characterizes as "true intellectual and spiritual nourishment for the people, with no impairment of the language and no descent to cheap and filthy colloquial" (*ibid.*, 340). All of this is offered as proof that the colloquial was a suitable language for literature to the extent that it could be made to approach the subject matter and style of classical Arabic, but that the colloquial by itself was still unsuitable for literature. Indeed, many of the examples of "colloquial poetry written by intellectuals" quoted by Said are nothing but fairly simple classical poems which are allegedly easy for the masses to understand.[17] Similarly, the colloquial poems of established figures such as Aḥmad Shauqī and Aḥmad Rāmī, both of whom wrote for popular singers of the day, were not, in Said's view, written out of respect for the colloquial, but to draw the masses closer to the classical. Development of colloquial style is equated ideally with its eradication.

Said's desire to eliminate colloquial Arabic, or for that matter, all nonclassical influences, is a common ideological position. For example, Dr. Yūsuf Zaydān, author of several books on Sufism, said in an interview that words do, in fact, accrete meanings. Nonetheless, his ideal language situation would be one in which words do *not* accrete meaning, or indeed, in which language does not accrete new words:

> I think [the use of foreign words in Arabic] is a scandal, and the greatest reflection of the decline of the indicator of general national consciousness. I am astonished when I hear someone use foreign synonyms when speaking Arabic as if he has penetrated a mine of cheap jewels. When we use a word we think, and I don't think we are in great need of thinking with the minds of others. Something even more amazing, and which gives greater cause for grief, is the naive use of foreign words, such as when the owner of some project sticks a "-co" on the end of its name.[18] The funny thing is that many who use these English contractions don't even know their meanings. *(B. Ramaḍān 1990, 14)*

Ibrahim Madkur, the president of the Arabic Language Academy in Cairo (1990), joins with Nafusa Said (1964) in his optimism that the colloquial has finally been extinguished:

> The situation today is that 95 percent of colloquial – at least – is classical in its original form. We've done many studies in this field which verify that the language is moving forward, and all we are concerned with now is to arrive at a spoken language which is shared by all of the Arabic regions. We are trying now to effect a linguistic erasing of the Arabic dialects, and to extract from them a shared language which is easy to use, doesn't contradict necessities [of daily life] and which enjoys flexibility and simplicity. *(Madkūr 1990, 46–47)*

Diglossia

For linguists a radical disjuncture between styles of language within a single community is termed diglossia. Charles Ferguson, who was among the first to define the condition, described diglossia functionally as a situation in which "high" and "low" varieties of a language exist side by side, the former a prestigious variant used in writing and formal situations, the latter a colloquial variant used in "everyday" situations (see fig. 3.1).[19] Most linguistic studies of Arabic diglossia are empirical and descriptive, focusing on the phonological and grammatical features that distinguish the low variety from the relatively well-documented high variant.[20] Studies in the Western literature on empirical diglossia are an echo of diglossic ideology expressed in Arabic writing.

Although most writing on diglossia takes place under the rubric of sociolinguistics, generally the sociological dimensions of the phenomenon receive only cursory attention.[21] Studies of diglossia that cast doubt on the notion that Arabic exhibits measurable linguistic parallelism (with some scholars assuming the existence of arbitrarily defined intermediate forms – see fig. 3.2) have little effect on linguists' efforts to define diglossia empirically. For example, one article in *al-ʿArabiyya* found no evidence that Egyptians either agreed on what modern standard Arabic (MSA) was, or could use it with facility (Parkinson 1991); another article in the same volume of *al-ʿArabiyya* allowed that the current generation "find it difficult and unnatural to use MSA spontaneously without referring to a written text" (Abu-Absi 1991, 118), but contended that future generations would close the gap between "high" and "low" styles through such means as classical Arabic versions of the American program "Sesame Street." In effect empirical objections to the idea of diglossia are circumvented by asserting that people might not *yet* speak MSA, but that they will achieve

Fig. 3.1 Ferguson's model of functional diglossia (Ferguson 1959a, 5)

High (classical)	Low (colloquial)
• sermon in church or mosque	• instructions to servants, waiters, workmen, clerks
• personal letter	• conversation with family, friends, colleagues
• speech in parliament, political speech	• radio "soap opera"
• university lecture	• caption on political cartoon
• news broadcast	• folk literature
• newspaper editorial, news story	
• caption on picture	
• poetry	

Fig. 3.2 An elaborated model of diglossia allowing for several intermediate forms of expression between "pure classical" Arabic and "pure colloquial" (sources: E. M. Badawi 1973, 104; Badawi and Hinds 1986, ix)

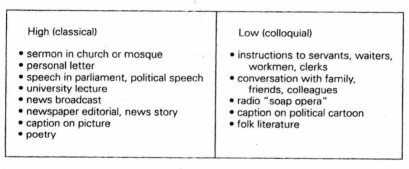

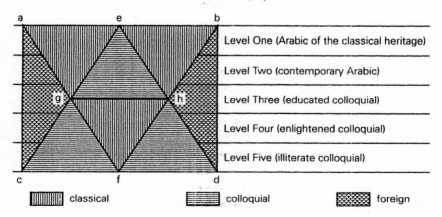

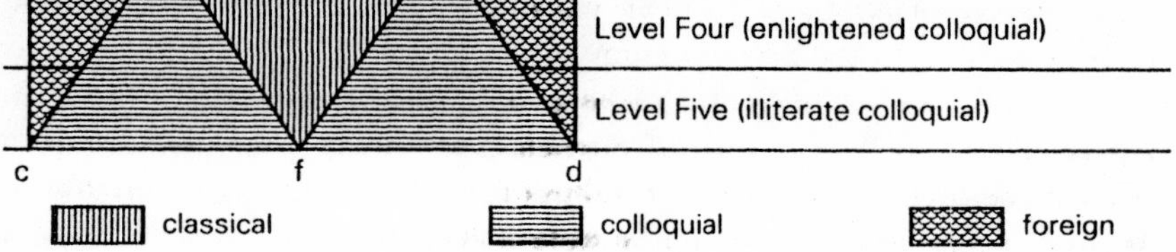

a "new linguistic state" (*ibid.*) at some unspecified future date. The Arab modernist dream, transposed to a Western scholarly venue, remains intact.

The linguistic model stipulates that the "high" language in a diglossic system should be used in formal situations, such as university lectures, public meetings, and news broadcasts. Most models of diglossia also assume a general correlation between register and social class. Yet even if one allows the substitution of a "high colloquial" for the classical variant, linguistic practice holds surprises. Indeed, linguistic register can often be the inverse of the situation prescribed by diglossic ideology.

Much of the educational system, in fact, operates in the colloquial medium, even though formal questions about language in education almost always yield the answer that all subjects should be taught in classical Arabic, and if they are not it is because of a failure on the part of students or teachers. The university *should* be a preserve of "proper" language use. That it rarely conforms to any empirical model of language use does not change this perception. For instance, an Arabic grammar class I attended on several occasions at Cairo University in the fall of 1989 was conducted almost entirely in colloquial except for the specific examples used by the instructor to illustrate how medieval grammarians defined their categories. The examples were taken from a medieval text, Ibn Malik's *al-Alfiyya* – the same text used in traditional grammar classes taught in the more classically oriented al-Azhar University, and therefore a pillar of classicism (Taha Husayn [1935, 129] mentions the text in his famous autobiography). The style of the colloquial may have been fairly "high," and the students insisted that ideally the course should have been conducted in classical Arabic; there was, however, no overriding ideological reason inherent in the subject of the class that would compel the use of classical Arabic. The teacher was on inherently classical ground by virtue of the subject.

Classical Arabic is more likely to be used when the subject matter is sensitive, when its relation to the classical heritage, and therefore its place in the university, is doubtful. A class on folklore, for example, proved to be a perfect opportunity for the professor to insist on stringent use of classical Arabic in its "proper" setting. When I attended such a class at Cairo University as an Arabic student in 1986 this was exactly what happened: the professor spent the first ten minutes of a lecture exhorting his students in impeccable classical Arabic to keep colloquialisms out of their term papers. The students, in turn, delivered questions to the professor in a much more formal manner than in the classical grammar class, and in "higher" language. The difference in style between the two classes very likely was due to more than just idiosyncracies of the two professors. "High" subjects allow low style, and "low" subjects require high style.

Linguists generally avoid the ideological assumptions that produced this feeling of separation between language types or registers. They often account for the obvious discrepancy between reality and the neatly bifurcated linguistic situation hypothesized by Ferguson by elaborating the empiricist model – creating "intermediate levels" between colloquial and classical types of language (e.g. E. M. Badawī 1973; Blanc 1960; Meiseles 1980; Zughoul 1980). Some even admit that the definition of "levels" of Arabic is an arbitrary exercise which depends on comparing the most widely separated styles possible (E. M. Badawī 1973, 11).[22] E. M. Badawi's elaborated model of diglossia, for example, recognizes the "messiness" of the linguistic situation, but still tries to impose on it a descriptive organization based partly on class, and partly on the prestige of classicism (see fig. 3.2). It is the middle range of Badawi's empirical model (level three – "educated colloquial") that controls the greatest range of linguistic expression, including colloquial, classical, and foreign languages. His model, one might note, is a perfect linguistic parallel of the middle-class position sketched out in "White Flag." The emphasis is on synthesis – competence in both the classical and the folk idioms, and in foreign technique.

If the metalanguage of cultural linguistics turns on an imagined sociology, so do people in the real world perceive others' language use through an unthought sociology. Viewers' perceptions of "White Flag" are a case in point. Since Dr. Mufid had mastered the link with foreign culture he must speak in a certain way: "He used a lot of foreign words," said a female college student. "He was obviously living the life of an ambassador." And yet if one refers to the serial itself – the text – it becomes quickly apparent that Dr. Mufid uses far fewer foreign words than the villains. He is, however, virtually the only character who uses any good classical Arabic at all in the show, particularly in the scene in which he begins writing his memoirs while contemplating the visages of Alexandria's artists. Almost all other use of classical Arabic was presented as vulgarity – Fadda or Nunu trying to give themselves a gloss of class through comical linguistic pretense, as in Fadda's speech to the artistic community (none of whom are shown in the audience), or Nunu's occasional painful efforts to read newspaper articles to Fadda.

"Colloquial" and "classical" can function as both markers of taste and as measurable phenomena. This is why colloquial poets can sometimes be considered "eloquent," and why a professor of folkloric studies must take care not to blur the line between the potentially vulgar nature of his subject matter and the civilizing and modernizing mission of the institution in which it is taught. A university that is to "represent advanced civilization . . . must inculcate faith in duty before right, greater concern for one's obligations to others than for theirs to oneself, self-respect, absence of pettiness, and refined taste" (Ḥusayn 1954, 127–28). It is the classically educated man, steeped in refined taste, who can be trusted to handle the colloquial in a suitably tasteful manner. The tasteful handling of colloquial material is, in the official view, designed to "raise the level of the masses" and only couched in the colloquial so that the uneducated can understand it.

The same dynamics of expression, dictated more by an awareness of ideologically distinct categories of taste than by empirical linguistic "competence," was in evidence during a debate over the legacy of the singer Muhammad Abd al-Wahhab held at the American University in Cairo on July 10, 1991. Abd al-Wahhab was the greatest singer and composer in Egypt from the 1920s through the 1940s. Although many of his compositions had colloquial lyrics, he, more than any other singer, is credited with having defined the high-art style of modern Arabic music. Abd al-Wahhab was, therefore, a symbol of modernized classicism.

The debate was to feature lectures by Ratība al-Ḥifnī, a Cairo Conservatoire voice professor, and Jihād Dāūd, a composition professor at the Egyptian Music Academy. Al-Hifni was to be the pro-Abd al-Wahhab speaker, and Daud was to assume a more critical stance – but not fiercely anti-Abd al-Wahhab because the entire event, which included the showing of two Abd al-Wahhab films, was intended to honor the singer only one month after his death. In fact the organizer of the event had intentionally refrained from inviting speakers who might have been more critical of Abd al-Wahhab's musical legacy.[23]

In theory, since the event took place in an auditorium before a small but formal audience, both speakers might have been expected to use fairly stringent classical language. As college professors both were likely to have sufficient facility with the classical medium to do so. Nonetheless, Daud, the "anti-Abd al-Wahhab" speaker, was noticeably more classical than al-Hifni, the appointed defender of classicism. This was not surprising. Al-Hifni was inherently on solid classical ground by virtue of her association with a potent symbol of high tradition, so her manner of speaking was of less concern. She expressed her thoughts in the ordinary colloquial of educated Arabic speakers. But Daud, by criticizing a cultural giant, was taking a riskier position. He delivered his criticism carefully, in classical Arabic, heaping fulsome praise on Abd al-Wahhab as a singer and, eventually, giving less enthusiastic praise of Abd al-Wahhab as a composer and musical innovator.

Daud took care not to give the impression that he was criticizing Abd al-Wahhab in favor of singers who might be considered vulgar. He quoted Abd al-Wahhab favorably to the effect that the salvation of Egyptian music would come only through *ʿilm* (science, knowledge), but then juxtaposed Abd al-Wahhab's words with the name of a singer – ʿAlī Ḥamayda – who is often mentioned in the press as an example of a "vulgar" performer. Daud was using Hamayda's "well-known" vulgarity to implicitly criticize Abd al-Wahhab, who had surprised many by refusing to criticize Hamayda who, as a graduate of the music academy, was widely considered to have betrayed the highest ideals of the institution.[24] Hamayda, in other words, had become known as a prime example of someone who should follow the master's injunction to compose music with *ʿilm* (knowledge), and not just through *mauhiba* (talent), which Daud noted "can bring popularity, but unlike *ʿilm*, can never be developed."[25] Daud's impeccably classical delivery helped him cast himself as a defender of the "true" legacy of Abd al-Wahhab, thereby assuring that his criticism would be construed as constructive and avoiding any suspicion that he was subverting the march of progress. In her rebuttal al-Hifni countered Daud's Ali Hamayda strategy by defending Hamayda weakly as a promising student who they had thought might use his folk heritage in novel ways, but who had gone wrong, veering into a vulgar commercial dance-hall style. In the end, despite their markedly different styles, both speakers managed to align themselves on the side of classicism and good taste.

In this case, as in the case of the classroom lectures, styles of speaking differed markedly. But it was not simply that "high-culture subjects" were discussed in high language. Instead, the language tended to be pitched higher when the speaker's subject threatened to blur the boundaries between categories of high and low culture. Such use of linguistic register is not so much a rule as a potential strategy. The most common strategy is to use a few lines of very high speech – as classical as possible – and then to "lapse" into a colloquial which varies according to speaker, audience, and setting.

The same pattern is often repeated in television and radio interviews; practical communication in "ordinary" speech is the norm except when the speaker cannot afford to give the impression of siding with attitudes that an audience might consider vulgar, or wishes to establish authority in a public talk. But when interviews or oral presentations are published they are often "translated" into classical Arabic unless there is some special reason to retain the colloquial. The ideology of diglossia demands that the written word be classical. Sometimes when colloquial is retained in written language it is to confirm the ideology of social separation by emphasizing a class difference between the interviewer and his subject, a practice that goes back further than does television.

This was done with exaggerated clarity in a pair of anonymous articles published in 1929 in *al-Dunyā al-muṣawwara*, based on interviews with *futūwāt* ("tough guys," sg. *futūwa*; women can attain the status of *futūwa* – f. *futūwāya* – as well as men ["*Kayfa yaʿīshūna* . . .," 5; "*Futūwāyat sūq al-khuḍār*," 9]).[26] The dialogue in both interviews was written in colloquial. Unlike the university lectures and the debate discussed above, the articles were devoid of didacticism. Indeed, they had more the feeling of a freak show – an "exposé" of crude and backward life in the parts of Cairo that have not been favored with enlightenment. In classical Arabic the interviewer says: "In the native quarters[27] of the capital there is a group of *awlād al-balad* ["sons of the town" – Dr. Mufid's allies from the traditional quarters in "White Flag" sixty years later] who care about nothing except rushing headlong into danger and committing acts [of violence]. No sooner do they get out of one scrape than they get into another one – out of one catastrophe only to plunge into a worse one. These are the *futūwāt*" ("*Kayfa yaʿīshūna* . . ." 1929, 9). The interviewer then pointedly notes that his subject replies to his questions "in a clear colloquial," thereby creating the illusion that he himself does not speak colloquially. He uses the same device – highlighting the crude speech of his interviewee by juxtaposition to his own refined style of expression – in the second interview, this time with a woman, a *futūwāya*. The interviewer asks her if she would mind having her photograph published. At first she warns him that this might make her angry, and he writes: "If I didn't use all of the tactful rustic phrases I had memorized with her I might have come back with a smashed head, so I smiled and said [and this is rendered in colloquial], '"Here is a tough woman" – that's all we'll say about you'" ("*Futūwāyat sūq al-khuḍār*" 1929, 9). However, the colloquial he uses is not in fact unusually slangy or "low,"[28] but ordinary conversational Egyptian Arabic with which the author, unless he was exceedingly odd, must have conversed with all his friends no matter what their level of education.

The importance of diglossia is as an ideological construct which can be – but is not necessarily – invoked through observable linguistic strategies. "Diglossic" situations can be expressed nonlinguistically, or merely suggested rather than stated explicitly. Ratiba al-Hifni, by defending the legacy of Abd al-Wahhab at the American University, was as "classical" as the more critical Jihad Daud even though any linguistic analysis would show that in fact she spoke a "lower" colloquial than he during her defense of the musical legacy of Muhammad Abd al-Wahhab; the Cairo University grammar instructor was as "classical" as the folklore professor, even though the latter used more classical Arabic in the classroom. One need not speak classical Arabic to evoke a sense of classicism.

Official heritage, folk parody

Not everyone accepts a state monopoly on culture and taste, or ever has. Literature oriented toward the *ibn al-balad* formulation of identity was often written in conscious opposition to the state's formula of modernity through classicism. Such writing has roots at least as far back as the mid-nineteenth century when it was presented in the works of Yaqub Sanu and ʿAbd Allāh Nadīm; it extends through Bayram al-Tunsi and other poets of the 1930s, and on to contemporary colloquial poets such as Salah Jahin, Ahmad Fuad Nigm and Fu'ād Ḥaddād. These are only some of the better-known colloquial poets, who are accepted in the media and the academy only to the extent that they can be seen as speaking "eloquent colloquial" (*ʿāmmīya fuṣḥā*) so as to "elevate the masses." Some of their work was indeed didactic. But they also had a keen sense of irony which often operated through association or contrast with classicism.

Bayram al-Tunsi's satiric *Maqāmāt* (a series of vignettes in a rhymed prose style generally associated with the classical past), written in exile during the 1930s, are typical of works opposed to an alliance between religious authority and the state. The *maqāma* (s. of *maqāmāt*) was both a logical choice as a vehicle for satire and completely out of character for a *shaʿbī* (popular) poet known for his colloquial works. It was a logical form to choose because the genre had, from its beginning in the tenth century, a satiric slant in exploring the "dregs of society" through stories of an eloquent *mukaddī* (trickster) told by a well-traveled *rāwī* (narrator [Booth 1990, 344–46; Beeston 1971, 1–12]). But the *maqāma* also became the model for *badīʿ* (stylistically ornamented) literature of the sort reformers such as Taha Husayn, and later Luis Awad, wanted to eliminate in favor of a clearer "technical" style (L. ʿAwad 1974). Although modern writers had revived the *maqāma* form to some extent (see Allen 1974), it never became widely accepted in modern Arabic literature, and was considered an anachronism "embodying a notion of the text as a showcase for the multi-talented litterateur-craftsman . . . neither wholly prose nor wholly poetry" (Booth 1990, 347). Neither prose nor poetry, but the emphasis on ornamented classical style in the *maqāma* made it a genre that evoked exactly the opposite tradition from the one in which al-Tunsi made his reputation.

Al-Tunsi makes the *maqāmāt* into popular contemporary works by inverting certain of the conventions of the medieval genre, but leaving enough of the form to be recognizable to the reader. Whereas the medieval form centers on the success of the trickster, in al-Tunsi's *Maqāmāt* the trickster is transformed into the butt of all the jokes; the medieval *maqāma* is set on the margins of society, but al-Tunsi's *Maqāmāt* portray the marginalization of moral exemplars (*ibid.*, 151). As in the medieval *maqāma*, the force of the narrative derives from juxtaposition of social and literary opposites, but where *shaṭāra* (cleverness) always brings victory to the trickster in the traditional genre, it often brings shame and ridicule to al-Tunsi's protagonists.

What gave al-Tunsi's *Maqāmāt* continuity with his more purely colloquial work – of which he wrote a great deal – was his practice of juxtaposing within the text a competent rendition of the classical *maqāma* style with elements of the "folkloric" *baladī* (rustic).[29] The would-be trickster, collapsed in al-Tunsi's *Maqāmāt* into the character of the narrator (in the medieval stories they are separate), is always a poor student at al-Azhar University, known as a *mujāwir* (an Azhar student living in the popular quarters near the university).[30] This character is often thrust, through greed or circumstances, into association with either a corrupt pseudo-Western character from the aristocracy, or into some other situation in which class distinctions are heightened.[31]

The ideological transformation used by al-Tunsi in the *Maqāmāt* is common to a great deal of popular culture in all media and throughout most of the twentieth century.[32] In "The Camp Caesar *Maqāma*," for example, he burlesques a pair of Azharī students in a manner consistent with film comedies from the 1930s to the 1980s. The two would-be clerics take an unlikely trip to the Alexandria beach in search of women. They start at a "popular" (low-class) beach, but the first *shaykh* has heard of a beach called Camp Caesar (a real beach in Alexandria) "where the rich women bathe, and German wenches too" (al-Tūnsī 1974, 20). The second *shaykh*, narrator of the tale, wants to stay, telling his friend that

> a beach is a beach, and where one finds water, one finds ducks [i.e. "chicks" – young women] . . . Anyway, look at these women! The water is filled with them . . . That one stretched out on her face might be the wife of a deputy secretary of state . . . and this one hanging her thighs in the air, and that one with blond hair – they might be from a princely estate! (*ibid.*)

The first *shaykh* – really a kind of "anti-*shaykh*" character – still wants to leave, but then a party of scantily clad women appear on the beach. The second *shaykh* exclaims: "I had, by God, reckoned them foreigners, but they were Egyptian!" (*ibid.*, 21). The girls, accompanied by a servant, proceed to revel in European pursuits such as sunbathing and gymnastics. Finally one of the girls stretches out temptingly before the second *shaykh*, who reels off a scandalous parody of a poem extolling her virtues:

> She sat, and stretched before her royally
> Were her silvery thighs, blinding the eyes.
> She inclined to the rear, leaning on her
> Elbows, coupled with the alabaster sand.
> Then she twisted, and I contorted a part of myself
> While she swished and swiveled her haunches
> And slackened her flanks, exposing
> To the sun her rosy red shanks.
> She turned to me suddenly and smiled,
> Then bashfully averted her face and nose
> As if something were causing her doubt. She squirmed,
> And my gaze was met with a rump all but unclothed!
> (*ibid.*)

The story ends with the second *shaykh* romping in the surf with the girls while the first, who originally wanted to go flirt with foreign women, nearly drowns due to his preoccupation with staring at immodest Egyptian girls.

The "Camp Caesar *Maqāma*" is a raucous parody of traditional Azharī students, which one might be tempted to interpret as a fulfillment of the textbook injunction quoted above – "renew what is authentic from our culture and tie it to what is useful from our modern lives." But the Azhar milieu is not usually portrayed as an incubator of buffoonery and sexual license, as in the "Camp Caesar *Maqāma*," or in a spirit of calculating greed, as in the "Phonograph *Maqāma*" (Booth 1990, 364), or as a breeding ground for sly beggars, as in "The *Maqāma* of Socialism."[33] Al-Tunsi's irreverent, sometimes grasping, but generally ineffectual student is almost the alter ego to the stock image of the sober, clean-living and intellectually vibrant traditional young scholar: almost, but not quite. For as Booth points out, the Bayramic student of the *Maqāmāt* is not corrupt by nature, but is marginalized by circumstances, specifically the adoption by Egyptian elites of European artifacts and customs: "While in the classical *maqāma* the hero is seen to triumph over those who are considered, in the social hierarchy, to be his 'superiors,' it is most often the opposite that occurs in those Bayramic *maqāmāt* which portray the Egyptian upper classes" (*ibid.*).[34] In such a world the student either conforms to the expectations of the new Europeanized bourgeoisie, or remains destitute. From this perspective the heroic reformulation of society planned by "official" intellectuals such as Taha Husayn or Luis Awad appears only as unobtainable material goods and licentious behavior: the aforementioned phonograph, fashion accessories ("The *Maqāma* of the Waterman [pen]"), conspicuous consumption ("The *Maqāma* of the Automobile"; "The *Maqāma* of the Telephone"; "The *Maqāma* of the Pajama"), or a bevy of scandalously immodest girls on the beach.

But the *Maqāmāt* did more than simply reverse the official ideology of modernized tradition: they consistently blurred the categories. *Ibn al-balad* in his traditional quarter is neither threatening nor problematic, even if he is an identity formed by virtue of opposition to the Europeanized bourgeoisie. He is not threatening as long as he stays in the traditional quarter, which is the case in the occasional patronizing "interview with a *futūwa*" or, in a more contemporary context, televised "coffeehouse stories."[35] Al-Tunsi blurs the boundaries of identity by bringing the characters out of their "proper" milieu. Their victories in this wider world are small, or more often they are humiliated by their experience of the unfamiliar; worst of all, they are irreverent, rejecting both the injunction to modernize the classical tradition and the facade of a modernity that is always beyond their reach. It is here, as much as anywhere, that we find the roots of contemporary film and television. But it is scarcely "folklore." Indeed, al-Tunsi's parody of classical form could not have been effective if he had not been conversant both with the tradition he was lampooning and with the process of modernization he was indicting. Nor would the satire have been effective if it had been aimed at the uneducated.

Ideology and practice

Works such as al-Tunsi's *Maqāmāt* leave no doubt that "popular culture" in Egypt is more than folklore or "naive" artistic expression appealing mainly to the uneducated and "unmodern." Indeed, some later colloquial poetry, despite its utilization of the "folk" idiom, is no more accessible to the masses than is classical material.[36] By the same token, the humor in such works as al-Tunsi's "folk" *Maqāmāt* could only be understood by readers who had at least some familiarity with the classical tradition. Yet the *Maqāmāt* share an essential feature with al-Tunsi's more "folkloric" work: both question the ideological structure of Egyptian modernity, refusing to recognize the officially sanctioned association of imported technique with the classical heritage. This formula for popular culture came late to the cinema and television screen – not until the 1970s, as we shall see – and when it did come was condemned as vulgar.

What poets, writers, and filmmakers do is scarcely covered by a diagram, no matter how complex (with tongue in cheek, see fig. 3.3). As social analogs to linguistic practice none of the Egyptian popular culture we have thus far encountered makes sense in terms of an empirical model of Arabic diglossia. In which "level" on Badawi's elaborated chart would one place "The Camp Caesar *Maqāma*"? Far simpler diagrams, however, do account for the place works and authors are given in *official* versions of cultural history. And these official versions are by no means remote. They inform what people see and are part of what people read.

Bayram al-Tunsi, one of the century's major colloquial figures, receives only cursory mention in Nafusa Said's Nasser-era *History of the Call to Colloquial*. But her refusal to recognize colloquial literature as anything but, at best, a means to draw the masses into modernity lives on. The same points were made about al-Tunsi more recently in mass-circulation literature (e.g. *al-Idhāʿa wa-l-tilifizyōn* – the Egyptian *T. V. Guide*): he could not have been really writing colloquial because the work was too good;

Fig. 3.3 Diglossic practice in ideological context

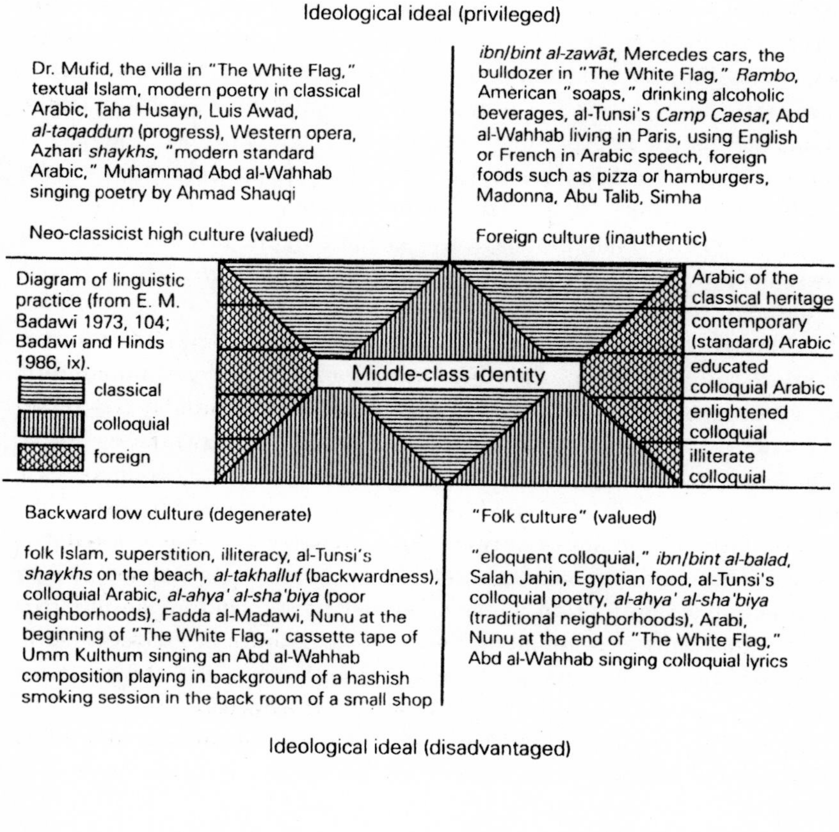

whatever colloquial he may have used was primarily a strategem to reach the people and thereby raise their cultural level; he actually loved the classical, had memorized the Qur'ān by an early age, as well as several books on *tajwīd* (rules for reciting the Qur'ān with proper intonation [Ghabn 1975]). The appearance of such articles in the equivalent of *T.V. Guide* suggests how fundamental *both* the colloquial ideal and the classical ideal are to discussions of popular culture, and how far into everyday life such discussions reach. Said's book on the history of colloquial Egyptian Arabic is not an irrelevant Nasserist artifact of academic discourse, but part of mainstream ideology – a part of people's lives. An ideological selectivity allows such works as al-Tunsi's into the canon only to the extent that they can be dissociated from the assumed naiveté of folklore (al-Rāwī 1986, 42–43).[37] Canonization of colloquial works requires that the works be somehow redefined as classical – al-Tunsi, by this reasoning, was actually writing *ʿāmmīya fuṣḥā* (eloquent colloquial), and was therefore not a *shaʿbī* (popular) poet at all (Ghabn 1975).

Salah Jahin was another artist (poet, cartoonist, lyricist) exempted from association with the assumed vulgarity of the masses. Like Said, he was a product of the modernist Nasser era, and was known as the semiofficial poet of the July 1952 revolution (ʿAyyād 1986, 44–45). But even in Jahin's case, while his cartoons, for example, were greatly admired, critics tend to submerge his wit and use of irony beneath his identity as "the [artist's] brush of July [the 1952 Free Officers' revolution] and its literary tongue," as the mass-circulation magazine *Ṣabāḥ al-khayr* put it (1582 [May 1, 1986], 20–21). Although the poet was inspired by the revolution, even the cartoons printed in the Salah Jahin issue of *Ṣabāḥ al-khayr* had little to do with the revolution.

Although the overview articles of the issue, which summarized impressions of Jahin, tended towards didactic nationalistic interpretation, several of the articles on specific aspects of his work were noticeably free of this rhetoric, such as an article on the *fahhāma* (al-Baṭrāwī 1986, 30–32). *Fahhāma*, "the understander," was a theme used in a cartoon series to satirize modern life. The *fahhāma* was an imaginary vise-like device clamped onto the skulls of various cartoon characters – usually people in modern occupations such as students or bureaucrats. It was a Rube Goldberg-like contraption intended to make the incomprehensible comprehensible, thus drawing attention to the absurdities of modern life; for example, an idle bureaucrat at his desk with three successively larger *fahhāma*s screwed onto his head, looking up from his newspaper. The caption reads: "Still he doesn't understand [what he is doing sitting at a desk when there is no work to be done]" (see plate 1). Or a seedy-looking

Plate 1 "From the offices of the government: 'And still he doesn't understand'" (Salah Jahin in *Ṣabāḥ al-khayr* 1582 [May 1, 1986]: 32; originally published in 1961)

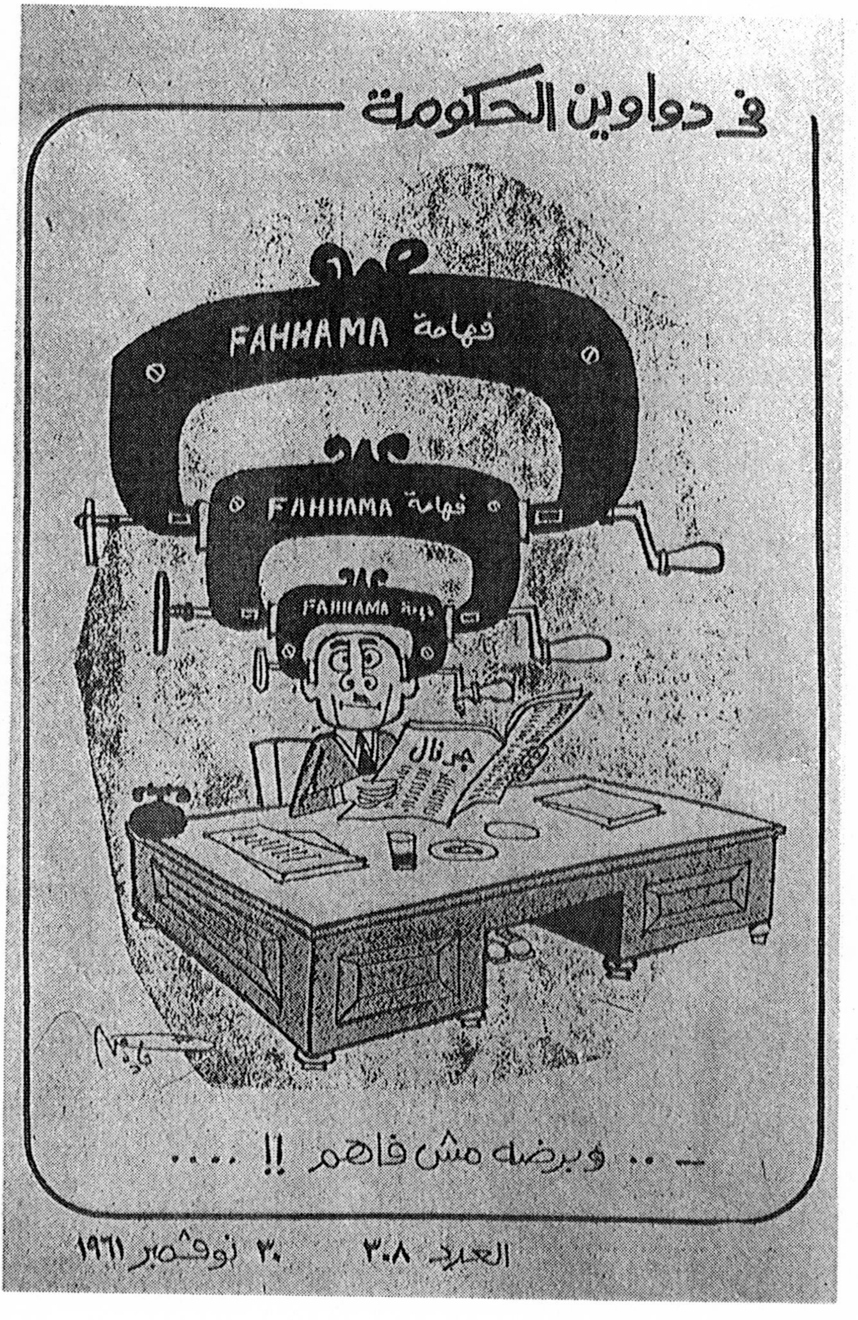

film star in sunglasses: "To the men of the cinema: the mechanical *fahhāma*. It's true – the machine that will push the cinema forward" (see plate 2). This is hardly the stuff of the nationalist heroics with which Jahin is associated officially. Indeed, the *fahhāma* serves as a powerful image of people trapped in a crowded world where modernity fails routinely and everyday life makes little sense – a modern image, but scarcely modernist.

Plate 2 "To the men of the cinema: the mechanical *fahhāma*. It's true – the machine that will push the cinema forward. Ladies' model for actresses" (Salah Jahin in *Ṣabāḥ al-khayr* 1582 [May 1, 1986]: 32; originally published in 1961)

4

The gifted musician

The artist of genius, no matter what era God creates him in, is a unique creature. He believes firmly that his natural place is among the vanguard. He studies public opinion thoroughly so that he knows its desires and inclinations. This helps him to present his message of musical innovation as a "pill" which the people can easily digest. He can lead the new generation – can inscribe his name in capital letters on artistic history.

Singer Muhammad Abd al-Wahhab on himself[1]

The legend I: 1990 looks at the 1920s

In the media Muhammad Abd al-Wahhab appears in different company to that of Bayram al-Tunsi. Although Abd al-Wahhab enjoyed widespread popularity in the 1920s and 1930s, his media associations now are not with the "folk," but with the canonized artistic giants such as Taha Husayn, Taufiq al-Hakim, Naguib Mahfouz, and Ahmad Shauqi. Abd al-Wahhab's current status as a key figure in the Egyptian iconography of progress and one of the holiest of the media's sacred cows makes it easy to overlook ambiguities in his image at the peak of his popularity. In the 1930s Abd al-Wahhab's own heroic modernism was coupled with precisely the sorts of images deplored currently as immodest, "Westernized," or *infitāḥī*.

Abd al-Wahhab died on May 3, 1991. There was little popular reaction to the Great Man's death, in contrast to that of his colleague Umm Kulthum, whose funeral procession in 1975 was one of the largest in memory, rivaled only by that of President Gamal Abdel Nasser in 1970 (Danielson 1991b, 74–75). However, media reaction to Abd al-Wahhab's death was immediate and enormous. Every mass-circulation publication ran a commemorative Abd al-Wahhab issue, and a number of biographies were either reissued or published for the first time.[2] As one would expect, the tone of the articles was eulogistic.

Most of this literature emphasized Abd al-Wahhab's authenticity as an Arab composer and his role as a synthesizer of Western and Middle Eastern cultures. He was "a giant with one leg in the East and one in the West, a great tree with its roots sunk deeply into the Arabic musical culture, its branches reaching into the culture of Western music" ("*Mā alladhī aḍāfahu* . . ." 1991, 26–27). As another commentator put it, Abd al-Wahhab was

> the main impetus to the musicians of our generation and to the hearts, minds and musical tastes of the generations that follow us. We cannot forget that when we talk about the history of the song in Egypt we find that the music of Abd al-Wahhab is the most sincere expression of all tendencies and composers. He . . . is like the river into which all tributaries flow. *(Kamāl al-Ṭawīl, quoted in al-Shināwī 1991, 6)*

Another article stressed that Abd al-Wahhab was the cultural property of the educated bourgeoisie, which the author pointedly distinguished from

> the new *infitāḥī* class [those who profited from the free-market policies of the late 1970s and 1980s] who travelled to the petroleum nations of the Gulf and returned laden with cassette recorders and VCRs, and whose hero is Adawiya. [Adawiya] is what one hears in taxis and at *fūl* and *ṭa*ʿ*mīya* stands, on the carts of vendors in al-ʿAtaba al-Khaḍrā and in popular quarters. *(A. Ramaḍān 1991, 17)*[3]

The same article firmly dissociates Abd al-Wahhab and his educated bourgeois fans from the "intellectually backward" Islamists, who tried to have Abd al-Wahhab's last song, "*Min ghayr lēh*" (Without asking "why," 1989), banned. The author portrays Abd al-Wahhab's (and his own) generation as the only one capable of making a smooth transition to Western-influenced modernity while maintaining Arab authenticity:

> Our generation should be happy with itself for having lived in the age of Abd al-Wahhab, and having savored this historic encounter between classical [Western] music and Arabic music which Abd al-Wahhab brought about. This great generation was able to enjoy composers who were influenced by Abd al-Wahhab like Balīgh Ḥamdī, Muḥammad al-Mōgī, Kamāl al-Ṭawīl, ʿAmmār al-Sharīʿī and others – the generation which took Arabic music a great step forward. Yes, our generation should be happy with itself, and should remember Abd al-Wahhab respectfully and humbly. *(ibid.)*

Abd al-Wahhab's "historic encounter" between Western and Eastern musical styles involved transforming traditional Arabic ensembles of four or five instruments into massive orchestras, and it thrust Arabic music into new contexts such as gramophone records and musical films. The "encounter" made Abd al-Wahhab ultrarespectable in polite society. Establishment history aligns the march of progress with the story of Abd al-Wahhab's life, but perhaps in a way different from that one would have predicted given the singer's marked association with Westernized bourgeois style in his heyday.

Abd al-Wahhab was old when he died, although his exact age was subject to speculation. He himself was cagey on the subject:

> An artist . . . does not work as a bureaucrat who will retire at age 60 and receive a pension, therefore his birthdate is of no concern to anyone. Also an artist . . . measures his life by his works and their artistic scope. The important thing is that the artist can make a contribution, no matter what his age. *(Tabārak 1991, 9)*

The official record, attested by two personal identification cards in Abd al-Wahhab's possession, showed that he was born in 1910. One of the cards lists the place of birth as Cairo, the other as the village of Abū Kibīr, Sharqīya province (*ibid.*). His contemporaries put Abd al-Wahhab's birth at around 1900, speculating that he changed the first zero to a one; or 1901, under the assumption that he reversed the last two digits (*ibid.*). Ratiba al-Hifni goes even further, saying that Abd al-Wahhab was born in 1896. According to al-Hifni, he worked with composer Sayyid Darwish on the operetta *Shahrazād* in 1922, at the age of twenty-six, rather than as a child prodigy, as others believe; and she has him meeting poet Ahmad Rami in 1915 while studying at the Arabic Music Club, at which time he would have been only five if he were born in 1910.[4]

Aside from the purely empirical problem of exactly how the events of his life followed one another, the question of Abd al-Wahhab's age is both trivial and important. On one hand, the later image of Abd al-Wahhab was built on a series of associations with representatives of various types of tradition. The character of such encounters changes markedly if one assumes that Abd al-Wahhab was actually twenty when he met a particular person, rather than ten. In some cases the publicized story is so completely undermined that the event could not have taken place. But in another sense Abd al-Wahhab's age is of little concern because his effect on the history of Egyptian culture in the twentieth century is contained in a series of recorded images – records, tapes, and films – which associate him with symbols of tradition and with a particular type of modernity. The Abd al-Wahhab legend was constructed much like the ideology of language: authentic modernity lies in its links to the past.

All accounts of Abd al-Wahhab's life agree that his formative years were spent in the Birgwān district of Cairo's Bāb al-Shaʿrīya quarter, which is sometimes known by its principal mosque as the Shaʿrānī quarter. His father, Abd al-Wahhab ʿĪsā, was *shaykh* of the Shaʿrānī mosque (M. ʿAwaḍ 1991, 43–44), that is, an Islamic scholar who was also the mosque's chief caretaker. Accordingly, young Muhammad attended a *kuttāb* (religious school for young boys), where the first order of business, and the foundation for continuing education in the traditional mold, was to memorize the Qur'ān, or at least as much of it as a young boy could manage. Although qur'ānic schooling is often invoked in cases of "legendary" public figures as the foundation of personal piety, in the case of a singer the importance of the *kuttāb* lay in the way the Qur'ān was taught.[5] Students learned not only the words of the Qur'ān, but specific rules for recitation called *tajwīd*. The slowest and most "song-like" style of *tajwīd* is called *tartīl*, and although religious scholars firmly differentiate *tartīl* from singing, it is nonetheless excellent training for vocal technique.[6]

Abd al-Wahhab is said to have played truant from the *kuttāb* because of his budding talent for singing (Naẓmī 1991, 27–28; M. ʿAwaḍ 1991, 48–49). Although his classmates and teachers praised his recitation voice, he first made his mark in the neighborhood by singing popular songs by Shaykh Salāma al-Ḥigāzī to other children. One of the first of the stories of Abd al-Wahhab's associations with significant figures occurs at this point. As Maḥmūd ʿAwaḍ describes it, Abd al-Wahhab was standing on a neighborhood street corner when a carriage passed by carrying a popular singer named Ṣāliḥ ʿAbd al-Ḥayy. The young Abd al-Wahhab, familiar with Salih only by reputation, jumped onto the running board of the carriage and said through the window, "Please, sir, may I kiss your hand?" The singer merely motioned to his driver and said, "*al-kurbāg*" (the whip). The driver duly whipped poor Abd al-Wahhab, who fell off the carriage and returned home with his face bloody but his enthusiasm for music undimmed (M. ʿAwaḍ 1991, 51–52).

Whether or not the story's particulars are factual, it serves as an example of how a popular singer could be turned into the legendary hero of Egyptian modernism eulogized in the summer of 1991. Awad makes the significance of the story clear by contextualizing Salih Abd al-Hayy, making him, in effect, an icon of the crudity of his age, from which Abd al-Wahhab escaped. He describes what a Salih Abd al-Hayy concert around the turn of the century might have been like:[7]

In any music hall, whether the singer was al-Kumsārīya or *al-ṣayyīt* [the Qur'ān chanter] Salih Abd al-Hayy or Salama al-Higazi, we will see the singer and the audience in a special state of harmony, interacting with each other. The singer comes on, and behind him the *sannīda* [accompanists] who sing behind him. Also there are the *muṭayyibāt* [sycophants, groupies] who are responsible for keeping the crowd interested.[8] The singer sits with his *takht* [traditional ensemble].

When the concert begins Salih Abd al-Hayy, for example, would sing: "*Fīk nās ya layl bi-tishtikī-lak mā wāgiʿ-hum*" [O night, there are people out there complaining about their bad times]. At that moment the crowd begins to divide into several groups.

The groupies whom the singer has brought with him cry out: "Again! Sing it again!" And again Salih sings, "Some people out there are complaining about bad times!"

Then the fans start in, the ones who came to spend the night wailing, sighing, looking about, smiling, flirting, and crying out "again!"

"Some people are complaining about bad times!"

Then the largest group starts to move: the drunks, their minds alcohol-hardened by the time the first word is sung. They cry out, "*Ya ʿayn-i ʿalayk*!" [how beautiful].

And Abd al-Hayy cuts them off: "Some people are complaining about bad times!"

Then the final and smallest group begins to move: the *futūwāt* [tough guys]. They are small in number, but loud of voice. They shout, "By the Prophet, again!"

And Salih Abd al-Hayy sings again: "O night, there are people out there complaining about their bad times!"

We can eat, drink, get up, move about, sit, and sleep. Then the voice burns into our ears again: "People are complaining about their bad times!"

We can leave the hall, go to Ezbekīya, Rōḍ al-Farag, even Maṣr al-Gadīda, and when we come back we still find "the chanter" singing, "People are complaining to you about their problems!" *(ibid., 41–43)*.

Awad plainly means to suggest that the musical culture of the day – just before the 1919 revolt against British rule – was coarse and backward. A pre-Abd al-Wahhab state of cultural decline (with a few prominent exceptions to be discussed below) is a common theme in much writing on the singer. Some of the lyrics from songs of the early twentieth century are quoted as evidence of cultural backwardness in much the same way that Nafusa Zakariyya Said quoted "backward" colloquial poetry in her book on "the call for colloquial." For example:[9]

> Watch over me and watch out, don't tickle me
> My body is delicate, can't take it.
> And I'm jealous when you touch me.
> My body is flexible, pliant and soft
> Like clotted cream, O sweet one

And:

> You tell me "take off your slipper
> On the bed, and do your duty."
> I'm afraid the neighbors will get you in trouble
> And hit you, so don't take me lightly.

Although such risqué songs have long been a part of Cairo's musical culture, it would be absurd to assume that they made up all or even the major part of Egyptian music at the turn of the century. There were also singers who had developed a reputation for "high style," such as the nineteenth-century singer ʿAbduh al-Ḥamūlī (1841–1901) who became known as an innovator through such means as reintroducing elements of Ottoman court style into Egyptian music, and singing classical Arabic poems composed by prominent social figures of his day, thus earning himself a place in the court of the Khedive Ismāʿīl (Kāmil 1971, 10–15).[10] Abd al-Wahhab himself, in his later life, when asked by a popular magazine to comment on al-Hamuli's legacy, confirmed the value of the music, but also pointedly mentioned its assumed faults:

> Abduh was the first to begin 'acting' in his singing. Before him singing consisted merely of homogeneous melodies sung for enjoyment, which expressed no salient emotion. Abduh was the first to voice pain in his songs . . . Most of his singing was improvised, so he sang with more heart than mind, drawing inspiration from whatever situation he found himself in when he was to sing . . . His most important attribute was his clear understanding of the psychology of the audience that would be listening to him. This helped him make the most appropriate choice of modality . . .
>
> Abduh was not interested in instrumental music. We never heard of him that this [instrumental music] was a musical necessity, or that he connected one passage to another in a composition. Nor was he concerned that his group play on the new *bashraf* or *samāʿī* forms [relatively recent instrumental forms of Middle Eastern music], even though he was in contact with some of the prominent Turkish musicians by virtue of his association with princes whose homes were never without music. Perhaps he can be excused for this, since art at the time was individualistic, and not a collective enterprise. This individualism prevailed over all aspects of Egyptian life, not over music alone . . . This "individualism," or egotism, affected the efforts of each musician such that the interests of the group were lost . . . And so the modalities mixed with one another; there was no systematization or order.
>
> *(ʿAbd al-Wahhāb 1938 [209], 18–20)*

Although the article purported to seek Abd al-Wahhab's expert opinion on al-Hamuli, Abd al-Wahhab's response was in fact little more than the received wisdom. Al-Hamuli died in 1901, before Abd al-Wahhab could possibly have had a chance to hear him, even assuming the earliest date for his birth. There were, however, a number of students and contemporaries of al-Hamuli active during Abd al-Wahhab's youth (see Kāmil [1971, 14]).

By the time Abd al-Wahhab spoke about al-Hamuli he had himself assumed the mantle of high art, and was known as "the singer of kings and princes" due to his introduction into high society in the late 1920s by the aristocratic poet Ahmad Shauqi. Nonetheless, he still had to build his fame through numerous public concerts not unlike those in which his "decadent" predecessors sang – such venues as weddings, saints' festivals, and concerts in outdoor pavilions.

Representing the pre-Abd al-Wahhab cultural milieu as rife with decadence has the effect of making his rise to prominence appear that much more meteoric when set against a background of lewd songs crooned to drunken men in tents. When discussing later aspects of his life, Abd al-Wahhab's biographers – and possibly Abd al-Wahhab himself – emphasized a different history. In particular, after Abd al-Wahhab "arrives" as a musical and cinematic star, all writing stresses his continuity with positively valued traditions. The two main traditions highlighted in this later phase are the folk tradition, represented by the singer Sayyid Darwish, and the classical tradition, represented by the poet Ahmad Shauqi. Further ties to his musical lineage, as we shall see, are suggested in the figures of Abduh al-Hamuli and Salama al-Higazi. These biographical constructions of Abd al-Wahhab strongly parallel the ideological treatment of sociolinguistic types: the "modern" Abd al-Wahhab contrasts with the "backwardness" of the cultural milieu from which he rose. The *kuttāb* gives him classical authenticity (not to mention superb voice training), as does his association with the neoclassicist Shauqi, but advertising his folk-based musical lineage keeps him firmly rooted in the best of the "colloquial" tradition.

The bottom rung of Abd al-Wahhab's ladder to stardom was, according to all the biographies, Al-Klūb al-Miṣrī (the Egyptian Club). This establishment was a musical theater in the Ḥusayn quarter near al-Azhar University and not far from Abd al-Wahhab's home quarter of Bāb al-Shaʿrīya. It was owned by Fauzī al-Gazāyirlī, a comedian who later acted in films. Abd al-Wahhab is said to have been introduced to al-Gazayirli by a Syrian tailor named Yūsuf Shamʿūn to whom the young Muhammad had been apprenticed by his father in an effort to distract him from his interest in singing. Unfortunately, the Syrian liked music, and sang in al-Gazayirli's chorus in his spare time. When he heard the boy's voice he promptly put him in contact with the person most likely to frustrate the senior Abd al-Wahhab's efforts to channel his son's life into sober pursuits (M. ʿAwaḍ 1991, 56–57). In keeping with the image of Abd al-Wahhab's inexorable rise from the ashes of backward decadence, Awad describes the Egyptian Club as a seedy place rife with drinking, dancing and hashish smoking. The men, listening to a coarse *baladī* singer, comment to each other:

Isn't that better than foreign singing? Honestly, Si Fahmī [Fahmi Sir], the English are occupying our land, but have you ever heard an Englishman sing "*yā layl yā ʿayn*"? Of course not. For this reason, by God, all is still well in the community of

Muḥammad. Another beer! All right! Sing for us man, sing! Give us a song, *shaykh*!

The *shaykh* sings . . . (*M. ʿAwaḍ 1991, 59*)

Abd al-Wahhab began working at the Egyptian Club in 1917, at the age of seven (if we assume that he was born in 1910). His job was to sing between the acts of plays for five piasters a night, which he did under the name Muḥammad al-Baghdādī. Unfortunately, the pseudonym was not enough to keep his family from discovering his job. His older brother Ḥasan came one night and took him home. Muhammad responded to discipline by running away in 1918 to sing in the circus, where the young boy was made to sleep with the animals. Such a life was not to his liking, and so, with the intercession of a relative, Abd al-Wahhab again returned to his family (*ibid.*, 61–63).

By this time Abd al-Wahhab had obtained reluctant permission to continue his performance career. He began singing in the troupe of ʿAbd al-Raḥmān Rushdī – now in the plays as a little girl and between the acts in a "smoking jacket" (ʿAbd al-Wahhāb and Wahba 1992, 34). Once again, the biographies tell us, the young boy was marked for future greatness. The poet Ahmad Shauqi came to the play one night and heard Abd al-Wahhab sing. What struck Shauqi most about the boy was not just his voice, but his extreme youth. As a progressive he was outraged at the sight of a child on the stage, so he had his friend Russell Pasha, the British ex-*ḥikimdār* (chief officer) of police, talk to Rushdi about the matter. The result was that Abd al-Wahhab was made to leave the troupe.[11]

In at least one interview Abd al-Wahhab is ascribed a tenuous connection with another major figure – Saʿd Zaghlūl, leader of the nationalist Wafd Party, inspiration of the 1919 revolution against British rule and revered as one of the founding fathers of the modern Egyptian state. Abd al-Wahhab related that he stood on the fringe of a crowd listening to the great leader speak at a political rally. After the speech, Abd al-Wahhab joined in shouting political slogans in the street, even though he was too young to understand what they really meant (Fauzī 1991, 10). The story clouds still more the issue of exactly when Abd al-Wahhab was born. In this version of his life he claims to have seen Zaghlul during the revolution, as a child of twelve. Zaghlul, however, was exiled from Egypt in 1919 and did not return to Egypt until 1923, hence the story suggests Abd al-Wahhab was born in 1907.[12] The vagueness of dates, always coupled with relatively specific accounts of real people, is a constant feature of writing on and by Abd al-Wahhab.

But this glimpse of Saad Zaghlul from the margins of childhood gives

Abd al-Wahhab the best of both worlds: he can be present at the greatest historical moment of Egypt's early twentieth-century history, but be absolved of any responsibility for participating meaningfully in it. This minor tie to the emotions of 1919 (generally not prominently mentioned in the biographies) is consistent with the tone of nonpartisan patriotism (often mentioned in biographies) which is stressed in the later description of his ties to Shauqi and Sayyid Darwish – both of whom were political icons, but of different persuasions.

In the biographies, Abd al-Wahhab was to be marked as a singer of destiny one final time before his rise to stardom began in earnest. After his early brush with Shauqi, which is supposed to have taken place in 1919, he did not remain outside the entertainment profession for long. Soon he was again performing, this time in the troupe of ʿAlī al-Kassār, which Awad describes as *khalāʿa* (dissolute). The reason for this, he says, is that the British had begun to defuse the heady vigor of 1919 through sham negotiations. "Dissolute" entertainment such as that performed by al-Kassar, he says, was an escapist reaction to the "defeat of the revolution" (M. ʿAwaḍ 1991, 69–70). Nonetheless, al-Kassar's troupe was famed for its frank use of colloquial Arabic and became extremely popular (Landau 1958, 90–91). In 1921, while Abd al-Wahhab was working for Ali al-Kassar, the great singer Sayyid Darwish entered the theater, heard the boy singing (Abd al-Wahhab was "officially" eleven at the time), and was extremely impressed.[13] Later that year Darwish formed his own troupe in order to perform the operetta *Shahrazād*, and he asked Abd al-Wahhab to join him.[14] Abd al-Wahhab agreed, but unfortunately, the play was a miserable failure with Darwish in the lead. It was suggested that Abd al-Wahhab had a better voice, and should be tried in the lead, but the play still proved unpopular. Awad ascribes the failure of *Shahrazād* to the still-undeveloped voice of Abd al-Wahhab (again the alleged 1910 birthdate looms large) and to the reportedly avant-garde nature of the material, which audiences were unable to appreciate (M. ʿAwaḍ 1991, 72–73).[15]

Abd al-Wahhab left Darwish and began to work with Darwish's old troupe, which was led by Nagib al-Rihani. With al-Rihani Abd al-Wahhab toured the Levant, but never achieved great success, so he left the troupe in 1922 to study music formally in the recently established Nādī al-Mūsīqā (Music Club).[16] In the early 1920s he finally got his big break. Ahmad Shauqi Bey, "prince of poets," attended a performance Abd al-Wahhab gave at the San Stefano hotel in Alexandria. In his first encounter with Shauqi the poet had admonished Abd al-Wahhab's mentor, Abd al-Rahman Rushdi, for exploiting child labor. In the San Stefano encounter

Abd al-Wahhab's youth seemed not to bother Shauqi. He invited Abd al-Wahhab to come visit him in Cairo. All the biographies pointedly note that Abd al-Wahhab was reluctant to speak to Shauqi because of his earlier experience with him, but he overcame his shyness, and the most important friendship of Abd al-Wahhab's life began (*ibid.*, 77–83).[17]

The friendship of Muhammad Abd al-Wahhab, "singer of kings and princes," and Ahmad Shauqi, "prince of poets," is always described as a Pygmalion-like relationship: Shauqi "created" Abd al-Wahhab from the rough clay of his traditional background, bought him new clothes, took him to France, introduced him to high society, and hired the best music teachers for him.[18] But the importance of Shauqi to Abd al-Wahhab's many admirers was not just that Shauqi made him into a commercial success, but that the poet's influence finished the process of making Abd al-Wahhab into a subtle hybrid of tradition, classicism and Western-inspired modernity. The following passage aptly illustrates the way this new identity was represented to the public on Abd al-Wahhab's death in 1991. It is worth quoting at length:

> It was an interesting encounter between Muhammad Effendi, the son of Shaykh Abd al-Wahhab Isa, muezzin of the mosque of Sayyid al-Sha'rānī, and Shauqi Bey, a man of rank, scion of a family in whose veins ran the blood of Arabs, Turks, Kurds and Greeks. An encounter between Muhammad Effendi, apprentice to a tailor, and Ahmad Shauqi, who had been sent by the Khedive Taufiq to study literature and law in France. A meeting between Muhammad Abd al-Wahhab who embarked on an artistic career to finish the work of Sayyid Darwish – the folk artist who ran behind children in the streets of poor quarters to hear their songs, who listened to the songs of migrant workers, wrote satiric songs, and compositions based on the voices of hashish addicts, chicken cluckings, water carriers and market vendors – and Ahmad Shauqi, "prince of poets," poet of prince 'Abbās II. An encounter which symbolized an important change in Egyptian society: a poor son of the people – weak politically – rising into the middle class which wanted to decide its own future through independence and the constitution; together with a son of high rank, confidant of princes, a man shaken by World War I and the fall of Turkey, who was exiled to Spain when Abbas was exiled . . .
>
> This encounter between Abd al-Wahhab and Shauqi symbolized a stage in the history of Egypt and of Arabdom . . . the "reconciliation" [*taufiq*] between the civilization and heritage of Islam, and the civilization and heritage of the West, which dominates the world politically and economically today. This reconciliation succeeds sometimes, and sometimes fails, becoming [in that case] "fabrication" [*talfiq*]. But effort, patience and challenge were the hallmarks of Abd al-Wahhab. He was acquainted with the European musical culture, tried to comprehend it and find agreement between it and the music and singing of the East. It is easy to see in his music what he borrowed from Tchaikovsky, Verdi, Offenbach and Beethoven in a serious effort to bring reconciliation between what came from the West and

musical lines [*jumal*] derived from the qur'ānic readings of Shaykh Rif'at, or Egyptian folk tunes, or the development of the musical vocabulary of [prominent contemporary singers] Shokōkō, Kuḥlāwī and others.

The effort to tie Arabic music to world music began with Abd al-Wahhab – with [Shauqi's effort] to introduce him into a more refined and civilized society. And so Shauqi entered into every part of Abd al-Wahhab's life, large or small. He found him sickly, and so took him to doctors, oversaw his treatment and his medicine. He reviewed his appearance, and then picked out some clothes that made him elegant. He taught him proper style in eating and drinking, how to speak. And through this arduous training he taught him how to be independent in his desires, and how to take pride in his superiority. There were many campaigns in magazines and newspapers attacking Abd al-Wahhab, the new star. Other singers and composers were threatened by his brilliance. (*Ghānim 1991, 8–9*)

Shauqi was involved in many of the political issues of his day, particularly the debate over allegiance to the Ottoman Empire. Abd al-Wahhab was, to some extent, caught in the cross-fire of these battles, but Awad contends that most criticism leveled at Abd al-Wahhab derived from the innovative nature of his music, and that he could always counter the nay-sayers merely by singing (M. 'Awaḍ 1991, 84–85; Zakarīyā 1991, 79). The problem with all this attention from prominent personalities was that Abd al-Wahhab risked acquiring the reputation of being a pet of the aristocracy – truly the "singer of kings and princes" rather than a symbol of burgeoning Egyptian nationalism. Association with the aristocracy was chic in the 1930s and 1940s, but acquired a very different significance after the 1952 revolution. Indeed, practically the only negative note struck in all the admiring prose published after Abd al-Wahhab died had to do with this point. The author Ṭāriq al-Shināwī, writing in the weekly *Rūz al-Yūsuf*, notes first of all that when two cassettes of post-1952 revolution patriotic songs were released a few years ago by the Ṣaut al-Fann record company, owned by Abd al-Wahhab, one by protégé Abd al-Halim Hafiz (composed by Kamal al-Tawil) and the other by Abd al-Wahhab, the tape by Abd al-Halim – who rose to prominence in the Nasserist period and is associated with its spirit – sold far better. Al-Shinawi ascribed the failure of the Abd al-Wahhab tape to a clear difference in the "degree of sincerity" in the voices on the respective cassettes – in other words, Abd al-Wahhab was less convincing as a national (and Nasserist) voice than was Abd al-Halim (al-Shināwī 1991, 5).

Other biographers insist even more strongly that Abd al-Wahhab's political role lay in his defining modern Egyptian identity, and that this definition transcended the world of party politics. Novelist Fatḥī Ghānim anoints Abd al-Wahhab the successor to Sayyid Darwish – balladeer of the 1919 revolution – but contends that the interwar years required different tactics from those of the stormy days of the revolution. In his view Shauqi was the decisive factor in Abd al-Wahhab's turn from vulgar practical politics to the transcendental definition of national identity:

> Muhammad Effendi Abd al-Wahhab had two choices: to continue the mission of Sayyid Darwish as it was – revolutionary songs expressing the views of the oppressed – in which case he would become by necessity a politician and end up oppressed and in prison; or to choose the way of art and rise, if only temporarily, to the [national] struggle and to politics. He chose the way of art because he found one of the rarest geniuses in the history of the Arab nation to guide and protect him and to look after his education: Ahmad Shauqi, who had the greatest influence on the future of Abd al-Wahhab. *(Ghānim 1991, 8)*

Whatever the political implications of Abd al-Wahhab's association with Shauqi, he does seem to have become a commercial success by about 1924.[19] He appeared in the hit play *Qunṣul al-wizz* (Consul of the geese) with Nagib al-Rihani, and then in 1927 was invited by the leading female vocalist of the day, the "*Sulṭāna* of song" Munīra al-Mahdīya, to finish Sayyid Darwish's uncompleted operetta *Anṭōniyo wa-Kliyūbātrā* (Antony and Cleopatra).[20] Al-Mahdiya was the leading female star of the day (although soon to be eclipsed by Umm Kulthum), and hung a sign outside her door saying "*Duktūra mumtāza fi-l-ghinā' wa-al-ṭarab bayn al-ʿālim al-sharqī jamīʿihi*" (distinguished doctor of song and music in the entire Eastern world).

Sayyid Darwish, dead for three years by the time the play was performed, had already become one of the most revered figures of the 1919 revolution against the British. Thus performing a Darwish operetta opposite Munira al-Mahdiya was the biggest gamble of Abd al-Wahhab's young career. Failure would be so humiliating that he felt it would end his singing career; success would make him the leading male vocalist of his age. The gamble paid off handsomely.[21] There were certain oddities in some of the performances, such as the incongruence of Abd al-Wahhab's slight physique in the role of Antony with al-Mahdiya's enormous Cleopatra (a serious problem in the final scene of Darwish's version of the story, in which Cleopatra throws herself into Antony's arms), and a long-remembered night when the lights in the theater went off at a critical moment during a scene in which Cleopatra enters singing "I left Egypt, my country," to be met by an embrace from Antony. The lights came on to reveal Abd al-Wahhab embracing an extra rather than al-Mahdiya.[22]

By this time Abd al-Wahhab was too well established to be derailed by gaffes. Shauqi had worked to get his protégé accepted by the aristocracy, bringing him to the "Ṣōlat establishment," a literary salon frequented by the leading intellectuals of the day. Abd al-Wahhab later described Ṣōlat's as his "third education" after the *kuttāb* and Shauqi. Shauqi formally consecrated what he saw as a passing of the mantle of authenticity and modernity in music from Sayyid Darwish to Abd al-Wahhab in a poem eulogizing Darwish:

Master of art, rest easy from a world	in which you have known the extent of its pleasures and pains
Though you may have wearied, and found no joy in it,	your inspiration flowed out, relieving you of your distress.
You have chosen your successor [Abd al-Wahhab] in artistic genius;	art urges him on to its banner.
[He is] a nightingale in the dominion of the heart,	the like of which is granted to no others.
Slender as tiny droplets, it emanates:	his voice – across the vast expanse of the globe.
He inspires art to extol him,	[art and] the beauty of living genius

(A. Shauqī 1925–36, 14–16)

This was the picture of Abd al-Wahhab in his golden age – a nightingale blessed by the highest ideals of artistic sensibility, singing sweetly across the landscape. Shauqi's neoclassical vision of Abd al-Wahhab was, substantially, what was handed down to the generation of the 1980s and 1990s in the media blitz immediately following the singer's death: Beethoven and Caruso rolled into one in the person of *al-mūsīqār al-nābigh* – the "genius musician."

The bourgeoisie on the beach circa 1934

It is not by the direct method of a scrupulous narration that the explorer of the past can hope to depict that singular epoch. If he is wise, he will adopt a subtler strategy. He will attack his subject in unexpected places; he will fall upon the flank, or the rear; he will shoot a sudden, revealing searchlight into obscure recesses, hitherto undivined. He will row out over that great ocean of material, and lower down into it, here and there, a little bucket, which will bring up to the light of day some characteristic specimen, from those far depths, to be examined with a careful curiosity. *(Strachey [1918], vii)*

When Lytton Strachey wrote about rowing out "over that great ocean of material" he referred to the Victorian age from the perspective of 1918. With the world in ruin and millions of his fellow Europeans dead, he was trying to reevaluate the spirit of an age that had, in his opinion, led to men rushing into hails of machine-gun fire like lemmings into the sea. His problem was that the Victorian age was barely over. How does one get perspective on an unfinished story? Dead history is easier to write; the sources are finite and very likely dwindling. This is the same problem Americans face with regard to their wartime legacies: the "good" World War II and the "bad" Vietnam experience. It is the same problem Egyptians face with the legacy of their "eminent modernists," among whom Abd al-Wahhab features prominently. What were the 1930s really like?

The weekly magazine *al-Ithnayn* was one forum in which the image of middle-class modernity was refined in Abd al-Wahhab's heyday.[23] *Al-Ithnayn* featured humor (much of which was in colloquial Arabic), cartoons, news of prominent entertainers, as well as occasional satire by serious writers. Abd al-Wahhab was a great favorite of *al-Ithnayn*, and was mentioned at least once in nearly every issue. One finds little mention of him in more sober publications such as the highbrow arts and literature journal *al-Hilāl* – issued by the company that published *al-Ithnayn* – which is a more likely forum for the joining of Western technique and Eastern classicism so central to ideological modernism. In fact, the December 1, 1933 issue of *al-Hilāl*, published just before the opening of Abd al-Wahhab's first film, contained an article entitled "The Language of Song as a Means of Education." The article found Arabic music badly deficient in higher values: "We have no music of the sort which educators and reformers crave. What we have are moans, sighs, weeping and laments – a mournful style which kills the emotions, inciting the soul to lethargy, fatalism and contentment with degradation" (Ṭanāḥī 1933, 217).[24] The article goes on to excoriate modern poets for not providing material up to the standards of the ancients which could be utilized in elevated music. The only exception mentioned in the article was neoclassicist Ahmad Shauqi, but the author says nothing about singers who adapted Shauqi's material, of whom Abd al-Wahhab was the most prominent.

Although Abd al-Wahhab, in his day, was of little overt concern to highbrow arbiters of refinement, he was nonetheless a regular feature in the middle- to lowbrow *al-Ithnayn*. What sorts of images were promoted on the pages of this weekly? In fact, the magazine has a logical format through from front to back. Often the front cover depicted something "folkloric." The first issue sported Kishkish Bey, a stage and film character played by comedian Nagib al-Rihani. Another issue (number two) sported the face of a Gypsy woman. Issue number four featured a vendor of *ʿirʔ sūs* (a drink made from licorice root) and printed his cry: " *ʿĀdi l-ʿagab, ḥilāwa min khashab, ya ʿirʔ sūs khamīr*!" (Here is an amazing thing, candy made from wood, fermented *ʿirʔ sūs*!).

The cover of the sixth issue featured drawings of two women. One was dark and brown-eyed, wearing a gauzy veil on the lower half of her face, leaving her large, languorous eyes exposed. Her face is turned to one side in modest "Eastern" fashion – no chance of looking a man in the eye. The second woman is light-skinned, blue-eyed, and wearing heavy lipstick. There is no veil on her face, and her shoulders are bare. Unlike her counterpart, she stares straight ahead into the eyes of whoever is looking on. The caption reads: "Beauty of today and beauty of the past" (see plate 3).

The inside front cover always featured a caricature of some famous Egyptian person, often an actor or actress. Issue number one contained the face – with exaggerated long nose – of Badīʿa Maṣābnī, the leading dancer of the time and famous as a nightclub proprietress. In issue four it was Yūsuf Wahbī, a heart-throb of the 1930s and friend of Abd al-Wahhab's director, Muḥammad Karīm. Abd al-Wahhab didn't get his turn until issue number eight. He appears looking rather older than in his early films, sporting extremely long sideburns and an enormous bow tie.[25]

In 1991 some of the articles on Abd al-Wahhab printed in mass-circulation publications pointed out that he was famed for his *anāqa* – his "elegance." His fashionable Western suits, regular trips to Beirut and Paris (where Shauqi always insisted they stay in the Latin Quarter [M. ʿAwaḍ 1991, 103]),[26] and hairstyle – marginal issues in 1991 – were central to the Abd al-Wahhab image of sixty years before. In fact, while the 1991 version of Abd al-Wahhab implies that his style is popular because of the avant-garde character of his music, the 1930s version may have done just the opposite: made the music popular because of the singer's style.

The inside of *al-Ithnayn*'s back cover usually carried an advertisement. Issue number two, for example, showed a bare-shouldered blue-eyed woman with hair uncovered. She clutches a bouquet of flowers to her breast, suggesting that she is wearing nothing. The advertisement proclaims: "Youth is not enough: *Pūmpīyā* lotion, the scent men love." In issue three the inside back cover sported a Jantzen bathing-suit advertisement: "Le costume de bain élégant et classique." Both men and women were shown in the advertisement, their bathing suits practically identical – backless and form-fitting, with the legs fully exposed. The beach theme was continued in issue four, which carried an advertisement for the government railway: "Lower rates for private cars in trains going to Alexandria on July 15. Trains to depart at 6:15 A.M., return at 8:30 P.M. on the same day. Leather-covered seats, buffet, reserved seats for the ladies. Price: 325 millimes" (*al-Ithnayn* 4: 47). The advertisement on the inside back page of this issue offered a practical product for anyone interested in the July 15 train special: Elizabeth Arden sunscreen. This advertisement featured two women, both with ample skin showing, one painfully burned and the other, presumably the Elizabeth Arden customer, comfortable and still pale.

The outside of the back cover generally featured the face of· a foreign actress. Issue number two – with an inside-front-cover caricature of actress

Plate 3 "Beauty of today and beauty of the past" (cover of *al-Ithnayn* 6 [July 23, 1934])

Bahīga Ḥāfiẓ threatening to shave her chin if she couldn't top Greta Garbo – had none other than Garbo. On issue four it was Toby Wing, fresh from Busby Berkeley's *Gold Diggers of 1933* and soon to dance in *Gold Diggers of 1935* and in *Gold Diggers of 1937*, which featured masses

Plate 4 "'Ustaz' Yusuf Wahbi heard that power [*al-ḥaul*] was half of beauty, so he got himself the most powerful [*aḥwal*] monocle" (from *al-Ithnayn* 8 [August 6, 1934]: 2). This is a play on words, as *aḥwal* (most powerful) also means "squint-eyed"

of girls dancing in geometric patterns. The dancing-girl phenomenon was noted in *al-Ithnayn* issue ten, which contained a drawing of chorus girls in short skirts doing high kicks. Looking at the poster are comedians Nagib al-Rihani in his Kishkish Bey persona, and his colleague Ali al-Kassar, who was known on stage as *al-Barbarī* (the barbarian).[27] Like al-Rihani's Kishkish, al-Kassar's routine revolved around the juxtaposition of a "hick" from the countryside with urban sophistication. *Al-Barbarī* says: "Why does the ministry want to ban pictures of women in bathing suits?" Kishkish replies: "Because the newspapers are putting the cinema out of business!"

The pattern of pictures displayed on the front and back covers of *al-Ithnayn* suggests a progression. Folkloric images at the beginning of the magazines led to advertisements for modern consumer goods on the inside of the back cover; caricatures of Egyptian actors (sometimes other prominent persons) on the inside front cover were matched by photos of foreign actresses on the back. In the iconography of *al-Ithnayn*, society appears to be headed away from "traditionalism" and toward a Westernized "modernity." But while Western glamor may have featured in the image of modernity popularized by *al-Ithnayn*, the contents of the magazine often functioned to suggest what sort of behavior was going too far.[28]

For example, while the beach theme emphasized prominently in the summer advertising campaigns of the first issues signaled the adoption of a new bourgeois habit, the contents of the magazine indicate that the limits and etiquette of beach behavior were still being negotiated. A cartoon shows two women on the beach wearing the latest in Western bathing fashion. One of the suits is a bit more revealing than the other – practically a bikini, with top and bottom connected only by a slender strip of fabric. The first woman, wearing the marginally more modest suit, says, "Wow! It's hot today!" The woman in the "ur-bikini" replies, "Didn't I tell you not to wear that heavy bathing suit?" (*al-Ithnayn* 3 [July 2, 1934]: 15). The reader is allowed to feel traditional indignation ("*we* don't dress like those women, how dare they do that") while participating in a thoroughly untraditional practice.

The magazine is rife with this sort of hyperbole. In issue number eight the "Laws for Bathing" are given:

Article 1: Everyone must obey the law.
Article 2: Male and female bathers must be good.
Article 3: "Good" means that boys must be handsome and girls pretty.
Article 4: Those who are not "good" can swim under the following conditions:
  a. they are rich
  b. they are cultured
  c. they are lighthearted . . .

Article 8: An old woman can come to the beach only on the condition that she drown herself in the water [*tighraq*].
Article 9: If she cannot meet the conditions of article 8 she must stand far away so as not to bother the girls and the children.
Article 10: We assume no responsibility for lost items such as false teeth, glass eyes, wigs or the lives of any other old women.
Article 11: Before swimming with wives and children men must know that morals are old-fashioned . . . *(al-Ithnayn 8 [August 6, 1934]: 26)*

Plate 5 Al-Kassar: "Why does the ministry want to ban pictures of women in bathing suits?" Kishkish: "Because the newspapers are putting the cinema out of business!" (from *al-Ithnayn* 10 [August 20, 1934]: 5)

A drawing of a bearded Azharī *shaykh* in robe and turban, strolling on the beach among reclining beauties who converse with boys in swimming trunks, accompanies the "Bathing Laws." The facing page displays an article on Kishkish and *al-Barbarī* at the beach.

Lampooning social conventions in this way took on considerable importance in the context of potentially threatening novelties such as mixed bathing. At a time when many people were experimenting with new (generally European-inspired) practices, such articles served to explore the boundaries of what was permissible Egyptian behavior. By making a joke of questionable behavior the magazine constructed an area of ambiguity in the new morals and at the same time made it less threatening than it might have been in real life.

Of course not everybody approved of mixed bathing. Bayram al-Tunsi's "Camp Caesar *Maqāma*," described in chapter 3, assumes that most of the readers would draw the line considerably short of merely putting the women in more modest suits, maybe even to the point of refusing any sanction for mixed bathing. Al-Tunsi occasionally used the image of women at the beach in a more explicitly political manner, as in his poem "Egypt is a Part of Europe":

> For ages she [Egypt] has scraped and crawled
> When passing by Vienna and Barcelona.
> Before you came we abolished religion
> And since Napoleon, we've done away with *sharīʿa* [Islamic law]
> Our Qur'āns, we've put in museums:
> From them we get memories and joy and prettiness.
> The age of cloaks and veils has ended,
> And women walk about with legs naked.
> My mother, my sister, my wife – are they going with us
> To the beach while the world looks upon us?!
> We're like you in everything, O people of culture [Europeans],
> Like you, staying up all night playing poker.
> We have bars of every sort, in every quarter.
> Shame on you – exploiting us after that!
> Leave us to enjoy our own country,
> Not your country. And let us forge our own steel,
> Not your steel. Crap? We want our own crap,
> Not your crap, O you who mean to butcher us.
>
> *(al-Tūnsī 1978, 41–42)*

Between "Egypt is a Part of Europe" and "The Bathing Laws" – between what was seen by some as corrupt aping of Europe, and by others as native adaptation of European custom – lay the potential for families and individuals to negotiate their identities as "modern Egyptians." Negotiation of identity within such limits was, more than any material criteria, what defined the Egyptian middle class.

Al-Ithnayn was not unconcerned with the trappings of wealth, but it catered more to aspirations than to the objectively wealthy. This was abundantly clear in the first issue, which ran a tongue-in-cheek advice column titled "*Isma' yā bēh . . . isma'ī yā hānim*" (Listen, your excellency . . . listen, my lady). The "advice" offered was largely about how to handle the servants, and about proper social behavior:

Listen, Your Excellency . . .

1. If you take "the lady" to the cinema . . . don't pay any attention to her.
2. If you bring guests with you . . . stop in at Groppi's.[29]

. . .

23. If your driver is handsome . . . don't leave him alone [with "the lady"].
24. If the phone rings . . . don't let "the lady" answer it.
25. If your mistress skips your rendezvous . . . go back to "the lady."

Listen, My Lady . . .

1. If you go to the cinema with "the bey" . . . blindfold him [so he doesn't see any other women].
2. If "the bey" brings guests . . . make like you're sick (*i'mili 'ayyāna*).

. . .

23. If your driver is late . . . tell him, "Shame on you."
24. If the phone rings . . . careful that your husband doesn't listen.
25. If your lover is late for your rendezvous . . . complain to your husband.

("Isma' yā bēh . . ." 1934)

The advice column was accompanied by a drawing at the top of the page of a man in a natty European suit wearing a tarbush, then commonly associated with the *efendīya* (men who were educated but not aristocratic, often office workers or bureaucrats). He is talking to a woman with wild, uncovered hair who wears a necklace. The same couple appears in the middle of the page, he with his arm around her and she quite *décolletée*. As in the "Bathing Laws," the point of "Listen, Your Excellency . . ." is not to sanction unacceptable behavior, but to "Egyptianize" it, at least for some.

The article was directed to a stereotypical image of upper-class society. Although many of the advertisements in *al-Ithnayn* were oriented toward the well-off reader, one need not assume that the hawking of high-priced goods and services is a sure reflection of the magazine's clientele. Probably most readers of *al-Ithnayn* did not possess cars, drivers, or servants any more than they had mistresses or, in "the lady's" case, lovers. The "bey" and "hānim" of *al-Ithnayn* covet the same luxuries as the middle class (sweets from Groppi's, a night at the cinema, an automobile), but they are not of the middle class. Indeed, they bear more resemblance to the slothful, immoral *ibn al-zawāt* aristocrats of the sort lampooned by Bayram al-Tunsi.

By the end of the 1930s the image of modernity had been substantially defined in popular magazines such as *al-Ithnayn* and other media. The hallmark of this newly defined identity was confident possession of such European customs as were deemed desirable, coupled with a fine discrimination of how far one could go in such behavior and remain truly Egyptian. In practice, everybody who ever dabbled in the manners and customs of foreigners saw themselves as practicing European ways "correctly" – that is, as a proper Egyptian. Evaluating the behavior of others was more problematic. In the censorious view of some (Bayram al-Tunsi for example) practically everything European could be considered un-Egyptian. The two points of view – self-definition as someone "who can handle it" and the attribution of "over-Europeanization" to others – are not mutually exclusive.

Other articles in *al-Ithnayn* were more explicit in differentiating a wholesome middle-class image from the presumption of unsavory behavior by the aristocracy. For instance, Abu Buthayna, a colloquial poet later excoriated by the literary establishment as "vulgar" (N. Saʿīd 1964, 338), offered advice to the young in a poem titled "*Yā afandī, il-maẓhar mā yihimmish*" (Effendi, appearances don't matter) by mocking the dandified airs of a young man trying to affect the appearance of an aristocrat:

Okay boy, put on makeup if you like, be foppish, dress up and show off,
But I want to say something to you, even if it bothers you.
Before you go out swaggering in your clothes, and looking pretty,
Look after your mind, your know-how, wise up, take care of your brain.
Go on prettying up from outside, dress up in brown and grey.
What good are your clothes, effendi, if your head is like a water jug.
In Europe when a boy goes out, you'll find he's ultrachic.
At work he looks out for number one, boasts of his artfulness, puts on airs.
Effendi, appearances don't matter: one's value comes from effort.
Many a worker in dirty clothes is wanted by a hundred factories.
One needs to be cultured, not just decorated from the outside.
My mind is better than my body a hundred million times over in this world.

(*Abū Buthayna 1934*)

A drawing in the margin of the page shows a man in tarbush seated at a conspicuously feminine vanity table looking intently into a mirror as he powders his nose. Another drawing at the top of the page shows him strolling in a garden dressed in his effendi finery (a wide-lapelled Western suit and tie) with a woman in Western clothes on his arm.

"Appearances Don't Matter," like "Listen, Your Excellency" and the "Bathing Laws," is concerned with exploring the limits of proper comportment. Although "Appearances" assumes a more directly didactic tone than the other articles, its appeal is the same. Poetry and humor of this sort simultaneously implicated readers in the practice of foreign customs, and absolved them of participating in the worst excesses of such behavior. It was through such articles that magazines such as *al-Ithnayn* could play an

Plate 6 "Effendi, appearances don't matter" (from *al-Ithnayn* 3 [July 2, 1934]: 31)

important role in defining and publicizing tastes that were considered markers of middle-class status for those who could not necessarily afford the material trappings of the middle class. The entry fee to the world of *al-Ithnayn* was only ten millimes and some ability to read.

The legend II: the 1930s

From an early age Muhammad Abd al-Wahhab himself probably played an active role in creating the heroic modernist image later so prominent in the press. For example, the idea for Abd al-Wahhab's first film, *White Rose* (which we shall look at in chapter 5), came from the singer himself and was initially autobiographical in nature. Muhammad Karim, director of *White Rose*, first met Abd al-Wahhab in February 1931 while in the provincial town of Zaqāzīq to film a documentary on the Ministry of Agriculture's efforts to foster peasant cooperatives as a means of lessening foreign influence in the countryside (Karīm 1972, 128–34). Abd al-Wahhab was staying in the Zaqāzīq home of ʿAbd Allāh Fikrī Abāẓa, a prominent lawyer and later editor of *al-Ithnayn*'s sister publication *al-Muṣawwar*.[30] The singer was to perform, and Karim was invited to attend by Abaza (*ibid.*, 161). Karim describes the Abd al-Wahhab of 1931 as a young man reminiscent of Abu Buthayna's "Effendi."

When Karim met Abd al-Wahhab it was afternoon and the singer was asleep at the house in Zaqāzīq: "The windows of the room in which Abd al-Wahhab was sleeping were shut, and were covered with drapes so that it was pitch-dark during the daylight hours. I wondered how Abd al-Wahhab could be sleeping at that hour and in such conditions" (*ibid.*, 162). Karim had just finished his first film, *Zaynab* (1930), and had not yet begun his second, *Awlād al-zawāt* (Sons of the aristocracy, 1932). When Abd al-Wahhab woke he chatted with Karim about *Zaynab*, and then said point-blank, "Would it be possible, *yā ustādh* ["professor," not literally, but in a respectful sense], to make a short film on my personal life?" Karim answered politely that such a film would make an excellent memento for Abd al-Wahhab, and the matter went no further. The concert, Karim said, was enjoyable, but he "felt that [his] nerves would be shattered and [his] breath stopped from the yelling of the crowd, their whistling, and all those tarbushes being thrown in admiration for the music" (*ibid.*).

Two years later (1933) Karim received a phone call from a friend who wanted to meet with Karim to discuss a "very important matter" which could not be mentioned over the phone. The friend was Taufīq al-Mardanlī, who eventually wrote the dialogue for *White Rose*, and the "important matter" turned out to be Abd al-Wahhab, who was making overtures about the film project he had mentioned two years before in Zaqāzīq. Karim agreed to meet the singer in his own home to discuss the project, and pointedly describes how Abd al-Wahhab was late because he had to attend a soccer match: soccer, at the time, was a new fashion, and Abd al-Wahhab as a trendsetter was bound to follow it. When Abd al-Wahhab did arrive at Karim's home, his behavior continued in its unreassuring path:

When we had taken our places in the small salon he snapped at me, "Please close the windows." Then my wife came into the room and I introduced him to her. He asked her not to smoke, so she put out her cigarette. Then he asked my permission to place a vase of roses in front of him. While doing all this he continually put his mouth to a handkerchief. He hadn't even taken off his coat, even though he was in the salon. I gave him some coffee, but he wouldn't drink it. Suddenly he asked for a glass of cognac. He sprinkled a bit of it on his hands and then raised it to his nose. My wife and I realized that he was afraid of microbes!

I knew then from his behavior here and from what I had seen in Zaqāzīq that he was very "delicate" [*dalīkāt*], and I asked myself what could this "delicateness" do in the cinema? *(ibid., 163)*

In the early 1930s Karim liked what he saw in Abd al-Wahhab (box-office potential), and wanted to do the film despite the opposition of his wife, who was horrified at what she considered Abd al-Wahhab's strange behavior. Karim was to meet with Abd al-Wahhab to finish the details of the contract in the office of the Bayḍāfōn record company, with which Abd al-Wahhab worked closely (*ibid.*, 164).[31] Some of Abd al-Wahhab's alleged cheapness seems to have infected the record company:

At the Bayḍāfōn office after we had exchanged greetings they all seemed to be absorbed by an extremely serious matter: buying an oke [1.248 kg] of apples from an itinerant vendor.

"How much is an oke of apples?"

"Five piasters."

"No, only four."

"Okay, five less a millime, *yiftaḥ alla* [that's the final offer]."

"For your sake we'll go to four and a half."

"*Yiftaḥ alla.*"

The haggling went on for a long time, finally forcing the vendor to pick up his box and start to go. One of the buyers grabbed him by the sleeve and pulled him inside. The haggling began again, the buyers swearing to break it off and the seller saying, "For your sake . . ." The bargaining and negotiation went on for a full half hour, after which the buyers were able to reduce the price of an oke of apples by no less than half a piaster. When the seller had taken his four and a half piasters he took a deep breath and withdrew.

During all this I became more and more depressed. I apologized without saying a word about the matter I had come to discuss, and withdrew. I had decided not to direct the film because working in the cinema is very different than buying an oke of apples; there was a part of one scene [in his last film] that we spent LE 200 on and then threw it in the wastebasket. *(ibid., 164–65)*

Abd al-Wahhab, however, convinced Karim that the company would spend whatever necessary to produce the film, and he seems to have kept his word, as Karim never complained – in his memoirs at any rate – about financial difficulties in dealing with Abd al-Wahhab or with Bayḍāfōn.

This prima-donna aspect of Abd al-Wahhab in the 1930s, along with his alleged miserliness, was not so vividly presented in 1991 when his hypochondria was often mentioned but not explored. Karim, himself from a well-off bourgeois family, suggests that Abd al-Wahhab's rise to the pinnacle of polite society may have been accompanied by a certain amount of overcompensation.

Karim's intimations of affectation in the great star were bolstered at the time by jokes in popular magazines. In an article published in 1938 just after the release of his third film, *Yaḥyā al-ḥubb* (Long live love), Abd al-Wahhab was asked about his experiences in Paris while shooting parts of the film. Abd al-Wahhab told the interviewer: "This was the first time I have seen Paris during the winter, and I was thrilled by the cold" (*al-Ithnayn* 191 [February 7, 1938]: 12). In the text after the word "cold," *bard*, the author adds, "*bi-fatḥ al-bā' wa-l-rā'*" – "with an 'a' on the 'b' and the 'r'" – "*barad*" rather than "*bard*." The implication was that luxurious life among foreigners was causing Abd al-Wahhab to forget his Arabic. At the end of the article the author asks Abd al-Wahhab which scenes of the film were shot in Paris. The singer replies that there were two songs. The second of these, *Yā dunyā* (O world), required a roomful of sultry beauties to ogle him while he sang.[32] Abd al-Wahhab tells the interviewer that "this type of girl is plentiful in Paris. At home . . . well, you know, sir. That's all there is to it." The final sentence, "that's all," is written "*wa-bathth*." It should be "*wa-bass*"; Abd al-Wahhab is made to appear as if he lisps, again due to affectation. The author drives the point home by telling the reader that "this *baththth* in Abd al-Wahhab language means *bass* in our own language [colloquial], and *faqaṭ* – no other word – in that of the [Arabic] Language Academy."

The joke was continued in later articles. In one of these he was chided for his growing popularity, especially with women. The author describes the perfumed letters sent by adoring female fans:

He spoke without embarrassment about the perfumes [from the letters]. In Abd al-Wahhab's office you smell "al-Kalkaflī," and "al-Lāntrīk" [L'Enteric], not "Anfān"

[Lanvin] and "Būrgwā" [Bourgeois]. And you smell "Mayyat al-Qays," "Muṭrān," "Filīb" [Philippe], "Flīrdāmūr" [Fleur d'amour], "Nūrī Bek" and others.

(al-Ithnayn 194 [February 28, 1938]: 21)

Later in the (perhaps fanciful) article a woman calls him on the phone and he replies, "*Aywa yā thitt*ⁱ *hānim*" (Yes, my lady). "Lady," *sitt*, is deliberately misspelled *thitt*, again to give the impression that Abd al-Wahhab was lisping (he didn't actually lisp, at least not in any of his films). The author contrasted the singer's affectation with jokes about the Arab Language Academy's efforts to substitute Arabic neologisms for foreign words; he notes how "elegant" the Academy's *irzīz* was compared to the foreign *tilifōn*.

Despite Abd al-Wahhab's later affectations, what Karim saw in 1932 when he began the planning for his first Abd al-Wahhab film was box-office potential: Abd al-Wahhab's flirtation with the margins of Egyptian identity was popular at the time. By the time of his death this element of Abd al-Wahhab's initial popularity was mentioned only obliquely. But aside from the issue of who got formal credit for writing *White Rose*, the guiding philosophy seems to have been Abd al-Wahhab's original wish expressed to Karim in 1931: to make a film about himself.[33] As we shall see, the film makes reference to a number of the elements highlighted prominently when Abd al-Wahhab died in 1991.

Music

Those concerned with the musical heritage of Abd al-Wahhab assert that he defined the style of modern Arabic music. In Western music the importance of style lies in its capacity to accomplish a progressive realization of an existing musical language (Rosen 1971, 57). However, while Western music has been analyzed through a detailed bar-by-bar reading of tonal patterns, there is as yet no analysis of Abd al-Wahhab's music by his many admirers that comes near to approaching the thoroughness with which, for example, Charles Rosen studies European classical style.

The issue of change in Egyptian music prior to Abd al-Wahhab's film period has, however, been explored by Ali Jihad Racy. Although Racy does not write exclusively on the music of Abd al-Wahhab, he does give a detailed exposition of how Egyptian music changed from 1904 to 1932 – the period in which phonograph recordings were the primary medium for disseminating Egyptian music to a mass audience (Racy 1977, 1). Given the extreme emphasis placed on Abd al-Wahhab's innovativeness in print media from the 1930s to the 1970s, it comes as a surprise that Racy's mention of Abd al-Wahhab's role in the prefilm era is muted. Racy essentially overturns one of the key claims for Abd al-Wahhab's role in musical innovation – responsibility for the expansion of the *takht*. A *takht* is the traditional Arab music ensemble the composition of which was not fixed, but usually included an *ʿūd* (lute), *qānūn* (a trapezoidal type of zither), a *kamānga* (violin), and sometimes a *riqq* (tambourine) and *nay* (reed flute) (Danielson 1991b, 41).

Certainly Abd al-Wahhab employed progressively larger ensembles. The difference between a recording of an early Abd al-Wahhab performance, such as "*Minka yā hāgiru dā'ī*" (My sickness is from you who has left me) in 1923, then "*Al-Gundūl*" (The gondola) in 1939, and then "*Al-Nahr al-khālid*" (The eternal river) in the 1960s is obvious. The latter two songs progress to a much fuller orchestral accompaniment in which the melody is carried alternately by different sections or instruments. In this respect the pieces are like a Glen Miller arrangement compared to a Dixieland sound.

But the development of the *takht* was a complex and lengthy process. According to Racy, by the turn of the century, when Abd al-Wahhab was either unborn or in his infancy, the first steps toward "Westernizing" the *takht* had already been taken, as the Arabic form of violin – the *kamānga* – had been replaced by the European violin (Racy 1977, 52). Racy also reports that by the end of World War I photographs in journals and in record catalogs show ensembles that "used a number of violins and admitted other string instruments, namely the cello and double bass" (*ibid.*). Racy's observations make it seem unlikely that Abd al-Wahhab's mere employment of an expanded *takht* even in the 1920s, let alone the 1930s when he began his film career, could be considered an innovation. Whether Abd al-Wahhab's use of the expanded ensemble was aesthetically superior to that of his contemporaries is a separate issue, but Racy says nothing about it.

Racy does mention Abd al-Wahhab several times in connection with his well-marked borrowings from European music. For example: "In the 1930s and 1940s, thematic borrowing from European art music earmarked the music of Abd al-Wahhab, who extracted melodic themes and assimilated them in fragmentary form into his compositions. These themes were taken mostly from Beethoven, Tchaikovsky, Rimsky-Korsakov, Saint-Saëns, and Verdi" (*ibid.*, 326).

Racy also says: "A 1932 Baidaphon catalog bestowed upon Muhammad Abd al-Wahhab the title of *Mujaddid al-Mūsīqā al-Aʿẓam* or '*The Most Magnificent Renovator of Music*,' a title obviously inspired by the prominent European influence upon the artist's compositions" (*ibid.*, 166). The title of "musical renovator" may have been chosen deliberately by Abd al-Wahhab, who had become part owner of Bayḍāfōn by the time the 1932 catalog was printed (*ibid.*, 113).

Obviously the issues at stake in analyzing Abd al-Wahhab's music would be very different from an analysis of European classical style, in which new configurations of harmonic patterns were the key. The music of Abd al-Wahhab was resolutely monophonic (although he is said to have occasionally inserted a line or two of harmony) and retained the quarter-tone system. In this he was actually more conservative than some of his contemporaries. The background music to some other early films, for example, was harmonic.[34] But the presence of harmonic music written by Egyptians points up a complication faced by Arab musicians of the early twentieth century that was not faced by the composers who created the classical European style, namely the overbearing and frequently unwelcome presence of an alien tradition. In music, as in literature, the goal was to adapt the alien tradition without effacing the old. But in one sense music had an even more immediate link to tradition than did literature. The audience for literature was inevitably restricted to those with the ability and inclination to read. In the case of music the audience was wider because it required less expertise to listen than to read, and as radios became more plentiful in homes and cafés, access by a national audience to a single performer became commonplace.

The great virtue of Abd al-Wahhab, in the eyes of his supporters, was that he steadfastly maintained a rapport with his audience. It is often said that his failed experiment with Sayyid Darwish's *Shahrazād* made him wary of being too far in the artistic vanguard. The audience's attention had to be held in order to get them to listen, and it was assumed that harmonic music would be too radical a departure from what the audience was used to. Shortly before his death Abd al-Wahhab was quoted as saying that he considered the audience finally ready for harmonic music:

> If I say that music elevated to the highest standards is still far from the apprehension of the masses, this does not mean that they don't already have bits of it. These are scattered through films – are heard in romantic or dramatic situations. They penetrate the minds of the masses unconsciously, leaving an impression which becomes a part of their nature, enabling them to hear music that is both Western and Arabic as a part of their heritage unsuspected by all but composers. Thus I envy the next generation [of composers]. *(Najmī 1991, 22)*

During his film period (the 1930s and 1940s) Abd al-Wahhab began to experiment seriously with European adaptations. His voice allegedly was beginning to decline by the 1930s, and this provided an impetus for making the music more interesting so that his individual voice would be less the focus of the audience than the musical composition as a whole (*ibid.*, 20).[35] The overall effect, for those who consider Abd al-Wahhab's experiments a success, was to move Arabic music away from "mere song" and put it on a par with European instrumental music:

> A song, in the hands of Abd al-Wahhab, changed into a repository for the expression of various compositional lines [*al-gumal al-laḥnīya al-mutanawwiʿa*] and creative musical phrases. This [repository] gave him a huge harvest of pure musical advances which gave the Arab listener the same scale [*maqām*] as the European listener. (*ibid.*)

The issue of harmony was another potential avenue for innovation. Arranging a monophonic piece does not present the complexity of a harmonic arrangement. The sophistication of Egyptian music of this kind lay in elements other than harmony, such as modality (*maqām*), meter (*wazn*), or solo recitals (*taqāsīm*). Racy suggests that the improvisational character of Egyptian music had, by the turn of the century, been significantly lessened by a new emphasis on musical notation, as well as a tendency to standardize performance repertoires according to the dictates of recording conventions (Racy 1977, 8).[36] This implies that Arabic music may, in a sense, have been *forced* to develop new types of sophistication to compensate for losing the older style's capacity to produce musical nuance. Harmony may have been a potential avenue for recapturing nuance. Abd al-Wahhab, however, was not considered even by his most fervent admirers to have been a leader in developing harmonic Arab music. By the film period he did occasionally use tonality in his rhythm section, as in a section of "*Al-Nīl Nagāshī*" (Negus the Nile – a song from *The White Rose*, 1933) in which the *qānūn* and lute strum behind the melody. But for the most part the instruments in Abd al-Wahhab's compositions played the same line except in the case of an improvisation, which was a convention of traditional Arabic music. The occasional harmonic film score, as well as magazine articles describing harmonic arangements, suggest that it would be an oversimplification to say that Abd al-Wahhab developed an orchestra against a background of thoroughly traditional *takht* arrangements.[37]

Although the importance of Abd al-Wahhab's films is generally considered to derive from the music, we cannot, in fact, untangle the purely musical elements of his legacy from the social context in which he became popular. Part of the problem is that analysis of the music remains relatively impoverished – we don't really know how it fits into its era.[38] Until historians of Egyptian music move beyond hagiography, all we really know is that the music is beautiful, that it was popular, and that in Abd al-Wahhab's films, as well as in the collective memory of the Egyptian media, popularity was often justified in the idiom of inexorable development of a modernized national identity.

5

Classic, clunker, national narrative

Al-mūsīqā, ya hānim, fann^i gamīl, fann il-iḥsān wi-l-ḥanān. Bass^i khasāra. Taʕdīrha maḥdūd.

(My lady, music is a beautiful art, the art of goodness and love. But what a shame. It isn't well appreciated.)

Muhammad Abd al-Wahhab as Galāl Effendi in *White Rose*

In 1933 Abd al-Wahhab's first film, *The White Rose*, played an important part in bringing his image to a large public. Like the magazine *al-Ithnayn*, the style of *White Rose* appears on the surface to be unabashedly Western, and yet the film is fundamentally "Egyptian modernist" in the sense that it attempts to couple an image of authentic tradition with one of revolutionary transformation. Critics tend to separate what they see as the high-art component of *White Rose* – the music – from the cinematic component, which seems today to be embarrassingly compromised because of its adherence to Western style. It is also true, however, that the film partakes of conventions intrinsic to the genre of popular cinema in Egypt. Most importantly, *White Rose* grapples with defining a middle-class identity. Like the elusive "middle language" of elaborated models of diglossia, the middle class of 1930s Egyptian cinema seeks to draw its identity from both classicist and folk ideals; but just as the "middle language" is conceptually unstable, so is middle-class identity continually in need of the images against which it defines itself.

White Rose makes an interesting contrast to another classic Egyptian film of the prewar cinema, *al-ʿAzīma* (Resolution, 1939). *Resolution* was written and directed by Kamāl Salīm, a promising director who died tragically young in 1945 after directing only nine films.[1] It was an immediate success at the time of its release, and later came to be regarded as the most important film made prior to the 1952 revolution because, critics alleged, it was the only film to depict "ordinary" people in *shaʿbī* (popular) quarters. Despite its popular setting, *Resolution* is predicated on a narrative development that complements, but does not contradict, the spirit of Abd al-Wahhab's *White Rose*.

The White Rose

The rationale of later critics trying to separate the allegedly sophisticated music of *White Rose* from the film itself becomes understandable in the opening scene. The pace is excruciatingly slow, and the images are all upper class. Although the focus of the first scene in *White Rose* is actually a cat, the audience also gets its first glimpse of Ragā', daughter of Ismāʿīl Bey, a prominent and wealthy lawyer. Raga lives in a sumptuous and conspicuously French-looking house. We see her playing with the cat – a white Persian. The camera alternates several times between scenes of the girl pretending to dance with her cat and of her mother Fāṭima, a large woman in *décolletée* (in contrast to the modest neck-high black dress worn by her daughter) who stands imperiously puffing on a cigarette as a dressmaker fits her. Finally the mother puts down her cigarette and goes into the parlor, where her daughter is now dancing the cat on a low doily-covered table, disturbing the lace. The angry mother walks up to the radio, showing still more of the enormous room with its sumptuous furnishing punctuated by French statues. She turns the radio off.

"Haven't I told you not to play *mūsīqā afrangiyya* [foreign music]? How bizarre. Is this good?" Raga's angry mother points to the crumpled doily lace. "Look what the cat did." French landscape paintings loom in the background as the cat jumps out of Raga's arms and runs from the parlor. "Cats in the salon? You're not a little girl anymore." The cat looks in from the next room past an expensive tapestry. "That cat! I'll wring its neck." The cat backs away as she says this. "It makes the blood boil!" The mother walks out as the camera cuts to the dejected cat.

Director Muhammad Karim presents Raga's dalliance with her pet as innocent and natural, if slightly frivolous.[2] The cat's fear of Raga's mother helps emphasize a thin but perceptible line between the two: innocence and purity in the case of Raga; imperiousness and rough immodesty on the part of her mother. Although Karim portrays Raga's family, especially the mother, in a negative light, for the most part the film suggests that the excesses of the rich can be mitigated through the development of a sophisticated and responsible middle class which can partake of the best

Europe offers without losing its authenticity (the same pattern promoted by *al-Ithnayn*). This becomes clearer as the film progresses and the woman's state of corruption becomes more evident.

Abd al-Wahhab, the star of *White Rose*, appears first as a hand with an enormous ring on one finger, which is pushing a buzzer on an elaborate wrought-iron gate. Immediately afterward the camera shifts to a medium-length shot of the singer, nattily dressed in a double-breasted suit and tie, tarbush on his head. Abd al-Wahhab plays the part of Galāl Effendi, a son of the aristocracy fallen on hard times. He has come to the villa of Ismail Bey, Raga's father, to ask for a job. Once Galal has been ushered into the bey's presence (another French-decorated room), Ismail asks after Galal's father, whereupon Galal looks even more downcast, and tells his potential benefactor that both his parents have died but that he himself has finished a baccalaureate degree. Ismail Bey asks, "Will you continue your studies?"

"I can't, Your Excellency," replies the singer mournfully. "I'm forced to look for a job."

Ismail Bey pontificates: "It's a shame, my boy, that our country's youth are in such straits that they can't finish their studies and have to go looking for government jobs. They are wasting their future."

Plate 7 Muhammad Abd al-Wahhab as Galal Effendi: at Ismail Bey's gate on his way to ask for a clerk's job (from *White Rose*, 1933)

Exactly Galal Effendi's thoughts, or so one assumes, since he has come to Ismail Bey seeking a nongovernmental job. The encounter ends with vague promises to let Galal Effendi work with the bey's *bāshkātib* (chief clerk). Galal leaves the mansion smiling. We then see Ismail Bey telling his family that the son of Galal Bey just came looking for a clerk's job. "That man used to play with money!" he exclaims. Then he asks if his daughter will wear a chic dress to tomorrow's social event. Mirth reigns in the mansion.

So the visual image of *al-mūsīqār al-nābigh* (the gifted musician), as Abd al-Wahhab's publicity posters called him, was introduced to the public. In later years some members of the press attempted bravely to put his acting abilities in the best light possible ("*'Abd al-Wahhāb al-mumaththil*" 1991, 62–65). However, in the end it must be admitted that Abd al-Wahhab was no actor. Wooden and mechanical, the best that could be said of him was that he was more at ease on the screen than Samīra Khalūṣī, the actress who played Raga.[3]

The opening scene of *White Rose* typified all seven of Abd al-Wahhab's films.[4] The high-society settings made them "salon films" in the eyes of many post-1952 critics (Ḥawwās 1986, 162–78).[5] But it was always high society with a twist. In *White Rose* Abd al-Wahhab plays the son of the deceased Galal Bey, but the family fortune is gone, forcing the character to rely on what he has in common with the middle class: his education. Even if he is literally the "son of aristocrats," he never plays the stereotypical *ibn al-zawāt* role in the sense of being overly Europeanized, lazy, effeminate, or otherwise corrupt. These roles are left to others. Already in the first scene Raga's mother, Fatima, puffing on her cigarette and immodestly dressed compared to her daughter, gives a hint of the *ibn* (or in this case *bint*) *al-zawāt*. This thread becomes stronger as the film progresses.[6]

Vice in *White Rose* has distinct class associations. The immodesty of Raga's mother is never played for laughs, as sometimes occurs with flawed characters in other films of the period. She spends most of the film plotting to get her daughter married to Shafīq, a heavyset, clean-shaven, and pleasant but weak-looking voluptuary from the mother's family who works in a *dīwān* (government office), and is as corrupt and indolent as she herself. He makes his first appearance in the film just after Raga has met Galal for the first time in the garden of Ismail Bey's mansion as Galal goes to the clerk's job granted him by the bey. Raga has been in the garden searching for pearls which had fallen from a broken necklace. Galal helps her search, finds the last pearl, and receives a white rose from the girl in exchange for it. As Galal goes to his office Shafiq appears and greets the girl in French.

We see throughout the course of the film that Shafiq is immoral and weak willed – the *ibn al-zawāt* to Galal's enlightened modern man. Not only does he use more French than is strictly necessary, but he appears at one point waking up at three o'clock in the afternoon fully dressed from a party the night before. As soon as he wakes he begins preparation for another party. He also carries on an affair with a married woman who lives across the street from him. He is such a spendthrift that he lacks the resources to pay for the *shabka* (a gift of jewelry given by the groom to his bride) that he must give in order to marry Raga, so Raga's mother *gives* it to him (presumably paid for by her husband, i.e. the *shabka* comes from the bride's family rather than the groom's as is customary).

We see Shafiq entering the mansion to talk to Ismail Bey about his stalled fortunes at the *dīwān*.[7] The bey promises to talk to the deputy minister in charge of Shafiq's office, and assures the younger man that he will be advanced once it is known that he is a relative of Ismail Bey's wife. Through this exchange Karim continues to build a case with the audience against Shafiq. His overuse of French already makes him suspect, and by seeking to advance himself through family connections he firmly identifies himself with the *ibn al-zawāt* camp.

The young hero of *White Rose*, Galal, in contrast to the villainous Shafiq, is practically a man of the people – at least he is not too proud to do an honest day's work. This comes through in scenes depicting Galal working for Ismail Bey. We see him with the bey's other clerk, Khalīl Effendi, a lovable but slightly bumbling representative of the old guard, whose occasional incompetence makes a counterpoint to Galal's college-educated abilities.

An extended sequence of Galal at work shows him collecting rent on the bey's properties – hardly a populist occupation. However, the director uses the rent-collecting device as a means to contrast Galal's modern-yet-authentic character with various other social types. First comes the *khawāga*, the foreigner. In many contexts (certainly here) the word *khawāga* approximates the sense of "gringo" – a resident alien regarded with suspicion. The *khawāga* from whom Galal is to collect rent is a recalcitrant Frenchman. The conversation is entirely in French. Galal tells him he wants the rent, and he wants to see the flat, presumably to check for any damage. The Frenchman replies that he will not pay the rent next month if repairs – probably necessitated by him – are not made. Later, when talking to Khalil, Galal mentions that he "didn't understand a thing the Frenchman said."

Following his meeting with the irritable Frenchman, Galal goes to another apartment. This time the door is answered by an Egyptian in a tarbush, presumably wealthy by virtue of his presence in the spacious modern building owned by Ismail Bey, but nonetheless possessed of a distinctly folksy manner of speech. The problem is that the tenant is hard of hearing, and misunderstands everything Galal says.

GALAL (cheerily): **Nahār**-*ak saʿīd.* [Good day.]

DEAF TENANT: *ʾĒh? in-***nahār***-da ʾēh? Mīn ʕāl kida?* [What? Today is what? Who said so?]

GALAL (to himself): Great . . . (then to the tenant) *ʿĀyiz* **il-ʾigār**. [I want the rent.]

TENANT (confused): *Tidfaʿ* **il-mahr?** [You want to pay the *mahr*?][8]

GALAL: *Il-ʾigār* . . . **filūs.** [The rent, money.]

TENANT: *Il-bayt fīh* **nāmūs?** *ʾAbadan. Dī shaʕʕa muʿtabara fi ghāyit il-bidaʿa.* [The house has mosquitoes (*nāmūs*) in it? Never. This is a good apartment, the epitome of modernity.]

GALAL: *Shūf yā ustāz, ana ʿāyiz il-ʾigār. Ana gibt* **il-waṣl**. [Look, mister, I want the rent. I've brought a receipt.]

TENANT: **Aṣl** *ʾēh wi-* **faṣl** *ʾēh*? [What is all this?] (He goes to get another man named Taufīq.)

TAUFIQ: Where's the usual guy?

GALAL: I'm his replacement.

TAUFIQ (yelling in the deaf man's ear): He wants the rent!

TENANT: He should have said so in the first place!

The second encounter – with the deaf man – pokes light fun at Egyptians, but also flatters the audience because it consists entirely of in-jokes comprehensible only to an Egyptian audience. The humor comes from the audience's familiarity with the language: confusing such phrases as "*ʿāyiz il-īgār*" (I want the rent) with "*tidfaʿ il-mahr*?" (you want to pay the *mahr*?); and "*il-īgār, il-filūs*" (the rent, the money) with "*il-bayt fīh nāmūs*" (the house has mosquitoes in it). The first encounter, by contrast, implies a mastery of French language and culture, but at the same time a distancing from it. The audience has seen that in fact Galal could communicate easily with the Frenchman, thus his later statement to Khalil that "he couldn't understand a word the Frenchman said" carries an implication that the Frenchman was behaving irrationally, or at least boorishly, which is how an audience that identifies positively with the virtues of an *ibn al-balad*, particularly in the context of Egypt's boorish imperialist "tenants," would assume a Frenchman behaves.

Karim distinguishes Abd al-Wahhab's Egyptian identity from that of the pseudoforeigner *ibn al-zawāt* identity by juxtaposing Galal's cool competence with the Frenchman's arrogance: he speaks their language but is emphatically not one of them, nor does he want to become one. By turning to the deaf man Karim takes Galal, his new Egyptian man, and roots him firmly in native soil. Galal's conversation with the Frenchman would have been a blur for most of the audience. His conversation with the deaf man would have been as familiar as the one with the foreigner was alienating. The scene reiterates the same point made implicitly by the front and back covers of *al-Ithnayn* – that the bookends of middle-class Egyptian identity are a romanticized "folkloric" figure oriented toward change, and a sophisticated consumer of Western technique firmly anchored in Egyptian authenticity.

Resolution

Whereas *White Rose* (1933) begins in a blaze of unapologetic European style later frowned upon by critics, *Resolution* (1939) opens with a scene of a modest lower- to middle-class neighborhood. Portrayals of such neighborhoods were rare in the prewar Egyptian cinema. *Resolution* was not the only film of the period to depict the lives of nonaristocratic people, but its portrayal of *baladī* life was by far the most sympathetic of the prewar cinema.[9]

While *White Rose* featured untrained actors in the main roles (Abd al-Wahhab and Samira Khalusi), *Resolution* used professionals trained on the stage. The main character is a young man named Muḥammad Ḥanafī, played by Ḥusayn Ṣidqī, who was one of the most popular actors of his day. The heroine was Fāṭima, played by Fāṭima Rushdī – also a major stage actress of the 1920s and 1930s, and married at the time to director Kamal Salim.[10]

Resolution's protagonist, Muhammad, is the son of a barber, *Usṭā* Ḥanafī ("master" Hanafi). The film is about Muhammad's determination, his "resolution," to better himself; his goals include getting a university education, becoming an independent merchant, and marrying Fatima, the girl next door. Although critics praise *Resolution* as a faithful representation of lower-class life, it is in fact about trying to transform the lower class into something other than the "traditionalist" society criticized in didactic descriptions of *ibn al-balad*; the film is about modernizing the popular quarters, not about life as lived there.

The tone of the opening scene in *Resolution* is very different from that of *White Rose*. In *White Rose* we see aristocrats who seem almost to be moving in slow motion. *Resolution* shows us a street scene in which animals and people move in clockwork fashion. Ironically, the contrived-looking villa in *White Rose* was "real" – a real French villa – whereas the realistic street of *Resolution* was, in fact, a thoroughly synthetic film set. This is how the opening scene was constructed in *Resolution*:[11]

The opening scene is a shot of a street lamp fixed to the wall of Muhammad's house, and below it a sign saying Maʿtūq Alley. We hear the dawn call to prayer, and the street lamp goes out as the call ends. The camera pulls back and pans to the left. We see Muhammad's house, the wooden stairs and railing. The door opens and *usṭā* Hanafi, the barber and Muhammad's father, exits. Wearing a woolen wrap, he descends the stairs and heads for the mosque. Other people enter with him, approaching from various directions. The pan shot continues until we see a meat cart pulled by a horse entering the frame. It stops in front of the shop of al-ʿItir, the butcher, which is being opened by his apprentice. The horse moves and is stopped by the driver, who jumps from the cart and is approached by the apprentice. A medium-range shot from above of the boy carrying meat into the butcher shop, then a pan shot of the boy and the driver carrying meat.

One says to the other, "Watch out for the meat, fella."

"What are you afraid of? You think we're carrying the boss?"

We cut to the house next to the shop and see a milk vendor on a donkey pouring milk into a bowl held by a woman standing in front of the door. The vendor cries out, "*Ḥalīb ya ʕishṭa*" [Milk, o clotted cream – a vendor's cry intended to alert the neighborhood to his presence].

The camera moves on until a bakery appears in the frame and we see the workers spreading bread onto sheets of paper. There is a small cart in front of the bakery, and on the door [of the bakery] hangs a gas lamp. The district police officer stands by the workers. *Muʿallim* ʿĀshūr approaches from a neighboring alley crooning, "The moon has nights . . . when it comes up carelessly . . ." A pastry vendor yells, "*Ghayyar rīʕ-ak* [Have some breakfast],[12] pray to the Prophet Muhammad!"

Muʿallim Ashur brings out a bottle of liquor from under his wool cloak and calls to one of the workers, "ʿAwaḍ, boy."

"Yes, master."

"Hand me a jug, boy."

The worker hands him a jug, and *Muʿallim* Ashur takes it, pours the water on the ground, and pours liquor in it as the workers comment on his actions.

Muʿallim al-Itir, the butcher, arrives at his shop on a donkey. In the barber shop we see Rūḥī the undertaker and *Usṭā* Hanafi. We hear a *fūl* [fava beans] vendor: "*Abyaḍ ya nābit*" [White, O bean sprouts].[13]

A medium-range shot: we see Fatima on the balcony watering plants. We see Muhammad in another shot in the salon of his house putting on a vest by a window that faces the balcony. He puts on his necktie in a closeup. We see Fatima, and he greets her: "Good morning, Fatima!"

She sees him and answers politely, "Good morning, *Si* Muhammad."[14] She moves to the side of the balcony facing al-Itir's butcher shop so she can hang the bed sheets. Al-Itir is cutting meat, his customers standing around him. One of the customers says, "Give me a pound of *mōza* [lamb shin]."

The butcher answers, jokingly, "*Mōza*? So what are you going to get from the fruit stand, liver?" [*Mōza* means either lamb shin or banana.] He raises his face from his work and sees Fatima on the balcony. He smiles, puts his hand on a tail of sheep hanging in his shop and says, "By the Prophet! *Baladī* is the best. O *baladī*, o *baladī*!"

Fatima looks at him scornfully and leaves the balcony.

As conventional wisdom would have it, the initial contrast between *Resolution* and *White Rose* is stark. The vendors' cries are a constant presence in the background of *Resolution*'s opening scene, reminding the viewer of the *baladī* locale; in the background of *White Rose* Nubian servants move silently through the French mansion. *Resolution* features Muhammad's loving mother sewing buttons on his vest; in *White Rose* we see the dressmaker fitting Raga's mother in a scandalous backless evening gown. In *Resolution* hearty men pirouette through a workers' ballet for the common man, each one cheerfully performing his appointed task; in *White Rose* Ismail Bey sits and reads the paper, waiting for others to come ask him for work. Fatima, the love interest in *Resolution*, hangs the sheets from the balcony, shyly greeting the man everybody assumes she will marry; Raga of *White Rose* sulks and plays with her cat. Muhammad's father in *Resolution* goes deep into debt paying for his son's education; in *White Rose* Ismail Bey muses on the misfortunes of Galal's father who "used to play with money." Muhammad's impending college degree is a momentous occasion for his family; Ismail Bey disapproves of Galal's cutting short his education, displaying a fine incomprehension of what it means to work for a living.

The only element of rough equivalence in the two films was their early intimations of vice. In *Resolution* it is the alcoholic father of Fatima who parallels in some degree the blatant immodesty of Raga's mother in *White Rose*. But in both films the early portrayals of vice are misleading. The alcoholic baker in *Resolution* is slightly tragic, but mainly his shortcomings are funny – unlike the immodesty of Raga's mother in *White Rose* or, in some cases, *Resolution*'s butcher. The baker appears throughout the film surreptitiously nipping at his jug of liquor. The real threat in *Resolution* comes from the butcher who leers at Fatima as she hangs the sheets on the balcony. When he exclaims "*baladī* is best" he means Fatima, not the sheep tail on which his hand rests. The line is a stock phrase in Egyptian films, usually rendered as "*aḥibb il-baladī*!" (I love the *baladī* [girl])" and said in coarse tones to a possibly flirtatious (or if the role calls for a "good girl," an indignant) *bint al-balad*. The effect of such a line is invariably to call attention to the rudeness of the man saying it. In *Resolution* the butcher's crudeness quickly develops into a more threatening vileness. He wants to marry Fatima, not because he loves her, but simply because he is jealous of Muhammad. Eventually he plots to break up the marriage of Muhammad and Fatima, and by the end tries physically to abduct her.

Calling attention to the crudities of the *awlād al-balad* as manifested by the alcoholic baker and the philandering butcher was an important part of the "realism" of *Resolution*, as was the contrast between these figures and Muhammad's educated "enlightenment." This is not to say that the film features no positive roles evocative of the stereotypically traditionalist *ibn al-balad*, but such roles are limited. The most extensive example of the positive version of *ibn al-balad* was Rūḥī, an undertaker who rescues Muhammad's father from *khawāga* (foreigner) creditors trying to repossess his property, which was used as collateral on the loans taken out to pay for Muhammad's education. Aside from the undertaker there is only a blacksmith and a shoemaker, neither of whom features prominently in the film. The only unequivocally positive *baladī* female roles in the film are those of Muhammad's mother and Fatima. Even Fatima displays a determination to escape some of the traditional practices of her class as the film progresses. She marries Muhammad, then demands and receives divorce when she later discovers that he has been fired from the prestigious middle-class job he had when they married.

Unlike *White Rose*, *Resolution* is often assumed to have championed the cause of the lower class in the figure of *ibn al-balad vis-à-vis* the aristocracy. And yet as we saw above, the film does not, in fact, center on "life in the popular quarters" in quite the way that some later criticism might lead one to believe. Those who fit the sociological stereotype of traditional merchants who wear *galālīb*, speak colloquial Arabic exclusively, and practice "folklore" are all of secondary importance in *Resolution*. Muhammad, the middle-class character in *Resolution*, is the opposite number of Galal in *White Rose*: they just come into the middle class from different directions – Galal from the aristocracy, and Muhammad from the *awlād al-balad*. Since the middle class is the point of *Resolution*, and not the "popular quarters," one might expect the same differentiation from both traditionalism and the Western-oriented aristocracy. We have already seen the contrast between the educated Muhammad and the familiar, but backward, butcher and baker in the opening scenes. Opposition to the aristocracy in *Resolution* is expressed in the character of a college friend of Muhammad, ʿAdlī, the son of Nazīh Pasha.[15]

Adli is basically kind-hearted, but utterly irresponsible – rather like a well-intentioned version of *White Rose*'s Shafiq, caught in an endless round of parties and completely oblivious of anything resembling a bourgeois work ethic. Unlike the middle-class Muhammad, Adli drives to school in a long, low convertible automobile. Where Muhammad and his family feel their future hinges on his success in college, Adli appears utterly unconcerned with graduation. Instead, Adli is preoccupied with personal matters such as an angry dancer named Regina having confronted his father the pasha with the fact of her relationship to his son (Salīm 1975, 70). In one scene Adli takes Muhammad to a bar to discuss his father's attitude toward his womanizing. In the bar we see Adli's *awlād al-zawāt* friends making fun of Muhammad's humble background:[16]

A group of Adli's aristocratic friends sit at a table[17] near the bar, including 'Izzat, Shaukat, Ra'fat and Rashād. Adli and Muhammad enter and go to the bar. Adli greets Rafat playfully. A piano plays European-style bar music in the background.

Adli greets one of his friends: "*Bonjour*, you 'joker.'"

Rafat replies, "*Bonjour*, 'Mickey Mouse.'"

A closeup of Muhammad and Adli seated at the bar. Izzat speaks to Adli as he enters the bar.

"Listen Adli, that girl Regina is mad as hell at you.[18] Watch out for her."

Adli turns angrily, and says in heavily accented English, "*Shut up, boorish*."

The bartender brings a drink to Adli, saying, "*Bonjour*, *Excellence*."

"*Bonjour* Nīkolā," he replies. "See if Muhammad wants some."

Embarrassed, Muhammad says, "No, thank you."

We see a closeup of the group as Adli turns to them, saying, "What's with you fine pashas, you made of wood? Why so sullen? Why don't you greet *Si*[19] Muhammad?"

We hear Izzat's voice: "*Si* Muhammad? Ahh, Muhammad Hanafi! My God, it's been a long time." Izzat, Shaukat and Rafat come into the frame and shake Muhammad's hand. Shaukat makes a show of friendliness. "Where have you been, Muhammad?"

"Congratulate him, you cold people," says Adli. "Give him your blessings."

Rafat replies, "Why, has he inherited?"

"Gotten married?" says Shaukat.

"He just found out he graduated from college today," says Adli.

Izzat gives a patronizing, "Congratulations."

"*Cheerio*," says Shaukat, raising his glass.

"Let's drink to us!"[20] says Izzat.

Izzat draws near to Shaukat and speaks in a low voice: "Man, look at that hick."[21]

"Yeah," says Shaukat, "and with a diploma. Check it out."[22]

Rafat joins in: "The son of a master barber to boot. And that says it all."[23]

Rashad, who was listening to the conversation, looks amused. Rafat raises his voice so Muhammad will hear. "No, he really deserved it."

Shaukat chimes in, "Of course." And Izzat adds, "Indeed."

This is typical of most of the scenes having to do with the aristocracy in *Resolution*. There is, however, a generational split in the aristocracy. Salim portrays Nazih Pasha, Adli's father, as an honest businessman. Eventually, with Muhammad's help, Nazih Pasha also turns his son into an honest businessman. Initially he is so taken with Muhammad that he capitalizes a joint business venture which the two young men are to run. Adli gambles away the money and allows his aristocratic friends to make fun of

Muhammad when he confronts his frivolous would-be business partner. Muhammad punches one of Adli's insolent friends, and tells Nazih Pasha what happened. Nazih Pasha rewards the young man's honesty by using his influence to find Muhammad an office job; the pasha banishes his errant son from the house.

Muhammad's office job gives him the security he needs to marry Fatima, saving her from the unwelcome advances of the butcher. Later Muhammad's office manager wrongly blames him for a clerical mistake, and he loses his job. Desperate, he takes a demeaning stockroom job in a department store. The butcher discovers Muhammad's condition, and through his machinations Fatima also learns of Muhammad's desperate circumstances. She rashly demands divorce, and Muhammad, angry that she seems to love him only for his prestigious job, grants it. But he only pronounces divorce twice. Under Islamic law he can still take her back within her *ʿidda* – a specified period, usually three months, during which she is not free to remarry (if he pronounces the third divorce he can only remarry her if she has subsequently married another man and been divorced by him or widowed). The butcher quickly makes his move, proposing marriage. Fatima's weak alcoholic father and coarse greedy mother accept the offer.

In the meantime Adli reforms and makes up to Muhammad by using his influence to see that the clerical mistake for which Muhammad was blamed is resolved. Exonerated, Muhammad and the new Adli go into business as originally planned. The business is a huge success. Fatima goes to Muhammad and asks to be taken back. He refuses, but Adli intercedes on Fatima's behalf. Muhammad goes to take her back, but discovers the wedding of Fatima and the butcher already in progress. Knowing that the *ʿidda* has not passed, Muhammad breaks up the proceedings, causing a huge fight. The butcher tries to abduct Fatima but Muhammad, in alliance with the undertaker and a handful of his *awlād al-balad* friends, defeats the butcher and his allies in a pitched battle.

The story ends with Muhammad having fulfilled his resolution to marry the girl he loves from his *baladī* quarter and to be, at the same time, a modern, educated man neither mired in traditionalism nor corrupted by the extravagances of Europe. This is not an unusual ending for an Egyptian film. *Resolution* is primarily about the imagined formation of a middle-class Egyptian citizen who is *ibn al-balad* and aristocrat in equal parts – the productive, hard-working tandem of the progressive *ibn al-balad* Muhammad and his reformed *ibn al-zawāt* friend Adli.

The popular *isnād*: authenticating strategies

Resolution attempts to show a convergence of social types into a middle-class national identity. Defining a middle-class identity was a common goal for the plot of Egyptian mass entertainment of the time, but arriving at the middle-class destination via the *baladī* road was unusual. Kamal Salim's perspective on *ibn al-balad*, however, was vintage social reformism – "raising" *ibn al-balad* from his ignorance, winnowing out the bad characteristics in favor of the good. The thrust of Salim's reformist attitude – quite common in Egyptian cinema – came through clearly in the character of Muhammad because the audience could see the familiar outlines of where he came from.[24] This was not true in the case of Adli, whose conversion comes as an improbable jolt. Showing Muhammad's roots is where Salim's masterful technique was most effective: the vendors' cries, the call to prayer in the opening scene, the men working, the butcher riding into the frame on a donkey, the final resolution of the plot hinging on a technical detail of Islamic law. Such images tie *Resolution* to an *isnād*, a line of descent – that of folk culture which, we have seen in chapters 3

Plate 8 Fatima, dressed as a middle-class lady, goes to ask Muhammad (left) to remarry her so that she can escape the unwanted attentions of the *baladī* butcher. Adli (right), the *ibn al-zawāt* with a new work ethic, urges his friend to do the right thing and take the remorseful woman back (from *Resolution*, 1939)

and 4, is perfectly respectable when viewed from the safe perspective of media-sponsored modernism. Folklore is safest as a relic, never to be shown as important in its own right, but to be represented as a picture of where the viewers (modern folk) have come from.

Salim accomplishes this most effectively not in scenes depicting the already modernized Muhammad, but through Fatima, less educated but also expecting to enjoy the fruits of his modernity. We see her hanging about the bakery office because the office has a phone, which Muhammad is to use to tell her the expected good news of his graduation. When Muhammad calls she rushes to the barbershop to tell Muhammad's father, who is taken aback that she knows the news before any of Muhammad's own family. Then the camera shifts to the salon of Fatima's home, where she and her mother are already receiving a coterie of women jealous of Fatima's good fortune, even though she is not yet even formally engaged to Muhammad:

Muhammad's mother appears, opening the door to receive Umm Bahiya and her daughter, Bahiya, who are giving ululations of joy. Umm Bahiya greets the lady of the house and they enter in a pan shot. We see that the salon is full of women there to give congratulations . . . Fatima enters from the kitchen carrying a tray of sweet drinks. She passes in front of them in a pan shot so that they all appear except for Firdūs and Umm Firdūs, who are seated at the table. Muhammad's mother speaks to Fatima.

"You've gone to too much trouble, Faṭṭūma my dear. God willing I'll do the same for you so that you can relax when you're married,[25] my dear."

Sikīna speaks up. "They're made for each other."[26]

Umm Firdus interjects, "It's true. Strangers flatter each other."[27]

Fatima gives a drink to Bahiya's mother. One of them draws more open attention to the assumption of Fatima's good fortune. "How are you?"

Fatima turns to Umm Muhammad. "I'm really tired, Auntie Umm Muhammad.[28] Waiting eagerly for the day *Si* Muhammad gets a nice job, God willing."

Firdus speaks quietly to her mother. "Look at that girl jumping about like a demon in a bottle.[29] How horrid."

Umm Firdus says to her daughter, "Show them your arms. There you are, look at them [her daughter's strong arms], look how they stare at them!"[30]

Fatima enters the frame between Firdus and her mother. Smiling, she presents sweet drinks to the two women.

"Why thank you,[31] my dear," says Firdus, barely concealing her jealousy.

Umm Firdus turns to Umm Muhammad. "Umm Muhammad, look at my girl Firdus. She won't even let me do the wash.[32] Still, congratulations from us. God willing, you won't have to do any washing."

Umm Muhammad replies, "May you live long, my dear."

A woman enters the room.[33] "Congratulations! By the Prophet, we are happy for *Si* Muhammad, and by God, if I am lying may I be ground up by the trolley car!"

Umm Muhammad looks taken aback. "God forbid,[34] Umm Zaynab."

Sikina speaks. "And me, ask Momma, when I heard the news I was in the kitchen, and I was so happy I started drumming on the onion pan. Here, smell my hands . . ."

The Turkish woman becomes agitated at all this cattiness. "Umm Muhammad, congratulations. What a lot of talk. What empty talk. Myself, I don't have any girls, nor do I have any of this toadying."[35]

Fatima's younger brother Balḥa comes into the room. "Can I have a sweet, Auntie Umm Muhammad? *Si* Muhammad is coming in down below."

Umm Muhammad stands. "Yes, of course."

Fatima heads for her brother, saying, "Get out of here, boy. What are you doing here? Get back to the house. I'm coming right behind you."[36] She turns to Umm Muhammad. "Excuse me, Auntie Umm Muhammad. I must go now."

"It's still early!" protests Umm Muhammad.

"I'm late for my prayer," says the girl. "Goodbye, all."

All the women reply: "Goodbye, sister."

Under her breath Firdus mutters, "Good riddance, God damn you."[37]

(Salīm 1975, 74–75)

Salim's depiction of the women's reaction to Muhammad's graduation contrasts the bumbling men, oblivious to the machinations of women, with a delightfully catty female group who know exactly the implications of Muhammad's graduation before the men even have time to finish congratulating themselves. Fatima must balance the need to pay homage to the conventions of modest women's behavior, the temptation to gloat over her good fortune in front of the women who had also had designs on Muhammad, and the expectation that she is soon to become a middle-class *hānim* married to a college graduate rather than a mere baker's daughter. Such scenes do not comprise a large portion of *Resolution*, but they serve to keep the characters associated with their *baladī* roots even as the plot suggests movement away from them.

Fatima shows that she can behave as a good *bint al-balad*, modestly trying to avoid obvious reference to what she and all the neighbors know: that she and Muhammad are in love and will marry now that he is able to support a family. The idea of a love match is problematic in traditional society because it implies an unacceptable premarital familiarity between the bride and groom. Here it appears heavily cloaked in a slangy style of speech and set in a thoroughly traditional milieu, replete with intimations of the evil eye (the women's jealousy of Fatima's good fortune). It is ultimately one of these women who sabotages Fatima's marriage by arranging for Fatima to discover her husband's fall from grace into the purgatory of clerking in a department store. The contrast between all these references to tradition and the assumed inevitability of the untraditional love match make the film at least an effective statement of modernist social policy, if not a completely unique cinematic experience.[38]

Authenticating Abd al-Wahhab

Imparting a sense of authenticity to Abd al-Wahhab's character in *White Rose* is more problematic than was tying Muhammad and Fatima to a *baladī* quarter in *Resolution*. The plot of *White Rose* centered on Galal's love affair with his employer Ismail Bey's daughter. In this film we see none of the subtle unspoken assumptions featured in *Resolution*, but rather a European-style love match: boy meets girl, they fall in love, but can't get married because the girl's father will only marry her to another aristocrat; boy becomes a star musician in an effort to impress girl's father, but to no avail; boy's rival (Shafiq in tandem with Raga's corrupt mother) successfully plots to discredit the would-be lover; boy ends film as a lonely artist, girl ends up married to the corrupt rival. The film devotes sufficient attention to the corruption of Raga's mother and Shafiq to suggest a differentiation between the Westernized *awlād al-zawāt* and the modern middle class. But by itself, the film's critical stance *vis-à-vis* the Westernized elite is not enough to establish Galal's cultural authenticity. Few Egyptians then or now would look happily upon the sort of love match Galal was trying to carry on with Raga. The film even shows two scenes of an unmarried man and woman kissing – completely beyond the pale for Egyptian society. Something more was needed to give this film "authenticity" so that it did not drift completely away from its audience.

It is often assumed that the most powerful authenticating element of *White Rose* was the music. There is no doubt that Abd al-Wahhab's generation loved the songs, and one speculates that to the listeners' ears Abd al-Wahhab's singing in *White Rose* tied the film to the high tradition of Arabic music just as the various scenes from *Resolution* mentioned above tied that film to the *isnād* of folkloric tradition. But one need not posit a mysterious alchemy between singer and audience. The film itself contains a scene that explicitly ties the music to *turāth* (the heritage). The scene visually accomplishes what all the later writing on Abd al-Wahhab claimed – that the singer is a "radical conservative," his music simultaneously evoking both an image of progress and a grounding in tradition.

The scene comes about two-thirds of the way through the film. Galal and Raga have met and fallen in love. Her father takes her to his estate in the countryside, from which she surreptitiously exchanges love letters with Galal. Her mother has arranged that Shafiq be present to inflict his unwanted attentions on Raga. Finally Galal gets a chance to go see Ismail

Bey in the countryside on an urgent business matter. The lovers tryst by a running brook, but Shafiq spies them and forces them to admit their transgression to Ismail Bey.[39] All is lost. Galal is fired from his clerk's position and returns to Cairo despondent. It is at this point that the film makes an explicit visual tie to an image of tradition.

We see Galal walking despondently on an old street in a poor quarter. Someone is putting up a poster. He stops and stares at the sign: "*Tiyātrū Ḥadīqat al-Ezbekīya, yuṭribukum al-muṭrib al-nābigh al-ustādh Maḥmūd ʿAṭīya*" (The Ezbekīya Garden Theater, the brilliant singer "Professor" Mahmud Atiya sings to you).[40] As he stares the name "Mahmud Atiya" fades to "Galal Muhammad," and then back to the original name. European music plays in the background. Galal walks on as the music fades.

In his apartment Galal paces nervously. Oriental music plays. Galal stops and inspects some pictures on a wall. The first is a portrait of a heavily mustached man in a tarbush wearing a dignified European suit. He is Abduh al-Hamuli, Abd al-Wahhab's musical "grandfather" and the founder of modern Arabic music, who died in 1901. Galal looks at the second picture: another man in European dress, this time seated. An old-fashioned, vaguely qur'ānic song begins in the background: "*Salām ʿalā Ḥasan*" (Salute to Hasan), a famous Salama al-Higazi song.[41] Finally he turns reverently to the third portrait: Sayyid Darwish, singer of the 1919 revolution.

It is after this that Galal decides to put all his energy into singing in an attempt to make the money he needs to marry. We see him several times rehearsing with his band. Later his success as a singer runs in inverse proportion to his fortunes in love; just as Raga's father demands that Galal stay out of his daughter's life we see his name on a poster for a performance in the Royal Opera House, then we see hordes of men in tarbushes streaming into the building.

The explicit musical turn in *White Rose* comes when Abd al-Wahhab pays homage to the masters. All the figures in the portraits were real persons, and whatever the extent of Abd al-Wahhab's actual involvement with them, he always sought to associate his name with them. The first figure, Abduh al-Hamuli, was mentioned in chapter 4; he was a major figure of mid- to late nineteenth-century Arabic music who died in 1901 before Abd al-Wahhab was born (or perhaps in Abd al-Wahhab's infancy). Salama al-Higazi was a student of al-Hamuli and the most prominent singer of Abd al-Wahhab's childhood. As a child Abd al-Wahhab memorized his songs, and when Fauzi al-Gazayirli hired him to sing between the acts of plays it was after hearing the boy sing Salama al-Higazi. The third figure, Sayyid Darwish, was actually someone with whom Abd al-Wahhab worked. We remember from chapter 4 that he had collaborated with Sayyid Darwish in the unsuccessful *Shahrazād* of 1920; and in 1927 Abd al-Wahhab broke into the big time by completing Sayyid Darwish's unfinished *Anṭūniyō wa-Klīyōbātrā* and performing it with Munira al-Mahdiya.

By publicly performing homage to his "ancestors" Abd al-Wahhab created both a musical lineage and a tidy *isnād* (chain of transmission)[42] into which he slotted himself. By making himself heir to both Sayyid Darwish and Abduh al-Hamuli, Abd al-Wahhab established himself as the spokesman for both the folk and the classical traditions of Arabic music. This was the most directly autobiographical section of the film – the fruition of his earlier request to Muhammad Karim to "make a film about his personal life" – and it bears an obvious resemblance to the biographical material on Abd al-Wahhab written later. In a sense Abd al-Wahhab had created himself long before the media took up the cause of making him into a sober hero of modernism. But his ubiquity amid the hyperbolic commentary of *al-Ithnayn* also suggests that in his day he was well appreciated for his bold forays into modern style and his revolution against tradition (kissing the bey's daughter!). The sober tie to tradition and the high-spirited youthful rebellion were linked in the film; later accounts of Abd al-Wahhab overwhelmingly stressed only the former as an antidote to tendencies in youth of the 1990s toward, oddly enough, many of the same luxuries coveted by Abd al-Wahhab's own generation. These included automobiles (featured later in the film after Galal has "made it" as a singer), foreign travel (his movements abroad were assiduously reported in *al-Ithnayn*), style (the much-ballyhooed long sideburns and his fine suits, mentioned in later accounts as his "elegance"), and bold attacks on the traditionalism of the preceding generation (his films all condone European-style relationships between men and women).

Films in historical memory

Resolution is one of the few pre-1945-era films to escape critical censure in later writing on Egyptian cinema. It is unambiguously considered to be both Salim's best film and the best film of the period. Film historian Saʿd al-Dīn Taufīq is typical in devoting 15 pages, in a 150-page text on the history of the Egyptian cinema, to *Resolution* and its effects on the industry as a whole. *White Rose*, by contrast, gets only three pages (Taufīq 1969).[43]

Samir Farid, a prominent Egyptian film critic, perfectly described the typical attitude toward early Egyptian cinema in the following statement:

> In Egypt, over the course of the more than two thousand films produced in half a century, and then shown again on television and destined to continue being aired on the video, the image of the Egyptian prevalent in Egyptian films is Egyptian in his clothes, his accent and manner of speaking, his movements. But he is not Egyptian in his traditions and customs, behavior, thoughts, actions and reactions. The reason for this is the prevalence of the Western model in Egyptian filmmaking. The filmmakers are Egyptian, and the films are made in Egypt, but their content is Western. *(Farīd 1986, 209)*

Excepting the music, many critics put *White Rose* in the category of "Egyptian in style, but Western in content." By contrast *Resolution*, because of its allegedly realistic portrayal of *baladī* life, is always characterized as the first thread of cinematic realism in Egypt – a tradition that was then developed in the 1950s and 1960s by Ṣalāḥ Abū Sayf (who was the assistant director in *Resolution*), Yūsuf Shāhīn and a handful of other directors.[44] But the way in which "realism" was construed in *Resolution*, in contrast to the sort of romanticism disparaged by the critics as "divorced from reality," needs further examination. *White Rose* and *Resolution* have a great deal in common, even though the former now appears as compromised as a Jantzen bathing-suit advertisement in a 1934 edition of *al-Ithnayn*, while the latter continues to be revered as a monument to true Egyptian authenticity.

Resolution was not just unusual in that it portrayed a *baladī* quarter; it was also a technical masterpiece. Very few other Egyptian films from the period (indeed, throughout the history of Egyptian cinema) were made to the same standard. The camera in *Resolution* is wonderfully fluent, as is the soundtrack, in which street noise forms the background to many scenes.[45] Indeed, it was the street scenes that gave the film its special flavor. The scenes are wonderfully choreographed, people and animals moving in and out of doorways and shops in an idealized "traditional quarter" that recalls Naguib Mahfouz novels of his realist phase.[46] *White Rose*, six years older than *Resolution*, appears leaden by comparison. But like Mahfouz novels, the realism of *Resolution* comes from a definite social perspective that cannot be separated from the ideology of modernization we have already seen in both *White Rose* and in the modernist discourse that runs the gamut from sober discussion of linguistic and educational reform to the humor of *al-Ithnayn*. The realism in *Resolution* is highly idealized and thoroughly modernist. It is the technique and the actors – almost all of them far more accomplished than those in *White Rose* – that give the film a much more natural feel than most of its contemporaries. In all the praise for *Resolution* as a realistic portrayal of lower-class life, the fact that the film still illustrates a certain perspective on the lower classes gets lost. Furthermore, this perspective has much in common with the dandified *White Rose*. *Resolution* is not an anomalous work of populism in a sea of elitist hegemony. In many ways the two films are variations on the same theme, and in both cases that theme is an Egyptian modernism that has always sought to distance itself from European dominance.

Although *Resolution* and *White Rose* exhibit more similarities than immediately meets the eye, it is *Resolution* that is thought of as the origin of "social realism" in the Egyptian cinema, and the ideal of social realism is associated explicitly with representing the life of the masses, of an idealized *ibn al-balad*. The idealization of the characters gives *Resolution* a highly structured feel. The hero is the perfect "son of the country," pulling himself up by the bootstraps to earn the title "effendi." His mother is the perfect mother with no thought but the welfare of her children. The *awlād al-zawāt* are perfectly horrible (except for the one who teams up with the hero to form a middle-class unification of society), obsessed with behaving like the stereotypical foreigner, playing games all day, revelling in shameful parties, never working.

However, it might also be argued that a famous scene in *Resolution* of bureaucrats shirking their jobs (just before Muhammad loses the office job that Nazih Pasha found for him), touted by one critic as "social criticism" (Taufīq 1969, 68), is a more elaborate, more naturalistic version of a scene in *White Rose*. In this scene, Abd al-Wahhab's superior, Khalil Effendi, is out of the office when his boss wants him and when asked later to explain his absence becomes defensive, protesting that he was out on work-related business, inadvertently pointing the finger at himself when in fact nobody had accused him of shirking. *White Rose* generally goes a bit beyond *Resolution* in its depiction of aristocrats taking advantage of their position, as in a scene where Shafiq approaches Ismail Bey in order to obtain his intercession at the ministry in which he works. Such scenes surely struck a chord in the middle-class audience – the same audience that was attracted to the meritocratic ethic of *Resolution*. Shafiq's inappropriate use of family influence was promotion through *wāsṭa* (personal, especially family, connections), and this was a sore point for many. The problem featured prominently on the pages of *al-Ithnayn*. For example, an article entitled " *'Ishmiʿnā*" (Why, especially. . .) featured a list of seemingly innocent questions, many of them veiled complaints, followed by sarcastic answers:

Q: Why did ʿAbd al-Ḥamīd Effendi advance so quickly?
A: Because he married a pasha's daughter.
Q: Why are the foreign quarters well kept and the native quarters [*al-aḥyāʾ al-waṭanīya*] . . . well, you know?
A: "Hospitality to guests."
Q: Why did Suʿād marry and not me, even though I'm prettier?
A: She's richer.
Q: Why did Ibrāhīm's family travel to Europe for the summer?
A: They found someone to loan them the money. ("*Ishmiʿnā*" *1934*)[47]

In its invocation of such middle-class preoccupations as advancement through merit rather than through influence *White Rose* could plausibly have been classed with *Resolution* as a work of social criticism. However, critics remember *White Rose* mainly for its music; as a film there is always a suggestion that it is a bit of an embarrassment. It and all of the films made by Muhammad Karim and Abd al-Wahhab are part of what the media sometimes characterize as the bad old days of cultural subservience to the West. Consequently such films are accorded only limited significance in the development of Egyptian cinematic language.[48]

Given the general disapproval by critics in later years of the social content of early films, it is surprising to learn that when *White Rose* opened – in December 1933, six months before the inaugural issue of *al-Ithnayn* – it was something of a nationalist cause. Egyptian students opposed to British rule had been trying to organize a boycott of foreign-owned theaters. They enforced the boycott by leaving chlorine stinkbombs in the aisles. *White Rose* was to open in the Royal Theater, which was foreign owned, but the students agreed to relax the boycott for the opening week, and a sign was affixed to the theater saying: "You are Egyptian, and it was Egyptians who made what you are seeing here. Be proud of your Egyptianness and see the film *White Rose* in the Royal Theater beginning on December 4, 1933" (Karīm 1972, 198–99).[49]

Politicians found the film irresistible. Ṣafīya Zaghlūl, widow of nationalist leader and Wafd Party founder Saad Zaghlul, wrote to Karim thanking him for his "nationalistic and futuristic project" (*ibid.*, 201). Muṣṭafā Naḥḥās Pasha of the Wafd Party found time to congratulate Karim on his successful "patriotic film," saying that it was "as good as any foreign film" (*ibid.*, 200–01). Taha Husayn, then editor of the journal *Kawkab al-sharq*, wrote:

I want to give my sincerest congratulations to Abd al-Wahhab after having seen the film. After seeing how pleased the people were with the film I didn't know whether to give more praise to the film's creativeness, or to the people's admiration for it, or both together. Both are worthy of congratulations. Abd al-Wahhab deserves the best of luck. (*ibid.*, *202*)

Aside from *White Rose*'s surprisingly straightforward nationalist appeal, there is no reason to assume that *Resolution*, the "good nationalist film" in the judgment of later writers, stands apart from the rest of the early Egyptian cinema as an anomaly. Since the film was a commercial success, one suspects *Resolution* had similarities with its contemporaries.[50] Furthermore, the claim that *Resolution* became highly emulated for its "social realism" contradicts history: certainly the upper-class setting of *White Rose* was the style most emulated in later films. The important point is that both the "salon style" of *White Rose* and the "realistic" style of *Resolution* focused on the interface between upper-middle and upper class.

Resolution, for all its dazzle and charm, performs exactly the same closure of social extremes as *White Rose*. In *White Rose* it is the fallen aristocrat Galal from one side and his suspicious hobby – Arabic music – from the other, both moving inexorably to the center; in *Resolution* it is Muhammad Effendi growing out of the *ibn al-balad* milieu and his friend Adli moving – hesitantly up to this point – into a healthy, hardworking middle-class life. In both films markers of style and taste function to construct a national Egyptian culture which remained salient in popular culture from the 1930s through the decade of the 1960s.

6

Popular commentary, real lives

*The issue of cultural identity is not a problem for Egypt. Egypt settled this issue, once and for all, way back in the 'twenties and the 'thirties of this century. Great battles were raged [*sic*] in the press by Egyptian intellectuals. Those battles have now become just memories, but sometimes it is worthwhile to evoke memories, especially as from time to time, the same arguments still appear.*

Mursī Saʿd al-Dīn (former chief censor of English-language publications in Egypt), in "Plain Talk," *Al-Ahram Weekly*, 1 (February, 28 1991).

The old formula of modernist synthesis still receives sympathetic treatment in some quarters. However, the media have changed. Some are now more heavily dominated by the state than ever before, while others are, to a greater or lesser degree, in private hands. The mixture of public and private ownership mirrors the situation of other Egyptian institutions in the era of *infitāḥ*: the line dividing interests of the state and those of wealthy players in the newly reconstituted private sector is not always clear. There has, however, been enough diversification in media production to permit significant deviation in some productions from the heroic modernism of such figures as Abd al-Wahhab. Whether such deviation is motivated chiefly by profit or by a desire to more accurately mirror "social reality" is hotly debated in the Egyptian press. What is not in doubt is that modernist ideology must now compete with other styles of popular culture that contest the glib unity of local tradition, Islamic tradition, and Western technique. Since the 1960s discrepancies between the ideology of establishment-approved culture and the lives of many Egyptians have become glaringly obvious. The expansion of both media imagery and state institutions into the lives of so many people – virtually every Egyptian in some way by this time – has brought a greater immediacy to the gap between ideology and practice. Let us start with a transitional case.

The university style: 1972

Although *Khallī bālak min Zūzū* (Pay attention to Zuzu, 1972)[1] was released thirty-nine years after *White Rose*, it was a logical extension of the earlier film. Zuzu, a vivacious and popular student at Cairo University, leads a double life. By day she attends classes and wins track meets. Her peers at the university vote her *al-bint al-mithālīya* (the exemplary girl). By night she is a bellydancer. Zuzu, the student-bellydancer, has an even more scandalous double identity than Abd al-Wahhab's bureaucrat-singer. At least in Abd al-Wahhab's 1933 film fantasy the art could be rehabilitated, raised to the status of modernity, and performed in the opera house before an audience of admiring middle-class men in tarbushes. This is not an option for Zuzu in 1972. Professional dancers in Egypt have traditionally been associated with prostitution, and though attempts have been made to adapt certain folk dances to the stage, the dances selected tend to be rural, communal (Riḍā 1968), and not at all sensual. Zuzu's style of dance can be performed honorably only in the company of other women; performed in front of men, it is one step from prostitution. And men, at weddings and parties – although significantly, not in nightclubs – are Zuzu's main audience.

Zuzu is not a prostitute, merely from a backward family. Her mother, herself a former dancer,[2] is in fact horrified at the idea of Zuzu being made to "put out" in order to get ahead. We learn this late in the film, when Zuzu's mother has a nightmare in which her daughter literally dances her way into a leering man's bed. The nightmare comes at a point in the film when Zuzu feels torn between her role as star dancer in the family troupe, which makes her everyone's primary meal ticket, and her desire for education and progress.

Early in the film we see Zuzu, clad in shorts and a tank shirt, running a race against similarly clad college girls. Zuzu wins her race, giving her *usra* (her student "family") victory over the other "families." They have won "the cup," a large metal thing that Zuzu hoists aloft exultantly. Zuzu's "family" is essentially a social club for students, although some "families" are more inclined to politics than to track and field.[3] Zuzu's group is called *al-Ḥaraka al-'īgābīya* (the positive movement). After the Positivists win the cup, the editor of the student newspaper sends a female reporter to the locker room to interview Zuzu, who was unknown to most of the students before she swept the track-and-field competition.[4] The reporter asks Zuzu, whose wet head appears above a shower curtain, why she took up sports. "Because I love old Abd al-Wahhab songs," is Zuzu's irreverent answer. The reporter fails to get her point. Zuzu elaborates: "Didn't Abd al-Wahhab say, 'Run, run, I want to get there fast'?" She refers to Abd al-Wahhab's song "*Igrī, igrī*" (Run, run), a hit song from his 1938 film *Long Live Love*. The joke wins points with the admiring reporter.

Zuzu emerges from the locker room in a *décolletée* red plastic minidress. She finds her "family" members completing a riotous caricature of her winning the cup on a large bulletin board festooned with bright pictures and announcements of happy social events. This is the group's "wall magazine," an inexpensive forum for allowing student groups to express themselves.[5] The leader of a rival "family" called *al-Ṣirāṭ al-mustaqīm* (the straight [Islamic] path) looks on disapprovingly.[6] He is ʿUmrān, an intense, unsmiling young man wearing a long-sleeved shirt and narrow black tie (all the other college boys wear bright-colored short-sleeved shirts open at the neck). Umran speaks a near-classical variant of Arabic, and is ever on the lookout for a chance to declaim publicly. One of the Positivists inspects the Straight Path wall magazine, and informs Zuzu that Umran has written an insulting poem about her. Zuzu laughs and asks him to recite it. Umran, happy at the chance to fulminate, complies:

Where is shame
If I had my sword with me
I wouldn't need my pen.
A hundred regrets
For morals and values.
O people, O people!
Today I saw a girl student
Running in shorts,
Making me speechless with anger.
We have all won, we have all won
A look at her charms.
We have won the cup of shame and repentance!

Zuzu's friends respond to Umran's anguished ode on lost morality by gleefully singing a lighthearted song in which they try to crown Zuzu as their beauty queen. She laughingly rejects this attempt, but allows them to decorate her head with a paper crown upon which is written *al-fatāt al-mithālīya* (the exemplary young woman).

Next we see Zuzu going home, and the extent of her double life becomes apparent. Home for Zuzu is obviously not in a smart neighborhood. The camera moves through a series of long-range street scenes, starting with modern downtown streets and moving to poorer, narrower areas. The general street shots fade into the sight of Zuzu tripping merrily along in her tiny dress – *de rigueur* for the cinematic college girl of 1972:[7] Barbarella meets *bint al-balad.* But surprisingly, no one says anything rude to Zuzu, despite her red plastic minidress which, if worn today on a crowded thoroughfare in almost any neighborhood, would at least attract incredulous stares if not outright harassment. The camera follows Zuzu past a café called *Qahwat al-Tigāra* (The commerce café) – a real establishment frequented by musicians and other entertainers where they rest and drink coffee between jobs. But the Commerce Café alone is not well enough known for the audience to link it automatically with the entertainment profession, so the camera follows Zuzu past the café to a row of shops displaying lutes and drums. As she passes by, the men in the café flirt with her mildly. She is known by musicians; she walks by the Commerce Café; she lives in a relatively poor area. This is enough for the audience to know where she lives – Muḥammad ʿAlī Street.

Muḥammad ʿAlī Street is famed as the street of traditional entertainers. Even today, when most of the entertainment business has moved to Pyramids Road in Giza, or other newer and glitzier neighborhoods, Muḥammad ʿAlī Street is thick with shops selling lutes and other musical instruments.[8] The area has an unremarkable, slightly run-down look today. The musical-instrument shops are mixed in among numerous ordinary shops selling household items and groceries. Judging from the film, it was much the same in 1972 when *Zuzu* was made. The dilapidated look of Zuzu's neighborhood was intentional. The point of the character is that she represents decadent traditional life trying hard to modernize.

Zuzu goes slightly farther than its cinematic predecessors in advocating the abandonment of low tradition in favor of modernity, but not to the point of wholesale condemnation of the folk heritage. Zuzu's mother may be backward, often expressing frustration at her daughter's incomprehensible love of learning, and unthinkingly pushing the girl into her own footsteps; but she is not hopelessly immoral. The idea of pushing her daughter into prostitution, conveyed in her lurid dream, is abhorrent. Zuzu also feels a commendable loyalty to her mother, even after she tries to make a break with her past.

Like *White Rose*, *Zuzu* is a boy-meets-girl story in which there is a disparity in the social standing of the would-be couple. This time the girl is poor and the boy rich. His name in the film is Dr. Saʿīd – a professor in the theater department fresh from a *biʿtha* (foreign-study mission). Immediately Zuzu falls in love with him. Dr. Said was played by Ḥusayn Fahmī who had, in fact, just returned from study abroad in the UCLA film program. *Zuzu* was Fahmi's breakthrough film. We see them at one point meeting on the "water taxi" dock. The water taxi is a ferry from in front of the Radio and Television Building on the Cairo (east) side of the river to a point near Cairo University in Giza on the other (west) side of the Nile. Zuzu, dressed in a new yellow minidress and looking for all the world like Disney's Snow White, is obviously a perfect match for the blond Dr. Said, who wears skin-tight short-sleeved shirts open nearly to his belly button.

Of course Zuzu can't reveal her background, which she fears the aristocratic director would consider sordid. When the love affair between Zuzu and the director blossoms, the director's jilted lover – his cousin – spies on Zuzu, and discovers her secret. The cousin gets her revenge by arranging for Zuzu's family to perform at a party. Zuzu and Dr. Said attend the party. When Zuzu's mother dances it becomes apparent that she is over the hill. The onlookers laugh at her. Zuzu responds by dancing in her mother's place, which of course reveals her hidden secret and causes scandal in the university.

Plate 9 Zuzu feeds Dr. Said at a riverside café (from *Pay Attention to Zuzu*, 1972)

Zuzu is heartbroken at what she assumes will be the loss of her aristocratic lover. She tries to put a brave face on the matter, and comes to school the next day wearing a ruffled black and white vaguely Tyrolean "Heidi" skirt. As she passes by the Straight Path wall magazine Zuzu is shocked to see a lurid drawing of herself in dance attire, bare arms raised and hip thrown provocatively to one side. The poster reads *Yā li-l-ʿār* (oh shame!). Umran, in the same fully buttoned long-sleeved shirt, but minus the necktie, stands smugly by. Zuzu challenges him: "Has the Straight Path become an 'arts magazine' [*magalla fannīya*]? Since when have you put up pictures of dancers?"

Umran begins spouting slogans in classical Arabic: *al-inḥirāf yu'addī ilā-l-inḥirāf* (deviance leads to deviance), *al-shurb yu'addī ilā badlat al-raqṣ* (liquor leads to dance dresses), *al-istād yu'addī ilā al-kābārayh* (stadiums [girls running in shorts] lead to cabarets).

"What do you want, then?" asks Zuzu. As she says this a girl in long skirt and *ḥijāb* comes and unobtrusively inspects the poster. She says nothing – this is still 1972 and most of the female students look like Zuzu – then disappears after a moment. Umran, however, is not as quiet as this anonymous girl. He answers Zuzu: "To cleanse the country of all evil."

Some students protest, telling Umran that he is not living in the modern age. "We have a national dance troupe. Farīda Fahmī is a student. Her father is a college professor."[9]

"That's different," says an angry Zuzu. "My mother is a Muḥammad ʿAlī Street dancer earning a living from dancing at weddings." The students defend Zuzu even when she will not defend herself. "There's no shame in working for a living." Umran's friends begin to drum and sing, as if to make Zuzu dance despite herself; they try to tie a scarf around her hips, bellydancer style, but Zuzu resists. A brawl ensues between Zuzu's group and Umran's neo-Islamists. Umran's white shirt is nearly ripped from his back. Zuzu rescues him, but then flees the university in shame.

Back in her Muḥammad ʿAlī Street home the despairing Zuzu tells her mother that she wants to throw her life into cabaret dancing in Pyramids Road nightclubs – the most lucrative type of dancing, but also the most shameful. It is at this point that Zuzu's mother has her Zuzu-dancing-into-prostitution dream. Disturbed, she tries to convince Zuzu to go back to school, but the girl's pride is wounded and she refuses. Then Dr. Said comes calling. He also tries to convince the sulking Zuzu to go back to school, and again she refuses. The progressive, foreign-educated Dr. Said then turns into a conservative *ibn al-balad*. He slaps the girl and orders her back to school, then stomps out of Zuzu's flat in a huff. Zuzu collapses in tears.

In Zuzu's absence, the students and some faculty members, including Dr. Said, convene a meeting to discuss the accusations of her immorality. Most of the students are on Zuzu's side. Dr. Said demands to know exactly what Zuzu is accused of. Umran, again decked out in a clean white long-sleeved and fully buttoned shirt, proclaims that "someone who gives up her studies is not worthy of them." It is at this moment that Zuzu, apparently chastened finally by her lover's show of manliness, returns to school.

Wearing a neat white buttoned-up blouse and a skirt extending well below the knees – her only outfit in the film that would have even a prayer of being described today as "modest" – she walks into the room saying, "I'll tell you what she's accused of." Shocked silence. She continues, referring to herself in the third person. "Zaynab ʿAbd al-Karīm [Zuzu's full name] walks the street of her mother, Naʿīma al-Almāẓīya ʿAbd al-Karīm. Her mother carries the mark of this pathetic street, and it carries the mark of a past age – the age of backwardness. This is the sin for which she should be punished."

Umran protests. "Have some respect for our intelligence. How can one be punished for something so paltry?" It seems he wants to have her specifically punished for her alleged transgression. One of Zuzu's friends rises in anger, saying, "Zuzu is blameless."

But Zuzu cuts him off: "She is at fault. Her sin is that she hid the truth about herself in fear of persecution. But she was the first to persecute herself. Zuzu the 'exemplary girl' persecuting Zuzu al-Almaziya."

"That's an illness," a professor exclaims. "Schizophrenia," says a student in hushed tones.

Zuzu will not be stopped. "We all suffer from that disease, Dr. Maḥmūd."

This provokes Umran. "Why? Are we all children of Naima al-Almaziya?"

"Yes, we are. Children of an environment that the world has left behind. And every time we try to rise, it weighs us back down to the earth. We don't know whether to hate ourselves or the world."

The director likes this. "Bravo, Zuzu, bravo." But a student asks, "What's the solution?"

"Everybody should know himself well," she replies, "and not look always at his origins, but to the future, always the future. That's why I came: to look after my future." She sits in the front desk of the classroom.

Umran is impressed. He comes to the front of the room, saying in his peculiar variant of almost-classical Arabic: "The university should be proud of any person with this mentality. I am sorry for all that I said about her." Zuzu and Umran shake hands. A professor exhorts the students to get back to their lectures. Everybody cheers. Dancing and singing begin.

Once again, the colloquial heritage, humbled by Zuzu's repudiation of her former profession, joins with classicism through the transforming offices of higher education. Now that the "schizophrenia" induced by the uneasy coexistence of conflicting cultural heritages is symbolically healed, Zuzu can be herself. In the last scene she appears in her "Snow White" minidress, frolicking through ʿUrmān Gardens (just beside Cairo University) with the director and an army of singing students. The film ends on an excruciatingly long kiss between Zuzu and the handsome young director.

Zuzu was an oddly popular film. "Oddly" because the fantasy world of miniskirted students singing in public gardens was so far from the reality of the times. Indeed, the professor's exhortation in the last scene to "get back to your lectures" comes perilously close to propaganda. The year *Zuzu* came out President Sadat had accused student leaders of treason, claiming that a small minority of students were troublemakers, and urging the majority to "rid themselves of extreme elements" so that students could concentrate on their studies "bearing in mind that study time is for studying" (Abdalla 1985, 185–86). One could forgive the students for a certain amount of skepticism toward such exhortations. Just four years earlier angry students had shouted such slogans as "Down with the secret-police state," "Down with the military state," and "Heikal [then-President Abdel Nasser's right-hand man and later editor of the semiofficial *Al-Ahrām* newspaper], you are a liar, stop lying, you cheat." In an effort to stop severe rioting, students were allowed to present their demands to the parliament. *Zuzu* contains not a whiff of these demands, which included release of arrested colleagues, freedom of the press, withdrawal of intelligence personnel from campus, and permission to reconstitute banned youth organizations (*ibid.*, 152). The students who presented these demands expressed fear of being arrested. Sadat, who was then Speaker of the Parliament, assured them that they had nothing to fear, and gave them his personal phone number in case they had any trouble. They were arrested at home that evening (*ibid.*, 153).

Students may well have been involved in track meets of the sort that Zuzu's "family" won early in the film. They had few other officially sanctioned outlets for their energies. During the 1960s many had noticed that students became excessively interested in soccer. As one observer put it: "From my personal experience I can assure you that 90 percent of student discussions at the university are on the subject of football . . . The young men on whom the future of the country depends are obsessed with an opium called football" (*ibid.*, 123). The 1968 riots were one result of this enforced abdication to the realm of sports, and the wall magazines were one of the fruits of the riots. In this respect, the pedantic and sloganeering Umran is much closer to the truth than Zuzu's happy friends. The only problem is that he isn't nearly angry enough. The wall magazines were described by one state security prosecutor in scathing terms:

> It is apparent that they contain an attack on the present regime and its policies, on the practice of socialism in Egypt, on the legitimate constitutional institutions of the state and its various bodies, such as the . . . People's Council [parliament], the armed forces, the media and the security forces. They also contain an attack on the foreign policy of the state since it represented what they call a policy of kneeling before the U.S. and of trembling before imperialism. They also attacked the policy of Arab states, alleging that the Egyptian govermnent is allying with the Shaikhs and Sultans against national liberation . . . These wall magazines also contain discussion of what they call the question of freedom and democracy, alleging that democracy is absent and that liberties are shackled and there is no free press in the country. Meanwhile, they alleged that the university administration applies repressive measures against the student movement, and that the legitimate Student Union is an agent of security bodies. *(ibid., 198–199)*

Pay Attention to Zuzu was, in the opinion of many, laughably out of sync with the student protests of the late 1960s and early 1970s. However, there were and are people who take it seriously as a politically committed work of art. For example, I met a young journalist who worked for the public-sector cinema magazine *al-Kawākib* who took the film as an expression of Nasserist ideology. He was quite offended when I suggested that much of the film's remaining popularity was due to the miniskirts and bellydance scenes. More often Egyptians I spoke to agreed that *Zuzu* was primarily a dance film. The journalist did, however, have a point. The confrontation between Zuzu's enthusiastic student friends and Umran's dour proto-Islamists has been replayed since the late 1960s on college campuses, usually with the Islamists gaining the upper hand (Kepel 1984, 129–71). *Pay Attention to Zuzu* was virtually the only film that attempted to depict this confrontation in any way. After the 1972 *Zuzu*, Islamists largely disappeared from the screen. It was not until twenty years later that Islamist politics resurfaced in the cinema, but the later cinematic treatments of Islamists located the phenomenon conspicuously (and uncharacteristically) *outside* the educational system.[10]

Zuzu was perfectly consonant with the character of Egyptian cinema throughout much of its history. Aside from the film's propagandizing, it promotes the same ideological message – a message to which some still respond positively – as *White Rose* or *Resolution*: the folk heritage shall be elevated to the level of a modernized classicism purged of its backward elements. *Zuzu* is more exaggerated than *White Rose*. The "backwardness" of the traditional musical milieu is never presented explicitly in *White Rose* because Abd al-Wahhab has already transformed it into "proper art." *Zuzu*, forty years later, attempts to rub our noses in backwardness. The dance itself cannot be transformed, but that does not mean that the dancer is irredeemable.

The contradictions between the hopeful resolution of *Pay Attention to Zuzu* and the tumultuous social and historical circumstances of its audience give the film an element of mild hysteria. It must be as obvious as possible to have any hope of drawing viewers in to a promise that is so divergent from the reality in which most of the audience lives. *Zuzu*'s immense popularity suggests that the battered modernist formula still retained considerable appeal, although cynics might have pointed out that it had to be dressed in scandalous minidresses to draw an audience.

The 1989 university style: in search of Zuzu

It is 1989. I am standing on the water-taxi dock by the Radio and Television Building where Zuzu and the director met on their way to Cairo University seventeen years ago. I am, in fact, there for a university-sponsored event – a day trip to a park located by the Nile sluice gates just north of Cairo. The low, relatively fast, blue-and-white water taxis speed off to the left of where I stand on the east bank of the Nile. Soon I will find myself sailing to the right on a much larger double-decked boat, open on the sides and top, and used by groups for day trips. Most of these trips are to the Nile barrages, a journey of about an hour and a half. At the barrages there is a good-sized park, in which the crowds now boarding the boat will disperse to eat the picnic lunches they have brought with them.

I am with a group of friends and their relatives: Farīd, his cousin Nabīl, his aunt Fatḥīya, Fathiya's two daughters Khadīga and Widād, and two women, friends of Fathiya.[11] Farid and Nabil grew up in the Upper Egyptian town of Sohāg, although their college education was entirely in Cairo. "Is" in Cairo, in Nabil's case. He is a third-year student in the Cairo University faculty of medicine. To get into medical school – an undergraduate degree in Egypt – Nabil had to get a high score on the *thanawīya ʿāmma* (general secondary exams). What one studies in the Egyptian higher educational system depends entirely on one's *thanawīya ʿāmma* scores. Medicine and engineering are at the top of the heap, and receive the most resources from the state. Nabil, therefore, is among the elite, and it shows from his polite, intelligent conversation. Despite his high status in the university system, Nabil is pessimistic about his chances of getting a decent job when he finishes his degree. "You have to go abroad for specialized studies to get a good job," he says: "I know doctors who are working in public-sector clinics who are only making a hundred pounds a month. But you need connections to go abroad for study." Fortunately or not, Nabil will not have to worry about either jobs or travel for some time. In two years he finishes his degree, and then he must do his obligatory military service. If Nabil is lucky, he will be made an ordinary soldier and finish his duty in one year. "One gets treated badly as a soldier," he says wryly, "but at least it's over quickly."

Farid is more bitter than Nabil. He is twenty-eight years old, and finished his degree several years ago at ʿAyn Shams, Egypt's second-largest university, located in northeast Cairo. His degree was from the faculty of education, his specialty mathematics. Farid now works as a math teacher at the *iʿdādī* level (preparatory, for students aged twelve to fifteen years) in a girls' school not far from the American University in Cairo. He does not like his job. "Why do these girls need to learn math? All they're going to do is get married." Nonetheless, Farid makes good money teaching. Although his base salary is a pathetically inadequate LE 60 per month, he can augment this tenfold or more through private lessons. In a good month (around exam time) he can make nearly LE 1,000. He needs the money because he is engaged to be married to a girl who is now in college. The apartment, furniture, and his contribution to the wedding will cost at least LE 20,000. He has saved approximately half this sum.

Farid's fiancée, who is not with us, looks nothing like Zuzu. In fact, she wears the neo-Islamic *ḥijāb*, much like the silent girl in *Zuzu* who briefly inspected the Straight Path wall magazine near the end of the film. "Of course the *ḥijāb* is not an absolute guarantee of a girl's good character, but any girl who doesn't wear it these days is obviously trying to make some sort of statement, and I'm having none of it." Farid looks askance at his cousin Khadiga, one of the few girls on the boat not wearing the *ḥijāb*. "A television is a necessary part of my wedding expenses. She's not going to be leaving the house after we're married, so I need it for her entertainment."

Farid, Nabil, and another medical student from Sohāg live in a three-room furnished apartment far from the center of Cairo, where Farid works. Rent is LE 120 per month. The apartment is relatively spacious by Cairene standards and has a phone, which is essential for Farid to arrange lessons. Each of the three would have preferred to live with relatives in an unfurnished apartment, but none of them have family in Cairo with extra space. Unfurnished apartments are synonymous with stable family housing, and are officially rent controlled, which means that one pays an enormous unofficial sum up front to the owner, and very little thereafter. Living in furnished apartments – not rent controlled and therefore more expensive per month, but requiring little or no money up front – is problematic for Egyptians because such apartments are temporary and regarded as potential havens for drug dealing, prostitution, con games, and foreigners (who are not allowed access to rent-controlled apartments). None of this applies to Farid and Nabil, but their landlord, a wall-eyed engineer who has found profitable employment with a foreign company subcontracting on a sewer project coordinated by the U.S. Agency for International Development, still does not trust them.

Farid's school is on the same street as the girls' dormitory for the American University. He professes boundless disdain for AUC students, most of whom are quite wealthy, and all of whom speak English well enough at least to survive AUC's English-language curriculum. The female students draw special ire. "Whores, all of them. You know that dormitory is the biggest whorehouse in Cairo." Not all of the AUC female students walk past Farid's school on their way to class. He claims to have seen large numbers of them – the majority of the female student body, he thinks – being dropped off at the gates of the university from new Mercedes and BMW cars. "Those are the worst. They all wear miniskirts and shorts. Whores."

Farid and I once sat next to a table of female AUC students in a nearby café. Women and girls do not normally frequent cafés, but this particular location was a kind of no-man's land – a place to wait for rides or to have a cup of coffee off campus.[12] Judging by their dress and manner of speech the students at the table beside us were very likely full-time AUC students (as opposed to part-timers taking much less expensive courses offered by the university in secretarial skills or basic English). They were the closest thing to Zuzu one saw in 1989. They wore no *ḥijāb* over their expensively coiffed, fluffed, and dyed hair. Our neighbors did not wear miniskirts, but they did show a lot of leg and arm. One of them wore tight imported jeans. I overheard one of them speaking in English. "I can't decide whether to take Italian citizenship, or to keep my Egyptian passport." I didn't bother to translate for Farid. Then we heard another say in a high, nasal voice, half Arabic, half English, "*Kunt*^{i} *ḥadris iṭ-ṭibb, bass . . . yaʿnī . . .* I can't stand the sight of blood!" (I was going to study medicine, but you know, I can't stand the sight of blood.) This time I had to translate for Farid, since he understood the first half of the sentence. When I told him what she said in the second (English) half he snorted. "She couldn't even get into medical school. None of them can even pass the *thanawīya ʿāmma*. They go to AUC because they're a bunch of rich failures."

Farid and I are wary of each other. He knows that I have friends in the American University, but I rarely try to defend the place to him. He is a frustrated Umran, surrounded by what appear to him like a multitude of sassy Zuzus. It would be useless for me to try to convince him that they are not all as bad as they look – that only the more overtly Westernized ones jump to the eye, that some wear the *ḥijāb* and that many of them are virtually indistinguishable from run-of-the-mill Egyptian university students. Farid is often exhausted and irritable from teaching, but he will never be able to afford a Mercedes with which to shield his wife from the streets, as he believes all of these AUC students are shielded; perhaps a Fiat, if he continues giving private lessons at his present breakneck pace, but never a long, low "crocodile." He has a low opinion of Americans in general, and believes that the foreign films and television shown in Egypt confirm this view. He sees the bed-hopping world of "Knots Landing" and "Falcon Crest" as documentary, confirmation of his worst opinions of America and the West. "Big-haired" AUC students wearing tight jeans and speaking broken Arabic are the finishing touch to his portrait of imported corruption.

Farid's cousin Khadiga, however, finds the place glamorous. Although her branch of the family grew up in Cairo rather than in Sohāg, they are also more distanced, both socially and spatially, from the glitzy world of fantastically expensive private universities (tuition at AUC was several thousands of Egyptian pounds per year in the early 1990s – far more than the usual middle-class family income). Khadiga, her younger sister Widad, and their mother Fathiya live in a single room in the neighborhood of ʿAbdīn. The room is in an old office building which has been converted into housing. Each floor of the building has a single bathroom, shared by approximately twenty-five people. They keep their room spotless, in contrast to the overused public space in the building such as stairwells and bathrooms.

Khadiga's mother Fathiya, a divorcée, works in a public-sector pharmaceutical factory in Giza. She is a gaunt woman who wears the *ḥijāb* and spends an hour and a half a day or more commuting to her job. The job requires her to be on her feet for most of the time she is at work, which causes chronic swelling in her legs, compounded by anemia. Years ago, shortly before the divorce, her ex-husband moved to Kuwait, where he ran a "supermarket." Long before the Gulf War destroyed Kuwait he had relocated to Eastern Europe, where he has now married a Hungarian woman. His child-support payments, never generous, have recently ceased altogether even though he is, in the estimation of Fathiya and her daughters, a "millionaire."

Half of Fathiya's monthly income goes to education, most of it to pay for private lessons in math, Arabic, and science. It is the younger daughter, Widad, who must have the lessons. The expensive tutors are a sore point with Fathiya: "They are parasites. If we don't pay they will flunk our children. Look at the girls upstairs. They refused the private lessons, and what are they doing now? Sitting at home." But Fathiya continues to pay for Widad's lessons, as she paid for Khadiga's when she was younger. Fathiya does this not out of belief in the need to forge a new modern Egyptian identity, but for status, which in their situation equates with a degree of wealth and security. As a divorcée she holds few cards in the marriage game which she must play on behalf of her daughters. If the daughters are educated, her hand is considerably improved.

Khadiga, the elder daughter, is a student in the Cairo University faculty of law. Cairo University, of course, was Zuzu's alma mater, and although Khadiga and her sister have seen *Pay Attention to Zuzu* repeatedly, she finds that even without the burden of a bellydancer mother the process of erasing the stigma of "backwardness" is more difficult than the film suggests. By this time Khadiga should have graduated, but is still in her junior year because she was temporarily expelled. She had been talking to a friend during a lecture, and the professor told her to stop. She hurled an insult at him, and found herself expelled from sophomore year and suspended for a subsequent year. Now that she is back, however, she is doing surprisingly well. In college, as in the lower levels of education, private lessons and "insider" lecture notes are sold, sometimes for reportedly phenomenal prices. Khadiga blames foreign Arab students and money earned by Egyptians in Saudi Arabia and the Arab Gulf for the inflated prices of private lessons. Of course the benefit of Arab oil money would have been hers but for her father having divorced her mother and then refusing to have any but the most minimal contact with them. Even so, she managed to pass the sophomore-year exams by joining study groups and getting some free tutoring from altruistic law-school graduates.

Khadiga did not do as well in the *thanawīya ʿāmma* as Nabil. Formerly the faculty of law carried a great deal of prestige, but those days are gone. Law now ranks well below medicine, engineering, and science in the

Egyptian education hierarchy. Classes overflow the lecture halls. This does not mean that there is no prestige in being a lawyer. As Khadiga puts it: "The professors are all advisers to the government – some of them even hold cabinet positions. Fatḥī Surūr [the minister of education at that time] is supposed to be a law professor. He never comes to the lectures. Who are we to them?" But one does not become a lawyer merely by getting a law degree. The Bar Association decides who actually practices law, and according to Khadiga there is a widespread belief that admission to the union depends on favoritism and family connections.

Despite her precarious prospects in marriage and life, Khadiga does resemble Zuzu in certain respects. Of course she does not wear Zuzu's miniskirt ensemble, nor would she if given the chance, and public dancing is out of the question. But Khadiga does share with Zuzu a certain vivaciousness, a trait of which her Umran-like cousin Farid disapproves in women. And she has a certain optimism, which was Zuzu's saving grace. The film *Pay Attention to Zuzu* may have been propagandistic and full of two-dimensional characters, but the important thing about Zuzu's character was that she struggled to get her education against stiff odds, and this is exactly what Khadiga has done. She is the only girl in the building without a father or brother to provide real or symbolic protection against the vicissitudes of public life, and she is also the only girl in the building who is likely to graduate from college. She was not always a good student, dislikes reading, and has very little love of learning. But she will graduate.

Whatever films Khadiga and her family see are from the television. They have seen *Zuzu* often enough to have learned the words to several of the songs. They do not, however, go to theaters. In all the years I have known these three women only Khadiga has gone, once with a group of girlfriends, to a movie theater. Fathiya and Widad have not gone at all. Part of the problem is expense, but theaters have also acquired a bad reputation in recent years. Film-industry personnel often blame an alleged decline of the Egyptian cinema on the audience, which they believe now to be made up entirely of coarse, uneducated *ḥirafiyya* (tradesmen, sg. *ḥirafī*). In fact one sees the occasional male–female "date" at theaters, a few groups of female friends, and sometimes families. But three-quarters or more of any theater audience consists of student-aged men.

I have watched a great deal of television with Fathiya, Khadiga, and Widad. As Khadiga's cousin Farid indicated by his insistence on buying a television to entertain his housebound future wife, many people consider television watching to be a largely female habit. The situation in Fathiya's house, where the device is on almost all the time except when lessons are being given, supports this contention. Khadiga, like her cousin Farid, tends to see exactly what she wants to see in the foreign shows broadcast every night in Cairo. Although she considers herself an avid fan of "Falcon Crest," she never seems overly interested in the plot. She does, however, like the clothes worn on the program very much, and frequently comments on them with an enthusiastic "*shīk ʕawī*" (very chic). She also comments on the commercials, which overwhelmingly feature blond Egyptians (and often blond foreigners with Egyptian voice-over), racy clothes, and a generally Western-oriented attitude. They all occasionally follow Egyptian serials, in which case the plot tends to be of more concern than in the foreign shows. The whole family saw most of the episodes of "White Flag," and commented much more enthusiastically on Fadda's wealth than on Dr. Mufid's high learning.

Khadiga laughs at a Cadbury chocolate-bar advertisement in which a singer made up to look like Abd al-Halim Hafiz (the only singer after Abd al-Wahhab generally considered to be of his stature) croons "*ya Snāk . . .*" (o Snack...) to the tune of a famous Abd al-Halim film song called "*Ahwāk*" (I love you). A girl in a short flouncy skirt hovers about the piano. The candy bar in question is being marketed as an excellent snack for two because it has dividers that allow it to be easily broken into two or four parts. "*Ya Snāk, wi-atmannā tigīb wayyāk, shūkulāta bi-ṭaʿmⁱ Snāk, iSnāk, wi-ana wi-inta itnayn ya malāk, wi-itnayn li-itnayn ya Snāk*" (Snack, I hope you bring one with you, chocolate with the taste of Snack, Snack, me and you, the two of us my angel, two [pieces] for us two, O Snack).[13]

Khadiga is fond of Madonna, and even more enamored of Michael Jackson. She wrinkles her nose in distaste at the mention of Abd al-Wahhab and Umm Kulthum. "They are old. Do you know what 'old' means? *Nobody* listens to *them* anymore." I protest that many people still love Abd al-Wahhab, and the press calls him "last of the giants" (meaning him, Umm Kulthum and Abd al-Halim). "'*Awāgīz*" (old folks), she says. She likes a pair of female Egyptian singers whose stage names are Anūshkā and Sīmōn. Both singers utilize Western vocal styles, dress like AUC students and sport "big hair" – dyed, blow-dried, and coiffed expensively.

On the day that we all go on the outing to the park by the sluice gates most of the groups of students on the boat and in the park at the barrages are heavily chaperoned. One group of three boys and three girls, who are not, sits not far from where we eat our picnic lunch. They indulge in nothing more wicked than playing a game in which two lines are drawn on the ground, between which is placed a handkerchief. Two competitors approach the handkerchief warily, each trying to grab it before the other can tag him. The boys play, while the girls watch.

At the end of the day we steam back up the Nile as the sun sets. A small rock band begins playing on the upper deck where we sit. Fathiya smiles politely. Widad is tired and cranky. Khadiga, Farid the thwarted teacher, and Nabil, however, all enjoy the show. The music comes to an end before we reach the dock, but the group of unchaperoned students bring out a tape deck and play a song by the popular singer Ahmad Adawiya. All the songs on the tape are up-tempo rock songs belted out by Adawiya, with none of the ornamented vocal technique of an Abd al-Wahhab. Fathiya looks a bit annoyed at the song. "*Balāsh il-aghānī il-habṭa di*" (enough of these vulgar songs). Surprisingly, Farid the Islamist smiles, obviously enjoying the music. The first song is about a girl.

Daughter of the sultan
The water's in your hand
On the ʿAbbās Bridge
Why don't you look at me
Water me, water me more,
Goodbye, my sweet, goodbye,
Call and I'll come
have pity on this wretch
and Adawiya is thirsty.
she walks and people walk.
my little fruit, my pineapple
the water in your hand is sugar
off to your far city,
all the way to Maṣr il-Gadīda.

(from the cassette album "Adawiya 91")

The ʿAbbās Bridge to which the song refers is the only bridge over the Nile with one lane for animal and bicycle traffic, another for cars – in effect one for the poor and one for the rich. The bridge passes from a relatively affluent neighborhood on the west bank to a series of quite poor neighborhoods on the east side of the river. The song also evokes a sense of place through its mention of Maṣr il-Gadīda, a neighborhood far from the ʿAbbās Bridge, like saying, "I'll follow you to the ends of the earth – even to Maṣr il-Gadīda!" – far enough, anyway, to be an excruciating commute for anyone not favored with access to a private car. And most of the people on our boat fit into precisely that category: commuters, poor people lost in the crowd, boys looking for girls without much hope of marriage.

As the song blares, a saucy girl in a rather tight-fitting dress begins dancing on the back of the boat. Nobody joins her, but many of the boys on the boat clap appreciatively. "Shame," says Fathiya. Farid, Nabil, and I look on, interested, but we do not clap. Khadiga laughs, not embarrassed at all by the spectacle. Widad has fallen asleep. The girl continues dancing as the sun goes down over the Nile. Our university outing is over.

Education: statistical reprise

Education plays an essential role in the lives of people such as this extended family. Likewise, all of the popular culture we have considered so far, from "White Flag" to *Zuzu*, has turned on the value of education. Without it there is virtually no way to discuss the issue of modernity in popular culture or in real life. Education is supposed to bridge the gap between official media theory of what modernity should be and social practice which often takes place under conditions that are far from ideal. But "bridging the gap" between the media sales pitch for modernity and lived experience of the modern world does not mean that the two interact harmoniously. As the grim statistics quoted in chapter 3 indicated, education was neither easy to acquire nor as likely to bring material rewards as the traditional media fantasy would have it. The point about "statistical reality" bears repeating here because the popular culture we have seen draws a certain relationship between success in the modern school system and worldly success.

It comes as no surprise that to be illiterate is very likely to be poor (see fig. 6.1). What is less obvious is that for those in the middle ranges of income (between LE 250 and LE 1,000), educational attainment does not translate into salary. In fact almost a fifth of those earning less than

Fig. 6.1 Income distribution according to education level, 1974 (source: Abdel-Fadil 1982, 368). Middle income is marked with connected lines, extremes of poverty and wealth with bars

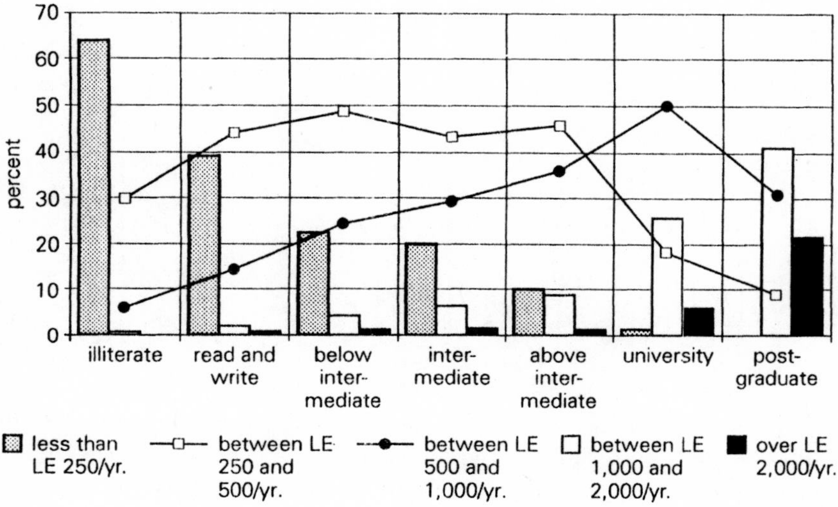

LE 500 per year – not a princely sum even in the early 1970s when *Zuzu* was made – had a university education.[14] Only at the upper income levels (over LE 1,000 per year) is there a correlation between income and paper qualifications.

A 1979 survey (Ibrahim 1982) found that while 15 percent of the sample were college graduates, being a college graduate was no guarantee of making even a relatively moderate income of LE 3,000 to LE 5,000.[15] Over 80 percent of this educated group earned an income that might be described as neither desperately poor nor extravagantly rich.[16] Even by the 1970s (when *Zuzu* was made) popular images that coupled middle-class educational attainment with material success no longer bore a solid relation to people's practical chances.[17] The discrepancy between the official view of education reflected in pre-1970s films and statistical reality, however, does not keep people such as Khadiga, Farid, and Nabil from wanting to be upwardly mobile. Education plays a prominent role in their strategies for achieving this goal. And despite their academic achievements, Khadiga and Nabil worry constantly about their lack of connections through which they can translate their institutional success into material gain. Figure 6.2 suggests that their worries are not unfounded.

By 1973 certain faculties and professions (engineering and law in this case) were in fact skewed towards sons and daughters of the bourgeoisie

Fig. 6.2 Class origins of subsamples of professional engineers, engineering and law students, 1973 (source: Abdel-Fadil 1982, 360)

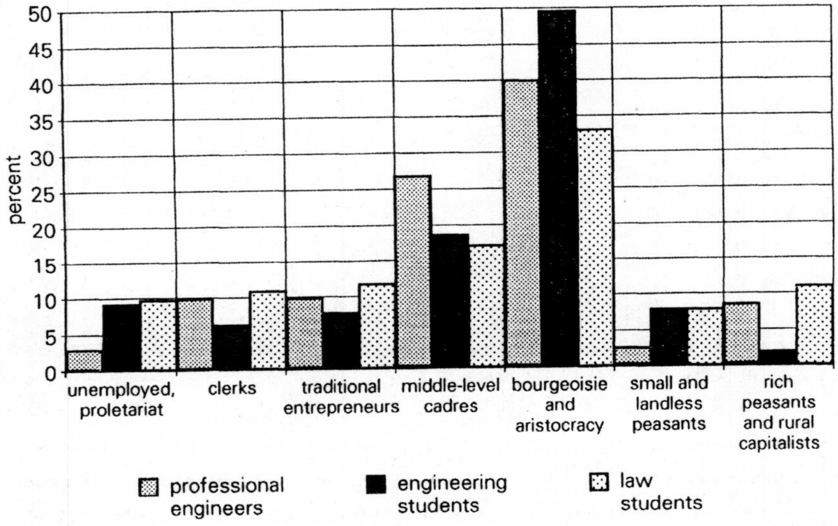

and the aristocracy. Medicine, like engineering, is among the prestige subjects (indeed, more prestigious according to Reid [1990, 182]), so it would not be unreasonable to expect the medical profession also to be skewed toward traditional elites. The overrepresentation of elites in the law faculty is slightly misleading. Graduating from law school is only a first step toward becoming a member of the Bar Association, and even bar membership is no guarantee of making the profession pay. One needs money and family connections. Even though the law faculty is the least prestigious among all the faculties (*ibid.*), only 10.6 percent of the law students were from petit bourgeois families (Abdel-Fadil 1982, 360), as was Khadiga. Medical training is similar to the legal profession in that graduating from the medical faculty alone does not grant access to training – preferably in a foreign school – in a specialty. For this, connections to the rich and powerful are necessary.

The relationships among class origin, profession, and income have not remained constant. If anything, social mobility seems to have declined. A survey in 1979 (Ibrahim 1982, 398) found that respondents – all heads of households – who counted themselves "professionals" had fathers from every category in the survey – professionals, executives, clerical workers, sales workers, production (factory) workers, service workers, and farmers. Clerical workers also claimed fathers in every category, as did executives and service workers. Those working in sales (a very broad category in most respects) also claimed fathers in every category except those of professionals and sales. The categories are crude, but the impression is of reasonable mobility. The following generation, however, were already in a different position. Professionals and executives of this generation (Nabil's and Khadiga's) were overwhelmingly sons of professionals. What class mobility there had been in that branch of society seemed over.

As class or occupational mobility froze, the figures for "education" seemed to keep on growing. Illiteracy was constantly being cut down. The number of people being put through school was increasing – the educational goals of the state appeared to have been met.[18] But being a college graduate, as we have seen, brought little in the way of security or income. Economically, education was an empty triumph.

Statistics suggest that it would be reasonable for the younger generation to view the modernism of their parents and grandparents with a degree of skepticism. The logic of education "raising the masses" is reflected hardly at all in correlations of income with diplomas and degrees. The hardening of occupational mobility, coupled with the stagnation in per capita income (see chapter 3), are problems to which modernist ideology has yet to provide satisfactory answers. The result, as we shall see, is that some makers of popular culture have rebelled against the optimism of *White Rose* and *Pay Attention to Zuzu*. Both are now just "old films" for those living in circumstances filmmakers had not envisaged, or at least not admitted.

1990: the wasteland

Another family I knew in Cairo was that of Yaḥyā Muḥammad Wagdī. Yahya died several years ago in a traffic accident. He was survived by three sons, ʿAbd Allāh, Ibrāhīm, and Yūsuf, two of whom are in college. Abd Allah, the oldest son, never advanced beyond the preparatory (junior high-school) level. Ibrahim is a senior English major in the college of education at ʿAyn Shams University. Yusuf is a sophomore in the college of law at Cairo University.

Yahya, who was a barber, could not afford to live close to the center of Cairo. Instead the family, comprising Yahya, his wife and children, and an elderly aunt, lived in Basātīn, a more recently built neighborhood to the south of Cairo which one can reach only through a tortuous journey in some combination of the Cairo metro, buses, microbuses (vans seating approximately fifteen that run on fixed routes), and walking. Basātīn is near Dār al-Salām, which was the home of Egypt's first television assembly plant, founded by decree in the early 1960s. Dār al-Salām was, therefore, a "popular" neighborhood by design. One official, whose titles included Deputy for Engineering Affairs at the Public Radio Company, Director of Planning and Broadcasting, and Chief of the Administrative Assembly of the Naṣr Company for the Manufacture of Television Sets, described the mission of Dār al-Salām's new factory as "to provide a means of culture and entertainment for each citizen . . . and among the important devices leading to the fulfillment of this goal is the television" ("*al-Tilifizyōn al-Miṣrī*" 1961, 28–29). Whatever the company's success in putting a television set in every home, it certainly succeeded in drawing vast numbers of people to Dār al-Salām, which is now one of the largest stops on the metro.

To get to Basātīn one boards any microbus heading east from where the street from the Dār al-Salām metro station joins the main road. At one point the main road veers to the south, and there the commuter disembarks. The entire trip from downtown Cairo to Basātīn costs 35 piasters – a very expensive commute for Yusuf and Ibrahim, who must go every day to Cairo and ʿAyn Shams Universities. Usually they ride a different microbus, which they pick up from an alley somewhere behind their house.

This microbus takes them cheaply to a road from which they can catch a full-sized bus into town for only 5 piasters. By metro the trip to central Cairo takes about an hour. The bus can require two hours in heavy traffic.

From a fruit stand on the outskirts of Basātīn, where our microbus lets us off, we walk through a narrow alley which becomes flooded in the winter when it rains. We pass a café named after the famous singer Umm Kulthum, and come to a large open space ringed by apartment buildings. During the day, laborers cut stone here for new buildings, and this activity covers everything with a fine dust. There is no vegetation in sight, and nothing is paved. Automobile traffic, bumper-to-bumper in much of Cairo for much of the day, is almost absent here, but the lack of paving is problematic when it rains. Not only do the streets become soggy, but so do the foundations of many of the buildings. Some of them collapse when the ground becomes muddy enough for foundations to shift slightly. At sunset this dusty plain is a remarkable sight. The buildings – a jumble of colors in different sizes and shapes – become lit by a fiery light. Dust rises from the plain, where boys play soccer in the evening. A few ruined and half-buried machines protrude from the ground.

Yahya's family lives in a small apartment located to one side of the dusty plain in the middle of Basātīn. Basātīn, which ironically means "gardens," is located on the edge of the vast cemetery on Cairo's southern limit. The neighborhood does not enjoy a good reputation. A wealthy young businessman I knew once described Basātīn as *in* the cemetery, but this was not true even metaphorically, at least of the part of Basātīn in which Yahya's family lived. In fact, many of the families in the area have middle-class aspirations. Yahya's family, in which two of the boys are in college, is not unusual. Although education is, for them and most of their neighbors, ruinously expensive, they pursue the modernist dream. There are few alternatives.

I met the family through Yusuf, the youngest son, who knew a mutual friend attending Cairo University. Periodically I visited them, and when Yusuf's older brother was studying for his final exams, I helped him study certain topics of English literature considered crucial for graduation.

Yusuf's father had been a barber, so there was no government pension after his death. His partners at the barbershop and several relatives give significant, if irregular, support. Abd Allah, the eldest son, had been forced to work cutting stone – arduous labor and very low paid – but now he is in the army. Yusuf and Ibrahim also work during summers and vacation, at stonecutting and occasional construction work, but their main focus is on school. The family's monthly income, irregular at best, rarely tops LE 100. They have not yet been forced to sell their belongings, which include an imported television (not manufactured in Dār al-Salām, or even in Egypt) and a refrigerator (which was manufactured in Egypt). At one point they looked into using their apartment, which they own, as collateral for a loan, but the foundations turned out to be unsound, making it impossible to borrow money against the property.

Yusuf is the less serious of the two brothers in college. He did not do particularly well in the *thanawīya ʿāmma* exam, and was therefore enrolled in the law faculty. He passed the freshman-year exams without undue strain, but his older brother fears that if Yusuf does not start to apply himself more seriously he will be forced to repeat his sophomore year – an indulgence the family can ill afford. Yusuf is a carefree, impressionable youth who wears a *kābūryā* haircut. The style – a "fade," shaved on the sides and about an inch long on top – comes from a popular film called *Kābūryā* (Crabs).[19] The film is an Egyptian cross between the American boxing film *Rocky* and the Japanese film *Tampopo*, which is about food and sex. *Crabs* is about food and class. One catches crabs by holding a light in or near the water, which attracts the creatures, allowing the crabber to net them. In the film corrupt rich people entice poor people with the lure of money.

The protagonist of *Crabs*, Ḥasan "Hudhud" (hoopoe), is the son of a glassblower in a poor traditional neighborhood. His hobby is boxing, and he dreams of one day making it to the Olympics. Early in the film we see Hudhud boxing in an impromptu ring set up in the street outside his *baladī* apartment building. The raven-haired daughter of a man who runs the gym where he works out looks down from a second-story window as Hudhud boxes. Distracted by the beautiful girl, he nearly loses his bout.

Hudhud and his *shilla* (a group of close friends from a common neighborhood or school) are tough young men, but good-hearted. They are reminiscent of the salutary images sometimes associated with the traditional *futūwa* – tough guys who unofficially protect neighborhoods (or, in the worst-case scenario, prey on neighborhoods). We see them rescuing an unfortunate man being thrown out of his apartment into the street by a heartless landlord. They fight off the landlord's goons and move the man's furniture back into his apartment (what happens after this we never find out).

The young men meet some bored rich people on the Nile in the dim light of dawn. Hudhud and company are singing their theme song about hunting crabs. The rich people sail by on a massive tourist boat. Most of the rich people are distracted by the spectacle of a cockfight arranged for their entertainment, but while they are betting on "the circassian" or "the red," two of their number wander to the rail and spy Hudhud and his friends in their tiny boat. The two are Madam Ḥurrīya, a stunningly sluttish woman, and her curvaceous young secretary, Nūr. Although Nur appears throughout the film attired in spectacularly immodest clothes, she is, in fact, from al-Gamālīya, a poor respectable neighborhood much like Hudhud's. Madam Hurriya speaks foreign languages, French and English, as much as Arabic, particularly when talking to her husband, Sulaymān. The couple also have a retinue of foreigners and foreign-language-speaking Egyptians in attendance. None of them seems to do anything except party and gamble on whatever events Hurriya and Sulayman arrange. Conversations in French and English in the film are fairly extensive – to the point that they are subtitled for the Arabic-speaking audience.

The women entice the boxers onto their boat, and later Madam Hurriya and Nur lure the young men out to their villa in the countryside. The purpose of bringing the *baladī* boxers to Madam Hurriya's sumptuous villa is for them to provide entertainment – a human-scale version of the cockfight that had been taking place on the boat when Hudhud first met the women. Hudhud and his friends are to fight each other and various challengers brought in by their rich patrons at parties. The boxers get a flat fee for their efforts – a few hundred Egyptian pounds per bout – while the wealthy spectators bet tens of thousands.

The secretary, Nur, like Hudhud and his friends, is trying to get what she can from her rich bosses. Her gimmick is to keep stringing along Sulayman Bey (Madam Hurriya's philandering husband) by wearing the shortest and tightest of miniskirts, but never actually putting out. She warns Hudhud that if he wants to be allowed to stay at the farm and make money he must devise a more entertaining gimmick than mere boxing.

As one might guess, part of the "entertainment" envisioned by the corrupt Madam Hurriya involves using the young men as sex toys. After the first boxing match she brings Hudhud into her bedroom and asks him for a massage. This kind of forwardness confuses poor Hudhud, and one sees him constantly fidgeting, trying to work out what strings are attached to this apparently open invitation to debauchery with a married woman. Madam Hurriya then turns to Hudhud and says, "Do you know, Hudhud, that I write poetry?" The young man's embarrassment increases. "I'll let you hear it," she tells him.

Just as Hurriya and company get all the foreign-language lines in the film, so Hurriya gets the only lines in classical Arabic. The poem is a parody of classical style – a clumsy attempt at seduction delivered as if it were high art – which, at the showing of the film I attended, elicited gales of laughter from the audience:

I dreamed of you yesterday
Undoing my braids and breaking my silence
  [Hudhud becomes visibly more uncomfortable as she continues]
Come and water me, release my madness
Come, surely, and allay my doubts
Come openly and rend my tranquility
Come rustling and caress my limbs
  [She pauses. Hudhud thinks the poem is over, and struggles to find something polite to say. Unexpectedly she starts again, laying on the faux passion even more stridently, bringing still more laughter from the audience.]
Come as you like
Come, a lion to my jungle, reaching out to my womanhood
Come as you like – you are delight
Other than death, and other than all legends

Madam Hurriya pauses, leaning forward almost into Hudhud's lap. Just at this moment Nur, the secretary, enters, telling Madam Hurriya that Sulayman, her husband, is looking for her. Hudhud is off the hook for now.

Plate 10 A poster from *Crabs* (1990). On the left Hudhud, crablike, brandishes his boxing gloves like claws. On the right Madam Hurriya throws herself at an embarrassed Hudhud

As time goes by a competition develops between Madam Hurriya and Nur over Hudhud. Of course Madam Hurriya's ready availability tempts the young man, but the fact of her marriage to Sulayman Bey stirs his conscience. In any case, the unmarried and relatively fresh Nur is more to his liking. Not only do his instincts lead the boxer to the secretary rather than her employer, but when all is said and done Hurriya wants a boy-toy, while Nur, still the canny *bint al-balad* despite her miniskirt, sees in Hudhud a potential husband – but only if he can use the rich people long enough to earn a pile of cash by which she can live in the style to which she has become accustomed. This, she warns him, will be tricky and requires that Hudhud develop a gimmick of his own.

The precariousness of Hudhud's newfound wealth becomes apparent at a party in which Sulayman complains that Hudhud and his boxers are becoming boring. Madam Hurriya, still lusting after the young fighter, bets her husband that Hudhud is a better singer than ʿAzīz, their bloated master of ceremonies. She throws this challenge at Hudhud, who fidgets nervously.

"Sing that thing you and your friends were doing when I first saw you on the boat," she tells him.

"But madam, that was just a trifle . . . you know . . . it has no . . ." He seems on the verge of saying, "it has no meaning." But he sings it anyway.

The song features almost no instruments traditional to an Arab musical ensemble: it has synthesizer, drum set, bass guitar, and electric guitar – and an amplified *ṭabla* (traditional drum). The first line, repeated several times to a driving rhythm, is "*ʕazʕaz kabūryā* . . . *ʕazʕaz* / *ʕazʕaz kabūryā* . . . *ʕazʕaz*" (crack open the crab . . . munch munch / crack open the crab . . . munch munch). Plainly the "crabs" are Hudhud and his friends, and the rich people are doing the munching. For anyone who does not get the point, there are film posters showing Aḥmad Zakī, the actor who plays Hudhud, with gloved fists raised in a crablike pose.

The full lyrics are as follows:

Crack open the crab	munch
Crack open the crab	munch
I'm at loose ends[20]	(chorus)
So what's to cry about?	(chorus)
Night and day, O Bey	(chorus)
I'm hunting for crab	(chorus)
And they're hunting me, O Bey	(chorus)
Hunting for crab	(chorus)
I get high on it – nothing beats it	(chorus)
Crack open the crab, crack open the crab	

> If they crack me open, what will I munch on?
> My father told me, "Throw out your net
> And don't forget the one who wants to net you."[21]
> My mother said, "The sea will eat you."
> *Ash-shinganinga nau* I'm not a fish eater![22]
> *Fīgā bīgā* doesn't nourish me
> And *ḥāgā fīgā* don't make me happy[23]
> Bravo to the tough guy who turns his back on the world
> Even when his punch misses the target.[24]

Hudhud's song, full of energy and wit (especially compared to Madam Hurriya's travesty of classical poetry) is a hit, but all this means is that Hurriya wins her bet with Sulayman. There is nothing in it for Hudhud but a chance to stay in the company of the rich. He still needs a gimmick.

Hudhud stumbles onto a plan to organize a tournament of chubby female wrestlers, each of whom is named after an Umm Kulthum song. In this game he controls the betting while others do the work. He begins making serious money and his dream of marrying the secretary seems within his grasp. The eventual winner of the tournament is a grossly fat woman wrestling under the name "*Inta ʿumrī*" (You are my life) – the massively popular collaboration between Abd al-Wahhab (who wrote the song) and Umm Kulthum (who sang it).[25] This mockery of Egyptian womanhood and a cherished Egyptian cultural icon causes one of Hudhud's three boxer friends to walk out.

Although Hudhud's stock with his corrupt patrons goes up, his position is still precarious. Eventually Hudhud rejects Hurriya's advances once too often. She and Sulayman devise a plan to finally break the defiant Hudhud. They will import a ringer – a boxer who is far larger, stronger, and better trained than Hudhud. Sulayman cautions her that it might not work. "The boy isn't stupid. When he started winning money he forgot his training. He might just keep his money and walk away."

But Hurriya's plan is more devious than that. Rather than throw the ringer directly at Hudhud she will feed one of Hudhud's friends to the ravenous new shark and lure Hudhud into betting on the bout. She has in mind ʿAntar, a hulking giant who joined the group of boxers at the beginning of the story. Antar is loyal and good-hearted, but no athlete, and lacking even the most rudimentary skill in boxing. The mere idea of putting Antar into the ring causes Hudhud's *shilla* to abandon him in disgust. Hurriya lures Antar to his destruction by matching him against an ordinary Egyptian boxer, who still punches the big man at will but is too small to do serious damage. Then in the middle of the bout, for "technical reasons," she substitutes her ringer. The match is over in seconds with

Antar lying flat on the canvas bleeding, and Hudhud has lost the last of his friends and all his money.

Following this, the blood-sated rich people sing another song about food. This number is sung to a Latin-sounding tune; the words are nothing but the names of expensive imported foods alternating with *baladī* foods, each dish sung in turns by Hurriya, Sulayman, and Aziz:

> Shatta . . . cha cha cha . . .
> Shatta . . . cha cha cha . . .
> Filet mignon [Hurriya]
> Chateaubriand [Sulayman]
> [E]scalope pané
> [E]scalope maison
> . . .
> *Shakshūka*
> *Bessāra*
> *Kammunīya*
> *Mulukhiiiiiiyaaa* . . . [drawn out operatically by Aziz]
> Dis-moi, pourquoi, al-shatta cha cha cha [all together]

The food song complements the *Crabs* theme song which Hudhud sang earlier, and which is also about food. In this case, however, the effect is to underscore the alienation of the bored cosmopolitans from any heritage, let alone their own. *Baladī* delicacies, to them, are nothing but novelties, much like *baladī* boxers or *baladī* female wrestlers named after Umm Kulthum songs: when the novelty wears thin they are easily discarded.

After Antar gets pounded it is up to Hudhud to avenge him. As Sulayman had predicted, Hudhud sees the dangers of his situation. But rather than go into the ring immediately, he goes back to his old neighborhood and asks his boxing coach to train him for his big bout. Of course all his old neighbors have heard about Hudhud's exploits, and they put on a great show of disgust at his apparent debauchery. Hudhud comes at night and stands in front of the building where his coach, "Captain" Ḥasanayn, lives. He yells for the coach to come down to talk to him. Instead, one by one, the windows light up and righteous neighbors heap abuse on the errant boxer. Finally he lashes back at them, cataloging all their evils so that his own dalliance with corruption looks mild by comparison:

> Ḥagg ʿAbd al-Salām, did God make you buy [subsidized] imported meat at the cooperative store and then sell it as [more highly prized] *baladī* for LE 25? All you people know you're no better than me. Sayyid (turns to man smoking cigarette in doorway), aren't you the one who plunged his wife and kids into poverty and then put her to work on Sulaymān Bāsha Street [a downtown street where much prostitution goes on under cover of "maid services"]? Shame on you letting your

wife spend money on you that she earns working in people's houses. You know what I mean. And you Amrād (turning to another man) – making furniture out of wood you know is rotten. You know what I'm saying? And Captain Hasanayn, "father of captains," "uncle" Hasanayn. Marrying your sixteen-year-old daughter to a man your own age – no, older than you. Shame. Any of you – if you found a piaster in the garbage you'd take it. I've gotten pounded, wrecked, just to make some money by the sweat of my brow. I'm not saying I'm better than anyone, but none of you are any better than me. If anyone thinks they're better than me then come down here. Come here. I'll wait for you right here.

Hudhud's *baladī* eloquence wins the day: Captain Hasanayn agrees to be his trainer again. We see a brief "*Rocky*" sequence where Hudhud jogs through the medieval sections of Cairo, Captain Hasanayn following behind on a bicycle. In *Crabs* the parallel to the "unorthodox training" scenes in *Rocky* (Sylvester Stallone pounding savagely on a side of beef in a freezer) is a brief glimpse of Hudhud puffing hard on a glassblowing pipe (his father's trade).

The actual bout is brutal. Hurriya announces that there will be no betting on the bout, but that she will give the winner a purse of LE 100,000. Scrawny Hudhud gives as good as he gets from the much larger and stronger boxer. Nur cannot stand to watch what she assumes will be a slaughter, and leaves the villa. We see her weeping on the steps of the villa, telling herself that she truly loved Hudhud, but that now Madam Hurriya will have her way. She vows not to return to the company of the corrupt rich people.

Madam Hurriya has her own soliloquy during the fight. We see her face in closeup: "Tell Aziz to get his roosters ready. They're better than human beings." She looks at Sulayman, and the camera switches momentarily to show him looking back at her curiously. Then back to her face. "Sulayman. To hell with you. To hell with all of you. You're all liars. Nobody understands Hurriya." The fight goes on furiously, and Hurriya continues her soliloquy. "Who told you to gamble?[26] You want to make lots of money from nothing? Okay – play on. Play so you can win. You are a bad boy, Hudhud."

The boxers land simultaneous haymakers and both of them collapse. Hudhud, however, has just enough energy to drag himself to his feet before the referee counts them both out. He wins. Hurriya enters the ring and hands the bloody but unbowed Hudhud a plate upon which piles of bills sit. "The money you wanted," she says.

Hudhud takes the money and replies, "I need every piaster of it." He pauses. "But now it no longer has any hold on me." He throws it into the air and leaves the ring, leaves the villa, and returns to his neighborhood.[27]

The last scene at the villa is of the corrupt but ultimately unhappy Hurriya and Sulayman embracing in the ring as a man in tuxedo walks slowly around them playing a sad tune on a trumpet.

The film itself ends with Hudhud and his *shilla* reconstituted now that they have all rejected the corrupting temptation of making easy money by entertaining the idle rich. The *shilla* has built a human ladder with the enormous Antar on the bottom and Hudhud on the top, looking into the window of the beautiful girl who distracted him in his fight at the beginning of the film. As Antar laughingly groans under the weight of four men, Hudhud professes his love to the girl, promises to get a job in the neighborhood, and then kisses her just before her father enters the room and he has to flee. The final scene shows the young men cavorting about the boxing ring as the theme song plays.

Yusuf has a cassette tape of the theme song to the film. He tells me that the words are nonsense but that he likes it anyway. The song actually contains no lines of nonsense. People who say the song "has no meaning" often elaborate by saying that "uneducated" people listen to such music. The most commonly mentioned context for uneducated people listening to "vulgar" music is in microbuses such as the one leading from the metro stop to Basātīn. However, Husayn al-Imam, the lyricist and composer of the song, is not from a low-class milieu, but rather lives (and always has lived) in a well-appointed apartment, and never uses microbuses or other modes of mass transit.[28] The songs – indeed the film itself – were al-Imam's attempt to imagine the tastes and discontents of people less well off than himself. Yusuf, with his *Crabs* haircut and cassette tape, is living evidence that he did this rather well.

The energy of the theme song meshes perfectly with images portrayed in the film – especially scenes from early in the film when the director is trying to establish the characters of Hudhud and his friends. When we see the boys roaming about the streets doing good deeds and thoroughly enjoying themselves early in *Crabs*, the streets appear friendly and colorful – energetic. Very few contemporary Egyptian films convey such a feeling. Recent films aiming for "cinematic realism" tend to portray the street as dirty and threatening. *Crabs* is practically alone in showing the street as an almost magical place, not without danger, but also not without charm. And despite the accusations of "nonsense," the *Crabs* theme song conveys a very straightforward meaning: the big fish eat the little fish. The song's appeals to a "bey" – an archaic, originally Turkish, figure once the focus of envy and resentment in Egyptian cinema – are in keeping with the film's content, as is the theme of hunting smaller creatures and cracking them open (*ʕazʕaz*) between one's teeth like a nut or seed.

Several wealthy people I knew objected to the film, telling me that nobody actually lives like the rich people in *Crabs*. Specifically they rejected the idea that there were people with nothing to do but organize boxing and wrestling matches for their own jaded entertainment. They also criticized the poor but honorable neighborhood shown in the film as unrealistic, asserting again that "people don't live that way." In both cases, they found fault with specific images: the idle rich hiring poor boys to entertain them; and in the poor neighborhood, a boxing ring set up in the street.[29] Yusuf, when confronted with such objections, does not dispute them. He is willing to admit that the images portrayed in *Crabs* may be grossly exaggerated, and regards extreme criticism of the wealthy as motivated by jealousy. He liked *Crabs*, he says, just because it was a *qiṣṣa gamīla* (a beautiful story), and says he enjoys listening to the songs from the film. But he is either unwilling or unable to explain the words to me.

This is not because the words to songs are unimportant in any general sense. Magazines such as the youth-oriented *Shabāb* (Youth), and even the public-sector "T.V. Guide," *al-Idhāʿa wa-l-tilifizyōn* (Radio and television), regularly publish the texts and translations of Western popular songs. I have told Yusuf that in American pop music the words are not always as important as the tunes, but this makes no sense to him. He constantly asks me to help him understand the words to the Bee Gees' song "Staying Alive." I can get as far as "You can tell by the way I use my walk I'm a woman's man, no time to talk." And naturally the chorus is clear: "Staying alive, staying alive . . ." After this the lyrics elude me. But I never succeeded in getting Yusuf to have a go at the words to *Crabs.* "There is no meaning to that song," he tells me. "The government banned it because it's *hābiṭ* [vulgar]." Other people tell me the same thing. There are also rumors that the song was banned because it was sung by an actor who was not a member of the musicians' guild.[30] In fact I had no difficulty obtaining a copy at an open-air market in downtown Cairo. But neither does the availability of the tape disprove allegations that it was banned, as this particular market – in al-ʿAtaba on Twenty-sixth of July Street just to one side of Ezbekīya Gardens – was often the target of police raids for *sharāyiṭ habṭa* (vulgar tapes).[31] Yusuf, with his devotion to the officially despised *Crabs* music and his *Crabs* haircut, inhabits a Cairene twilight zone – not openly rebellious and yet unabashedly attracted to the symbols of "bad taste" regularly denounced by the establishment. The official path of optimistic modernity is a distant rumor to him.

Yusuf's brother Ibrahim is the more serious of the two. He cannot afford to be frivolous because his final exams are fast approaching. Final exams include sections on translation – both into and from Arabic – composition, novels, linguistics, and poetry. Linguistics and poetry are the most feared subjects. The linguistics book, he says, is hopelessly complicated; none of the students can make head or tail of it. I examine the book and concur. It makes no sense to me either. I tell Ibrahim he is on his own here. I have no expertise in the subject, and can't even guess what some of the technical passages are supposed to mean.

The poetry is even more problematic. Ibrahim has no trouble with most of it. The old poetry seems rather formal and predictable. He feels confident from lectures on romanticism and naturalism that the more modern poetry will also cause few problems for him in the exam. Even Yeats appears relatively straightforward. But the one obstacle – the only barrier standing between him and a chance to help his family escape grinding poverty – is T. S. Eliot's "The Waste Land." Ibrahim pleads with me for help on this poem. "Please, Mister, what is he talking about? I've read it and read it, but that poem makes no sense."

I am taken aback by his desperation. "The Waste Land," I tell him, doesn't make sense to most of us. It is so full of allusions to mythology and literature that only experts in literature can really understand all its nuances. Since Ibrahim is not in an English-literature program, and can barely speak the language, it seems preposterous for him to be forced to learn such a poem. Ibrahim looks grim. "But one professor insists that no student will pass who cannot satisfactorily answer a question on 'The Waste Land.' He is a very nice man, but on this point he won't budge."

Although I never understood the poem well, I decide to do the best I can to explain what "The Waste Land" might be about. It transpires that the professor has hinted broadly that the question will require the students to discuss whether the poem is hopeful or pessimistic. "Usually in America," I tell him, "people think of it as a pessimistic poem." I go on to give him a few general pointers about the state of Western civilization immediately following World War I, the feelings of devastation and loss. I tell him that even before the war people felt a sense of dislocation due to the effects of the industrial revolution. This seems to be working. Ibrahim begins to look hopeful.

"Don't try to memorize the entire poem," I tell him, warming to the task. "Just get a few lines so you can quote them on the exam. The opening lines – 'April is the cruellest month, breeding/Lilacs out of the dead land . . .' – are extremely famous, and set the tone of everything that follows." We pick out a few more strategic lines, some of which make sense to him, and some of which remain obscure. "Madame Sosostris" is a tough one. "Why does he suddenly start talking about her?" asks Ibrahim. "Where does she come from?" I don't really know why she is in the poem, so I start guessing. "It's sort of a joke. He brings in the image of some superstitious old biddy dealing cards with mythological pictures on them, trying to tell the future. 'The wisest woman in Europe' is just a pathetic hag trying to fool some other foolish woman into thinking she knows the future. And of course, the future is grim: 'Fear death by water.' More pessimistic stuff. It just adds to the feeling that European culture is fractured and decrepit. Look, he even throws in lines from Shakespeare: 'Those are pearls that were his eyes' [I am reading the notes now]. In fact, the poem is full of fragments" (I show him the notes, which reference a multitude of works neither of us has read).

Ibrahim looks a bit dubious. He has heard plenty of criticisms of Europe from the neighborhood fundamentalists – *sunniyīn* (literally people who follow the *sunna*, or traditions of the Prophet Muhammad) as Ibrahim and Yusuf call them – who drop by often to remind Ibrahim to pray, and stare suspiciously at me. But this image of a dotty old hag dealing cards doesn't quite hit the spot for Ibrahim. We move on to the lines about the secretary whose date

> Endeavours to engage her in caresses
> Which still are unreproved, if undesired.
> Flushed and decided, he assaults at once;
> Exploring hands encounter no defence;
> His vanity requires no response,
> And makes a welcome of indifference.

"Aha," says Ibrahim, "they've lost religion, and now they just have sex with anyone they meet." "Yes," I reply, not liking where our conversation is going, but not wanting to interrupt a basically sound reading of the poem.

We locate a few more grim images of cultural decay in "The Waste Land." Corrupt old Tiresias laughing at casual fornication, rats' alley, bones, corpses, unfaithful women, aborted babies, neglected churches, and all the rest start to make more sense to Ibrahim. We finally arrive at the last section of the poem, "What the Thunder Said." "Water seems to be the important thing here," I tell him. "Before we've got all these drowned sailors and polluted rivers. Now the symbols are reversed. We've got an arid plain and all these 'hooded hoardes swarming/ Over endless plains, stumbling in cracked earth,' and 'Dead mountain mouth of carious teeth that cannot spit.' We're through all this to the other side, dangling our feet in the water and fishing. All through this section we get hints of rain, which symbolizes salvation from cultural ruin." Ibrahim takes this as a sign that the poem is, finally, optimistic. I tell him, "You could say that, but look, he's saying, 'Shall I at least set my lands in order?' and 'These fragments I have shored against my ruins.' He's made it to safety, but lost most everything in the process."

"Yes," Ibrahim replies, "but by the end he's turning to the East. See, the notes say that the voice of the thunder, 'DA,' '*Datta*,' '*Dayadhvam*,' and '*Damyata*' are from Indian religion. The water comes from the East. He wants to renew civilization through Eastern religions." I maintain that this represents scant hope for Europeans, but I don't challenge his interpretation too vigorously. He is sure that what his professor wants to hear in the exam is that the poem is primarily optimistic, and this is what he will say. I see fragments, but Ibrahim sees a watery Eastern-inspired resurrection of European culture, so resurrection it is.

Several weeks after the exams I go to visit Ibrahim and Yusuf. The results were to have been announced in early July, and it is now late July. For the two brothers the outcome of finals is mixed. Yusuf's negligent ways have caught up with him. He has failed several subjects, and will be forced to repeat a year of law school. Ibrahim is not pleased. "You think we can afford for you to stay in school forever? Why didn't you study harder?" Yusuf looks sheepish, but says nothing. His *Crabs* haircut has grown out now, but he has moved on to new fashion statements. Now it is high-topped sneakers, worn unlaced in the style of American youth. I don't inquire where the money for the sneakers came from.

Ibrahim has good news and bad news, and bad news again. He is one of only three students in a class of several dozen education-school English majors who passed the poetry section of the exam. The bad news is that he failed the linguistics section. I offer condolences, but Ibrahim assures me it is not complete disaster, because students who fail only one or two subjects during their senior year are allowed to retake these sections of the exam during the summer. He is confident that given time to concentrate on one subject he can pass. The really bad news is that Ibrahim has received a letter from the army. Within a few months he is expected to begin his military service. He considers it unlikely that he will be required to serve as an officer – something that occasionally happens to new recruits. (No one wants to be an officer, because it means three years of service instead of just one. The slightly higher officer's pay is considered scant consolation for having to serve two extra years.) Only-sons are exempted from military service, but of course Ibrahim has two brothers, one of whom is already in the army. Rumor has it that for LE 30,000 one can buy one's way out of military service, but this is an astronomical sum to Ibrahim's family.[32] There is no way out, and Ibrahim worries that his absence will be detrimental to his already unstudious brother Yusuf. His older brother Abd Allah should be getting out of the army at about the time Ibrahim enters, but he will be little help to Yusuf at school, and the money he can earn from menial labor will only help the family marginally.

Ibrahim expects to come home in worn olive-drab fatigues, desperate for some decent food after months of minimal army fare. If he is really unlucky there will be some crisis which results in an extension of his military service (in fact, the 1991 Gulf War occurred, but it was too brief and decisive to necessitate the extension of military service). People still speak with dread of the late 1960s and early 1970s, when chronic conflict with Israel made the need for manpower so great that some draftees served as long as seven years.

I leave Yusuf and Ibrahim's home at sunset. They accompany me to the main road where I will pick up the microbus. As we pass through the open space in the middle of Basātīn the hot sun turns the ring of apartment buildings into fiery pillars. Feral dogs bark from a half-buried bus. Little puffs of dust rise from where some boys are playing soccer. Not a drop of water in sight, and no vegetation.

> Here is no water but only rock
> Rock and no water and the sandy road

As we pass the Café Umm Kulthum a few tired men in *gallabiyya*s are listening to the "Umm Kulthum Show" – a period around sundown each day when a government radio station plays songs by the great singer. Today they are playing "You Are My Life," the name of Hudhud's champion female wrestler taken from the first Umm Kulthum–Abd al-Wahhab collaboration. When "You Are My Life" was first broadcast over the radio in 1964 it stopped traffic in the middle-class neighborhood of Shubrā while people listened to the song as it played over loudspeakers set up in cafés just for this event.

> Your eyes return me to my days gone by,
> Taught me to rue my past and its wounds.
> All that I saw before my eyes saw you
> Is a life wasted, how can I reckon it?
> You are my life, which began with the light of your morning.

Ibrahim and Yusuf stop at the café for a cup of tea. I go on to my microbus.

Madame Sosostris

Many of my friends, such as Farid, the math teacher, or Nabil, the medical student, vehemently denied that Egypt's intellectual elite lived in a cosmopolitan milieu in which competence in foreign languages was an important marker of sophistication. Not that they were hostile to the study of foreign languages in principle: Nabil in particular defended the need for medical professionals to have some competence so that Egypt could "catch up" with the latest developments in medicine. But at the same time, speaking foreign languages (especially English, the dominant foreign language taught in the Egyptian educational system) was, for them, an unbearable act of snobbishness. "It's necessary only for science," Farid allowed, "but not for anything else." Their assumption was that Egyptian English speakers were a social and economic elite, but not an intellectual elite.

Al-Ahrām, the largest, most authoritative Egyptian newspaper, had a more expansive view of the value of English. The establishment of an English-language weekly version of *al-Ahrām* was, by the late 1980s, a high priority for the *al-Ahrām* organization, which in recent years had aggressively expanded the range of its publications, adding a sports magazine (*al-Ahrām al-riyāḍī*) and a women's magazine (*Nuṣf al-dunyā*) to its roster of publications, which already included a daily newspaper and an economics magazine (*al-Ahrām al-iqtiṣādī*). Farid reacted unenthusiastically to the news that *al-Ahrām* was about to begin publication of an English-language paper. "What, in English? '*al-Ahrām lil-khawāgāt*' [*al-Ahrām* for foreigners]? Why don't we just become the fifty-second state?" But I could not afford to be so dismissive, since I needed a job.

I began working at *al-Ahram Weekly* four months before the paper began publication. During the time I worked at the paper weekly "editorial meetings" – really brainstorming sessions since there was not yet a paper to edit – were held to discuss what the new publication would be like. Approximately half those attending the meetings were foreigners with varying levels of journalistic experience (I, for example, had absolutely none). The Egyptians at the meetings ranged from hopeful recent graduates sitting on the outer margins of the room to a number of editors, former editors, and journalists with many years' experience working on the local staffs of such foreign agencies as UPI and Reuters. The meetings were held in English to accommodate those who could not understand Arabic. We met around a large round conference table on the fourth floor of *al-Ahrām*'s modern twelve-story office building on Galā' Street, a narrow, dusty artery overshadowed by a massive "flyover" – really a highway raised twenty feet above ground level – and paralleled by a trolley-car track which was occasionally, and frighteningly, shared by buses.

Al-Ahrām is often referred to in the foreign press as a "semiofficial" newspaper. In the course of our early meetings Muḥammad Salmāwī, the managing editor of the new project and foreign editor for the parent organization, attempted to dispel the notion that *al-Ahrām* was a government paper.[33] This was largely for the benefit of the foreigners, who were worried that the government would place severe restrictions on the content of the publication. "Yes," Salmawi told us, "*al-Ahrām* was nationalized during the time of Abdel Nasser, and yes, it is still a public-sector company, but this no longer means that the paper is censored. We have assurances from Ibrāhīm Nāfiʿ (the editor of the parent organization) that the English weekly will be fully independent." Our paper would, however, be run by *al-Ahrām* editors, would use *al-Ahrām* facilities and would carry *al-Ahrām* opinions on its editorial page.

Most of the foreigners on the staff in those early days assumed that the readership of the new publication would be mainly foreigners. But this was not the assumption of the senior Egyptian staff. Salmawi affirmed that of course the paper would serve as an "authentic Egyptian voice" to the outside world, but he also insisted that there was a large English-speaking nonforeign constituency within Egypt. Perhaps his assumption was correct, although I never met large numbers of Egyptians who would prefer to read a newspaper in English when numerous Arabic papers were available.[34]

Salmawi himself spoke English fluently, and with very little accent. He was a graduate of Cairo University and then had attended the American University in Cairo for a master's degree in mass communications. He also received two "diplomas" in Shakespeare and modern English from Oxford and Birmingham Universities respectively. Neither of the two British journalists working on the paper, one of whom was an Oxford graduate, knew what a "diploma" in Shakespeare was. They assumed it was something awarded for attending one of the summer programs for foreigners held by Oxford to raise money. Salmawi was proud of his accomplishments as a writer of plays, short stories, and nonfiction.[35] He lived in a villa in the cosmopolitan section of Maʿādī, which is the foreigners' ghetto of Cairo and lies two or three stops further south from Cairo on the metro than my friends in Basātīn. He drove an olive-drab Mercedes 190, a "*zalamukka*" (chicken's backside in street slang), which is one of the smaller models, and presumably somewhat less expensive than the quarter-million-pound "crocodile" driven by Fadda al-Madawi of "White Flag."

I was asked to meet with Salmawi after one of these early editorial sessions to discuss which page I would be assigned to. His office was huge by the standards of Egyptian bureaucrats, although it was not a private office. Private offices only go to the ultraelite, and while Salmawi aspired to the *crème de la crème*, he was not yet there. The office was blue, and carpeted. Modernist paintings by his wife, Nazlī Madkūr, a prominent Cairene artist, hung on the wall behind his desk.

He began describing the paper. The first three pages would be news: on page 1 regional news and, when necessary, world news of pressing importance; local news on page 2; foreign news on page 3. Pages 4 and 5 would be economics and features respectively. Pages 6 and 7 would be opinion, 8 and 9 culture. Page 10 was to be "living," a nebulous category which never gained a solid identity. Sports was to be on page 11, and 12 would be "people" – a sizeable profile of some notable person, and a gossip column. He smiled and said, "We need someone very cultured and witty to do the gossip column." I did not volunteer, and he did not appear to expect me to. In fact an Egyptian publication could never have a true gossip column. Digging up dirt on the powerful would be unthinkable, and even the opposition papers – freer at this time than for a long while – had to be careful about criticizing officials by name.

I volunteered for culture or features, and let it be known that I would like to do some translating if possible. He smiled politely, and said, "What about sports? Our culture page is already filled, but we need someone on sports. Are you interested in sports? I myself like to run. You look like someone who enjoys sports." In fact there was a substantial oversupply of talent for the culture page, including the economics-page editor (who wrote book reviews, and eventually lost his economics-page post for including too many pessimistic articles), the assistant editor of the opinion page, the two English journalists (who made most of their contacts in the arts world through the assistant editor of the opinion page), a film reviewer (who eventually resigned in protest because his articles on popular culture were not taken seriously), and of course the editor of the culture page (a former official in the Ministry of Information whose brother had been a prominent composer for Umm Kulthum). I replied that while I was never fanatically devoted to sports, I was sure I knew enough to manage, and if that was all there was I would take it. The deal was done. For a short time I was assistant sports editor of the nascent *al-Ahram Weekly*.

In the early days of my short tenure on the *Weekly* I was given a lift several times by Salmawi in his Mercedes as far as Garden City, which he passed by on his way to Maʿādī, and was close to where I lived. Once Muḥammad Shebl, the film reviewer, who also lived in Maʿādī, accompanied us. Shebl talked briefly of his current project, directing a horror film about a murdered woman who comes back to haunt her husband. When my own interest in Egyptian films came into the conversation, I mentioned that I was partial to films by a comedian named Adil Imam, who is the highest-paid actor in the Egyptian film industry, and who had made a number of what I had thought were perceptive satires. The director seemed interested, but the managing editor appeared to be embarrassed and changed the subject.

A week later after the next brainstorming session the managing editor introduced me to my boss, the sports editor of the *Weekly*. Her name was Ṣāfīya Tharwat (known to us as Sophie Sarwat) and she was, I was told, the person who introduced synchronized swimming to Egypt. Sophie was a fit woman, approximately fifty years old, with short hair and an impish smile, who told me she was happy to welcome me onto her team. Later I discovered that she was a world-class bridge player (both the Egyptian men's and women's teams are perennial world powers in this game), and that she had had a brief acting career. Muhammad Shebl informed me that my boss in fact had a very famous line in a film called *Bayn al-aṭlāl* (Among the ruins, 1959). Her character in the film was the daughter of a character played by Fātin Ḥamāma, an actress "discovered" as a child by Muhammad Karim and cast in *Happy Day*, his fourth Abd al-Wahhab film. By the time *Among the Ruins* was made, Hamama was one of the most popular leading ladies in the Egyptian cinema, and Sophie was the budding star.

This, I thought, was a stroke of luck. My assumption about popular culture was that it reflects certain aspects of social life, and even helps create the social milieu in which people live. Now here I was observing a bit of "real life" (the *al-Ahrām* office), and suddenly my boss is a part of popular culture history. Life really is cross-stitched with references to films. Perhaps being assistant sports editor would be a useful exercise.

Among the Ruins begins with a young college girl (played by Sophie) falling in love with her professor, and he proposing. When her mother (played by Hamama) discovers the identity of the prospective groom she is inexplicably struck by terror, and turns over a sheaf of papers to her daughter. *Among the Ruins* is mainly an enactment of what the daughter (who disappears until the end) reads in these papers. The Sophie-character's mother, it turns out, is not her real mother; her real mother died giving birth to her. The woman she had thought was her mother is in fact her dead father's (unrequited) lover who, through a series of tragic circumstances, ended up raising the orphaned girl. The prospective groom, it turns out, is her foster mother's natural-born son by another man whom she never actually loved. When the character played by Sophie finishes reading this tangled tale her adoptive mother asks her whether she wants her to stay. The Sophie character bursts into tears and utters her immortal line, the one for which my boss on the sports page is still known: "*Inti māmā, inti kull^i ḥāga*"(you are mama, you are everything).

Among the Ruins takes place largely in sports clubs and fine mansions. Oddly enough, this is precisely the milieu in which Sophie was raised. Although she acquitted herself rather well as an actress, her acting career was subsequently abandoned in favor of a sports career. She was passionate about sports, and the idea of using the *al-Ahram Weekly* as a forum for sports education immediately appealed to her. "The African Games are to be held in Egypt next year," she told me. "We will run a weekly feature on our preparation for the games. Also we will have a sports editorial each week. We will deemphasize what all the other papers run – news about the local soccer leagues."

My own inclination, based on the assumption that foreigners would constitute most of the *Weekly*'s readership, was to include extensive baseball and basketball statistics gleaned from the wire services, and perhaps soccer for the European readers. She accepted this, but when we discovered that we would only have one page, the statistics were dropped. In the end our page contained regular swimming articles, and a bridge article photocopied from one of my boss's many books of bridge problems. Most of the articles, however, came from the regular *al-Ahrām* sports writer, and were about the local soccer league. This was because none of the reporters would attend the events our editor wanted to cover. Our inability to escape from reporting on the Egyptian soccer league – the only sport most Egyptians really care about – drove Sophie to distraction. Eventually she resigned in frustration. I was not present at the resignation, but rumor had it that harsh words were exchanged between my erstwhile supervisor and Salmawi. In fact I really only lasted two weeks on sports, after which I was allowed to move to translating the opinion page.[36]

The opinion page was run by Ḥasan Fu'ād, an *al-Ahrām* editor with considerable seniority, who had, in the 1970s, been coeditor of *Ṣabāḥ al-khayr* magazine. Hasan Fu'ad was one of the kindest and most efficient men on the *Weekly* staff, who could make time even for such relatively menial tasks as helping me decipher the handwriting in the regular *al-Ahrām* editorial. The regular editorial was written by a grubby-looking man who wore a devilish smirk, and whose chaotic handwriting hid a great talent in writing classicist prose. He took delight in confusing me. Of course he was told what to write – this was, after all, the official editorial of the paper – but then proceeded to render the official opinion in a highly baroque style which defied English syntax, and often left me bleary-eyed from staring at it. At the other end of the opinion-page spectrum was the weekly feature by Muḥammad Sīd Aḥmad which, while complex, seemed to fall naturally into English sentence patterns. Sid Ahmad's editorial was the only one that regularly came to us typed. I was surprised to learn that many people found Sid Ahmad's writing difficult. It was said that he wrote French but used Arabic words, and it was rumored that the man in fact spoke better French than Arabic.

Between the official editorial and Sid Ahmad was a variety of regular features – mostly *al-Ahrām* regulars such as Naguib Mahfouz and Salāma Aḥmad Salāma – and whatever contributions were sent to either the Arabic paper or the new English offshoot. The opinion page was sometimes arduous work, but was one of the first pages on the new publication to settle into a weekly routine which allowed for plenty of time to dabble in other parts of the paper.

Since I was interested in popular culture I naturally gravitated to the arts and culture page. Our film reviewer, Muhammad Shebl, made horror films. One of his films was *Anyāb* (Fangs, 1981) – an Egyptian version of *Dracula*, with a few nods to *The Rocky Horror Picture Show* – which even he admitted was not a big hit. Like Sophie, he resigned from the paper in anger. Shebl wanted to write about popular culture, which was not considered a worthy subject by the editors. Worse still, he wrote most of his articles in a "gonzo" style – very colloquial and full of hyperbole – which was appreciated by the editors even less than his preferred subject matter. The final straw came when he did a serious interview with Ṭāriq ʿAlī Ḥasan, director of the newly constructed Cairo Opera House. The new Opera House was a gift from Japan to Egypt.[37] The Japanese intended it to be a cultural center for average citizens, but many believe the result to be unforgivably elitist – an institution patronized mainly by foreigners.[38] Most of my friends outside the newspaper and the American University were intimidated by the Opera House's elitist reputation. Farid was openly contemptuous of it. The film *Crabs* contained a scene that commented on the Opera House's dress code. Flush with cash from the first boxing matches at the rich woman's villa, Hudhud wants to go to the Opera House because his sweetheart from the old neighborhood works there at the concession stand. He and his friends pay LE 50 for tickets to a foreign opera. Unaware of the dress code, which requires neckties for all men, they get turned away at the gate. Only Hudhud manages to slip through by cutting a strip off his friend's red shirt and winding it around his neck.

Initially Shebl's interview with Tariq Ali Hasan was, like Hudhud, turned away at the gate. Although Shebl's article was long and hard-hitting – by far the best article he had written for the *Weekly* – it was rejected on the grounds that it was too critical. Shebl had words with Salmawi and, like Sophie, found no option but resignation. An abridged version of his interview was later printed in zero issue number three (there were ultimately five zero issues), but this failed to entice him back. In fact he was immediately hired by the *Egyptian Gazette*, a rival Egyptian English-language paper published by the Gumhūrīya publishing group (home of another public-sector newspaper).[39]

The big picture on the culture page was managed by Mursi Saad al-Din, an affable former chairman (from 1977 to 1979) of the State Information Service. "Dr. Mursi," as the *Weekly* staff affectionately called him, was largely retired by the time he took on editorship of the *Weekly* arts and culture page.[40] A long life of public service had left him with such an extensive web of patronage and influence that he was constantly besieged with requests for intercession at all levels of private and public life. On the *Weekly* Dr. Mursi was mainly a source of contacts for others to exploit. Our culture editor was not a "hands-on" manager, but he did not have to be, since the two English journalists were able to do all the editing and a substantial amount of the writing. The culture page was also the part of the paper most likely to receive outside contributions, although the quality of these contributions was often not good. Dr. Mursi nonetheless encouraged the development of new talent. Whatever his shortcomings in terms of editorial vitality, it could not be said that he neglected the young; many were the times that I entered the seventh-floor *al-Ahram Weekly* office to find Mursi in intense conference with an earnest young prospective writer.

Dr. Mursi was fond of recalling his days as an assistant cultural attaché in London – his first diplomatic post as a young man. His long stays abroad, and association with the British cultural establishment in Egypt, made him the right man for the *Weekly*. The introduction to his latest book boldly states his rejection of the idea that "cultural invasion" from the West is an appropriate concern for modern Egyptians, who should feel secure enough in their own identity to venture into the ideas of others (Saʿd al-Dīn 1989, 5). This was the theme of Dr. Mursi's regular feature in the *Weekly* titled "Plain Talk." The first installment of "Plain Talk" was a commentary on a series of photographs published on the same page. The photographs were of sculptures by the Egyptian artist Maḥmūd Mukhtār, and the accompanying article was by Nagwā al-ʿAsharī, one of Dr. Mursi's young protégées. In his presentation of the Mukhtar sculptures Dr. Mursi ruminates on the character of Egyptian modernity, and boldly declares victory in the cultural struggle that bedeviled so many of my friends and acquaintances:

I remember representing Egypt at a symposium entitled "Cultural Self-Comprehension of Nations" . . . The symposium called for the rights to cultural self-realisation of all national cultures, support for all national cultures, and the promotion of tolerance towards other cultures. Apart from the patronising tone of the resolutions, the symposium showed clearly how colonialism had worked against indigenous cultures.

But the issue of cultural identity is not a problem for Egypt. *(ibid., 9)*

Dr. Mursi put the principal combatants in this great struggle into two camps: on one hand, those who advocated adherence to Arab culture (there is only brief mention of Islamic culture as one element of the "spiritual aspect of our culture"); on the other hand were intellectuals who called for a revival of pharaonic culture and for blending the restored pharaonic spirit with European culture. In Mursi's view it was the great modernizer (and former minister of education) Taha Ḥusayn who synthesized these opposed views:

It was Dr. Taha Hussein, the *doyen* of Arabic literature as he was called, who struck a balance between the two schools of thought when he wrote . . . that the spirit of Egypt: "Consists of three elements, the first is pure Egyptian inherited from the Pharaohs, the second is Arab, which comes from language, religion and civilisation, while the third is foreign which has always influenced Egyptian life."

That put an end to the controversy. In fact if one examines modern Egyptian culture, in the plastic arts, literature or music one will appreciate the truth of Dr. Taha Hussein's statement. *(ibid.)*

Al-Ashari, Dr. Mursi's protegée, echoes these sentiments in her own description of one of Mukhtar's works, which stands near Cairo University and symbolizes the Egyptian modernist view of the educational mission. Whatever its failings now for ordinary people, the modernist message is set before Cairo University quite literally in stone:[41]

Egypt Awakening, his great manifesto piece, stands as a political document as well as an artistic statement. Erected in its present position [on a wide avenue leading to the front gate of Cairo University] in 1928, this monumental statue is a perfect simulcrum [*sic*] of Mokhtar's technique. He takes ancient glories, in this case the monumental figure of the Sphinx, and juxtaposes them with modern elements. The peasant woman, removing her veil, looks steadfastly to the future, though her feet remain firmly planted in the traditions of the past.

> Mokhtar . . . lived in a popular quarter of the city. There he was daily exposed to the frustrations of a population increasingly alienated by the urban milieu to which they had moved, came increasingly to appreciate the need to attain some sort of synthesis between the traditional and the modern in Egyptian society.
>
> *(N. al-ʿAsharī 1991, 9)*

Al-Ashari, like the peasant woman she wrote about, wore no veil of any kind, unlike the majority of female Cairo University students who pass by Mukhtar's statue daily, for whom "looking to the future" means donning the neo-Islamic *ḥijāb*. While the *ḥijāb* is not exactly a "veil," and is very much a creation of the educated middle class (or of middle-class aspirants) rather than of the peasant woman in the statue, neither does it evoke al-Ashari's "traditions of the past" or Dr. Mursi's "balance between . . . two schools of thought." The emphasis in the cultural synthesis taking place on the campuses lies heavily on religion, specifically Islam, as the solution to all daily and metaphysical problems. Furthermore, students assume that resolution of the cultural conflicts they feel so acutely is yet to come, contrary to Dr. Mursi's confident assertion that the solution to whatever cultural contradictions Egypt may have faced was found sixty years ago.

Oddly enough, Dr. Mursi need not have gone far to witness the enactment of this Islamic response to his own solutions of the 1920s and 1930s. The door to our seventh-floor office was periodically blocked by long prayer mats unfurled so that those Muslims on our floor who were inclined to pray – mostly employees of *al-Ahrām al-riyāḍī* (Sports *al-Ahrām*), another recent special project carried out by the parent organization – could do so communally. The mats were invariably placed on our side of the hall, making it impossible for us to enter or exit our office for ten to twenty minutes, depending on how long the prayers lasted. This was inconvenient when one was facing a deadline. But we were expected not to cross the mat during prayer time, as I discovered when I respectfully (I thought) removed my shoes and slipped across, only to be faced by an angry *al-Ahrām* employee, after the prayer had ended, demanding to know who it was who had broken the rules. Nagwa al-Ashari, however, never faced such barriers because her desk (she was one of the few *Weekly* employees to have her own desk) was on the fourth floor in the office of the executive editor in chief of the *Weekly*. Most of the offices on the fourth floor were occupied by high-ranking officials in the *al-Ahrām* organization, and consequently it would be unthinkable to block their office doors with prayer mats.

Aside from my translation duties and my informal contacts with the

Plate 11 Mahmud Mukhtar's *Egypt Awakening*, unveiled for the public in 1928 and still standing on the street leading to Cairo University

culture page, I had relatively little to do with the news sections of the *Weekly*. In the early days of the paper most of the news was culled from wire-service reports, correspondents' reports (*al-Ahrām* had a handful of correspondents in American and European cities, but no permanent staff in Arab capitals) and the Arabic *al-Ahrām*. A few articles were written by the *Weekly*'s own staff, and the hope was that eventually most of the *Weekly*'s material would be separate from the Arabic daily.[42] I did get some exposure to the news when we began putting together serious zero issues (five in all, from January 17, 1991 to February 14, 1991). We were told to be present on Wednesday – the day before the paper would hit the streets if we were doing real editions – no matter what our regular page. It was during these last hectic weeks that Maḥmūd Murād, another relatively senior *al-Ahrām* employee, began to appear regularly. He was a tall, dour man who wore expensive suits, and was either unwilling or unable to speak English, unlike most of the staff. It was rumored that he was a "spy," or at least a watchdog planted by the government, but I had no way to confirm this.

There was no disputing that Murad was closely connected to government sources. On the last Wednesday of my short tenure at the *Weekly* I was given one of his articles to translate. Like most articles filed by *al-Ahrām* reporters, it was handwritten, but the script was worse than usual. I had to ask some of the Egyptians on the staff to help me read it, and found that in their opinion the prose style was as bad as the script – ungrammatical, repetitive, and nearly incoherent. I despaired of making anything out of it, and cut it to about a fourth of its original size, leaving it to the central editorial desk to restore what material they wished. To my surprise, it turned out to be the lead article on the front page. The article dealt with post-Gulf War security arrangements for the Middle East, and centered on a meeting of Arab foreign ministers that was to take place in Cairo on Friday, the day after the paper was published. As Mahmud Murad (or at any rate, the article published under his name) put it:

> The nine Arab foreign ministers meeting in Cairo Friday will try to agree on principles for postwar security arrangements in the region. The most important item to be discussed will be prospects for the withdrawal of foreign forces from the Gulf, and the formation of an Arab force to fill the void left by the departure of these forces. Egypt and Syria, already involved in the ongoing war, are expected to provide troops for this force, with other countries also participating.

Of course the security arrangements were, in the end, quite different. Several months later an obviously enraged Ḥusnī Mubārak announced on national television that the Egyptian troops were to be withdrawn, and responsibility for security in the Gulf was to remain in the hands of American and European forces. But of course none of us knew at that time what the outcome of the war would be. What struck me as odd about the article was not that the reporter knew what would be discussed in the meeting – presumably that would have been revealed to the press by the relevant government officials. What was odd was that the article I was given to translate on Wednesday, describing a conference that was to be held on Friday, had actually been written in the past tense. Presumably this high level of certainty as to the contents of a still-to-be-held conference was one of the advantages *al-Ahrām* enjoyed as a public-sector enterprise.

Along with all the other disparate elements of the *Weekly* that were hastily settled during the final five weeks of preparations for true publication (as opposed to practice issues) was the gossip column. The matter of a gossip column had been discussed with considerable animation during our early editorial brainstorming sessions. It had appeared that the idea was discarded, but when the zero issues went into production we found that this was not true. On the back page, together with a weekly profile and a column by managing editor Muhammad Salmawi, was a feature called "Pack of Cards" – by "Madame Sosostris." In the editorial meetings Salmawi was coy about the identity of Madame Sosostris, just as he had been coy in mentioning that we needed "someone very witty" to write a gossip column. But as the weeks went by it became obvious that "the wisest woman in Europe" was none other than our managing editor. Eventually the gossip column became a collective endeavor, but in the early days it was kept afloat mainly by Salmawi's efforts, and there was no doubt that the theme and the title were his creations.

As in most gossip columns, "news" consisted of reports on the activities of the rich and famous, or at least of the well connected. Unlike Madame Sosostris of "The Waste Land," who turned up cards printed with mythical figures of general significance, the *Weekly*'s Madame Sosostris peered at cards printed with the faces of those whom the audience was to assume were Cairo's movers and shakers. The diplomatic circuit featured prominently. The public's first experience of Madame Sosostris was the following item:

> Laurice Nasri is a dear friend of mine. She is a prominent Alexandrian lawyer. I was invited by the French ambassador Alain Dejamet to his home in Giza to attend a reception in her honour on the occasion of her receiving the "Legion d'Honneur." Laurice is of Greek origin. She has long been taking care of the embassy's legal affairs. It seems to me that she is doing a good job too. The party was attended by the ambassadors of Britain, Canada and Spain as well as Mrs.

Boutros Ghali [wife of the current secretary general of the U.N.] and Mrs. Frank Wisner [wife of the former American Ambassador to Egypt].

(*Madame Sosostris 1991, 14*)

The profile for that week was entitled "Challenges and Responsibilities." It was about Suzanne Mubarak, wife of the president. The page was rounded out by Salmawi's own column, an intimate feature titled "Entre Nous." In his first installment of "Entre Nous" our managing editor tipped his hand about the identity of "the wisest woman in Europe" by focusing on a dinner party he attended at the residence of "a Nordic ambassador in Cairo." The ambassador, it seems, saw fit to apologize for their "untimely entertainment" (they were about to open the wine, according to the article) during the Gulf War. Salmawi used the apology to point out what he considered a fundamental difference between Egyptians and foreigners:

What a world of difference in outlook, I thought, between the attitudes of people. Egyptians have a totally different approach to life which not all their guests are quick to know. Throughout thousands of years Egyptians have learned to make life go on despite setbacks and agonisings about what they have often had to put up with. Many wars have come and gone, but Egyptians have made sure that everyday life continued uninterrupted. (*Salmawi 1991, 14*)

Salmawi then gently admonished the ambassador for his grim attitude, and suggested he "go to any first-class hotel of his choice, on any evening of his choice, to watch the lavish splendour of Egyptian traditional weddings, beside which his dinner party, albeit more to my liking, would seem like a working lunch" (*ibid.*).

I always wondered what my friend Ibrahim, the young student in Basātīn whose struggle with "The Waste Land" had a direct bearing on his and his family's future livelihood, would have thought of "Entre Nous," and the *Weekly*'s Madame Sosostris. Unfortunately I could not ask him because when the paper started to come out he was in the army. Fortunately for him he couldn't have been in long enough to have even finished basic training when the Gulf War broke out. Madame Sosostris did garner a following among foreigners. For many the column was endearingly kitschy – an Egyptian version of Herb Caen, the gossip columnist for the *San Francisco Chronicle*. But those who took their sycophancy seriously also found much to praise in Madame Sosostris's "Pack of Cards."

Long after I stopped working on the *Weekly* I saw and heard reminders of its continued existence. One evening I was startled when a television announcer blurted in rising intonation "*al-Ahrām* . . . in English! Pack of

Cards! Ibrahim Nafi! Get all this in *al-Ahram Weekly*!" True to form, they were trying to develop their local audience. The advertisement was broadcast on Channel 1, which broadcasts mostly Arabic programming, unlike the more foreign-oriented Channel 2. My last brush with the paper while I was in Egypt was on my way to the airport. A large billboard standing in the desert carried an advertisement for it in English: "*Al-Ahram Weekly*: for an *authentic* Egyptian voice." The emphasis on "authentic" was in the original.

7

"Vulgarity"

Ya ahl al-maghnā dimāghna wagaʿna
Wallāhi kalāmku malhūsh maʿnā

(You singers, our heads hurt
By God, your prattle is meaningless.)

from the song "*al-Ustāz*" on the cassette
tape "*Ṣayf sākhin giddan*"

School of Troublemakers

Since the 1970s those media heavily dominated by the state, such as television, radio, and newspapers, have continued unabated the optimistic modernism of previous generations, although as we have seen, by the time of "White Flag" in 1989 a certain defensiveness had crept in. In other media, the cinema in particular, the post-Nasser market-oriented *infitāḥ* loosened state control in the economic sphere, and to some extent in the artistic sphere as well. Technical innovation also wrought changes in the character of mass art, particularly the advent of cheap cassette technology, which opened up the music industry to new influences to an unprecedented degree. Much of the new mass culture fares poorly at the hands of establishment critics.

Theater, while perhaps less affected by technological innovation than the electronic media, was also partially reprivatized, and it too began to change in ways that did not please critics or the state.[1] One early commercial production often denigrated by critics as "vulgar escapism" was the play *Madrasat al-mushāghibīn* (School of troublemakers), written by ʿAlī Sālim and directed by Galāl al-Sharqāwī.[2] *School of Troublemakers*, although contemporary with films we have mentioned, was in many ways a more perceptive production than more orthodox commercial fare such as the film *Pay Attention to Zuzu*. Like *Zuzu*, *School of Troublemakers* was a smash hit in its day, remaining in the theaters for three straight years (1971 to 1974). *School of Troublemakers* retains considerable vitality with younger audiences, whereas *Zuzu* has become a period piece for most.

I first heard about *School* from Farid, the prep-school math teacher, and his medical-student roommate Nabil. They told me that it was a play written by Ali Salim, a well-known writer whom I had heard casually referred to as "the Neil Simon of Egypt," and whose work I had read as an Arabic student. Farid and Nabil claimed that the play was considered subversive, and had been banned from television. "It shows the students attacking the principal – they even blow him up at one point. They sexually harass a female teacher. And the students smoke dope in class." The rumor about the ban proved untrue, although in the two years I was in Egypt I noticed that the final scene in which the problems were resolved was aired more often on television than the anarchical early scenes.[3] *School* was, however, available on video, and with very little prodding from me they agreed to rent a copy and bring it to watch on my VCR.

Farid and Nabil came to my rooftop flat at the appointed time, tapes in hand (the play lasts a good four hours), and two of their friends in tow. From the very beginning of the play they were in stitches, even though they had all seen it often enough to have memorized many of its lines. *School of Troublemakers* begins with a simple sequence showing the teachers of the school – Madrasat al-Akhlāq al-Ḥamīda (the school of commendable morals) – dancing to an oddly infantile tune which they chant: "*liiy liiy liiy liy liy liy* . . ." All are young men, most of them wearing the long hair, sideburns and bell-bottom trousers that were fashionable at the time. One of them wears a tarbush – emblem of the old days when the holder of a high-school degree could have reasonable hopes in the civil service. One wears the robe and felt-capped turban of an Azharite *shaykh*. They dance in geometric patterns, form lines, link arms, all slightly out of sync. Farid and Nabil howl with laughter. The *shaykh* breaks ranks with the rest and starts doing the twist. Farid and Nabil practically roll on the floor, guffawing loudly.

The principal enters. He is a lumpy, balding man wearing spectacles and a suit. His voice is gravelly and nasal at the same time. He sings:

> Tenhut! Salute! At ease! Be seated!
> Which one of you teachers
> Is refusing to do his lessons?

You? (No!) You? (No!) . . .
Stand up, you with the pop-bottle glasses!
Who is it making this mess?
Speak or you go straight to Maghāgha!

Maghāgha is a town in Upper Egypt. Not only is it in the "middle of nowhere," but it was the birthplace of Taha Husayn, hence a particularly humorous place to be mentioned in the "school of troublemakers." The song and dance are performed raggedly, the movements deliberately ridiculous, and the principal brays his song like a donkey, making no attempt to varnish his lack of vocal talent. Finally the teachers pick up the principal and carry him out on their shoulders chanting "*il-nāẓir il-gād bi-yigīb il-gād*" (a serious principal promotes seriousness).

The story is simple. Teachers and administrators can find no satisfactory way to deal with a group of troublemaking students, all of whom seemed destined to lives of crime. A female teacher comes to the school. She has a theory, which she is attempting to prove in a doctoral thesis, that the troublemaking students are not at fault, and that society makes them act the way they do. She believes that if they are treated with respect they will in turn treat their teachers and institutions with respect. The principal tries to reject her, but higher officials force him to give her a chance with the class full of bad apples. Eventually she proves stronger than the students, and is able to transform them into decent and useful citizens. The only wrinkle in the story comes from the presence of a poor student, Aḥmad, whom the principal constantly patronizes, telling him that he is only in the school at the principal's sufferance, and that if he makes one wrong move he will be expelled.[4] Ahmad has been placed in the class of troublemakers only because he is poor, and therefore automatically suspect. The other boys are all from wealthy families (one is even the principal's son), and are still in school only because their parents are rich and powerful. It is Ahmad's maltreatment at the hands of the principal that precipitates the crisis leading to the new teacher's gaining the students' confidence. The principal catches Ahmad smoking a water pipe in class. Ahmad did not, in fact, bring the pipe, but merely received the mouthpiece from one of the other students. The principal, ever one to apply the double standard, immediately expels the luckless boy, but the new teacher stands up for him, thereby getting through to the students finally, and convincing them that she is not like the others.

The play took a cast of young actors, led by journeyman comedian Adil Imam in the role of Bahgat al-Abāṣīrī, the chief "troublemaker" in the play, and catapulted several of them to stardom.[5] Imam and his fellow "troublemakers" took this simple story as merely a framework, within which they took whatever liberties they could get away with. It was mostly the ad-libbed lines and situations that captivated the audience and established the actors' reputations.

Watching *School of Troublemakers* with Farid and Nabil was like attending a performance of *The Rocky Horror Picture Show*, the bizarre American Frankenstein-in-drag film that played a night or two each week in repertory cinemas throughout the United States for years. Farid and Nabil, like the *Rocky Horror* audience, had memorized substantial portions of the performance, and said them out loud before the actors said them. For example the teacher, talking to the father of the ringleader of the students, picks up an object stolen by the man's son, which the son apparently had sold to the hapless principal, and yells in frustration, "*Yaum ibn-ak huwwa, bi-yiḍḥak ʿalayya ana, wi-yibīʿ il-bitāʿ da huwwa, wi-yiʕūl da bi-yiʕashshir baṭāṭā*" (one day that guy, your son, cheats me. Me! Sells me this thing here, and tells me it "peels sweet potatoes"!). "Peeling sweet potatoes" is part of a kind of *baladī* rhetorical question: "What do you think he's doing, peeling sweet potatoes?" The principal repeats the line three times, substituting different phrases – "cooking greenbeans," then "hulling sunflower seeds" (*yiʕashshir libb*), by cracking them open in one's teeth, and spitting out the husks. Eating *libb* in this way, especially in public places such as movie theaters, is considered a low-class habit. Farid and Nabil cackle with laughter as they join in this last line.

Many of the lines spoken in the production were not only absent from the printed text, but were actually alien to its spirit. The principal, for example, was supposed to be corrupt, coarse, and dimwitted. The actors had, however, identified a situation that was likely to bring laughs, and amplified it far out of proportion to the original script. This particular situation focused on an authority figure being mocked, and twenty years after the play was performed on the stage, it still struck my friends as hilarious, even though they were only young boys at the time of the original performance.

Critics have always found Imam, ringleader of the "troublemakers," problematic. Ever since *School*, writers in the national media have recognized him as a potentially great comedian, but rarely do they praise him for more than his promise. Initial reviews of *School* set the pattern. Galāl al-ʿAsharī, writing in *Rūz al-Yūsuf* when the play first came out, adopted a condescending tone. The play, he said, was fairly good for the commercial theater, "but we hope that the comic theater adopts a better plan in the coming season" (G. al-ʿAsharī 1971, 44–45). Al-Ashari's faint praise was most pronounced when discussing Imam. In a fairly long review (four two-by-seven-inch columns) Imam's performance was allotted half an inch of one column: "Adil Imam clearly put great effort into his part, although his exaggerated affectation . . . and his egotism . . . ruined the spontaneity of his movement and expression" (*ibid.*, 45).[6] One would never suspect from al-Ashari's review that the play was Imam's breakthrough performance, or that twenty years later it would be fondly remembered in its video version by people too young to have seen it on stage, or that of all the cast, Imam's performance would have the most staying power in the eyes of the public (Saʿīd Ṣāliḥ, Imam's partner in troublemaking, ran a close second). In fact the emphases of the reviewer were nearly opposite to those of the four young men with whom I watched the play.

In the article, the principal and female teacher get the most attention, the troublemaking students the least. Al-Ashari passes lightly over the first two-thirds of the play, saying only that

> after a long and bitter struggle in which the students use all manner of troublemaking, including violence, the female teacher succeeds in winning over the leader of the students [Adil Imam]. Through him she is able to dominate the other students, a dominance which is made complete by her use of modern educational methods. But no sooner does she succeed in this task than she faces a new problem. (*ibid.*, 44)

The "problem" is that the students fall in love with the teacher. Nabil and Farid were uninterested in such matters: one by one they and their friends excused themselves after the first two acts, in which most of the "troublemaking" took place, were finished. When I mentioned this to some of my other friends, they were not surprised, and confessed that they did not remember what happened in the last act even though they, like Nabil and Farid, had memorized many lines from the play. The lines most often memorized were inevitably the ad-libbed parts, about which al-Ashari had nothing good to say: "If the director Galal al-Sharqawi had eliminated these excesses and additions to which some of the actors resorted, such as a scene in which Adil Imam and Said Salih argued repetitively, the work would have been more disciplined and unified" (*ibid.*). Al-Ashari was undoubtedly correct in his assertion that the production lacked discipline. It was, however, the absence of discipline that made the greatest impression on the audience.

Much of the antidisciplinary spirit of *School* was expressed through slapstick – exaggerated voices, funny walks, threatening motions made by students toward teachers, a mock "burning" of the principal, a teacher speaking with such machine-gun rapidity that everything he says comes out as nonsense. Slapstick has long been a staple of the Egyptian commercial theater and cinema, so it was easy to overlook, amid all this low clowning, that the play thrived on its propensity to mock education – the institution portrayed for decades in literature and films as the solution to all problems of the modern world and, furthermore, an institution that, over these same decades, played an increasingly important role in the real lives of ordinary Egyptian citizens. This was a radical departure from the modernist formula prevalent in mass media from Abd al-Wahhab to *Pay Attention to Zuzu.*[7]

The physical humor in *School of Troublemakers* was augmented by a great deal of verbal jousting – all outside the published text – at icons of the educational institution. For example, early in the first act Adil Imam enters the principal's office and finds that his father is present. He greets his father with exaggerated enthusiasm – so exaggerated that one assumes he despises him: "*Abūyā*! *Abūyā*!" (my father! my father!). He administers bear hugs and warm kisses to his father. "*Abūyā*!" Then Imam leaves the stage momentarily muttering "*Abī fōq al-shagara*" (my father is up the tree). *My Father Is up the Tree* is the title of a film that came out in 1969 just two years before *School. Tree* was a musical, produced by Abd al-Wahhab and starring Abd al-Halim Hafiz, the most popular singer in Egypt after Umm Kulthum and Abd al-Wahhab himself. *Tree* still plays occasionally in second-run theaters.

Like so many other films, *Tree* was about students grappling successfully with modernity – a *Zuzu*-like scenario diametrically opposed to the first two acts of *School of Troublemakers*. Boy (played by Hafiz, who was far too old for the role) meets girl. Boy feels frustrated at girl's conservative attitude: not only won't she put out, she won't even spend time with him alone. Boy meets prostitute and decides to go for the sure thing. Boy and prostitute cavort happily, including a "road trip" to Lebanon, until boy starts to regret his lost innocence and to feel jealousy at the prostitute's continued dalliance with other men. Father comes looking for son, but finds prostitute first, and begins to fall prey to her charms. Boy finds father before things get out of hand. Both feel embarrassed. Boy goes back to girl, who forgives all.

Adil Imam's mention of *My Father Is up the Tree* was a throwaway line, but twenty years later it still brings laughs. A single line inserted *dehors du texte* invokes another text, but more importantly, it puts the modernist edifice built up through films such as *Tree* in a pointedly ridiculous context: a rebellious son responding to his father's pressure to conform by pretending exaggerated affection. The juxtaposition of Imam's surly dissembling hugs in *School* and the synthetic resolution of the generational conflict in *Tree* – one instant in a four-hour play – was deliciously absurd for an audience grappling with an increasingly unwieldy vision of modernity. Since the 1970s many people, particularly the younger generation, have found that the vision never seems to deliver its promised rewards, and never seemed to allow the swift resolution of problems depicted in films such as *Pay Attention to Zuzu* and *My Father Is up the Tree*.

When Imam returns from offstage after his "father is up the tree" line he brings a suitcase filled with smuggled goods, telling the principal that it was filled with "review notes" that he needs to pass his finals. Through threats and cajoling the principal gets Imam to open the suitcase. One by one he extracts Imam's "notes." First is a carton of imported Kent cigarettes. "Al-Gabartī's chronicles," says the principal sourly, in reference to ʿAbd al-Raḥmān al-Jabartī, the man who wrote what is still considered the most important Egyptian account of Napoleon's invasion of Egypt (and presumably a standard text in the high-school curriculum). The principal continues, pulling out a piece of fine wool: "*Encyclopaedia Britannica*," he intones. A bottle of whisky: "*Risālat al-ghufrān* (The epistle of forgiveness)," a work by the medieval philosopher Abū ʿAlāʾ al-Maʿarrī dealing with who gets to enter heaven. The next item is a massive bra: "*The Prolegomenon of Ibn Khaldūn*," a medieval work of protosociology written by a Tunisian scholar. "This is no longer the 'School of Praiseworthy Morals,'" says the principal, "but the 'School of Shawārbī Street.'"

Shawārbī Street was another icon of the times that still carries resonance for the present generation. The early 1970s, when *School of Troublemakers* was produced, marked the first blossoming of the *infitāḥ* – the Open Door economic policy through which Egypt allowed greater contact with the West than it had experienced during the Nasserist 1950s and 1960s. Shawārbī Street in downtown Cairo was known as the "street of the smugglers" – a semitolerated place where Western goods were allowed to trickle into the country. Imam, with his suitcase filled with imported luxuries, would have been known as *tāgir al-shanṭa* – a "suitcase merchant" selling furtively on the sidewalk. Before *School of Troublemakers* this was not a subject that could easily be discussed in mass entertainment. After *School* a steadily increasing torrent of *infitāḥ* commentary and criticism began to appear on stages and in cinemas.

The performance was filled with such dual references to modern events and to the modern/classicist agenda of the educational system. For example, Imam's partner in crime, played by Said Salih, carries on the "suitcase merchant" theme by talking like an auctioneer hawking cheap goods at a saint's festival. Then he makes a prescient reference to the private-lesson syndrome that plagues the education establishment of today (it was not yet as pressing a concern in the early 1970s), but he does it in a way that also evokes contemporary social and political stereotypes. The principal asks him why he was absent from school, and the boy replies that he was "giving private lessons" to girls in Beirut. At that time Beirut was famed for its allegedly libertine ways. *My Father Is up the Tree* made use of this stereotype, showing the errant Abd al-Halim Hafiz living it up on Alexandrian and Lebanese beaches with his prostitute. Said Salih plucks the same string in *School* by talking to the principal about how the "lessons" (i.e. the girls) are very easy in Beirut. In another scene Imam delivers a speech to the principal in the style of the recently deceased Gamal Abdel Nasser, echoing a point made by the principal earlier that Imam was "*markaz min marākiz il-quwwa*" (one of the centers of power – one of the few jokes in the performance that was actually in the text). This was a reference to the divisive power struggles that had taken place among Abdel Nasser's Free Officer cronies during the 1960s and which, many felt, had contributed greatly to Egypt's crushing defeat in 1967. Later Said Salih gets thrown unexpectedly to the ground by the new female teacher who, it transpires, knows judo. He returns to class, arm in sling, and announces his "defeat" in the style of an official radio broadcast prefaced by martial music and a qur'ānic invocation.

Farid and Nabil pointed out that this style of speech had particular resonance in the late 1960s and early 1970s, when Egypt was frequently at war, when Abdel Nasser was often preempting regular programming to make special announcements, and finally, when Abdel Nasser died in 1970, just one year before *School* opened its three-year run in the theater. Even twenty years later Nabil and Farid, who were too young to remember such events, had been told the significance of Salih's apparent clowning: the event had entered the vernacular to the point that both of them had memorized parts of Salih's mock-Nasserist speech.

Despite the actors' undeniable (and undeniably effective) resort to slapstick, and despite the cursory treatment given *School of Troublemakers* by critics, the play's appeal did not lie in any simple pandering to "the tastes of the masses." When the *al-Ahram Weekly*'s editor reacted to my mention of Adil Imam's name with embarrassed silence he was implicitly siding with the critics, condemning the actor and his performances on the stage and screen as hopelessly vulgar. Occasionally such criticism finds voice. When Imam's *al-Lu'b ma' al-kubār* (Playing with the grownups) was released in 1991 the *Weekly*'s opposite number in the public-sector

Gumhūrīya organization, *The Egyptian Gazette*, published an editorial on Imam. The article claimed that Imam "is the only actor on whose standing and assessment critics are far divided" (ʿAbd al-Qādir 1991, 3). Some critics, the article claimed, accuse Imam of pandering to the "desires of the poorly educated but well-off moviegoers," whereas others praise him for "cheering up his fans," and for taking his latest play to the provinces against fierce opposition from fundamentalist groups, thereby playing a key role in "driving the forces of darkness and backwardness from Egypt."[8] Although the writer allows that Imam has produced "some gems," he does so grudgingly. *Playing with the Grownups*, he says, was mostly wasted in Imam's slapstick acts, but nonetheless "effect[s] the impossible equation: appealing to the Egyptian 'philistines' and the intellectuals alike." But the writer also distances himself from the strawmen critics who praise Imam:

> Imam has carved out for himself a stature so soaring that he has become the idol of the majority of the Egyptians – but alas they mostly include the noveau rich [*sic*] whose phenomenal earnings can by no means obscure the fact that they are predisposed to ear-shattering songs, obscene jokes and trash films. *(ibid.)*

Contrary to Abd al-Qadir's accusation that the Adil Imam-loving majority of Egyptians are *nouveau riches*, Nabil and Farid were dirt poor. Nor did they consider themselves "predisposed to ear-shattering songs, obscene jokes and trash films." Rather they thought of themselves as intellectuals. The relentless ad-libbing of Imam and his fellow "troublemakers" turned the play, for Nabil and Farid, from yet another didactic reaffirmation of state-sponsored modernism into a cultural icon expressing their own doubts.

"The Master"

Fast forward from the 1970s *School of Troublemakers* to the late summer of 1990. The hit song in Cairo that year was a novelty piece called "*al-Ustāz*" (The master). I first heard of "*al-Ustāz*" from Muḥammad Zādah, a sound engineer and occasional poet, with whom I was working. Our job was to edit an English-language phonetics tape to be used in conjunction with a text being developed to teach English in Egyptian universities. I was given the tape-editing job by Longman's International, a publishing house hired by the Egyptian Ministry of Education to produce the phonetics materials. Muhammad had been hired by a subcontractor working for Longman's.

The text had been reorganized – the chapters shuffled and some lessons deleted. Using twenty-six cassette tapes made from the old quarter-inch reel-to-reel tapes, I had determined which parts were to go where. Muhammad's job was to do the actual cutting and splicing of the tape in a sound studio equipped with a quarter-inch reel-to-reel machine, and then make a cassette copy so that the Longman's employee responsible for editing the written text could check the tape against the book.

The studio rented for us by the subcontractor was located in the Muqaṭṭam Hills, a posh new neighborhood built on the limestone plateau east of Cairo. This was a very inconvenient location for both of us, as neither Muhammad nor I had a car. We were taken to the studio on the first day by the subcontractor's driver, but once in the studio we were practically stranded. The job took two entire nights and the better part of several days. Much of our time in the studio was idle. It generally took Muhammad only ten to twenty minutes to perform the necessary cutting and pasting. But since the studio was designed for working with music, which must be recorded at slow speed, it did not have facilities for high-speed dubbing. Therefore after every ten-minute cut-and-paste job we had to rewind the quarter-inch tape and wait the full time required to transfer the contents onto cassette at slow speed. The result was that Muhammad and I spent most of our two nights in Muqaṭṭam talking and sitting on the studio's balcony listening to military transport planes flying over every ten minutes or so carrying Egyptian troops and supplies to Saudi Arabia in preparation for the Gulf War.

Muhammad had majored in social sciences at Cairo University, graduating nearly twenty years before. He expressed little regret that he was not making a living in a profession related to his field of study. After graduation he had spent some time in Saudi Arabia working as a martial-arts instructor. Then he returned to Egypt and learned his current profession, which he enjoyed immensely. Most of Muhammad's work involved recording and mixing music, but he had also worked on some film soundtracks, and had learned how to build soundproofed studios.

His hobby was reading and writing colloquial poetry, which was occasionally used in songs. This I discovered during one of our all-nighters in the Muqaṭṭam studio. I mentioned that I had a minor interest in colloquial poetry, because the official rhetoric about colloquial poetry often mirrored the discourse on other art forms that were of more central concern to me. This was the right button to push with Muhammad. He started citing a line from the *Rubāʿīyāt* (Quatrains) of Salah Jahin, a popular collection of a hundred or so cleverly worded homilies: "*Walad-i, naṣaḥt-ak lamma ṣaut-i itnabbaḥ / Mā-tkhaf-shⁱ min ginn walā min shabaḥ*" (My boy, I've told you till my voice went hoarse / Don't fear *jinn* or spirits). Wonder of wonders, he had quoted from the one quatrain I had been made to memorize as an Arabic student in 1985. I finished the line: "*Wi-inn habb^{i} fīk ʿafrīt ʕatīl / Is'alu lēh ma-dāfiʿ-sh ʿan nafsu yaum^{i} ma-ndabaḥ*" (And if the ghost of some murdered man springs on you / Ask him why he didn't defend himself on the day he was slaughtered). I admitted to him that this was the only quatrain I knew, but he nonetheless went on talking for hours about Jahin and Bayram al-Tunsi, from whose *oeuvre* I exhausted my stock of memorized poetry with a few lines of "*Hatgannin ya rayt ya ikhwān-na ma-ruḥti-sh Lundun walā Bārīs*" (I'll go nuts, brothers, I wish I had never gone to London or Paris) – a satirical poem juxtaposing earthy images from *baladī* neighborhoods with a tone of mock awe at the civilizational advances of Europe. Most of the poetry Muhammad had memorized was from the work of Fuad Haddad, a highly philosophical poet who combined both classical and colloquial forms to express ideas as diverse as Marxism and Sufism (Booth 1992, 474–75). Although Muhammad made his living working with his hands, his interest in Fuad Haddad – a more difficult poet than Jahin or al-Tunsi – marked him as an intellectual, although a slightly unorthodox one since Fuad Haddad, like most colloquial poets, remains outside the institutional mainstream.

Muhammad first mentioned "*al-Ustāz*" one evening when we were sharing a taxi home from Muqaṭṭam, or actually from Sayyida ʿAysha, a neighborhood at the bottom of the limestone cliffs on the eastern edge of Cairo, which we had reached by picking up a microbus on a road about half a kilometer from our isolated studio.

"Have you heard the song by *al-mughannī al-aṭrash* [the deaf singer]?" he asked with a grin.

"What do you mean, 'deaf singer,'" I replied. "How can a singer be deaf?"

"He sings 'ee ah ee' – the way deaf people talk. It's a huge hit." I laughed, assuming he was pulling my leg.

"I'm serious," said Muhammad. "A friend of mine wrote it. He made a bet that he could write a hit for a deaf singer, and he did it."

The next day, before we began our frustrating search for a taxi driver willing to test his transmission on the steep hill to Muqaṭṭam Muhammad ducked into a knickknack shop selling cigarettes and other small items. He emerged with a cassette tape emblazoned with a blond sunbathing girl: "*Ṣayf sākhin giddan*" it read – "a very hot summer." He stuffed it triumphantly in my front shirt pocket. "There it is. There's your deaf singer. Enjoy."

When I played the tape a couple of days later, I found it began with an old-fashioned *muwashshaḥ* – an Andalusian poetic form used in many songs. I knew the *muwashshaḥ* from an old tape I had by the Lebanese singer Fayrūz. When I first heard it I had liked Fayruz's version of the song, but I had since encountered the tune in a number of films, always used to represent the idea of classicism gone stale. Even *Pay Attention to Zuzu*, champion of modernity, had mocked this hackneyed tune. In *Zuzu,* the modern young professor (Zuzu's lover) shakes his head in disgust when attending a rehearsal for a play to be performed by a local troupe that had not had the advantage of the professor's foreign-influenced expertise. The scene that provokes the professor's ire consists of a dance performed to the Andalusian *muwashshaḥ*. "*Al-Ustāz*" also begins by mocking the stale classicism of the Andalusian *muwashshaḥ*. It is sung with an exaggerated seriousness and at a draggy tempo: "*āmaaan āmaaan ḥubb-i gamālu itnassā āmaaan*" (*āmān* . . . the beauty of my love forgotten, *āmān*). In Egypt it is the perfect musical cliché, calculated to bring rolling of the eyes and an exasperated, "not *that* again." But it isn't *that* again. In "*al-Ustāz*" a brassy male voice breaks in, cutting off the *muwashshaḥ* singer: "Hey, guy, what is that you're saying? Get down from there, guy, the *ustāz* [master, 'professor'] has arrived. Come on up here, *ustāz*. See you later, guy." A snappy accordion plays the *baladī* equivalent of a drum roll. Then a synthesizer rock tune begins, backed by a heavy *baladī* beat. Another voice comes in, electronically modulated to a high nasal pitch *à la* "Chipmunks": "ee ah ee ah ee ah ah oh, ee ah ee ah ee ah ah oh . . ." – the "deaf singer."

Later I had a friend write out the rest of the words to the song. I copied it out in my own handwriting and had him check it. He laughed. "No, you've got it wrong, it's two 'ohs' and one 'ah' at the end." But the interesting part was what came between the lines of the "deaf singer" 's chant. Altogether there were three separate voices: the "deaf singer," a counterpoint "rap" voice (unnaturally low as the "deaf singer" was unnaturally high) asking disingenuously what the "deaf singer" was up to, and finally a normal male singing voice belting out an answer to the second voice.

RAP VOICE: Look at our friend, what does he want? Why is he angry, why does he frown?

NORMAL VOICE: He fancies himself a singer, thinks he can sing. Wise him up, make him understand, not just anyone can be a singer.

DEAF SINGER: Ee ah ee ah ee ah ah oh . . .

RAP VOICE: He wants to say something, give him a tape, everybody cheer and jump about.

NORMAL VOICE: You singers, our heads hurt us, by God your prattle is meaningless.

What kind of "star" is this keeping us up? Whose "moon" is this gathering us together?[9]

DEAF SINGER: Ee ah ee ah ee ah ah oh . . .

RAP VOICE: Look at our friend, what does he want? Why is he angry, why does he frown?

NORMAL VOICE: In our tunes we have authentic Easternness. In your tunes drumming and witlessness.

So drum on, he's in his element – get him a girl 'cause he's a dance-hall singer.

DEAF SINGER: Ee ah ee ah ee ah ah oh . . .

Almost everyone found the song funny. The voice defending "our Easternness" delivered its ostensible message of cultural conservatism in frenetic "dance-hall" style even more revved-up than that of "the master," who sounds like a schoolyard nerd playing rock star next to the ferocious accents of the "conservative" voice. After Muhammad gave me the tape I began noticing it blaring out of numerous cafés and workshops. It was, indeed, a "very hot summer," with the Gulf crisis threatening to explode into the Gulf War, and the usual problems with day-to-day life in crowded Cairo taking their toll on everybody's patience. "*Al-Ustāz*" 's mildly subversive mocking of high-art pretense provided momentary relief, and after a couple of months it disappeared, part of the ephemera of 1990.

One line in "*al-Ustāz*" was particularly revealing of a way of talking about entertainment that challenged the version of "heritage" promoted in the media: "By God, your prattle is *meaningless*." As we saw in the case of the theme song to *Crabs*, "meaninglessness" is often attributed to songs or films straddling the boundaries between sober "high art" that seeks to invoke the classical heritage and "folk art" derived from the premodern local Egyptian tradition. The theme song to the film *Crabs* was one such song, even though the words were meaningful in the context of the "*ibn al-balad* in the corrupt modern world" theme of the film. "*Al-Ustāz*" snickered at both the folk and classical traditions. The little accordion "drum roll" that introduced "the master" suggested the tired old classical theme being pushed off the stage by a sly and disrespectful newcomer. Then the hint of *ibn al-balad* is submerged beneath the frantic disco pace propelling the "deaf singer." Classicism comes through in the pedantic content of the "normal voice" complaining about splitting heads and witlessness. The classicist voice is belied, however, by the disco-inspired force with which the lines are delivered. And the "rap" voice, lower and slower than the others, is a caricature of an ignorant public that falls too easily into "cheering and jumping about" for the witless singer who is the target of critical displeasure. All together "*al-Ustāz*" was a splendid parody of the contemporary musical scene and, like all successful parody, it worked because it had the various voices in the musical equation down pat, and because the music itself was good. "*Al-Ustāz*" was also gentle satire, so that it passed without anyone objecting to it too strongly. This was not true of all popular songs labeled as "meaningless."

The king of "meaningless" songs in the late 1980s and early 1990s was a rap tune called "'*Ēh il-ḥikāya*" (What's the story). "*Al-Ustāz*" made reference to "What's the Story" in its last line: "*asitok-lu ma huwwa muṭrib ṣāla*" (get him a girl, 'cause he's a dance-hall singer). *Asitok-lu* means literally "elasticize him." I was told that the phrase refers to voluptuous girls. As one of my friends told me: "In the old days they liked really big girls – so big they had to hold up their clothes with elastic. Now people prefer smaller girls, but *asitokī* is still a reference to those big girls of the old days." In "What's the Story" the chorus chants several times, "'*Ēh il-asitokī da. . .*" (what's with this chick). So when the singer in "*al-Ustāz*" says "*asitok-lu*" the earlier song comes to mind. The earlier song, unlike "*al-Ustāz*," drew a great deal of critical ire – resulting, it was rumored, in the singer being expelled from the musicians' union.

The creator of "What's the Story" was Ḥamdī Baṭshān, a popular singer from Alexandria whose style and musical imagery is more traditional than that employed in "*al-Ustāz*," although still completely different from the respectable *takht*, or the expanded version of the *takht* employed by such critically approved singers as Abd al-Wahhab. Like "*al-Ustāz*," "What's the Story" takes a dig at convention, but this time it is a sharper dig at a more sensitive target: misbehavior of men and women in public. The song is about a dirty old man leering at a pretty girl. She is perhaps up to no good (depending on how much flirtatious intent one reads into the tone of the female voice in the song). The man, despite his advanced age, wants to take advantage of her. The song begins with a fairly long overture – a combination of synthesizer and orchestra (or perhaps a synthesizer made to sound like an orchestra). Then the chorus enters and the words begin:

MALE CHORUS: Whaaat . . .
FEMALE CHORUS: What's the story
. . .
BATSHAN: Tell me . . . wise me up . . .
MALE RAP VOICE: What's with this chick, what kind of walk is that, what is this rose, what is this waking up the sleeping?
FEMALE RAP VOICE: Sisters, what's with this man, why is he walking pestering us, what is this boorishness, what is this getting on my nerves?
BATSHAN: What is this, man, what are you doing, shame on you at your age, cut that out.
Tell me . . . wise me up . . .
(rap voices)

BATSHAN: What is this Casanova, what is this Travolta, what's with these clothes you're wearing, what's this with someone your age
(same line, with "Michael Jackson" instead of "Travolta")
Tell me . . . wise me up . . .
(rap lines)
BATSHAN: What's this, you with the grey hair, you dirty old man, you with the worn-out nose,[10] what an age of wonders this is.
Tell me . . . wise me up . . .
(rap lines)
BATSHAN: What is that noise he's making,[11] what is this insensitivity, why doesn't he hear me, someone talk to him.
Tell me . . . wise me up . . .
(rap lines and fade out)

"What's the Story" became the quintessential *ughnīya habṭa* (vulgar song). Though it was released in 1988, by 1991 it was still being employed to invoke the idea of vulgarity. "*Al-Ustāz*" echoes "What's the Story" both in its trivocalic structure, in which the voices comment on each other, and in the final line telling the audience to go ahead and *asitok-lu* – "get him a chick," or at least allow the girls to dance to his music.

"What's the Story" also appears in *Crabs*. Hudhud and his friends are working out in their "street gym" (a boxing ring constructed in the street). Suddenly Nur, the sultry secretary, wearing a tight and tiny miniskirt, sways into the scene. As she makes her way toward Hudhud the other boxers follow behind her, clapping their hands in the rhythm of "What's the Story" and chanting, "'*ēh il-asitokī da*, '*ēh il-asitokī da* . . ."

The reference to "What's the Story" in *Crabs* was a throwaway line – a touch of realism and a demonstration of how popular culture gets woven into everyday language, but is not really an integral part of the story. In another film, *Sūbirmārkit* (Supermarket), however, the song provides the defining moment of the narrative. The film is about a man and a woman, Ramzī and Amīra, who have grown up as neighbors. Although they have gone their separate ways, the film's plot throws them together again. One feels that of all the characters in the film Ramzi and Amira are made for each other. Unfortunately, a series of events concerning money, Amira's daughter by her first marriage, and various superficial *infitāḥī* men in both of their lives keep them from ever consciously considering marriage.[12] At the end of the film Ramzi sits in his car, bitter from having seen that Amira, his childhood friend whom he has loved platonically, is both literally and figuratively in bed with a grotesquely materialistic *infitāḥī* doctor. Ramzi sits listening to Western classical music – the one element of beauty in his life that seems unaffected by the sleaze of modern society. An anonymous man pulls up in a white Fiat. With no explanation the man throws a cassette through the open window of Ramzi's car and drives away. Curious, Ramzi shuts off his Beethoven tape and replaces it with the mysterious new tape: Hamdi Batshan hammering out an insistent "*fahhimnī . . . kallimnī . . .*" – "wise me up . . . tell me . . ." "Tell me," in other words, "what's the story," what is going on here? What is going on is a world in which there is no room for refinement or love because everything is dominated by the power of money. *Supermarket* ends with Ramzi looking bewildered for a moment as he hears the sound of Batshan's voice, then laughing bitterly.

Al-Mughannī al-hābiṭ

Another singer frequently accused of pandering to low tastes is Ahmad Adawiya, the singer the college students and their chaperones were listening to on the Nile excursion described in chapter 6. Once when I mentioned his name to a pair of students, I received simultaneous conflicting commentary. One said, "He is a *sha'bī* [popular] singer." At the same instant the other said, "He is a *hābiṭ* [vulgar] singer."

I asked the Adawiya detractor to bring me a "vulgar" Adawiya tape. The album he brought was "Adawiya 91," his latest release, which was not actually new but contained medleys of old material, much of which had been released originally in the mid-1970s. At the time I asked my friends to bring me a representative Adawiya tape, the fan magazines were touting this "Adawiya 91" as the number-one tape of 1991.

Adawiya, like Hamdi Batshan, displays little of the vocal technique characteristic of classical Arabic music, relying instead on volume, vocal range, and tempo. The rhythms alternate between a fast disco pace and a slower bump-and-grind pace, all played *'ala waḥda wa-nuṣṣ*, a traditional "folkloric" rhythm. Many of the songs Adawiya sings draw frankly on folklore in their words as well as in their rhythms. The song that originally made him famous in the early 1970s was called "*Is-Saḥḥ id-daḥḥ ambū.*" *Is-saḥḥ id-daḥḥ* is a phrase said by country children when trying to make a pair of rams fight. *Ambū* is another child's phrase, said when asking or offering a drink of water. On "Adawiya 91," however, the song apparently has little to do with rams or children, or so I was told by the young man who claimed that the album was vulgar. In his view the song was essentially a lighthearted trifle, and the "Adawiya 91" version did indeed seem designed to do nothing more serious than urge young people to dance. Of course urging young people to dance – especially boys and girls together – was often condemned as improper by many in both the older and younger generations.

Although Adawiya rose to national fame from a "folkloric" background, his appeal is broad. Some of his songs, especially his post-1970s productions, are fast-paced *aghānī shabābīya* (youth songs). For some the entire category of "youth music" is disgraceful – an Egyptian version of the "sex, drugs, and rock and roll" so feared by conservative American adults when the Beatles became popular.[13] For others "youth music" is a healthy phenomenon of modernity, includes patriotic songs broadcast on television, and is distinct from the untamed (or frankly commercial, in the view of detractors) music performed by such singers as Adawiya and Hamdi Batshan.[14] Those who object to Adawiya as a contributor to "youth music" do so prescriptively: they view him strictly as a denizen of nightclubs (a venue, however, in which virtually all commercially successful Egyptian musicians perform), and not as a proper role-model for young people. At the same time there is no doubt that certain of Adawiya's songs have a much wider appeal.

Adawiya's emphasis on folkloric imagery, with none of the mediating influence of classical convention, immediately sets him apart from the approved icons of musical modernity, such as Abd al-Wahhab and Umm Kulthum. Supporters of Adawiya, however, see no inconsistency in comparing Adawiya to the musical "giants." It is mainly the professional critics who see a fundamental incompatibility between Adawiya and "proper" singers; the fans tend to be more eclectic in their tastes. Even Muhammad Abd al-Wahhab, the icon of establishment good taste described in chapters 4 and 5, occasionally had a good word to say about him.

Many of Adawiya's songs are *mawāwīl* and *azgāl* (poetic forms adapting colloquial language to classical meters). The content as well as the form of the songs tends to evoke images of life in traditional quarters. For example, one of the "boy–girl" songs on "Adawiya 91" repeats the phrase *gōz walā fard*, "pair or single," meaning, are he and a girl described in the song a couple, or are they separated. *Gōz walā fard* is also a children's game – odds or evens – and by using it he contextualizes the song, situates it in the popular quarters. Adawiya often uses references to local places to transgress the bounds of the stereotypical premodern "folkloric" images. But despite Adawiya's relatively straightforward use of colloquial forms – easily recognizable to native speakers of Egyptian vernacular and sometimes praised as an element of authenticity in other singers[15] – many of the people who considered Adawiya a vulgar singer claimed that his music had no meaning, just as they had asserted that the words to *Crabs*, "What's the Story," and "*al-Ustāz*" were meaningless.

What all these songs have in common is that they make an open appeal to lower-class sensibilities, but not in terms of modernizing ideology. Even "*al-Ustāz*" does this with its sendup of pompous critics lecturing a slow, witless audience. All of them employ a fusion style in their music (just as Abd al-Wahhab did), but they sin in the eyes of the establishment by blithely ignoring the high musical tradition in favor of the *baladī* tradition.

What Adawiya does, perhaps more successfully than any of the other allegedly vulgar singers, is blend his class appeal with a certain sexiness. I asked one of my friends who wavered between the anti-Adawiya camp and the pro-Adawiya faction to write out the lyrics to one of the medleys on "Adawiya 91." As with all the other "meaningless" songs, he had no trouble recording the words. Some of the lines, however, struck him as particularly salacious. For example, some of the lines from "*Bint al-sulṭān*," which we have already encountered in chapter 6:

Daughter of the sultan have pity on this wretch
The water's in your hand and Adawiya is thirsty.

Although the driving rhythm and insistent tone of the singer doubtless contributed to the perceived raciness of the lines, there is certainly nothing in them inherently more salacious than much popular music, or indeed, much classical poetry. Nonetheless, the juxtaposition of music, images, and perhaps of class makes the song seem provocative to some. Another line in the song, mentioned by many as particularly "vulgar," describes a girl strutting provocatively on a particular bridge in Cairo:

On the ʿAbbās Bridge she walks and people walk.
Why don't you look at me my little fruit, my pineapple

The ʿAbbās Bridge, we remember from chapter 6, spans a distance over the Nile that is social as well as physical – a perfectly liminal, almost carnivalesque, spot for a pretty young girl to engage in risqué behavior.

Other parts of the "Adawiya 91" tape evoke the social gulf characteristic of modern Cairo, but no longer effectively bridged by an ideological fusion between the classical heritage and the modern present. Following "Daughter of the Sultan" the medley shifts into "*Zaḥma ya dunyā*" (Crowded world), which contains the lines quoted at the start of this book:

How crowded is the world
Crowded and friends lose their way
Crowded and merciless
A free-for-all

The last line is *mūlid wi-ṣaḥb-u ghāyib* – "a saint's festival with the principal absent." A *mūlid* – saint's festival – is a large gathering of people for the purpose of celebrating the birthday of some person thought to have special religious knowledge, or extraordinary insight into spiritual matters. These events can be unruly at the best of times, so the image of a *mūlid* with the saint absent is particularly evocative of chaos.[16] The version of this song on "Adawiya 91" is even more energetic than "Daughter of the Sultan."

The songs on "Adawiya 91" are a medley, and can be seen as simply boy–girl songs typical of "youth music." The object of desire in the first song, "*Balāsh il-laun da*" (Don't be that way – lit. "get rid of that color"), is a girl who has jilted her would-be boyfriend. A later section of the medley, "A Bit Up," describes a girl who lives "upstairs" and won't look at a young man who admires her. This section contains one of the lines most remembered by both proponents and detractors of Adawiya: "*Ḥabba fōq ḥabba taḥt / naẓra naẓra fōq naẓra naẓra taḥt* (a bit up, a bit down / a look up, a look down). This could refer both to the girl looking down at the boy or the boy looking the girl over. But the fact that she lives upstairs, and he down, is also suggestive of a difference in class between the two. A bit further in the tape he sings:

Hey, sweet thing living upstairs, why don't you look at what's down below?
And I living upstairs don't ask about what's down there

This is followed by another fragment from a song with the refrain "*kullu ʿalā kullu*" (everything on top of everything). This is suggestive of what one sees from "upstairs," and implies a certain feistiness, if not outright protest:

Everything on top of everything When you see him tell him
What does he think we are? Aren't we good enough for him?

Of course "him" can still, technically, be the girl, since poetic convention in Arabic does not demand that a feminine noun be marked by feminine pronouns or endings. But whether the person for whom "we aren't good enough" is a rich girl or a rich man, she (or he) is still "upstairs" while we remain "down."

Another section of the medley begins with the words:

Boy, O lad
There's nobody your stature, nobody with your beauty
Boy, my lad, O those who took you from me

In this passage Adawiya transposed *waladi* and *wādi*, two colloquial forms for "my boy," or "my lad," with *baladī* and *wādi*, "my country" and "valley" (i.e. the Nile valley), or at least this is how my scribe heard it.

"Valley," *wādi*, is distinguishable only by context from "my lad," also pronounced *wādi*. In the case of *waladi* and *baladī* the transposition was so difficult to hear that the person writing the text for me wrote it sometimes one way, sometimes the other; that is, by changing a single letter the song continues the same parallel resonance suggested by the earlier parts of the medley:[17] longing of the jilted lover on the one hand, and on the other longing of the dispossessed looking up at those "living upstairs."

This combination of musical fusion, *baladī* lyrics, and sexiness made Adawiya into one of the most popular – some say *the* most popular – singers in Egypt. Almost everybody claimed that Adawiya tapes sold well, although there were no reliable figures to prove it.[18] But unlike the "giants" of Arabic music, Adawiya is almost invisible in the print media and television (although he has made cameo appearances in a number of films). Adawiya's status in the media contrasts strongly with that of Abd al-Wahhab, who two generations earlier had employed the same principle of musical fusion as Adawiya and who, like Adawiya, had been assiduously associated in the media and in his own films with a much freer attitude toward relations between the sexes than was prevalent at the time. It is Adawiya's frank appeal to the masses – without any of the rhetoric of "raising their cultural standards" – that sets him apart from singers backed by the cultural establishment in print and on television.

Conversations on "vulgarity"

I spoke to a number of people about "vulgar art." Some of the people I spoke to were well known to me, and others were not. One group I spoke to were friends of one of my friends. All of them considered themselves middle class, and most had been to college. I was present at the conversation, but asked my friend to present the questions in the hope that this would produce more natural responses. He first asked them if they had heard of Hamdi Batshan's "What's the Story." One of them replied:

> I've heard it, but I wish I hadn't. It is meaningless. He [Batshan] wants to push a tape, no more. I don't want to say that a modern song, or a *shabābīya* [youth] song, as they say, is necessarily bad, but there is no connection between "What's the Story" and these other types of song.

Another maintained that only uneducated tradesmen (the famous *ḥirafiyya*) listened to such music, but was contradicted by his friend, who insisted that the problem was one of artistic taste, not of class. Yet another admitted that he listened to the songs, but disavowed any interest in the words: "The music is good. Of course I don't like the words at all. They are very bad – incomprehensible. Whoever sells these tapes is just trying to make money, nothing more. They don't present any new taste or elevated art, just nonsense." The questioner asked again who listened to such music:

A1: Most of the class who are factory workers or tradesmen. Or you might see some kid or some other people who listen to it because it fills up their time. When they are in the middle of problems and worries they want something to lighten their load, something new to make them happy.

Q: I asked some tradesmen about these songs, and they said it was educated people who listened to the stuff.

A1: We're throwing insults at each other, it's an epidemic. It's just that taste differs from one person to another. You can find someone who is very educated sitting listening to it. I won't tell him, "You're a *kāfir*" [an unbeliever, i.e. he will not hurl insults at him for listening to the song]. But I don't listen to such songs.

Q: What about the songs of Ahmad Adawiya? Vulgar or popular?

A1: Some say popular, but I say vulgar. The songs have no meaning. These songs are only made for tradesmen, not for the educated class. I can't listen to them.

A2: I don't think they are vulgar songs. As a person, his voice I mean, it's enough that Abd al-Wahhab acknowledged him. His voice is very powerful and beautiful. And he is also an excellent performer. I think he is the foremost popular singer in Egypt.

A1: Can I ask you something? If his voice is so good why hasn't he been played on the radio for so long?

A2: The radio and television usually record people I don't like.

A1: But if Abd al-Wahhab recognized him he should be played on the radio and television. It was Abd al-Wahhab who kept him off the television and radio.

A2: If it were up to me he would have been on the radio.

A3: Adawiya is a good singer, a good performer, but some of his songs were not good. Some were popular and some vulgar. "*Is-saḥḥ id-daḥḥ ambū*" for example, you feel like the words are meaningless. Because of that you feel like most people won't accept him. He makes these tapes for particular people, "people of the microbus" or whatever. These songs are just cheery little things.

A2: But I once saw Adawiya on television. The announcer was about to cry from the song. If some of the words are vulgar then why is everybody in Egypt singing them to themselves? "A Bit Up, A Bit Down" and "Pick the Boy Up Off the Ground" [titles to two Adawiya songs] and things like this. I consider these songs folklore because they elevate the people. And like they say, he's a popular singer. I mean all the people like him, not just a particular class. I have some of his tapes. Ahmad Adawiya was on a par with Umm Kulthum and with Abd al-Wahhab. Lots of people listen to him. I like him.

These young men often formulated the issue of whether singers such as Adawiya and Hamdi Batshan were legitimate artists in terms of the degree to which media icons of good taste – Abd al-Wahhab in particular – accepted them. They did this with no prompting from me. The value of the icons themselves was never questioned by these young men or, indeed, by most of the nonprofessionals I talked to about music. Within the entertainment business, however, the attitude toward Abd al-Wahhab as a musician was much more critical.

For example, I spoke to Hānī Shenūda about performers, both "vulgar" and those favored by the media. Shenuda is himself a celebrity due to the success in the 1970s of his own group, "The Egyptians." He now runs a recording studio. As a composer Shenuda has written for his own group, which is considered important in the development of modern Egyptian pop-music style, and on the side he writes film scores, which he also synchronizes with the action in the films. His credits also include having composed for both Muḥammad Munīr and Adawiya.[19] One of his most successful songs was "Crowded World," sung by Adawiya and part of the medly in "Adawiya 91." Shenuda claims that "Crowded World" was used in film soundtracks more than any other song in the history of Egyptian cinema.[20] In addition to pop music, Shenuda also composed the orchestral music used in a 1986 production of Taufiq al-Hakim's play *Izīs* (Isis, a political allegory set in pharaonic times) performed to inaugurate the opening of the newly renovated National Theater.

Hani Shenuda is a jovial man in his late forties with sparkling blue eyes. Although he was a busy man at the time I met him, he found time to talk about cultural matters, and even drove me to his studio once or twice. On one of these journeys he demonstrated that he had the common touch by stopping to buy a melon from a farmer who had brought his cart into town to sell his produce. The poor farmer didn't know quite what to make of this lively man who jumped out of his Peugeot sedan, insisted that the farmer tell him his name, and then proceeded to talk with him as if he had known him all his life. We left the farmer with a discounted melon, and Shenuda's promise that if it weren't perfectly ripe he would be back to exchange it for another one.

Hani Shenuda has always been a strong supporter of the colloquial arts, both in terms of what he calls *al-funūn al-shaʿbīya* (the folk arts) and in terms of contemporary colloquial poetry. Knowing this, I began my formal interview with him by asking his opinion of Abd al-Wahhab and the "high" tradition.

> Abd al-Wahhab had a detrimental influence on the generation that followed him. He worked actively to keep them from succeeding. One good thing he did, however, was to set a precedent for allowing other singers to sing his own melodies. But he still exercised great influence on all composers and arrangers in Egypt. He used to say, "Your *aghānī shababīya* [youth songs] should be stopped. They are a

mūlid [saint's festival, i.e. chaotic], empty songs without meaning, songs with vulgar words." He meant, for example, "*Firqat al-Maṣriyīn*" [The Egyptians], which I founded. One of the worst things about Abd al-Wahhab was that he took the *takht* [traditional ensemble] and kept adding to it without changing it. You see all those instruments in his films – violins and cellos and basses – but it was all show. He depended on appearances, not on content. They say that Abd al-Wahhab was an innovator because he was a musical symbol. Whenever a musician in Egypt had a success the credit always went to Abd al-Wahhab. What he did was always called "progress" but what it really was was fashion.

Some refer to Abd al-Wahhab as a "Turkish singer." A "Turkish singer" doesn't have to carry a Turkish passport. When the Turks were here they used to run a thing called a *tekiyya* [an establishment run by a Sufi order, also used as an inn]. What kind of entertainment [did a *tekiyya* feature]? People singing and dancing, and this kind of singing featured repetition, exaggeration, and elongation. Everything the singer says would be repeated. In my opinion that's what Umm Kulthum was [a *tekiyya* singer]. Real Egyptian songs are something other than these slow things where they keep repeating the words. In the style of the *tekiyya* the singer improvises and the band follows him exactly. That's a *takht* and an Ottoman thing.

I then asked him why the younger generation seems to ignore Abd al-Wahhab's music even when they often follow the critics in praising him. This, I suggested, seemed hypothetically analogous to American critics gushing on in the 1990s about Benny Goodman; American youth do not necessarily say Goodman was bad, but neither do most of them spend time listening to him. Certainly they would not think of evaluating current performers in terms of how 1940s performers regarded them.

When the critics write about Abd al-Wahhab they are merely writing about nostalgia. "If everyone sang like Abd al-Wahhab maybe the prices would return to what they were in the 1960s. Maybe we'll be able to find a place on the bus . . ." But kids aren't interested in nostalgia, they're interested in reality.

As for younger singers like Adawiya, the media, and especially the newspapers, call him vulgar. You know, often writers can't find anything to say, so they write, "Save us from vulgar songs," and Ahmad Adawiya is one of them.

I don't consider him vulgar. What does vulgar mean? It seems to me they say he is vulgar because of two or three songs. Suppose I'm a rational person. Would I want to listen to a song by Ahmad Adawiya, or a song on television that says "I love you my age, my place, my time"? I think that [television music] is what is vulgar. They are always saying "I love you, my country." This looks literary, and refined, but it's not really. Beneath the surface it is completely vulgar, if I can use their term. Is it better to sing a young people's song such as Adawiya's "*Zaḥma yā dunyā zaḥma*," which are *shaʿbī* [popular] – well understood by all of us. Or should we listen to some Abd al-Wahhab song which says "the world is a cigarette and a glass of wine"? I'm not saying people shouldn't drink or smoke if they want to, but the world just isn't like that. Then if Adawiya sings things that are a bit risqué, still nobody can say that he was worse than Umm Kulthum. She sang, "come, and we will finish our love in one night." She doesn't mean platonic love. She means, "Let's have sex tonight and never see each other again." You can't say that one's vulgar and one's elevated so easily.

Whether or not Shenuda is correct in attributing the Egyptian musical tradition to mainly Ottoman influence, his reading of the state of "official" Egyptian music has the effect of throwing the legitimacy of official culture into question. Official music, he says, is not only of questionable pedigree, but is divorced from reality, whereas his own brand of music speaks to the "reality" of modern Egypt. The "reality" as he sees it is steeped more in the colloquial tradition than in the high tradition. His strategy is to align himself with the *ibn al-balad* world view, in which case the opposing image is that of Westernized decadence: "The world is a cigarette and a glass of wine."

I also spoke to Muhammad Zadah, the sound engineer who introduced me to the "deaf singer," on the same topics. With us during the conversation was Nāṣir, a friend of Muhammad who worked for the state radio company. Zadah, like Shenuda, questioned the official view of the high-culture value of Abd al-Wahhab. His friend Nasir did not.

MUHAMMAD: Abd al-Wahhab the last of the Ottoman singers? No, he's not, because there are still some. Let me tell you something: the younger generation can't listen to Abd al-Wahhab. I'll give you some evidence. There was a concert in the *Nādī al-Shams* [a club where concerts are given]. Many different people were singing at this concert, and among them were two from the Abd al-Wahhab school. Those two were hit with bottles. Twenty thousand in the audience, and they were chanting in one voice "*ḥarām, kifāya*" [shame, enough]. Can you imagine? I'm serious. (To Nasir) Isn't that right?

NASIR: Of course Abd al-Wahhab was fantastic, no need to repeat this . . . I'm saying this for a reason. People still listen to Abd al-Wahhab's stuff, even today. People still do new arrangements of his music – new singers – and people listen. The difference in generations is the only problem – we're completely different as a generation than Abd al-Wahhab. Nonetheless, if you make some changes in the form of Abd al-Wahhab's songs . . .

MUHAMMAD: When today's voices, the drums, the bass, and all these things are put with Abd al-Wahhab's music maybe people listen, but that's not the point. That song of his, "*Min ghayr lēh*" [Without asking why – Abd al-Wahhab's last song, released in 1989],[21] he wasn't "standing" or anything. The man died, but not on his feet. You can see this in that last song, it wasn't written for the age we're living in. Did it sell? Of course not. Don't tell me that Abd al-Wahhab sells.

NASIR: I've got a copy of "Without Asking Why," many people have copies.

MUHAMMAD: Nonsense. This happens all the time. They make a big hullabaloo over it. The man was consecrated by the media – the papers wrote, the radio and television broadcast, the man did all these advertisements, and for nothing.

When it came out I went and heard the first few lines, and it was the same old stuff. I gave it back to the man and said, "give me anything else."

Take a song like "'*Āsh al-rūḥ*" [May the spirit live].[22] You know that tune . . . (he hums it)? Did this great classical theme come from the same person who sang . . . (he hums another, rather formless, tune). How can the same person put such a horrible thing in the same song as he puts great things? Artistically Abd al-Wahhab wasn't even up to the level of many of his contemporaries . . . I admit I don't like these kinds of songs, maybe I'm against him – but there are things that when we look behind them . . . we say, "My God, what a beautiful melody" – but then you find that he stole the tune from someone else. The thing I like best about him is the stuff that doesn't come from him.

Later the conversation turned to other types of music – specifically "vulgar" music. The two remained true to form, with Muhammad defending "low" culture, and Nasir advocating strictly the "high."

MUHAMMAD: If you really want my opinion, I don't think there are some songs that are vulgar and some not. Some people say, "it came to the world and nobody knows why" [presumably a line from a "proper" song], and they're free to like this stuff. But maybe I can say, "*ḥabba fōq wi-ḥabba taḥt*" ["a bit up, a bit down" – a line from Adawiya] or that "*hissⁱ biss*" [a sound made to get someone's attention – from Hamdi Batshan] stuff, and it's my right too to like this stuff. This is what my social position accustoms me to. Among the things they say about these songs is that they are nonsense. But whether it's vulgar or not – vulgar from whose point of view? The ones who say it's vulgar just don't like it.

NASIR: But you have to ask "vulgar in what way?" When someone says, "*Kaddāb ya khaysha kaddāb ʕawī*" ["you're a liar, you old piece of burlap (used to wipe the floor), a real liar" – a line from a "vulgar" song]. Is this vulgar or not? Is there some higher meaning to these words? Or even some nice sound?

MUHAMMAD: Nasir, maybe you don't like this phrase, but what if I do?

NASIR: No, nobody likes this stuff. There's no subject, no significance to it. It must be said by someone sitting in a café or something like that. All that kind of talk is . . .

MUHAMMAD: Maybe some who say that line might also say something beautiful. I think the man who wrote that is really good – "*Aḥmad Ḥilmī itgawwiz 'Ā'ida katab kitābu Shaykh Ramaḍān*" ["Ahmad Hilmi was married to Aida by Shaykh Ramadan" – all the names are well-known public squares in Cairo]. It's a really good idea and deserves respect.

NASIR (agreeing with Muhammad this time): He also said, for example, "*Qena, Sohāg, al-Ismā'īlīya, bint aṣ-ṣa'īda Baḥarīya* . . ." ["Qena, Sohāg, al-Ismā'īlīya, Upper Egyptian girl and Baḥarīya" – a poem consisting mainly of the names of Egyptian cities and regions]. In the days of the wars – all of them [1948, 1956, 1967, 1973] – there was this thing called "evacuation" here in Egypt. These cities were emptied – Suez, Ismā'īlīya, Fayed . . . Where did they go? They traveled to Upper Egypt, there was work to do there, buildings to build, so they traveled to places like Qena and Sohāg. And they lived there. So when the man talked, he had an idea.[23] And people considered him popular.

MUHAMMAD: But that's not exactly what I'm talking about. I'm not saying anything against Fuad Haddad [the poet who wrote the words to the song they both like], you know I've studied him very well. But why are these words good? There are many, many people who have written on the subject of the country – and this is always a popular subject, you can find a lot of these songs on al-Darb al-Aḥmar [the Red Alley – a narrow lane in medieval Cairo that has become a cliché for the stereotypically *baladī*] and al-Azhar [the area around al-Azhar University, another stereotypically *baladī* area] and these things, you can find people singing them at bus stops and so forth. But "Ahmad Hilmi was married to Aida," this was the first time that the subject [the nation] was cast in such a way that there was a story, and an excellent idea that I really liked. I don't care if some people say it's nonsense and all that.

NASIR: There's an idea in a joke as well – something said in jest. I think this type of song is a kind of a joke. Like when they say "*kurūmb quṣūr*" ["cabbage of palaces" – a vendor's cry]. It gets said and then becomes like custom. There are a lot of sayings that get written and we still use them even now. But the "popular song" – no, I shouldn't say that because I don't consider them so [popular in the sense that they are steeped in "authentic" folk culture]. Truly popular culture is the stuff in books on folklore and folk songs. But this [vulgar stuff] I don't consider popular, I consider it a wave which has come because of the economic conditions – Egypt's economic conditions.

MUHAMMAD: That's only natural. But when Adawiya had his success they called it "nonsense" and "very vulgar" [i.e. despite the fact that many of his songs were based heavily on the sort of officially sanctioned "folklore" that Nasser advocated]. You can get any donkey [i.e. any officially sanctioned singer] and put a lot of money on him. If you're running the television, why do you put on that guy and leave Adawiya out? But that's what they did. They won't acknowledge him. When Adawiya first came out there were people who listened to him secretly – really respectable businessmen – they would shut the doors to their offices so nobody would see them. And if you ask them, they say, "No, I listen to Umm Kulthum." They just won't admit to listening to him because people say he's vulgar, not respectable.

A hundred years of the modernist paradigm

The rise of "vulgar" art and the decline of direct subsidies to the arts do not keep the state from promoting its agenda. Indeed, as doubts about the modernist enterprise become more widespread the "official version" of modernity may, in some ways, be more stridently proclaimed than at any previous time. The ideology of nationalist modernity was expressed nowhere more clearly than in a poster issued in 1990 by the Egyptian Ministry of Culture. It was titled *A Hundred Years of Enlightenment* (plate 12), and the purpose of the painting was to symbolize the *nahḍa* – the cultural "renaissance" experienced by Egypt during the past two centuries.[24] Caricatures of twenty-three assorted Egyptian artists and intellectuals, plus a few symbols of "the people," are shown standing and sitting

Plate 12 A Hundred Years of Enlightenment, by Salah Inani, reproduced by the Ministry of Culture

on pedestals, peering out of the poster. These were the state-approved icons of authentic Egyptian modernity, the short list of cultural heroes with whom all Egyptians who had been through the educational system should be familiar.

The scene depicted in the painting is dominated by the unmistakable figure of singing sensation Umm Kulthum, Abd al-Wahhab's rival from the 1920s until 1964, when they collaborated on "You Are My Life" (see chapter 6). In the poster her stately figure is dressed in bright red, her eyes turned toward heaven, hand held high in a classic singing pose. Abd al-Wahhab stands to her left, and is much smaller, appearing as a small dapper man holding a conductor's baton with which he directs an invisible orchestra.

There are only two women in the poster, Umm Kulthum and a peasant woman dressed in black (seated on the ground with a peasant man and a worker, identifiable by his overalls and a wrench protruding from his back pocket). The token peasants are shown listening raptly to folksinger Sayyid Darwish who, along with a few other colloquial artists represented in the picture (Bayram al-Tunsi, Salah Jahin and Fuad Haddad, and painter Mahmud Said, who stands in the painting with brush in hand before a famous canvas of traditional women from Alexandria) was allowed into the canon of modernity on the condition that he only be depicted "raising the people from their ignorance." Said and Darwish were among the modernist heroes featured in Dr. Mufid's *Artists of Alexandria* in "White Flag" (chapter 2). While most of the figures in the poster look resolutely outward, or skyward, the primary colloquialists, Darwish and Bayram al-Tunsi, mostly face either each other or their peasant "students." More typical are a group of classically inclined authors seated on the lower-right side of the picture.[25] Although all of them feature prominently in the development of modern Arabic literature, the focus of the literary circle is Taha Husayn, first dean of Cairo University and an influential former minister of education, and Nobel laureate Naguib Mahfouz, seated to Husayn's left. A group of actors, including Yusuf Wahbi, Zaki Tulaymat, and Nagib al-Rihani occupy the center-left area of the picture, and are similarly oriented to the outside.

The figures shown in *A Hundred Years of Enlightenment* are static, but the image still suggests temporal and spatial movement. The sense of movement begins on the top right-hand corner of the picture where one sees a pair of turbaned and bearded *shaykh*s stepping out from a dark, vaguely medieval and definitely urban, stone passage. The *shaykh*s' appearance would have been unremarkable in the early nineteenth century from which they are symbolically emerging. But in the televised and cinematic representations of tradition to which the younger generation had become accustomed by the late 1980s, the robes, beards, and turbans of these emerging figures suggest a religious scholar – perhaps an Azharite *shaykh*.

The *shaykh*s are the only figures in the scene who are in motion. One carries a lamp, and the other a book, probably *the* book – the Qur'ān. It is possible that the figures are meant to represent specific people – perhaps the nineteenth-century Egyptian Azharite traveler and translator Rifaa Rafi al-Tahtawi and Islamic reformer Muḥammad ʿAbduh – but a reading of the poster does not require that they be anyone in particular. The darkness from which the *shaykh*s emerge is not tradition *per se*, but a shroud over the authentic Islamic heritage of Egypt; the *shaykh*s themselves represent salutary aspects of heritage, not the diminution of it.

The sense of motion begun by the *shaykh*s on the top right-hand corner continues as one "reads" from the top right side of the poster to the left, as if in an Arabic text. First comes a statue of a mounted leader, probably Muḥammad ʿAlī,[26] the Mamluk ruler presented to Egyptian students as the first modernizer and founder of the state. Just to the left of Muhammad Ali is the dome of Cairo University's administration building. Next we see a statue of a peasant woman lifting her veil from her face with one hand, with the other hand draped over the shoulder of a sphinx. This was the neopharaonic style of Mahmud Mukhtar, whose caricature stands beside the statue, pipe in hand and green felt beret on his head. The statue's combination of pharaonic and modern elements restates the theme of the past carried unbroken into the present. Just past the statue we see the Nile. Although only a bit of the river shows, it reaches back behind the Cairo University dome, and thus suggests a frame for the whole picture. Of course the river also symbolizes the territorial extent of the nation. In the top-left corner of the poster a village sits on the riverbank, complementing the urban medieval ruin from which the *shaykh*s emerge.

Finally, just below the village, we see a figure that both affirms the "past in the present" theme begun by the *shaykh*s, and suggests an element of transformation: a happy scientist peering into a microscope. Like the *shaykh*s, the scientist with his microscope is probably intended to represent a particular person, but unlike the various intellectuals and artists who only make sense if one knows who they are, he is also intelligible as a symbol.[27] The idea of tradition suggested by the *shaykh*s on one side of the picture and then merged with images of the state (Muhammad Ali on horseback), education (the university dome), the progressive modernization of antiquity (Mukhtar's statue), and territoriality (the Nile) leads to another idea, namely scientific progress. The friendly and inviting faces of the state-sanctioned heroes of modernity all occupy positions below the line of symbols connecting the *shaykhs* to the scientist. They are modernity's figurative children. The poster is a textbook display of Egyptian modernism: an unbroken journey from the shadows of traditionalism to the satisfying labors of science, together with the artistic offspring of the transformation to modernity. *A Hundred Years of Enlightenment* is both an *isnād* – a chain of figures who transmit the values of the traditionalist past into the progressive future in the same way that the companions of the Prophet Muhammad transmitted his statements to later generations – and a cultural lineage.

The modernism portrayed in *A Hundred Years of Enlightenment*, like its Western cousin, seeks to promote the march of rationally ordered progress toward "objective science, universal morality and law, and autonomous art" (Harvey 1989, 12). But unlike Western modernism, it rejects making a break with tradition. The Egyptian modernist, as portrayed by the state and by many intellectuals, is a conservative radical.[28] Given that the modernist is seen as both the vanguard and rearguard of culture, such a representation of simultaneous time – what Anderson characterizes as a prenationalist style[29] – makes perfect sense to Egyptian nationalists trying to establish the ideological underpinnings of a state that can compete with Europe without being European. Egyptian modernism allows for Europe as a cultural catalyst, but insists on continuity between present and past: no rejection of tradition, and therefore none of the uncomfortable dislocation of European modernism.

This view of unbroken modernist evolution is not confined to intellectuals, but is heavily embedded in state policy, of which officially approved art such as *A Hundred Years of Enlightenment* is an element. The same *isnād* model of modernity, in which cultural change goes hand in hand with the image of an unbroken vessel of cultural authenticity handed from one authoritative figure to another, appears in textbooks read by millions of Egyptian high-school students. Recall, for example, the high-school science text mentioned in chapter 2: it was taught through the medium of modernist *isnād*:

> We must search for the roots of our authenticity and its distinguishing marks, and combine what is authentic with what is new in a way that leads us finally to the creation of *the authentic Egyptian type* [emphasis in the original] – a type derived from the new to an extent that makes it "contemporary" but gives it authenticity to an extent that makes it "Egyptian" . . . inevitably some basic aspects of the past

> must be "modernized" so as to make those currents grow. But if the present clings to the past, then it makes itself a handed-down and mummified imitation, unaffected by the florescence of life. If authenticity means that there is no present without a past, then the continuation and advancement of life means that there is no past without a present. *(ʿAbd al-Gawwād and ʿĀmir 1988, 9)*

"No present without a past," and "no past without a present." If the text had added "no future without a past" it could as easily have been describing *A Hundred Years of Enlightenment* as introducing scientific method to second-year high-school students.

The problem with both *A Hundred Years of Enlightenment* and science texts is that neither is an effective means of propagating the idea of modernism to the Egyptian populace. Indeed, the poster of *A Hundred Years of Enlightenment* marketed in 1990 was sold overprinted with an English translation of the title (and an attribution in English to "Ministry of Culture, Egypt"). Accordingly, it tended to be most available to the people who were least able to understand it. I found it on sale in the bookstores of five-star hotels, and occasionally in other large downtown bookstores. No Egyptian I knew had bought a copy. In an effort to identify the handful of faces with which I was not familiar, I showed it to a friend – an Arabic literature major at Cairo University, and near the top of his class. He chuckled, and told me that I knew more of the faces than he did. While I ran across *A Hundred Years of Enlightenment* often in government institutions or at government-sponsored events, I never found any indication that the poster was as interesting to Egyptian students as it was to foreign researchers. Students knew the lines to the allegedly meaningless *Crabs* theme song; they listened to Adawiya in cafés and during school outings; chuckled at the "deaf singer"; smirked at the heavy beat of "*What's the Story.*" But the students – raw material to be molded by the hand of modernism – were never visibly moved by the symbols of "enlightenment."

Neither were the people who gave me the text on scientific method enamored of it. It had been used by the daughter of a family living next door to Khadiga and Fathiyya in ʿAbdīn. The girl had managed to pass the exam, her family told me, but had not really understood it because it was too dull and pedantic. The girl herself proved them wrong. "It means we should change, but that we should remain Egyptian," she told me. But as a means of reaching the hearts and minds of potentially modernizable Egyptian citizens, the scientific-methods text left much to be desired. Indeed, most of the girls in this particular apartment building hadn't even got as far as secondary school, and would therefore never be exposed to the admonition to keep the past in the present (but only what is "useful" from the past), and vice versa. If the modernist transformation of the "authentic Egyptian type" was to be made palatable to the masses, some means other than textbooks and posters must be used.

The means for disseminating modernity to the masses was supposed to have been popular culture. The state, however, has never been able completely to monopolize popular culture. We have already seen several examples of films, songs, and poetry that deviate from the approved formulas: Bayram al-Tunsi and other even more "vulgar" colloquial poets, Ali Hamayda, Ahmad Adawiya, Hamdi Batshan, the cassette tape "A Very Hot Summer," and Adil Imam. All of these performers are condemned in the press, if they are mentioned at all, as "vulgar."

As Hani Shenuda suggested above, in formal situations many people are reluctant to admit liking such "vulgarity." Their reluctance is not necessarily specific to Egyptian culture. If one were to ask college-educated Americans about Madonna or "Married with Children" one might well find a similar hesitancy to express a favorable opinion. The iconoclastic Camille Paglia, a harsh critic of American universities, knew she could infuriate academics by taking Madonna seriously as an artist rather than as a social phenomenon relevant to the masses, but analyzable from the safety of academia (see Paglia 1992). We deal with popular culture by carefully circumscribing the "kitsch" that we like: television film critics Siskel and Ebert doing a show on "ten films we shouldn't like (but do)." College-educated Americans often take their pop culture on the sly, much like Muhammad Zadah's image of the man in his office switching the Adawiya tape to Umm Kulthum when he hears someone coming.

Americans may view classically "bad" films with a kind of ironic detachment.[30] I rarely noticed this with my Egyptian friends, but it is very hard to judge irony even in a tradition one knows thoroughly and even among people one has grown up with. To be sure of attitudes is hard. But the areas of deadpan seriousness or didactic solemnity are, as readers will have grasped by now, sometimes unexpected.

This point was driven home to me in 1985, when I was an Arabic student. One night I had seen a program called "*Garrāḥ al-mukhkh yuqaddim*" (The brain surgeon presents). It was a variety show hosted by the leading brain surgeon at Cairo University. The program mixed film clips with medical insights about the brain. I saw the solemn brain surgeon in a natty blue suit sitting in a comfortable lounge. In impeccable classical Arabic he announced, "*Wa-al-ān urīdu an uqaddima la-kum ḍayfanā al-*

ʿazīz . . ." (and now I want to present to you our honored guest . . .) "*al-mukhkh al-basharī*" (the human brain). As he said it, he reached on to the table beside his easy chair and picked up a plastic model of the human brain. I was rolling with laughter. Later the program showed X-rays of the brain being cushioned from shock by its lining. "We must be careful with our brains because they are very fragile," intoned the surgeon. Then the X-rays were replaced with a scene from a 1950s Egyptian film starring a bleached-blond female singer known as Ṣabāḥ. She was in the passenger seat of a car, which was being driven by a smiling man. A third actor, probably a rival for the woman's favors, was stuffed in the trunk. The picture alternated between scenes of Sabah singing sweetly "*sūʕ ʿalā mahl-ak su-u-u-uʕ . . .*" (drive slowly, dri-i-i-ive . . .) and scenes of the man in the trunk grimacing as the speeding car hit bumps in the road, subjecting his brain to an unconscionable pounding. I was in stitches.

The next day I was discussing the show with a fellow Arabic student, who also found it funny. An Egyptian employee of the Arabic program saw us laughing and asked what about. "You should have seen it," we said, grinning, "a variety show, and it was presented by – you'll never guess – a *brain surgeon*!" We guffawed, but he looked slightly taken aback. "Yes, '*Garrāḥ al-mukhkh*,' I saw it. It was an excellent show. I learned a great deal about the brain."

Of course he was right. The show was surely intended to teach about the brain, and it had worked tolerably well. Our ironic viewing was out of place; "*Garrāḥ al-mukhkh*" was serious television, not deliberate camp. Most of the time my experiences with Egyptians' views of popular culture conformed to this same pattern: my own sense of irony was not to be trusted.

But despite the earnestness of "The Brain Surgeon" and at least some of its audience, it should be stressed that irony is by no means lacking in Egyptian popular culture, only that it tends to be employed differently. We have already seen some of it: the "deaf singer" or "A Very Hot Summer," for example, would never have been funny unless one sensed the clash between the earnest advocacy of "good" music (i.e. music that makes at least a nod toward classical conventions), the song's juiced-up "dance-hall" beat, and the chipmunk imitation of a "deaf singer." The same could be said of the rap-inspired patter of Hamdi Batshan's "What's the Story?" And of course the vice-grip-headed bureaucrats of the *fahhāma* were funny because they comment on the absurdity many people face in their dealings with institutional life. But solemnly didactic messages are sometimes absorbed straight faced.

Teaching the puppets: Fatima Rushdi's final bow

Compared to many officially organized cultural events, *A Hundred Years of Enlightenment* was light-hearted and full of subtlety. On May 12, 1991 I was invited by a British journalist working for *al-Ahram Weekly* to attend what was billed as a "Day of the Egyptian Theater." The event, intended to honor major figures in the Egyptian theater, had been postponed for several days because of the death of Muhammad Abd al-Wahhab, which plunged the artistic community into unofficial mourning. Although I attended the event with an *al-Ahram Weekly* employee, on the "Day of the Egyptian Theater" I was no longer working for the paper, having found a slightly better-paying job elsewhere.

The "Day of the Theater" was to be held in the National Theater, a plush neo-Islamic oasis located in al-ʿAtaba Square, an old and rundown neighborhood on the edge of the European-style part of downtown Cairo – an area often recommended as a good place to buy "vulgar" tapes and suspiciously cheap (buyer beware) merchandise. The National Theater was less dilapidated than its surrounding neighborhood, due to a renovation completed in 1985. As previously mentioned, the renovated theater had been inaugurated by a production of a Taufiq al-Hakim play put to music by Hani Shenuda. When we arrived a *baladī* band consisting of *mizmār* (a double-reeded wind instrument) and *rabāba* (a simple stringed instrument often used to accompany the reading of epic folk poetry) was playing in the courtyard. The band struck up a tune each time a limousine pulled up in the courtyard to disgorge its wealthy occupants. Few of those arriving were really big stars, but there were some notables. One was Karam Muṭāwiʿ, director of the National Theater, who would be delivering the keynote address. Another was Minister of Culture Faruq Ḥusni. The honored guest for this evening, however, was none other than Fatima Rushdi, heroine of the 1939 film *Resolution* (see chapter 5) and an important stage actress in her day. She was much the worse for wear, climbing slowly out of her limousine, and not moving with a great deal of focus. The limousine was not Rushdi's. Rumor had it that the great actress had been all but forgotten, and had only been located when Mutawi placed an advertisement in the paper inquiring as to her whereabouts (Kāẓim 1991, 41). Whatever the truth behind these rumors, Rushdi received the most enthusiastic welcome from the band and the cheering onlookers.

With the minister of culture seated in the top balcony, accompanied by some guests from the Arab Gulf states, Mutawi gave the opening address, in which he let it be known that awards would be given for the lifetime achievements of a number of prominent playwrights (*ibid.*). He described the mission of the theater as promoting progress for the good of the people, and congratulated his colleagues on having achieved an atmosphere of complete artistic freedom. The centerpiece of the evening, however, was a kind of musical revue organized around an educational theme. The show began with a pair of *arāgōz* (Punch-and-Judy theater) puppets, one female and the other male. These were to represent the uneducated masses, which we knew from their exaggerated colloquial speech. As *arāgōz* puppets, the pair also represented the state of Egyptian theater before it was invigorated by the progress that Mutawi spoke of so glowingly. They came in from the back of the theater, and were told to stay "so that they could be educated." The girl puppet's role called for her to be marginally brighter than the boy.

The lesson was presented as an *isnād*. The theatrical tradition began with Yaqub Sanu, an Egyptian Jew who entertained Khedive Ismail – the Egyptian ruler who uttered the infamous phrase "Egypt is a part of Europe" – with satirical plays modeled on (sometimes translated from) Molière. But when Sanu became too critical of the authorities he was exiled by the khedive. Next up was Aḥmad Abū Khalīl al-Qabbānī, a Syrian playwright active in Egypt during the latter half of the nineteenth century. He was also critical of the regime, as a result of which his theater was burned down, and he died of grief.

The girl puppet noted that the modern Egyptian theater also has many works full of political criticism, such as *al-Malik huwwa al-malik* (The king is the king), *al-ʿAsal ʿasal* (Honey is honey), and a number of other plays which had been shown in Cairo recently. She ended her recitation with *al-Fatā Mahrān* (The lad Mahran), a historical play in verse by ʿAbd al-Raḥmān al-Sharqāwī about a fifteenth-century Egyptian peasant revolt against foreign (Circassian) rulers. Al-Sharqawi was known both for his sympathy toward socialist realism and for his frequent use of Islamic themes in his plays – another impeccably conservative radical in the mold of Shauqi and Abd al-Wahhab. When the puppet mentioned *Mahran*, a silver-haired man (presumably the actor who played the part in the production of the play) jumped out of the audience onto the stage and began declaiming lines from the play. It was a powerful, energetic, and incredibly loud performance. The audience was impressed, many exclaiming "*Allāh*!" as he recited.

There was another of several musical interludes, and then we proceeded to Abd Allah Nadim, a turn-of-the-century poet, playwright, and journalist, who falls into the colloquial rather than the classicist *isnād* – Bayram al-Tunsi, Salah Jahin, and Fuad Haddad rather than Ahmad Shauqi, Taha Husayn, and al-Sharqawi. Nadim, at some point in his career, fell foul of the British. The narrator made a statement about *sulṭa* (power, authority), which the dim boy puppet mistook for *salaṭa* (salad). The narrator corrected him, and the boy puppet went into a frenzy of fear, until the girl puppet calmed him, saying, "*Sulṭa* is a thing of the past. Now there is no such thing as *sulṭa.*" I could not resist glancing up at the minister of culture, seated high in the balcony, conversing with his Saudi friends fresh from their triumph in the Gulf.

We observed a few more songs and dramatic presentations illustrating more links in the *isnād* of Egyptian theatrical tradition. We heard of George Abyaḍ, an early dramatist who translated Shakespeare. Then we saw Nagib al-Rihani, a low but beloved comic from the 1930s, arguing with *Hundred Years of Enlightenment* alumnus Zaki Tulaymat, founder of the first national theater, and a believer in elevated drama. Tulaymat admonished his competitor for pandering to low tastes. Finally we came to Fatima Rushdi.

When Rushdi was mentioned, the heroine of *Resolution* received thunderous applause. She smiled, obviously delighted to be in the limelight one more time. The venerable actress was seated in a balcony on one side of the theater with Amīna Rizq, another beloved actress who still takes some roles in films and television. On Rushdi's other side was a garishly dressed younger woman with expensively coiffed hair (later at the newspaper my British friend was told that she was Mutawi's wife, but I was never able to confirm this). The young woman was brandishing a copy of Rushdi's memoirs, *Kifāḥī fi-l-masraḥ wa-l-sīnimā* (My struggle in the theater and cinema). She thrust the book into Rushdi's hands and invited her to read. Poor Fatima seemed a bit confused at this request. The woman goaded her, but Rushdi merely smiled faintly. Finally the young woman took the book back and read a bit herself. We moved on to other notables of the Egyptian stage.

The list was long, and there was a real attempt at comprehensive coverage of the entire field of the Egyptian theater. The program ended with a roll call of the actors, writers, and critics for whom there was not enough time to stage an enactment of their work. But suddenly there was a glitch in the proceedings. Amina Rizq, Rushdi's neighbor in the balcony of honor, went down onto the stage. Obviously angry, she ripped the microphone from the hands of the narrator, al-Sayyid Rāḍī, a short, balding man whose last role had been as an Israeli spymaster on a popular television drama.[31] "You have forgotten Yusuf Wahbi!" she thundered. "How can you talk about the Egyptian theater without mention of Yusuf Wahbi? He was our *ustāz* [master]! How can you forget *Sons of the Rich* and *Sons of the Poor*?[32] This is scandalous. I won't accept it."

It *was* a bit peculiar that Wahbi had not been given a prominent place in the program.[33] He was an important figure in the Egyptian theater and cinema, especially from 1923 until the 1940s. An impressive roster of talent passed through Wahbi's *Firqat Ramsīs* (Ramsīs Troupe) at one time or another. Fatima Rushdi was, in fact, one of the earliest members of the Ramsīs Troupe, followed shortly by Amina Rizq.[34] Later she married Wahbi's partner Aziz Id (a name that had featured prominently in the program) and formed her own troupe. Fāṭima al-Yūsuf was another star of the early Ramsīs Troupe; she gave up acting in the mid-1920s to found the magazine *Rūz al-Yūsuf* (after Fatima al-Yusuf's nickname, Rose), which remains one of the most important weeklies in Egypt (see Yūsuf 1972).[35] Another member of the troupe was ʿAzīza Amīr, who in 1927 appeared in *Layla*, the very first Egyptian film.[36] Nagma Ibrāhīm played Rayyā in *Rayyā and Sikīna*, an early Salah Abu Sayf hit. Amīna Muḥammad formed a production company in the 1930s that provided the first cinematic experience for directors Kamal Salim and Salah Abu Sayf, worked as an assistant to Cecil B. deMille on *The Ten Commandments*, and starred with Husayn Sidqi (the leading man in *Resolution*) in a 1938 film about a Chinese girl in Cairo called *Tītā wa-Wang* (Tita and Wang). Daulat Abyad (who played the mother of Abd al-Wahhab in *White Rose*) was in the Ramsīs Troupe at one time. Farid Shauqi (the model for tough men in Egyptian cinema throughout the 1950s and 1960s) got his first acting break from Yusuf Wahbi in the 1940s. Wahbi, a childhood friend of *White Rose* director Muhammad Karim, also formed a film production company called Studio Ramsīs, which financed Karim's first film, *Zaynab.* He starred in Karim's (and Egypt's) first talkie, *Awlād al-zawāt* (Sons of aristocrats), and between 1932 and 1973 directed thirty-one films (in most of which he was also the star), and acted in fifty-four films (Rushdī 1971; F. Shauqī 1977; Shūsha 1978; Wahbī 1973; Yūsuf 1972). Taken at face value, such an impressive list of accomplishments should have lifted Yusuf Wahbi to Abd al-Wahhab-like adulation in the media, but as the "Day of the Theater" showed, this has not happened.

In fact, Yusuf Wahbi seems to have had many detractors. For example, Ṣāfīnāz Kāẓim, an art critic for the public-sector magazine *al-Muṣawwar* (a descendant of the Dār al-Hilāl publishing house, which formerly published *al-Ithnayn*), condemned Wahbi a few weeks after the incident at the

"Day of the Theater."[37] In Kazim's view Amina Rizq's outburst was not just about Wahbi, but was a true expression of Wahbi's spirit:

> He respected only one institution, and that was "Yusuf Wahbi." His interest in Amina Rizq was an extension of his concern for the female image of himself. Because of his long life, his extensive relations with the media and his aggressive personality, he was able to a great extent to dictate the history of the Egyptian theater from his own view, in conformity with his passion to be singled out as the "dean of the Egyptian theater," thereby effacing traces of other pioneers of the theater who fought him in their own time, and triumphed over him after his death.
> *(Kāẓim 1991, 41)*

Kazim goes on to ridicule Wahbi's contribution to Egyptian theatrical arts as nothing more than melodrama. Amina Rizq, despite her long experience in the Egyptian entertainment industry (from the early 1920s to the present), "lacks the critical facility to give an objective appraisal of the theater, and is biased, having no panoramic view of the long history of the Egyptian theater" (*ibid.*). Kazim attributes Rizq's outburst to blind adherence to the theater of Yusuf Wahbi and, since she was an important part of this theater, to an egotistical desire to hog the spotlight. Rizq's fanatical support of Wahbi, she says, is nothing more than fanatical support of herself.

Another reason, one presumes, that Wahbi was not slotted into the theatrical *isnād* even as a substantial artistic presence contributing to the success of later figures (on the level of, for example, Umm Kulthum's composers, who are given an honorable, if lesser, place in the pantheon of Egyptian music) was that Wahbi effectively wrote himself out of theatrical history. He did this by writing an autobiography that was not only shockingly frank (or perhaps inventive) about his sexual exploits, but which also makes little effort to connect himself to the great figures who preceded him or even to his contemporaries.[38] Instead, Wahbi focuses, arrogantly in the view of such critics as Kazim, on himself. Indeed, he is almost gleeful in reporting the exploits of a young man who seemed to be thoroughly out of control. Unlike Abd al-Wahhab's biographies, in which we hear almost mystical accounts of a young boy being repeatedly touched by the hand of fate – or at least by the hand of Shauqi – we hear of young Yusuf losing his virginity at the age of twelve to a friend of his mother (Wahbī 1973 vol. I, 30–36). He tells of being a circus wrestler (*ibid.*, 53–57); spins a tale of smoking hashish with an Armenian actress (who later became a member of his troupe), having sex with her, killing her husband (a Cypriot drug dealer), who caught them in the act, in a pitched battle, and then telling his worried mother that he and some friends had been involved in a fight with

Australian soldiers (*ibid.*, 58–62); describes seducing a Greek girl with a magic amulet, keeping the girl in a rented apartment near his home, getting her pregnant and having the baby aborted (*ibid.*, 70–81).[39] All these tales are from Wahbi's teen years. Among his later exploits is a tale of being robbed by a prostitute in Paris (*ibid.*, vol. II, 58), and another of having a protracted affair (described in some detail) with a sadomasochistic Italian woman who was an ether addict (*ibid.*, 24–36).

By contrast, the autobiography of Muhammad Karim, who grew up with Wahbi, is extremely straitlaced, and has more the air of inexorable destiny that we see in Abd al-Wahhab's biographies. The media admire Abd al-Wahhab for his friendships with the rich and famous: Shauqi "finishes" Abd al-Wahhab, makes him cultured, takes him to Paris only so that he can better appreciate his Egyptianness. Yusuf Wahbi, however, describes sitting in a Parisian café with Shauqi only as a lead-in to a story about a beggar girl who approaches them asking for enough money to return to her village, is taken to a hotel by Wahbi, but then ends up robbing him while he is in the shower (*ibid.*, 58–60).

Given Wahbi's admitted taste for low life, it is not surprising that the education doled out to the two ignorant *baladī* puppets during the "Day of the Theater" glossed over his contribution to Egyptian art. Actually the narrator, al-Sayyid Radi, had (as I recall) briefly mentioned Wahbi, a fact he tried unsuccessfully to impress on the near-hysterical Amina Rizq when she jumped onto the stage to protest at the omission of her mentor. But this was not enough for her. She saw to it that the show ground to a halt. People in the audience started talking to each other, some in support of Wahbi, some against, others merely aghast at what was happening. Finally Karam Mutawi appeared on the stage and consolingly wrapped his arm around Rizq's shoulder. He gave her the microphone, allowing her to repeat her protest, somewhat more calmly. When she had said her piece, Mutawi grandly announced that there was no thought of carrying out a campaign against the legacy of Yusuf Wahbi, and that next year the National Theater would do an entire show on him. Al-Sayyid Radi muttered audibly that he had, in fact, said Wahbi's name. Having healed the rift in the artistic community opened by Amina Rizq's pained protest, Radi, Mutawi, and the actors and singers involved in dramatizing the lives of selected giants of the stage could complete the education of our two ignorant puppets. Once the honor roll of Egyptian thespians and critics had been verbalized all that remained was one final song, followed by a few special awards to leading personalities, and then another song. When the show was over the audience stampeded for the doors of the theater, eager to board waiting limousines, private cars, and public transportation. This was how the heroine of *Resolution* had her last moment in the spotlight.

Descent to "vulgarity"

While the sun was setting on the career of Fatima Rushdi (and perhaps on the modernist establishment that honored her in the "Night of the Theater"), the careers of several of the actors in the much-ridiculed *School of Troublemakers* were flourishing. Adil Imam, the comedian who played chief "troublemaker" Bahgat al-Abasiri in *School*, has done particularly well on the commercial stage and screen since his early 1970s breakthrough. Before *School* Imam had appeared in a number of films, but never played the lead. By the time *School*'s run in the theater was over (1974) he started getting leads, and over the next fifteen years became the most popular actor in the Egyptian entertainment industry.[40] Many of my acquaintances joined with the critics in asserting that Imam had become arrogant in the last few years, and that he was interested only in making money. Imam is, however, still king at the box office. He is said to command a fee of a quarter million Egyptian pounds per film – more than twice that of any other actor or actress except, some claimed, Fatin Hamama.[41]

Plate 13 Fatima Rushdi on the staircase, with Husayn Sidqi (from *Resolution*, 1939)

Imam has maintained his popularity in part by continuing to do live stage performances throughout the 1970s and 1980s. Imam's second play in the mid-1970s, *Shāhid ma-shāf-shi ḥāga* (The witness who saw nothing), was a political farce and enjoyed popularity similar to that of *School of Troublemakers*. His third star vehicle in the theater, *il-Wād Sayyid ish-shaghghāl* (The boy Sayyid the janitor), played for eight consecutive years, ending in 1992. Following *Sayyid* he built his own theater and opened up a new production in 1993, *al-Za'īm* (The leader, directed by Sharīf 'Arafa), which promises to be as popular as its predecessors.

A few years after *School of Troublemakers* finished its four-year run, Imam began to appear in a number of films that carried the antimodernist theme of his breakthrough performance a step further. Among these productions was a pair of films that both sharpened the criticism of modern institutions begun in *School* and developed a more coherent (and even bleaker) image of "postmodern" Egyptian society. I first discovered these films by asking several college-student friends to suggest some "good" Adil Imam films.

Among the films most often suggested were *Ragab fōq ṣafīḥ sākhin* (Ragab on a hot tin roof, 1979, directed by Aḥmad Fu'ād) and *Sha'bān taḥt al-ṣifr* (Shaban below zero, 1980, directed by Henrī Barakāt).[42] Although the films represent a break with the sort of ideology symbolized in *A Hundred Years of Enlightenment*, they begin from a perspective that can be mapped onto the painting, namely the knot of *awlād al-balad* at the bottom of the poster – the illiterate peasants and worker listening raptly to the officially sanctioned vernacular artists. Their place in *A Hundred Years of Enlightenment* is to represent the virtuous characteristics of the traditional Egypt that is to be transformed by modernism. The films are about *ibn al-balad* in the sense that they chronicle the corruption and humiliation of the conceptual ideal of the highly moral, tradition-minded ordinary Egyptian. This struck Muhammad Zadah as simply realistic. He told me:

> *Ibn al-balad* is dead. He might live on in cartoons . . . on paper in the media, but that's it. The real thing is dead. You want to know why? It was a symbol, a sense of gallantry [*shahāma*] that is no longer there. Not a real person, but a moral thing, and this morality has died. Modern conditions have killed off the values which made up the character of *ibn al-balad*.

His friend Nasir, who consistently stood on the other side of the line between "high" and "low" culture, disagreed:

> It's not true that *ibn al-balad* is dead. I'm from the south, from Upper Egypt, and *ibn al-balad* is still there. I see it in myself, in my family. It's in my hometown of

Qena. It's in the popular quarters of Cairo, places like ʿAbbāsīya. Especially in the moral sense – *ibn al-balad* is still clearly here.

Muhammad countered: "I disagree. Maybe the character exists in Upper Egypt as you say because people are still living undisturbed by the modern world. They haven't been shaken from their basic humanity. But here in Cairo, or in cities in general, that's another matter altogether." I suggested that the concept of *ibn al-balad* was still used in films, if only negatively as in *Ragab on a Hot Tin Roof*. Muhammad still disagreed:

The film isn't saying that the character *ibn al-balad* exists, only that he wishes it existed. I've seen that film. It was good. The important thing in the film is that he tries – tries, mind you – to appeal to the character, to reclaim it from the past so that it can be present in our own age. He wishes it were here, that's the best thing about it.

What Muhammad saw in *Ragab* and these other Adil Imam films was an artistic treatment of *ibn al-balad* that differed sharply from the officially sanctioned stereotype. In *A Hundred Years of Enlightenment*, *ibn al-balad* moved up from the bottom of the poster and into the constellation of modernist heroes. In each film Imam starts out as a beleaguered *ibn al-balad*, crude but honest. But though Imam moves progressively closer in the two films to the urban center of enlightenment, he never prospers materially or morally other than by foul means.[43] The firmament of modernist stars is conspicuously absent. Some of the characters Adil Imam meets along his journey into modernist hell dress like the proverbial "enlightened" figures in the Ministry of Culture's poster – they possess all the material marks of success that had been mainly the preserve of the "enlightened" class in Egyptian cinema from *White Rose* in 1934 to *Pay Attention to Zuzu* in 1972. But these characters are "Westernized," not "enlightened"; there are no modern characters in these films in the *Hundred Years of Enlightenment* sense – the sense of a "radical conservative" who can successfully adapt to the new because he is in firm possession of the best characteristics of the old. The handful of decent characters in the films are mostly figures who have either rejected the modernist transformation or simply have not been reached by it.

The mock-modernist transformation begins in *Ragab on a Hot Tin Roof*, a production adapted from the American film *Midnight Cowboy*. *Midnight Cowboy* might seem to be an unlikely candidate for adaptation to the Egyptian screen. Not only is the original nihilistic, but the film's protagonist, Joe Buck, is intermittently homosexual.[44] *Ragab* retained the nihilism, but carefully excised the homosexuality by substituting women for some of the characters and in some of the events that centered around men in the American film.

The eponymous protagonist of *Ragab on a Hot Tin Roof* is a peasant (played by Adil Imam). We first see him laboring in the fields, hacking at the hard earth with a *fās* (a heavy hoelike implement). He and a fellow peasant decide that if they and their neighbors are to prosper the village must improve its irrigation of the hard earth which had been watered by means of a waterwheel turned by a worn-out buffalo. If there is to be progress they must buy a tractor for the purpose. The village elders agree, and after the Friday prayer they announce that they will collect money from each family to buy the tractor and then set about choosing someone to go to the big city to buy it.[45] Initially they want the *ʿumda* (headman) to go, but he is afraid of not being able to cope with the crowds and confusion of the city. Instead, Ragab is selected as the most trustworthy man in the village. Before he goes, one of his fellow peasants, who has been to the city, gives him the address of a woman named Shūshū scrawled on a slip of paper. Then off he goes to the big city.

Although this opening sequence occupies no more than five minutes of the film, it is one of the most important devices for making *Ragab* an Egyptianized reworking of *Midnight Cowboy* rather than a purely derivative film. In *Midnight Cowboy* Joe Buck starts out in amoral squalor and goes nowhere. He goes to the city planning to make a living as a male prostitute, not realizing that most of the clientele for male prostitutes are men. There is no question of "spoiling" Joe Buck: he is already ruined. Ragab, however, starts off as naive as Joe Buck, but not particularly corrupt. In fact his fellow peasants choose him to make the journey to the city because they consider him morally outstanding. *Ragab* starts off from the same modernist premise as countless other films, but then goes in a different direction. This is not to say that many other films do not feature peasants, but such films tend to depict an urban view of peasant life, and to be concerned with bringing "progress" to the countryside (or are a commentary on an assumed lack of same).[46] *Ragab* is unusual in that it portrays the countryside as a site of both morality and progress. It may be a fragile morality rooted more in the absence of temptation than in true conviction, and a pale, somewhat rudimentary progress, but compared to what Ragab encounters in the city the countryside appears enlightened.

Ragab arrives in the city on the train. We see him clad in *gallābīyya* (robe) and a brown felt peasant's *ṭaqiyya* (a simple cap), hanging out of the window, eyes practically popping from his head at the sight of so many people. When the train pulls into Cairo's Ramses Station we start to hear music, not Arabic music, but American bluegrass "hillbilly" music – banjos and fiddles. When I watched the film with my college-student friends they told me that the scene was funny because of Ragab's obvious naiveté – because he was a "hick," but that bluegrass music by itself would not evoke such an image for all viewers. Nonetheless, virtually all of the music in *Ragab* was Western, and the way it was employed in the film suggests that at least the director saw it as an additional element of irony. The exceptions to the overall prevalence of Western music included a singer at a nightclub in which Ragab gets swindled, and a bellydance song. Arabic music is also heard in scenes that feature heavy drinking and licentiousness; all other scenes are accompanied by Western music.

For example, Ragab is taken by the swindler (the Egyptian equivalent of *Midnight Cowboy*'s Ratso Rizzo) to a shish-kebob restaurant, where he wolfs down roasted meat as a bemused Ratso character looks on – all this

Plate 14 Ragab the worthy peasant (center, holding stick), discussing the need for agricultural modernization with the village notables (from *Ragab on a Hot Tin Roof*, 1979)

to a recording of a wordless 1960s American novelty song called *Manamana*. Later the swindler robs Ragab and leaves him with a bill for whiskey at a nightclub. The owner calls in three bouncers to shake down the frightened peasant. As Ragab eyes the huge men the theme from *The Sorcerer's Apprentice* starts up. The *Sorcerer's Apprentice* theme continues when a policeman discovers Ragab wandering the darkened Cairene streets. Ragab runs, so the policeman pursues as the *Sorcerer's* theme becomes wilder. In another scene Ragab is about to have sex with a hideous old woman who has bought him a meal in a restaurant: we hear the high-pitched pulses played in the background of the murder scenes of *Psycho*; the woman's face appears distorted and threatening, and Ragab flees. When Ragab is searching for the Ratso character we see the peasant-turned-avenger lurking by a sleazy hotel where he hopes to find his tormentor: the James Bond theme plays. When "Ratso" dies at the end of the film, it is to a tune from *Ben Hur*. Whether or not the audience understands the irony in the use of any of these tunes, the point still comes across that this city moves to alien rhythms, never to familiar Arabic sounds.[47]

The "Ratso" of *Ragab on a Hot Tin Roof* is named Bulbul – "Nightingale." Bulbul, an unsuccessful gambler and hustler like his American predecessor, spots Ragab lost in the crowd at the train station, looking around himself and muttering "*minēn yiwaddī ʿalā fayn*?" (from where heads to where?). Bulbul hooks his bewildered prey by pretending to recognize Ragab, telling the peasant that he comes from the same village. Then he keeps the gullible Ragab from spending his money on the tractor by asking the tractor salesman if the machine comes with a *siks^{i} bīs* (six piece). Both Ragab and the salesman are embarrassed to admit that they don't know what a *siks^{i} bīs* is, and the negotiations quickly break down. A few scenes later Bulbul has Ragab guzzling whiskey and ogling the women at a nightclub thick with Bulbul's fellow con-men and women. "*Di lābsa min ghayr hudūm*" (she's dressed without any clothes) says the astonished Ragab when he sees the bellydancer.

One of the other hustlers working this nightclub is Bulbul's mistress Iglāl, a buxom redhead wearing a skintight, strapless top, who leads Ragab into thinking he will sleep with her when the night is through. Ragab gives his money to Bulbul "for safekeeping." Bulbul quietly makes his exit while Ragab is drinking toast after toast to the smiling Iglal; the hapless Bulbul quickly loses the money in a card game. Ragab is freed from having to pay his bill at the nightclub by another of Bulbul's accomplices, a fat man dressed as a peasant, who claims that he was rescued in similar circumstances when he first came to the city. When Ragab is sent on his way the man promptly goes to Bulbul's card game, removes his fake peasant outfit, and collects his cut of the booty.

The remainder of the story is similar enough to *Midnight Cowboy* for no detailed plot summary to be necessary. Ragab searches for Bulbul, finds him, and eventually befriends him after a fashion. Along the way he endures numerous indignities. Ragab tries to repent, but repentance is expensive: how will he live? In the end only Bulbul can help him, but he does so by turning Ragab into himself. Finally, Bulbul is killed by an angry loser in a card game that Ragab has won through beginner's luck. The angry loser tries to stab Ragab, but Bulbul throws himself in the way of the knife – the only decent thing he has done in his life.

Ragab communicates degradation by putting the protagonist into an emasculated world. There are no manly men in *Ragab on a Hot Tin Roof*. In fact, there are not even any successful men. Scantily dressed women live alone in splendid villas while men literally scavenge the ruins, which we see near the end of the film when Bulbul takes Ragab to his lair in a ruined building. The most humiliating scene in *Ragab* – very much the equivalent of Joe Buck's first descent into homosexual prostitution in *Midnight Cowboy* – is of Ragab washing a (female) prositute's feet. He finds the prostitutes through the slip of paper given him in the village with the name and address of Shushu. But by the time he finds them he is no longer a potential customer, so the prostitutes make him into their servant. Ragab protests that "this is women's work," but he washes the prostitute's feet anyway because his only alternative is starving in the streets.

The uplifting side of Joe Buck's relationship with Ratso is adapted to *Ragab* by inserting a female character. Her name is Inshirāḥ, and Ragab stumbles upon her when fleeing from the police. Inshirah is another red-haired woman – a poor, modest girl who looks like Iglal, but who functions in the film as Iglal's opposite.[48] Inshirah lives with her ailing father in a desperately poor area, and works preparing *fūl* (fava beans, a staple in the diet of the poor) in large pots which are distributed all over the city after a night of slow cooking. When we first see Inshirah she is ascending from a sooty pit where the pots of beans bake. Ragab thinks she is an *ʿafrīta* (demon). Periodically Ragab returns to Inshirah and her kindly old father. They try to help him, but the uncorrupted characters in the world Ragab now inhabits are marginalized and helpless. Ragab eventually leaves Inshirah and sleeps with Iglal, only to discover that she was in league with Bulbul all along. Scenes featuring the two women are often paralleled: several times the good Inshirah is shown directly after the corrupt Iglal so that the contrast between the two is obvious. The scene in which Ragab washes the prostitute's feet is also immediately juxtaposed to a brief scene of Inshirah massaging her poor father's tired feet. The two women in *Ragab* take on the human characteristics, both good and bad, of *Midnight Cowboy*'s Ratso, but avoid the homosexuality of the original, which would almost certainly have been cut by the Egyptian censors. Bulbul is only a shell of *Cowboy*'s Ratso, and Ragab only becomes friendly with him in the final ten minutes.

Midnight Cowboy features flashbacks to Joe Buck's squalid past. These are transferred in *Ragab* to occasional scenes of Ragab's village showing his fellow peasants wondering what has happened to Ragab, but blissfully unconcerned about life in the big city.[49] There is surprisingly little inclination to condemn him. Instead, the villagers gather more money and send someone else to buy the tractor. By the end of the film the villagers have their machine, and are still wondering what happened to poor Ragab whom they will never see again. The flashbacks remind viewers that somewhere there is a place where small bits of modern life can be absorbed without corrupting the salutary aspects of tradition. But as the tenuous position of Inshirah and her father shows, there is little hope of integrating village life with the city. And even the villagers are not completely

Plate 15 Ragab's big adventure in the city: a series of humiliating "look but don't touch" situations (from *Ragab on a Hot Tin Roof*, 1979)

innocent. The last village scene shows the man who gave Ragab Shushu's address in profile against a sunset. He is talking about Ragab to the headman. They are concerned about Ragab, but not enough to do anything about him.

The sun sets on modernism

The contrast between the reception of *Ragab* by the public and that by the critics was as simple as Muhammad Zadah arguing with his friend Nasir over the relative merits of Abd al-Wahhab and Adawiya. Critics hated the film in much the same way that Nasir despised Adawiya. As one of them said:

> [*Ragab on a Hot Tin Roof* is] the story of a simple peasant living in a small village, most of which is inhabited by naive villagers living as their grandfathers had lived a hundred years ago, knowing nothing of progress and civilization except rumors. We find ourselves confronted not just by a character representing ignorance, but by a real contempt for the intelligence of the viewer. [The director] treats the audience as intellectually backward. The ultimate moral conclusions of the film completely ruin it – make it a despicable work. One cannot tell if it is criticism or an admonition, a lesson in morals, or a view of society . . . How I wished that Ragab would actually jump from that hot tin roof and stop the affected convulsions that we saw through three-quarters of the film . . . and tell us what ignorance and backwardness do to a good man who comes from a green branch of a tree rooted in the generous soil of Egypt. *("Ragab . . ." 1979)*

In the view of this critic it was entirely Ragab's backwardness that was the problem, not the savage milieu into which he fell. Ragab was living as his "grandfathers had lived a hundred years ago." In other words, he had completely missed out on "a hundred years of enlightenment" – the real thing, not the poster – and it was the duty of the filmmakers to show how Ragab could be enlightened, not how he could be morally perverted. "Enlightenment" is a reality in the official view of modernism, thus to leave it entirely out of a film is a perversion of reality. The critic implies that the institutions of modernism are imbued with traditional values – the values inherent in classicism – and that these values will raise the naive man from the "generous soil of Egypt." His criticism is pure *Hundred Years of Enlightenment* (the poster): the peasant sitting at the feet of the colloquial artists carried into the ranks of the progressive intellectuals.

The audience, however, did not feel that the makers of *Ragab* were contemptuous of them. Not only were my college-age friends fond of the film, but when the film came out *Ragab*'s fans kept it in the theaters for thirty-three straight weeks (*ibid.*) – an extremely long run for the Egyptian cinema. Ten years after *Ragab*'s initial run it was not the "unenlightened" who found *Ragab* appealing, but college students – the very audience that was supposed to be most conversant with the "progress and civilization" the critic saw as the natural antidote to *Ragab*'s assumed vulgarity. This is not to say that the students who recommended *Ragab* as a good film could not readily replicate the official discourse if asked. I discovered this with regard to another frequently recommended Adil Imam film called *Shaban below Zero*, which featured Ahmad Adawiya, the man considered by many to be the quintessential "vulgar singer."

Shaban was a remake by the same director (Henri Barakat) of a 1942 film called *Lau kunt[i] ghanī* (If I were rich). The differences between the old and the new versions of the two films is much the same as the difference in opinion expressed by many of my acquaintances and friends (or even expressed by the same person in different contexts) over "vulgar" and "high" art.

The original film featured a "Beverly Hillbillies" scenario in which Maḥrūs, an endearing but cloddish barber (considered a typical *ibn al-balad* occupation), inherits a lot of money from a despised relative who had been a beggar, but had never spent a piaster of the meager sums doled out grudgingly to him by Mahrus and the other small merchants of his *baladī* neighborhood. Early in the film, before he inherits the beggar's unsuspected riches, Mahrus makes a great show of his disdain for the rich, refusing to marry his daughter to a man who presents himself to the foolish barber as a bureaucrat working for the railroad. Mahrus, unimpressed by the man's obvious education and social refinement, and so backward that he fails to understand that the man's stated bureaucratic salary of LE 40 per month is a modest sum, is afraid the suitor is too wealthy for them. In reality the situation is even more absurd: the suitor is actually the son of a pasha – a fact of which even his would-be fiancée is unaware. He presents himself to her and Mahrus as a bureaucrat in order, he thinks, to ensure that she wants to marry him for his merits as a man, and not for his money.

But when Mahrus comes into really big money (thousands of Egyptian pounds stuffed into the walls of the beggar's hovel) he moves his family to Zamālek, the "Beverly Hills" of Cairo. We see them riding in a fine car, an *autrōmbīl* as Mahrus calls it in his garbled colloquial: the daughter who had been wooed by the incognito pasha; Mahrus's dissolute son, formerly an employee in a nearby publishing house; Mahrus's corpulent wife Fulla; and her lascivious brother, also an employee in the neighborhood publishing business, and a dabbler in organizing the workers to oppose the establishment's owners.

The unfortunate suitor approaches Mahrus again, but this time the barber rejects him because he doesn't appear to have *enough* money. The men of the family squander vast sums on dancers and prostitutes, and buy the publishing company at which Mahrus's brother-in-law and son had been employed. Mahrus and his brother-in-law, uneducated and unworldly, are uniquely unsuited for any modern business venture, let alone publishing. They proceed to run the operation into the ground, but are eventually saved when their affairs are taken over by the daughter's suitor, who finally reveals his aristocratic background. He not only bails them out of the huge mess they have made of the publishing house, but marries Mahrus's daughter, who is conspicuously more modern and middle class than her parents. Mahrus and company return to their idyllic, but backward, "folkloric" life; the future belongs to Mahrus's daughter and the hardworking rich man – a new middle class which avoids the pitfalls of both "backward" traditionalism and corrupt *awlād al-zawāt*.

The film features two songs by Sorāyā Ḥilmī, a popular *mūnūlūgist* (an entertainer who sings humorous songs, usually in a nightclub, which he or she dramatizes with dramatic gestures and jokes) of the 1940s. As Mahrus and his brother-in-law dive into the shady world of prostitutes and singers, Hilmi's songs entice them to lose all control and spend ever more recklessly on their sinful new habits. At one point she chides the nightclub audience for their decadent lives by shining a flashlight on male spectators, putting a symbolic "spotlight" on their transgressions while singing tales of their corruption with the refrain "*inta garī*" (you are impudent). Mahrus and his brother-in-law are in fact more than merely impudent. Mahrus nearly ruins his marriage to Fulla, and the pair run up debts higher than they could ever hope to repay. But the rich man's last-minute intervention is really the point of the film, because it sets the stage for the transformation of both *ibn al-balad* (actually *bint al-balad* in this case) and *ibn al-zawāt* to middle class. In other words the neat resolution of problems in *If I Were Rich*, a low 1942 comedy, leaves the viewer in exactly the same place as the 1939 classic *Resolution* and the 1934 melodrama *White Rose*.

Enter the 1980 version of the story, which starred Adil Imam in place of Mahrus and also featured Adawiya in Soraya Hilmi's role (Adawiya appears three times in a nightclub frequented by his protagonist, compared to Hilmi's two). The presence of Adawiya seemed to be a red flag for my friends. They liked the movie and were more than happy to view it with me, but direct questions about it brought the same sort of standoff as the one I had experienced between Muhammad and Nasir, with one side claiming the film as "popular" while the other denounced it as "vulgar."

In *If I Were Rich* the singers and prostitutes were there mostly to relieve Mahrus and company of their money. Everyone in the audience knows what they are – primarily a way to symbolize and facilitate Mahrus's slide down the slippery slope of sin. In *Shaban* the prostitutes are separate from the singer, and the songs act as narrative markers, signaling shifts in the film's tone. In the first song Adawiya appears dressed like a James Brown clone in colorful print shirt and white leisure suit, amid bottles of whiskey and bellydancers. He sings Hani Shenuda's "*Zaḥma ya dunyā*" (How crowded is the world), which was rereleased a decade later on the "Adawiya 91" tape: "How crowded is the world / crowded and friends lose their way, Crowded and merciless / a free-for-all."

In his second appearance Adawiya is again in the company of a bellydancer, but "James Brown" is now dressed in the traditional *gallabiyya* (robe). In the third song he still wears the traditional garb, but the dancer is gone. The significance of the transformation is clear both from the events in the film and from the general associations the audience has with the actor playing the protagonist.

In *Shaban below Zero* the protagonist, played of course by Adil Imam, is a partly educated and semiurban character who lives and works in a small town somewhere in the vicinity of Alexandria. The new film takes the characters of Mahrus and the wealthy suitor from *If I Were Rich* and collapses them into one – the character of Shaban. Whereas the money in the original film comes to Mahrus from a destitute relative who possessed unsuspected riches, in the remake Shaban attains wealth by participating in a scheme to defraud a distant relative of an inheritance. Ultimately, of course, the scheme unravels and plunges Shaban into ruin.

The part of Mahrus's modern daughter in the old film corresponds to a character named Zaynab, Shaban's coworker in the Bureau of Land Reclamation. In the old film it is Mahrus's stupidity that keeps his daughter from marrying, but all problems are eventually solved by her suitor's wealth and bureaucratic expertise. In *Shaban*, however, the protagonist's marginal position in the bureaucracy prevents the marriage. Shaban, in the late 1970s, actually has a *lower* salary – LE 28.14 per month – than the bureaucrat in the 1942 original. He has some education – always touted by the establishment as the route to upward mobility – but no money, no status, and no chance of marrying Zaynab. The solution to the problems of the old film has become the obstacle in the new.

Adawiya's second song in the film, which he sings in *gallabiyya*, but still in the company of a gyrating bellydancer, is also on the "Adawiya 91" tape. The title is "*Sulṭān ahl il-hawā*" (Sultan of the lovers). It comes in the film as Shaban reaches the depths of depravity, which is also the moment he begins to feel a faint twinge of guilt about leaving Zaynab.

Shaban's late-blooming guilt is ironic, because several times in the course of the film Shaban and Zaynab part in a welter of promises to remain faithful to each other. Shaban says to his fiancée, "Wait for me at sunset, exactly like Fatin Hamama and Imad Hamdi in *Bayn al-aṭlāl*." In the final scene of *Shaban* he repeats the line as he is being taken to prison in manacles. *Bayn al-aṭlāl* (Among the ruins, 1959) was a saccharine romance about an unconsummated love affair between a man and a woman, played by Fatin Hamama and Imad Hamdi (see chapter 6).[50] For Egyptians the film is a symbol of endless devotion and refined love – exactly the opposite of what *Shaban below Zero* is all about. Invoking the contrast between *Shaban* and *Among the Ruins* was also a way to contrast the degenerate present with an image of a golden past, an image constantly defended by the older generation, but increasingly meaningless to the younger generation.

Shortly after Shaban hears Adawiya singing "Sultan of the Lovers" Zaynab reenters the narrative, dragging Shaban back into the unsolvable contradictions of middle-class life. When she finally finds him in his villa three prostitutes are calling to him from the bedroom. He tries to explain the voices away, telling Zaynab that they come from the next apartment and are audible because of the *zaḥma* (crowdedness) of the city. His feeble explanation invokes Adawiya's first song, "*Zaḥma ya dunyā*" (Crowded world), which signaled his initial plunge into immorality.

But it is too late for repentance. Zaynab despairs of ever recovering the old Shaban, and leaves him. Then we get Adawiya's third song, a very traditional-sounding *mawwāl* – a "folkloric" lament, which he sings again in peasant clothes, with no electronic accompaniment and without the belly-dancer. The content of the song has also changed dramatically: no more life in the fast lane, no disco beat, no "*Zaḥma*" or "Sultan of the Lovers." This time the song is a folk ballad protesting against the injustices of the world:

> How incredible, our age, that you reward some people on this earth
> And some are lost at sea, suffering trials and torment.
> Some people are wretched – their sustenance passes through the eye of a needle,
> Living in hardship, not a moment for happiness,
> And other types, sated, pushing out the hungry,
> People in love with their own laughter
> Some people drying their tears, and others drinking honey
> Other people drinking bitterness
> How incredible – two branches, originally one

One branch, planted in the mud, coming up as one
You doling out sustenance [God], don't let [a single] one be forgotten

The song marks a progression that is entirely opposite to the transformation that lay at the heart of *If I Were Rich*. In the original film the movement was from the milieu of "sons of the country" to the middle class; in *Shaban* the characters start out middle class and retreat to the folkloric milieu. The final song signals Shaban's return to his roots, and to his senses. He tries to repent and looks futilely for morally acceptable ways to invest his ill-gotten gains, but it is too late. This time there is no convenient wealthy suitor hiding his identity as a pasha's son to provide a convenient escape, as there was forty years ago in *If I Were Rich*. The authorities discover the scam pulled by Shaban and his relatives to inherit the money fraudulently. In the last scene Shaban marries Zaynab, but then bids her farewell as he is taken to prison: "Remember me at sunset – just like Fatin Hamama and Imad Hamdi in *Among the Ruins*."[51]

Modernism is dead. Long live . . . modernism?

Clearly between *If I Were Rich* (1942) and *Shaban below Zero* (1980) something changed. Was it the audience? Part of the change is undoubtedly due simply to a generational difference. But a generational explanation begs the question: why does the younger generation prefer a different style to the older generation? What is the essence of this difference in style? And why do young people go to see such films, actively shun more orthodox modernist fare, and yet still occasionally produce the same rhetoric against "vulgarity" as the critics?

With regard to the much-promoted image of a "radically conservative" modernism, the structure of films has also changed. It is not just that new films are racier. Old films often depicted prostitutes, nightclubs, and even more exposed skin (especially on women) than the new films. Abd al-Wahhab's first film even showed an unmarried man and woman kissing – an extremely daring scene for 1934. The difference is that the new films are antimodernist – they do not assume a transformation of the "simple" *ibn al-balad* into the "modern man." Unlike the critics, these films do not blame lower-class victims for falling into immorality due to their ignorance and backwardness. *Ragab*, *Shaban*, and dozens of other films, plays, and songs produced since the mid-1970s are not even primarily about the immorality that critics condemn. Instead, they are about humiliation of the common man and the failure, corruption, or simple nonexistence of modernist institutions that are supposed to prevent it.

But if *Ragab* represents a conscious turning away from tradition, it is important to remember which tradition is being broken. *A Hundred Years of Enlightenment*, we remember, had two starting points: the upper-right-hand corner of the poster where classical tradition emerges from the shadows, and the bottom of the poster, just left of center, where the peasants and worker sit listening to the colloquial artists. The old modernist plan would have Abd al-Wahhab's films starting from the classicist corner, and Adil Imam's films coming up from the peasant foundation. Somewhere in the middle they should meet. What the new films reject is the middle space in which classicism and colloquialism are supposed to forge a new modern nation that preserves all the best characteristics of the old – a kind of an omelette made without breaking eggs. But the anti-modernist art developed by Adil Imam and other allegedly vulgarian entertainers leaves the starting points of *A Hundred Years of Enlightenment* intact. Ragab's village gets its tractor without Ragab's help. Shaban repents his debauchery and dreams of reforming society. It is the hundred-year-old tradition of conservative modernism that has been broken, not the ideas of tradition that lie behind modernism.

What comes after modernism in Egypt? Islamists would like to start the modernist transformation over again from the point on *A Hundred Years of Enlightenment* where the *shaykh*s emerge from the darkness holding the lamp of enlightenment. They would try to reestablish the link between classicism and technology, but with a much more stringent view of where Western technique ends and Western culture begins. But it would be wrong to assume that the vernacular path is completely exhausted. Adil Imam's latest films may foreshadow a rapprochement with modernism.

One of these films was playing in Egyptian theaters just before I left Egypt in 1991. I had spent as much time as possible during my last two months in Egypt just going to films. Sometimes I went by myself and observed the crowds in anonymity, as on the night I had to literally fight through the crowds to see the premiere of Khayri Bishara's followup to *Crabs*, a film luridly titled *al-Raghba al-mutawaḥḥisha* (Bestial desire). The film was arty, which might be expected to put off "the masses," but it also showed lots of skin, especially that of Nādiya al-Gindī, who was known for her frankly sexual roles. Artiness won out. The audience that had fought so fiercely for tickets grew bored before the end and began leaving.

On other occasions I went with friends. One night I was out with a couple of my college-student friends. We had checked all the downtown cinemas clustered around ʿImād al-Dīn Street and the Ezbekīya Gardens – the old theater district described so vividly in the memoirs of Muhammad Karim and Yusuf Wahbi. This was the stomping ground of Abd al-

Wahhab and, on occasion, his mentor Ahmad Shauqi. By 1991 the area had become seedy. Nobody came to theaters there anymore except crowds of half-wild and frustrated *shabāb* such as the small group I was in. Power and commerce had moved to other parts of town. Some cinemas remained: the Cairo Palace, the Diana Palace, the Pigalle, the Karīm I and II (showing art films), and the Radio. All were showing films I had seen. We turned away from ʿImād al-Dīn to Ṭalʿat Ḥarb Street, named after the Egyptian financier who had founded Studio Miṣr, Egypt's first homegrown studio. We passed by the Metro, but the Metro was showing *Another 48 Hours*, which I had seen, and though Eddie Murphy appeared to be popular with the ninety or so young men scattered through the cavernous theater, I had no wish to see the film again.

We came to the Miami, another huge theater built in the 1930s or 1940s. It was showing Adil Imam's latest, the hugely popular *al-Luʿb maʿ al-kubār* (Playing with the grownups, 1991, directed by Sharif Arafa). The film had a good reputation with the critics: *finally* a good film by Adil Imam, they said; a film in which he returns to true comedy (he had been trying his hand at drama in recent films) and fulfills his huge potential. The crowd seemed to agree with the critics. The theater was sold out. Someone was actually trying to scalp tickets, which we did not buy because the price demanded was LE 5 each – far above the normal price, and there were three of us. We decided not to see the film that night. But the next night I went by myself to see the film at a different theater, the Taḥrīr.

The Taḥrīr is more Fadda al-Madawi than *School of Troublemakers* – an *infitāḥī* theater geared more to the budgets of Arab tourists from the Gulf than to those of Egyptian bureaucrats. It is one of the few cinemas in Cairo built in the last decade (many others have been closed), and caters to a decidedly upscale market. I was shocked to find that I had to pay LE 7 for my ticket, and my seat was not in the most expensive section. Surrounded by well-heeled families and a few young men and women in expensive clothes who appeared for all the world to be out on dates, I settled back in air-conditioned comfort to enjoy the film. After a preview for *Blind Fury*, a Rutger Hauer karate film, *Playing with the Grownups* finally began.

The film was oddly appropriate for the rarified setting in which I saw it. Adil Imam plays an unemployed college graduate who enters into a "conspiracy of good" with an agent of the much-feared *mabāḥith amn al-daula* (national security officers – the Egyptian secret police) in order to expose plots to undermine the state. The *mabāḥith* agent was played by Husayn

Fahmi, the actor who had played Zuzu's lover in *Pay Attention to Zuzu*. *Ibn al-balad* meets the drama professor: classic Egyptian modernism. We no longer have one man being forced by impossible circumstances to make a pact with corruption, but brave souls martyring themselves in order to save society. If *Playing with the Grownups* is any indication, the answer to a failed modernism may well turn out to be a retrenched modernism. The polite audience in the Taḥrīr was certainly happy to pay the price for such modernity. The crowds of frustrated young men outside the Miami seemed willing to pay. One cannot help but wonder whether their willingness indicates an endorsement of the film's neomodernist message, or loyalty to the actor's antimodernist roots – which suggest an absurdist response to any didactic message from whatever quarter.

Notes

1 Introduction

1 By "popular culture" I mean expressive culture presented in mass media, including the print media, television, cinema, and recorded music on cassette tapes – roughly what Appadurai and Breckenridge have dubbed "public culture" (Appadurai and Breckenridge 1988, 5).

2 The issue of cultural hegemony was initially framed by the Frankfurt School (mainly Max Horkheimer and Theodore Adorno, but also their associate Walter Benjamin), and later disputed – too far in the opposite direction – by Raymond Williams and others in the cultural studies movement. For a concise summary of this debate see Dickey (1993, 11–12).

3 Some examples of the writers to whom Jameson and others concerned with the idea of Third World literature refer are: Salman Rushdie, Lu Xun, Ousmane Sembène, Mario Vargas Llosa, al-Tayyib Salih, Achebe Chinua.

4 Edward Said, for example, is typical in his disdain for cultural artifacts produced outside the languages of metropolitan societies – what he calls "other" literatures, which cannot be studied "respectably" (Said 1990, 13–14). Ahmad (1992, 216) severely criticizes Said and poststructuralism generally for devaluing non-metropolitan tradition but, as previously noted, offers no alternative save a fruitless search for "uncontaminated" culture.

5 In some ways non-Western filmmakers from other countries have greater difficulties than Egyptian filmmakers – sub-Saharan and North African filmmakers, for example, must make do with minimal national filmmaking infrastructures. However, this also means that the films they do manage to make are produced with heavy European involvement, which gives them some advantage in marketing their product to European audiences, and an enormous advantage in film festivals. See, for example, *Film and Politics in the Third World* (Downing 1987), which contains ten articles on sub-Saharan and North African filmmakers, but not a single article on any aspect of the Egyptian film industry. It is, of course, possible that Western audiences would not enjoy Egyptian film productions. The point is that we should not assume, without further investigation, that we actually understand everything that happens in an Egyptian film, or that audiences are "fooled" by what critics such as Said see as mere "mimicry."

6 The intent of Spitulnik's article, of course, was not to deny that any work has been done by anthropologists, but to identify how the anthropology of mass media is developing at a still relatively early stage. Recent work by anthropologists working on Middle Eastern mass media include Abu-Lughod (1989; 1993a; 1993b), Armbrust (1992), Starrett (1995), Swedenburg (1994). Other disciplines have also begun contributing usefully to the study of Middle Eastern popular culture (e.g. Douglas and Malti-Douglas 1994).

7 The late 1960s to early 1970s are considered by many to mark a transformation in the West from modernist to postmodernist sensibility (Harvey 1989, 39–65). The extent to which Egypt is part of or influenced by the same postmodernity is an open question.

8 It should be emphasized that the basic tension in nationalism between a rationalist present and a constructed image of a people's antiquity has been recognized and discussed for some time. For example, Ernest Renan, in 1882, wrote about nationalism in a way that is similar in spirit to Fishman, Anderson, and others: "A nation is a soul, a spiritual principle. Two things, which in truth are but one, constitute this soul or spiritual principle. One lies in the past, one in the present. One is the possession in common of a rich legacy of memories; the other is present-day consent, the desire to live together, the will to perpetuate the value of the heritage that one has received in an undivided form" (Renan 1990 [1882], 19).

9 Homi Bhabha, for example, sees this combination of modernist rationalism and nationalist invention of a past as important less for the way they are balanced than for what he sees as the way it creates an interstitial "space" between different kinds of discourse within which identity can be continually renegotiated (Bhabha 1990). This formulation works particularly well in analyzing the literary production of middle-class migrants to metropolitan societies – people who cross boundaries, real and metaphoric, from a position of relative strength. As Ahmad notes, it is precisely migrants who are positioned to enjoy "the pleasures of self-exile much more often than those of forced exile" (Ahmad 1992, 210) who have the most to gain from a poststructuralist deemphasis on the kind of "grand narrative" that constructs nationalist ideologies. See Ahmad (*ibid.*, 68–69) for an elaboration of this kind of criticism of the poststructuralist position typified by Bhabha's *Nation and Narration* (1990).

2 "The White Flag"

1 This is a figure given me by people who were in no position to buy a Mercedes. Whatever the exact cost, the price of a legally purchased (all taxes paid) Mercedes is probably in the hundreds of thousands of Egyptian pounds.

2 I attended two of these meetings. The first was held in Alexandria's Palace of Culture on January 20, 1990, and the second was in the Palace of Cinema in Garden City, Cairo, in early February. "White Flag" director Muhammad Fadil said that he had attended meetings all over the country, and that all of them had been very well attended. For example, despite a hard rain a meeting held in the Delta city of Zaqāzīq was attended by over six hundred people.

3 However, Brooks (1976) argues that melodrama should be taken seriously as a literary genre, and others have sometimes found melodrama's exaggerations appropriate as a description of social conditions:

> What a sombre, violent and emotional scene these early Victorian novelists present. Did they create those melodramatic plots to relieve the peaceful boredom of prosperity? A glance at the social history of the nineteenth century shows that this cannot be so . . . Victorian melodrama was only a very slightly exaggerated picture of Victorian life. The riots, shipwrecks, fires, lunatic asylums and deportations we read of in novels, the awful family splits about legacies and estates, the sons told never again to darken the door, the rejected lovers trekking off to the brutal colonies, all are real enough . . . Everything we can learn of Victorian life confirms the picture. People did turn out to be the missing sons of earls, honest families *were* ruined by the markets, clergymen *were* able to work themselves up to crises of conscience on what seems to us a mere point of order. *(Pritchett 1970, 128)*

4 Mahfouz, of course, won the 1988 Nobel Prize for literature; Idris and Haqqi are also prominent Egyptian novelists, less well known outside Arabic literature circles. All three have had a great deal of work adapted to the screen.

5 Some of Ukasha's other work includes "*Ḥārat al-Maghribī*" (The quarter of al-Maghribī, 1968), taken from his short story "*Al-Bayt al-kabīr*" (The big house), which was published in 1967; "*Al-Insān wa-al-ḥaqīqa*" (Man and truth), his first story written specifically for television; "*Al-Ḥiṣār*" (The siege); "*Al-Mashrabīya*" (The wooden screen); "*Abwāb al-madīna*" (Gates of the city), a two-part serial and his first big hit; "*Riḥlat Abū al-ʿAlā' al-Basharī*" (The journey of Abu al-Ala al-Bashari); "*Al-Ḥubb wa-ashyā' ukhrā*" (Love and other things); "*Adraka Shahriyār al-ṣabāḥ*" (Shahriyar knew it was morning); "*ʿAṣfūr al-nār*" (The firebird); "*Wa-qāla al-baḥr*" (And said the sea); "*Mā zāla al-Nīl yijrī*" (The Nile still flows); and "*Ḍamīr Abla Ḥikmet*" (The conscience of Miss Hikmet), a 1991 show broadcast after "White Flag" dealing with the problems of education in Egypt.

6 The *infitāḥ* (Open Door) began in the early 1970s when Anwar al-Sadat turned away from Soviet patronage. From 1974 to the present economic "liberalization" has been a consistently stated policy of both the Sadat and Mubarak regimes, although the actual implementation of a free-market economy has never been complete (see Lofgren 1993; Springborg 1989). Since the mid-1970s the *infitāḥ* and its alleged excesses of greed and corruption has been a major presence in Egyptian cinema, and sometimes television.

7 I met Sana Gamil through her husband, Louis Greiss, a former editor of the mass-circulation weekly *Ṣabāḥ al-khayr* and now editor of the magazine *Satellite Guide*. In 1991 he was director of public relations at the American University in Cairo, where I worked under him for several months writing press releases. Greiss also introduced me to Gamil Ratib.

8 Some of the Egyptian public may also be aware that Sana Gamil has performed in French. *Uktōbir* magazine reported in 1976 that she was to act in a French production entitled *Dance of Death* with Gamil Ratib. She was to go to France to perform the play in Paris, after which it was to be brought to Cairo

and performed in both French and Arabic ("France Wants Sana Gamil," *Uktōbir* 31 [1976, no. 1]: 71).

9 The gloss "my spirit is light" was suggested to me by Louis Greiss, Sana Gamil's husband. It was he who suggested to me the idea of malapropism in Nunu's trademark phrase. Mr. Greiss also emphasized that the crucial element of Nunu's character was his state of semieducation.

10 Private lessons are one of the sorest points in the Egyptian educational system. The steps that have been taken to regulate after-school teaching have hardly made a dent in the formally illegal practice of teaching individuals or charging more for small groups than the law allows. As a practical matter, however, it is almost impossible for teachers to survive without doing so. Rightly or wrongly, most people believe that educational success is impossible without private lessons. Not surprisingly, wealthy people have a tremendous advantage in being able to afford them.

11 The practice differs from American soaps such as "Dallas," where both the villains and the "good guys" dress uniformly in accordance with an American middle-class sense of glamor. Indeed, many characters in the prime-time American soaps "Dallas," "Knots Landing," and "Falcon Crest" tend not to remain either "good" or "bad," but to vacillate, always justifying their actions on the basis of personal need. Certain core characters, however, typically only threaten to vacillate, always drawing back in the end to their "true" character.

In Egypt at least one prime-time American soap opera was shown at all times during the period of my field research from 1989 to 1991. Many people claimed to be avid fans of these programs, although I rarely witnessed people I knew watching them. The clothes in American soaps were generally thought to be indicators that the events took place "at a certain level of society" – namely high society. This was, in fact, more true of some of the American programs than of others. But the programs were assumed overall to be extremely realistic (one person I spoke to even characterized "Falcon Crest" as a documentary). For many the programs confirmed their assumptions about America: that American society bore great similarity to the most negative images of the Egyptian upper class; that Western women were without any moral sense; that Western society was fantastically wealthy.

12 El-Messiri, for example, quotes a passage by Muḥammad al-Muwayliḥī from his *Ḥadīth ʿĪsā Ibn Hishām* in which two youths talk about another youth who was so enamored of Western fashion that he killed himself when he heard that suicide was fashionable in Paris (el-Messiri 1978a, 35).

13 The *muʿallima* has long been a stock film character. The emphasis is generally on *small* business, however, as in the film *Shabāb imrāʾa* (A woman's youth, 1956), in which a pipe-smoking *muʿallima* corrupts a young student. But the *muʿallima* of *A Woman's Youth*, unlike Fadda, has a strictly circumscribed view of the world. She threatens to drag the modern character back into her world, not to invade his world.

14 The correct colloquial transliteration according to Badawi and Hinds (1986, 96) would be *ibn*ⁱ *balad* (and the associated *ibn al-zawāt* would be *ibn*ⁱ *zawāt* – "son of aristocracy"). I have used *ibn al-balad* (fem. *bint al-balad*) throughout the text to simplify reading, and because others who have written about the

term (el-Messiri 1978a; Booth 1990) have used the literary Arabic transliteration. Associated terminology, such as *shahāma* and *ḥāra*, is transliterated in colloquial.

15 The newspaper was *Al-Ahram Weekly*, an English-language edition of the Arabic paper *al-Ahrām*. I worked there as a translator from late 1990 to 1991 when the paper was in the final planning stages.

16 In the context of manufactured goods *baladī* is almost always the less preferred category. The distinction is sometimes cast as *bitāʿ hina* ("of here," i.e. locally made) versus *bitāʿ barra* ("of outside," i.e. imported). Many Egyptians decry the practice of downgrading the local in favor of the imported as a manifestation of *ʿuʕdit il-khawāga* (a foreigner complex, essentially an inferiority complex).

17 Or so el-Messiri (1978a, 30) assumes. The evidence is largely negative; el-Messiri notes that the term *ibn al-balad* does not appear often in pre-nineteenth-century sources. She finds that only with al-Jabartī does the term begin to appear with regularity and with something like the sense that it carries today.

18 Early (1993, 51–84) describes the distinction through the terms *baladī/afrangi* (local/foreign), and notes that while the terms are semantically distinct, they are employed much more ambivalently in daily life (*ibid.*, 14).

19 There are other variants of the same idea, such as *muḥdisīn* (colloquial for *muḥdithīn*) *in-niʿma* (literally "newly comfortable," "upstarts"). New phrases are coined or applied continuously. Abdel-Malek, for example, points to a reference to *nouveaux riches* by the poet Aḥmad Fu'ād Nigm as *tanābila* – "loafers" (Abdel-Malek 1990, 32). Cartoonist Aḥmad Ḥigāzī also used the *tanābila* theme to satirize the corruption of business interests, the media and politicians (see Douglas and Malti-Douglas 1994, 62–80). Today people sometimes distinguish between *ibn al-zawāt* and other phrases applied to the newly rich *infitāḥi*s. The latter are supposed to be coarser, more grasping, less educated. There is a good deal of nostalgia tied up in a fond image of the old aristocracy, especially in the context of the current hard times in Egypt. As we will see in later chapters, the image of the aristocracy may not always have been so benevolent when the old films were originally released.

20 The *isnād* Dr. Mufid contemplates is a metaphoric one. *Isnād* means "support," specifically of a statement's trustworthiness. It is not the *isnād* itself that is of primary importance, but the tradition upon which commentary is made. Usually the practice of constructing *asānīd* (pl. of *isnād*) aimed to assure authenticity of statements (*aḥādīth*, s. *ḥadīth*) of the Prophet Muḥammad. The development of a means to assure accurate transmission of statements considered fundamental to the correct practice of religion was a natural development of a pre-Islamic concern to preserve the *sunna* (tradition) of one's forefathers. *Sunna* is now understood by Arabic speakers to mean predominantly Islamic religious tradition (see Juynboll 1927).

21 The text of the book Dr. Mufid is looking at reads "Nagi travelled to France in 1919, where he painted in the village of Giverny in Normandy, working with the artist Monet, one of the pillars of the Impressionist school" (Buṭrus 1964, 129).

22 *Shaʿbī* ("popular" or "of the people") covers very nearly the same semantic range as *baladī*. *Al-shaʿb* (the people) is sometimes interchangeable with *awlād*

al-balad. Frequently both *al-shaʿb* and *awlād al-balad* can denote a lack of sophistication outside a narrowly defined local sphere associated with a stereotypical image of the "folkloric." But in other contexts, such as political speeches, both terms can be used to equate the speaker with "the people" in a salutary sense. For example, Fārūq Ḥusnī, the current minister of culture and a prominent modernist painter, was quoted in an interview as saying, "*Anā wazīr shaʿbī*" – I am a *shaʿbī* (popular) minister (Husni 1992, 92). Ḥusnī had been asked by the interviewer to exhibit his modernist art in the provinces. When he said he was *shaʿbī* he did not mean that he practiced folklore, but that he was "one of them," i.e. from the same background.

23 Alexander the Great is sometimes called *Iskandar dhū-l-qarnayn* (Alexander of two horns) because he is depicted in the Qur'ān (XVIII. 83–98) and in contemporary Egyptian iconography with ram's horns, as the son of Amon.

24 This was the second time in the past few years that the opposition between bulldozer and domicile had been presented to an Egyptian audience. The film *Karakōn fī sh-shāriʿ* (Police station [or a type of prefab structure sometimes used as a police station] in the street) ended with virtually the same face-off. The object of the bulldozer's threat, however, was a handmade trailer-home – a symbol of the aspirations of the common man rather than of the heritage. In the film the situation is saved by a *deus ex machina* intervention from the highest levels of government.

25 Rent in Cairo is officially controlled. Nonetheless, landlords charge enormous under-the-table payments for tenants to be able to obtain apartments. A schoolteacher I knew in Cairo told me that in 1990 the absolute minimum for housing was something in the neighborhood of LE 4,000–LE 6,000. This was for an extremely tiny place – at most a bedroom and dining room – in a distant suburb of Cairo far from where he worked. Others confirmed that a range from LE 4,000 to LE 6,000 was about right for the most minimal housing. Anis's apartment in "White Flag" was very far from minimal. For a detailed breakdown of a typical lower-middle-class family's budget see Macleod (1991, 58–59).

26 The problem goes back at least to the 1950s (Reid 1990, 162). The issue was also alluded to once or twice in "White Flag." Another Usama Anwar Ukasha serial aired about a year after "White Flag" dealt with the problem more directly. This was "*Ḍamīr Abla Ḥikmet*" (The conscience of Miss Hikmet), in which idealistic teachers were shown working overtime with no extra pay to help their students.

27 People feel especially pressured to pay for extra lessons if their children are doing poorly, because the classroom teacher is often the same as the tutor. They feel that if they don't pay, the child will not be given the benefit of the doubt in exams or in the classroom. One family I knew spent over half the family budget on lessons for two girls, one in college, the other in primary school; the family had only one parent.

3 The split vernacular

1 Awad's essay was part of a series of articles published on folklore, which were instigated by Abd al-Hamid Yunis's "defense of folklore" (Yūnis 1970) quoted earlier.

2 Egypt's population grew from 9.7 million in 1897 to 19 million in 1947 (Ikram

1980, 106), 43 million in 1981 (UNESCO 1984, I-9), and will reach a projected 59 million by the year 2000 (Ikram 1980, 106).

3 In 1976 the country's urban population nearly equaled its rural population – a marked change from 1907, when around 80 percent of Egypt's population was rural (Waterbury 1982, 308). Furthermore, over three postrevolutionary census years (1947, 1960, and 1966) not only has the shift in population from rural areas to urban areas intensified, but there has also been a tendency for people to move from provincial urban conglomerations to the largest cities (see World Bank [1978 vol. II, 42]).

4 See World Bank (1978 vol. VI, 2) for a comparison of Egypt's inhabited area with its population density. Egypt's population density is among the highest in the world, rivaled only by Java and parts of India and China (Richards and Waterbury 1990, 53). Almost all of the population is packed into the Nile Valley, which has a population density of 3,333 persons per square mile (*ibid.*). Land reclamation can affect the situation only slightly. Richards and Waterbury (*ibid.*, 168) describe such efforts in Egypt as "economically questionable," and attractive to the government more as a way to consolidate centralized control (newly reclaimed land can be planned from the top down) than to increase agricultural production.

5 In 1897 there were 0.5 square feddans of cultivated land per person in Egypt – 10 square feddans per person allowing for double and triple cropping. In 1975 there were 0.2 square feddans, 0.3 allowing for double and triple cropping (World Bank 1978 vol. II, 15).

6 In 1984 Egypt spent 9.4 percent of its GDP on education, down from 15.8 percent in 1970 (UNESCO 1984, III-5). Total spending on education rose from LE 41 million in 1960 to LE 918 million in 1981 (Abdalla 1985, 103), but much of the gain was eroded by inflation (Leila, Palmer, and Yassin 1988, 24) and population, which increased by 10 million – heavily skewed toward those of school age.

7 The program's pessimism is unusual, but not the focus on crime and poverty. Magazines of the 1920s and 1930s (e.g. *Al-Dunyā al-muṣawwara*, 1929–31) and certain films of the 1950s (particularly those starring the actor Farīd Shauqī) suggest that fear of crime bred by poverty and ignorance is not unique to the age of *infitāḥ*. However, the images of crime popularized in earlier periods generally portrayed crime and backwardness as on the defensive in the face of a modernist onslaught.

8 Since the mid-1960s, when "White Flag" 's Dr. Mufid is meant to have left the country to fulfill his ambassadorial post, per capita income in Egypt has been stagnant (Ibrahim 1982, 283).

9 Belief in a perfect classical language from which the various dialects descended is itself a historical development. When Arabic was first recorded in writing there were many dialects. Beeston (1983, 4–6) notes that early Arab grammarians were "purely descriptive" rather than "normative and prescriptive," and thus recorded much data on dialects, and that gradually linguistic disparity was reduced, so that there could be a definitive reading of the Qur'ān. However, "reading" the Qur'ān or other Arabic texts in a classical context never meant reading silently as Westerners do today. Rather, the recording of texts through oral transmission is a general feature of all literate Arab culture. For more on

the issue of transmission in the writing of Arab history see, for example, Khalidi (1994, 17–82); on law Messick (1993, 15–36); on the practice of writing generally Pederson (1984, 20–36).

10 Fishman notes that the adoption of a national vernacular indexed to spoken languages was problematic in all the Asian and Middle Eastern cultures already possessing a written tradition before European colonialism. In such societies language seems to have been initially viewed for its large-scale integrative potential rather than as a means for more localized national integration (Fishman 1972, 32).

11 Cachia (1967, 20) quotes Naguib Mahfouz as saying that "the colloquial is one of the diseases from which the people are suffering." Cachia (*ibid.*, 21) also quotes ʿAlī al-Najdī Nāṣif, a professor in Dār al-ʿUlūm (a teachers' college now affiliated with Cairo University), as saying that "the colloquial is the protégé of ignorance and imperialism together."

12 Others echo Badawi's position, although not always uncritically. The Lebanese scholar Adonis (also based in the West), for example, sees Arab modernity as a progressive ideal rooted in the Qur'ān (Adonis 1992, 49). His reading of recent Arab history resembles Badawi in its insistence on continuity with the past above all else, but contends that such an emphasis is a misreading of classical Arab civilization with disastrous implications for the present:

> Opinions [over Arab modernity] were divided into two general tendencies: the traditionalist/conformist (*uṣūlī*) tendency, which considered religion and the Arab linguistic sciences as its main base; and the transgressing/non-conformist (*tajāwuzī*) tendency, which saw its base, by contrast, as lying in European secularism.
>
> It is the first philosophy that has prevailed, especially at the level of the establishment, encouraged by economic, social and political conditions, both internal and external. *(ibid., 77)*

13 This attitude had the effect of sharpening the perceived demarcation between colloquial and classical styles. In the mid-nineteenth century, when intensive contact with Europe was still relatively new, the issue of classical versus colloquial could be cast in less polemical terms, according to Said. She quotes Rifāʿa al-Ṭahṭāwī, a nineteenth-century Egyptian scholar who was one of the first Egyptians to travel to Europe in an official capacity, and an important early translator of European works, to the effect that language styles should be functionally determined:

> It is fine for the colloquial of a country . . . to have easily understood rules and principles, which the people of a region can know as much as possible. All could benefit [from such a language] and books of general usefulness and public interest could be written in it. But the beauty of the Islamic nations, which shows the true worth of Arabic, is knowledge of the true Arab tongue – possession of the ability to speak eloquently. *(N. Saʿīd 1964, 77)*

14 Cachia (1967, 20, n. 37) notes the ideological character of Said's book: "Although not without bias against any attitude that would seem to favor the colloquial, it is a well-documented study."

15 Dropping the regional variations is exactly what one might expect in a developing national vernacular as described by Anderson (1991) and Fishman (1972). But note that this commonplace nationalist standardization of vernacular took place with little reinforcement by print media. With the exception of the relatively small body of published colloquial work cited by Said spoken vernacular was utilized much more heavily in aural media such as recorded music, radio, theater, and cinema.

16 Said cites Riyad from *Adab al-shaʿb*, p. 71 and the introduction to his translation of the Rubāʿiyāt of Omar Khayyam, p. 23 (she lists no publisher for the book).

17 Said (1964, 339–44) quotes from a 1929 edition of *Muwashshaḥāt Naẓīm* (poems by Maḥmūd Ramzī Naẓīm in a postclassical style called *muwashshaḥa*) and from *ʿAbīr al-wādī* (a collection of poems in the classical *rajaz* meter by the same author).

18 As in "company." The practice was parodied in the film *Ramaḍān fōq al-burkān* (Ramadan on the volcano, 1985), a film in which the main character, a bureaucrat turned thief and con-man, forms a bogus company called "*Ramaḍānkō lil-Istīrād wa-l-Taṣdīr*" (Ramadan Import–Export Company). The language parody extended beyond the name to the first scene, in which one of the main character's sleazy friends, an ex-con, is seen at a desk dressed in a Western suit with phone in hand saying "nooo. . . yeees. . . nooo. . . yeees . . ." It is very much like the Sanu poem with English lines that Said dismisses as a naive early attempt to invest colloquial expression with social commentary. In this case it is not exactly foreigners who are being lampooned, but Egyptians making money by accommodating foreigners. The film was condemned as vulgar by most critics.

19 As Ferguson described it, diglossia is "[a] relatively stable language situation in which in addition to the primary dialects of the language (which may include a standard or regional standards), there is a very divergent, highly codified (often grammatically more complex) superposed variety either of an earlier period or in another speech community which is learned largely by formal education and used for most written and formal spoken purposes but not used by any sector of the community for ordinary conversation" (Ferguson 1959a, 325).

20 For example: Altoma (1969), E. M. Badawī (1973), Blanc (1960), Ferguson (1959a), Heath (1989), Mahmoud (1986), Meiseles (1980), and T. F. Mitchell (1986). There is also a large literature on diglossia in other languages such as Tamil, Greek, and German. See Stetkevych (1970) for an extended description of the modernized variant of the "high" variant of Arabic. It is generally assumed that the high variant of Arabic is highly standardized either in a medieval form as defined by classical grammars, or as a "modernized" Arabic often referred to as modern standard Arabic (MSA). The standardized nature of MSA has been challenged by Kaye (1972), who asserts that in fact it is colloquial Arabic that exhibits very little variation, whereas there is no agreement on what constitutes MSA. El-Hassan (1979), however, gives numerous examples that cast doubt on Kaye's hypothesis. El-Hassan also casts doubt on the accuracy of several other prominent treatments of the subject, including E. M. Badawī (1973), Blanc (1960), and Ezzat (1974), leading the reader to the suspicion that all empirical studies of Arabic diglossia are flawed.

21 Heath (1989, 15), for example, devotes four pages of a three-hundred-page study on Moroccan Arabic to the sociological background of diglossia, in which the local theory of how different variants are used in practice is only outlined: "Classical Arabic," he says, "is . . . the primary language of schools at all levels . . . In principle, teachers even in primary schools are supposed to use [classical Arabic] as the classroom language; in practice what they often do is code-switch from [classical Arabic] to [Moroccan Arabic], often repeating the same explanations in both languages to insure clarity" (Heath is unusual in that he examines diglossia and code-switching together. Code-switching may be relevant to Egypt as well [see Scotton 1986; Gumperz 1982]). Altoma (1969, 4) is also brief in discussing nondescriptive aspects of diglossia, noting only that "[colloquial Arabic] was never viewed, prior to the nineteenth century, as a serious challenge impairing the new drive for universal literacy and other cultural efforts in the Arab world. Similarly, the adequacy or the efficiency of the Classical as the language of culture or literature has only been seriously questioned by Arabs in modern works." One exception to the tendency of linguists to restrict themselves to descriptive studies is Somekh (1991), who examines at some length the place of colloquial Arabic in literature under the assumption that the colloquial is better suited for modern literature than the classical. Somekh's position, however, was received with little more warmth than Seldon Wilmore's nineteenth-century attempts to promote the colloquial as a literary language (see Siddiq 1992).

On the sociological side the issue of how colloquial and classical styles of expression articulate with modern Arab culture also receives little attention. A notable exception to social scientists' neglect of the issue is Sharabi (1988, 85–103), who claims that "a major implication of this rift [between classical and colloquial] has been the reinforcement of traditional social divisions and the concealment of the modern material and class basis of cultural disparity" (*ibid.*, 85), and that "colloquial or oral culture is . . . like the culture of children or the counterculture of rebels – both of whom turn away, withdraw, and remain silent without engaging in overt or direct opposition" (*ibid.*, 89).

22 El-Saʿīd M. Badawī (al-Saʿīd Muḥammad, cited as E. M.) does, however, allow for somewhat greater separation between what he calls *fuṣḥā al-turāth* (Arabic of the classical heritage) and all the other varieties of Arabic which he defines as due to the set historical nature of the style, and its circumscribed usage in very formal religious situations.

23 At the time I was an employee of the American University public relations office, which arranged the debate.

24 Hamayda, who is originally from the Awlād ʿAlī bedouin tribe of the Marsa Maṭrūḥ area (the western desert not far from the Libyan border), was a graduate of the Cairo music academy (see "*Lōlākī*" 1991, 16–19; Ḥasanayn 1991, 198).

25 The song that made Hamayda famous was "*Lōlākī*" (If not for you) – a fast dance tune with lyrics in the bedouin dialect of Egypt's western desert. It was released in 1988, and although tape-pirating makes it impossible to get accurate information on how many copies a given cassette sells, there was no doubt that the song was an unprecedented hit. Probably millions of copies, both legal and

illegal, were sold, and "*Lōlākī*" was dubbed "the earthquake of '88." For more on the milieu from which Ali Hamayda came, see Abu-Lughod (1989, 7–11).

26 Colloquially the term would be written *fitiwwa* (pl. *fitiwwāt*, f. *fitiwwāya*). Since the term appears here in the context of an article I have used the literary transliteration. Also, as with *ibn al-balad*, el-Messiri (1978a) uses the classical transliteration. To avoid confusion I will do the same.

27 For "native quarters" the author uses the now obsolete phrase *al-aḥyā' al-waṭaniyya. Waṭan* (homeland) is now associated almost exclusively with the idea of nation and nationalism, and is pointedly distinguished from anything having to do with a *ḥayy* (traditional quarter, pl. *aḥyā'*). This is indicative of a semantic shift away from the "traditionalism" associated with "native quarters" and towards a "modernism" coupled with notions of progress and scientific advancement.

28 "*'Ahí kida il-gadʿāna.' 'Ahú da illi iḥna ḥ-anʕul-u ʿannik*" ("*Futūwāyat sūq al-khuḍār*" 1929, 9).

29 Booth (1990, 345), drawing on Bosworth (1976), notes that the tendency to juxtapose elite speech with common language was a feature of the literature contemporary with early *maqāma* writers: "The literature . . . not only portrayed the shadowy 'dregs of society' to the aristocratic strata, but did so by appropriating the jargons in which thieves, beggars and prostitutes conducted their business, incorporating lexica from these jargons into a description of their speakers' motives and means."

30 Al-Tunsi's *Maqāmāt*, originally published in his periodicals *al-Shabāb*, *al-Funūn*, and *al-Imām*, became known collectively as *Maqāmāt al-mujāwirīn* (Booth 1990, 341).

31 Al-Tunsi carries out his dual satirization of classical form and the uneven modernity promoted by the Egyptian bourgeoisie generally by juxtaposing the *baladī* world to the Europeanized one through the inclusion of both colloquialisms and neologisms in the text as well as the titles. The *Maqāmāt* focus on things as diverse as boxes, bags, cars, bread, pennies, amulets, psychology, cocktails, American women, and beaches. But the development of each narrative centers on an opposition of poor to rich or of tradition to modernity (Booth 1990, 374–84).

32 Such work is usually dismissed by critics as hopelessly vulgar. In the cinema and theater antimodernist films only begin to appear in the 1970s (more on this in chapters 6 and 7). Music and poetry have a long tradition of such "vulgarity," as we have seen from Nafusa Zakariyya Said's description of colloquial poetry (in chapters 4, 6, and 7 we will see similar examples in the musical medium). There seems, generally, to be a technological hierarchy of "vulgarity." The more centralized media, such as television, show far less antimodernist art than less easily controlled media such as the musical cassette, which can be easily duplicated and cheaply sold.

33 A down-and-out *shaykh* goes to a public bakery to beg "like a rabid dog" and ends up stealing another customer's food.

Al-Tunsi's rough treatment of Azharīs makes a splendid contrast to Taha Husayn's autobiography *Al-Ayyām*, which is required reading for Egyptian students, and very much a part of the canon of Egyptian modernism. Husayn portrays the Azharī life as hard, but honorable, and he clearly marks the traditional Azhar education as a first step on his educational journey toward modernity, not as something to be discarded as incompatible with the modern age.

34 This is not to say that the Azharīs are exempt from criticism. Booth (1990, 373) notes that "the declamations of Bayram's *shuyūkh* are a recognition – if a back-handed one – of the gap between their classical culture and the demands of a new age, which they try to bridge through a change in content."

35 "*Ḥakāwī al-Qahāwī*" – the title of a 1990s program in which an elegant and "folklorically" dressed woman (she generally wears a dress of the type worn by women in Sīwa Oasis, although her hair and makeup are pure sophisticated Cairene) conducts interviews with various "folkloric" characters such as artisans or traditional musicians.

36 This point was made by Kamal Abdel-Malek with regard to the work of Ahmad Fuad Nigm, a colloquial poet who first rose to prominence in the 1960s. He quotes Nigm as lamenting the fact that he could not reach his target audience, but notes that Nigm's poems, when made into songs and sung by the "folk singer" Shaykh Imām, became much more popular (Abdel-Malek 1990, 23).

37 By *shaʿbī* (popular) al-Rawi means "folkloric," in the sense that the work is part of an oral tradition in which the collectivity dominates the individual to the extent that one cannot attribute individual authorship to a given poem or song.

4 The gifted musician

1 The Abd al-Wahhab quote is from "*ʿIndamā yaktubūna ʿan nafsihim*," in *Al-Kawākib* (19 [August 1950]: 32), and was also the frontispiece of al-Ḥifnī (1991, 7).

2 Some of the biographies available from street-corner book vendors at the time of Abd al-Wahhab's death: M. ʿAwaḍ 1991; Ḥasanayn 1991; Raḍwān 1991; Tabārak 1991. This is only a fraction of the total number of books on Abd al-Wahhab. Publishing accounts of Abd al-Wahhab's life, opinions, and music remains a growth industry in Egypt.

3 Adawiya is a singer who rose to prominence in the mid-1970s, and who is often invoked in the press as a symbol of vulgarity. His musical style draws on the folk heritage rather than the classical Arabic music tradition. Despite the hostility of the press, Adawiya does have his proponents, including some intellectuals (see chapter 7).

Ṭaʿmīya is a fried fava-bean paste usually used in inexpensive sandwiches. *Fūl* is a kind of stew made from fava beans, again, inexpensive and filling. Both dishes are staples in the diet of many poor people in Egypt. Ironically, *fūl* is one of the dishes that Abd al-Wahhab and Shauqi were meant to have been pining for while in Paris (see M.ʿAwaḍ 1991, 103).

4 Al-Hifni says this in *Uktōbir* magazine (*Uktōbir* 760 [May 19, 1991]: 73). Mahmud Awad and Luṭfī Raḍwān both agree with the 1910 birthdate. Awad never actually lists a date in his book, but has Abd al-Wahhab singing between the acts dressed as a "nine-year-old girl" (an alias to protect him from the wrath of his family) in the theatrical troupe of Abd al-Rahman Rushdi in 1918 (M. ʿAwaḍ 1991, 64); Radwan (1991, 11) gives Abd al-Wahhab's birthdate as 1910.

5 Ali Jihad Racy notes that the most important religious affiliation for musicians prior to the twentieth century was with Sufi orders, in which "it was customary for male concert singers to train their voices and learn singing techniques by participating in the musical rituals of the dervishes, especially those belonging to the Laythī order" (Racy 1977, 47). Singers with a strong Sufi association were called *shaykh*. During the post-World War I era this association of musicians with guild-like Sufi orders declined. Racy considers Abd al-Wahhab to have been at the forefront of the first musical generation to have *no* formal association with the religious institution most relevant to traditional Arab music, although several of the 1990 commemorative publications associated him with musicians carrying the appellation of *shaykh* (e.g. Najmī 1991).

6 Much singing in classical Arabic music is based on the techniques of *tartīl*. Vocalizations in this style use the head as a resonating chamber much more than the chest, as in much Western singing. The resulting sound tends to be more nasal than Western singing, but with great carrying power and, if the singer is well trained, tremendous facility. Such facility is important in Arabic music because it is played and sung on a quarter-tone scale having finer gradations than the Western half-tone system (see Nelson 1985). Abd al-Wahhab's model for *tartīl* was said to be Shaykh Muḥammad Rifʿat (Naẓmī 1991, 28; M. ʿAwaḍ 1991, 49).

7 The story is presented as if it were an eyewitness account of an early twentieth-century concert. It was, however, written in the late 1960s. The general atmosphere of the concert described by Awad tallies fairly closely with a description of a 1930s Abd al-Wahhab concert by Muhammad Karim, who directed all of Abd al-Wahhab's films. Karim's concert, ironically, sounds closer to the Abd al-Hayy concert described here than to the dignified high-art "opera house" atmosphere stressed by most accounts of the literature on Abd al-Wahhab. Danielson (1991b, 44–46) also notes that performances of commercial music (as opposed to those at religious festivals or in the homes of wealthy patrons) were, in fact, often subject to rowdy behavior. Danielson also elaborates on musical culture at later periods (e.g. *ibid*., 93–105).

8 Popular singers often found it necessary to keep themselves surrounded by friends and supporters who functioned as a buffer between them and the sometimes rowdy crowds (Danielson 1991b, 247). Awad's *muṭayyibāt* (*muṭayyibāti* [sg.] *muṭayyibātiyya* [pl.] in Badawi and Hinds [1986, 553]) sound similar to what Danielson, citing journalists from the 1920s, calls a *balāṭ* (court). A polite term for the *balāṭ* is *al-samāʿīyīn* (listeners [Danielson 1991b, 247–53]).

9 The following two examples are from Kamāl (1991, 74–75). Mahmud Awad (1991, 40) quotes a similar series of songs which convey images of drinking, drugs, and sex.

10 This scenario is not necessarily a complete falsification of the spirit of the times. Much had changed in the musical milieu of urban Cairo by the time of World War I. Patronage was no longer as significant as it had been once commercial recording and public concerts became the main sources of income for musicians (Racy 1977, 47). Music was taught frequently in a conservatory and included instruction in notation rather than in the traditional oral style (*ibid*., 36–39). The musical theater became a major conduit for Western musical styles

following World War I (*ibid.*, 64–71). It was surely a fluid and possibly unsettling period in Egyptian musical culture. Racy also suggests that between the end of World War I and the 1930s when the film-music period began the most popular musical genre became the *ṭaqṭūqa*, a "light" song previously associated with female singers and considered by many to be "vulgar." The spread of the phonograph was held responsible for the spread of such "vulgarity" (*ibid.*, 54). The same rhetoric disapproving of "vulgar" music surfaced with a vengeance after the mid-1970s when cheap cassette technology flooded Egypt.

11 All accounts of the story put the first meeting of Abd al-Wahhab and Shauqi in 1919 (e.g. M. ʿAwaḍ 1991, 66–67; Raḍwān 1991, 73–77; ʿAbd al-Wahhāb 1938 [203], 22; ʿAbd al-Wahhāb and Wahba 1992, 37–38).

12 Muṣṭafā Amīn (1991, 24) repeats nearly the same story about Abd al-Wahhab's encounter with Saad Zaghlul in the 1919 revolution. In another interview Abd al-Wahhab describes the demonstrations of 1919 in general terms, and claims to have shouted slogans and thrown bricks at British soldiers as a child of seven or eight, but says nothing about seeing Zaghlul (ʿAbd al-Wahhāb and Wahba 1992, 32–36).

13 Sayyid Darwish (1892–1923) is considered to have been the foremost composer before Abd al-Wahhab himself. Unlike Abd al-Wahhab, he experimented chiefly with the Egyptian folk tradition rather than with "high" art influenced by Turkish and Persian musical traditions. Darwish is also revered as the "singer of the 1919 revolution." Since he rose from a lower-class background and achieved fame largely through his novel use of "low" artistic traditions, the associations with Darwish are very different from those with Abd al-Wahhab's other main influence, Ahmad Shauqi.

14 When Abd al-Wahhab first met Sayyid Darwish he was working in the troupe of Nagib al-Rihani, yet another famous comic of the early stage and cinema. Al-Rihani was familiar with French theater and, while in the troupe of ʿAzīz ʿĪd during World War I, was given parts as an extra in plays featuring such foreign stars as Sarah Bernhardt, Coquelin, and Mounet-Sully. His predecessor, Id, was famed for the "Franco-Arab revue" – a comedy act that was very close to French vaudeville. Al-Rihani developed this style a step further, Egyptianizing the plays to a point where they hardly resembled the original material (Landau 1958, 86–90).

15 Mahmud Awad (1991, 72) says that the play began with Darwish in the lead, and Abd al-Wahhab took the part when he failed. Abd al-Wahhab himself, in a much earlier description of the event, said that Darwish never performed in his own production and that the young Abd al-Wahhab was hired to sing the lead from the start (ʿAbd al-Wahhāb 1938 [196], 16). In the article Abd al-Wahhab makes no mention of his age at the time, giving the impression that Darwish treated him as an equal despite his youth (he would have been as young as eleven years old, assuming a 1910 birthdate).

16 In an interview Abd al-Wahhab claimed to have been nine years old the first time he travelled abroad (to Beirut) with al-Rihani's troupe (ʿAbd al-Wahhāb and Wahba 1992, 227). He does not, however, mention a date in the interview.

17 Biographies of Shauqi do not mention Abd al-Wahhab prominently. Journalist Mustafa Amin, for example, makes no mention of Abd al-Wahhab in his

account of Shauqi's death, although a long list of prominent personalities who interacted with the poet on his last day is given (Amīn 1987, 257–58).

18 Mahmud Awad (1991, 83–84) says that Abd al-Wahhab studied harmony with a Russian teacher named Shatalov (Shaṭālūf), but that after his experiences with conservative audiences, he gave it up as too avant-garde. He later described giving up his studies in harmony as "the biggest mistake of his life." His Arabic music teachers at this time included Muṣṭafā Riḍā, Ḥasan al-Anwar, and Shaykh Darwīsh al-Ḥarīrī (see "'*Abd al-Wahhāb ʿalā ṭarīqat . . .*" 1991, 12–15).

19 The first Abd al-Wahhab–Shauqi collaboration was either "*Shabikti qalbī yā ʿaynī*" (You've caught my heart, my love) in colloquial, or "*Yā gārat al-wādī*" (O girl of the valley) in classical Arabic (M. ʿAwaḍ 1991, 83). On the compact disc *Mohamed Abdelwahab*: *Archives de la Musique Arabe*, vol. I, 1920–25, another song collaboration with Shauqi is listed: "*Minka ya hāgiru dā'ī*" (My sickness is from you, O departed one), dated 1923. As already noted, Abd al-Wahhab was not supposed to have met Shauqi until 1924.

20 This was Abd al-Wahhab's second performance with al-Mahdiya. The first was in the operetta *Al-Maẓlūma* (The oppressed woman) by Shaykh Yūnis al-Qāḍī (M. ʿAwaḍ 1991, 90–91). For more on al-Mahdiya see Danielson (1991b, 101–02).

21 Danielson (1991b, 135–37) points out that staging *Cleopatra* was a gamble for al-Mahdiya as well. Her popularity was waning at a time when the economy was also on the downturn. She hired Abd al-Wahhab not only to perform, but also to complete Darwish's music. Critics noted that Abd al-Wahhab wrote excellent songs for himself and inferior ones for al-Mahdiya. *Cleopatra* was the beginning of the end for Mahdiya, and the long-awaited breakthrough for Abd al-Wahhab.

22 Abd al-Wahhab recounted the story to Naṣṣār (1975, 43–45). The story was mentioned, for no apparent reason other than to poke fun at Abd al-Wahhab, in the second issue of *al-Ithnayn* (June 25, 1934) – seven years after *Antony and Cleopatra* opened.

23 *Al-Ithnayn* was published by Dār al-Hilāl starting in the summer of 1934. The title, which literally means "the two," probably refers to two earlier Dār al-Hilāl publications, *al-Fukāha* (Humor – published 1926–34) and *al-Kawākib* (The stars – a cinema magazine published 1932–34) which were combined under the title *al-Ithnayn* (al-Ṭamāwī 1992, 211).

24 Racy notes that such views were common "after the 1920s," but that they were always balanced to some extent by conservative writers who deplored the blind imitation of Western musical tastes. Racy characterizes the idea that Eastern music was somehow inferior, however, as the majority opinion in the press (Racy 1977, 44–45).

25 Abd al-Wahhab's hairstyles, particularly the sideburns, were followed by the public just as the styles of pop stars in contemporary America are followed and imitated. See Karīm 1972 (169–70) and *al-Ithnayn* 3 (August 2, 1934: 46) for descriptions of how Abd al-Wahhab's hairstyle was of concern in the making of two of his films.

26 Awad is, however, quick to point out that while Abd al-Wahhab and Shauqi

may have gravitated to the center of bohemianism in Paris of the 1920s and 1930s, they devoted considerable energy to searching for restaurants that served humble Egyptian food such as *mulukhīya* (a soup made from a type of mallow) and *fūl midammis* (a staple dish made of stewed dried fava beans).

27 Another gloss for *al-Barbarī* is "the black African," an obsolete (but probably not in 1934) derisive term for black Africans (Badawi and Hinds 1986, 60). Pierre Cachia translates al-Kassar's nickname as "the Berberine" (al-Hakim 1964, 191). There was, however, nothing Berber about al-Kassar. The actor and the character he portrayed were Nubian. Al-Kassar appears in *al-Ithnayn* 9 (August 13, 1934: 21) in a presumably Nubian outfit (it actually appears vaguely pharaonic). The degree of "Africanness" ascribed by Egyptians to Nubians, Sudanese, and sub-Saharan Africans in 1934 is a matter for conjecture. The "blackness" of Nubians was occasionally alluded to in *al-Ithnayn*, as on the inside front cover of *al-Ithnayn* 9 (August 13, 1934), which shows al-Kassar colored darkly and wearing some sort of "ethnic" costume. The caption reads: "He chose the role of *barbarī* because we live in an age that blackens the face." There were, in general, few positive images of Africans in *al-Ithnayn*. The magazine carried many images of exaggeratedly black (presumably Sudanese) servants (e.g. *al-Ithnayn* 6 [July 23, 1934]: 11). A black eunuch appeared on the cover of *al-Ithnayn* 27 (December 17, 1934). Another article mocked Maḥgūb Thābit, a writer involved in negotiations over relations between the Sudan, Egypt, and Britain (*al-Ithnayn* 4 [July 9, 1934]: 14). The article had Thabit married to a Sudanese woman, who was presented as repulsive and primitive. A cartoon acompanied the article, showing a caricature of a bare-breasted grass-skirt-wearing "native" dancing on the beach with a corpulent Thabit. Clearly Africans were portrayed as primitive, much as might have been done by the British, and Sudanese were shown as essentially African. Exactly how Nubians related to the categories of African and Egyptian is less clear.

28 After the first year, issues of *al-Ithnayn* were not as balanced in their presentation of the "folklore to modernity" progression. The themes of drawings on the cover were more varied, as were the contents of the inside front and back covers. The back cover, however, always sported a foreign actress. In late 1938, for example, the magazine featured photographs – often of the Egyptian royal family, as well as of other royalty such as Britain's or Iran's – instead of drawings.

29 Then a fashionable Cairo restaurant and patisserie, frequented by intellectuals and prominent members of society. In recent years it has gone badly downhill.

30 Abaza was editor of *al-Muṣawwar* from 1934 to 1962 (al-Ṭamāwī 1992, 208). Like *al-Ithnayn*, *al-Muṣawwar* was published by Dār al-Hilāl.

31 The company was owned by a Lebanese family, two of whom are mentioned by Karim – Jibrān and Ra'īsī Bayḍā.

32 In the scene Abd al-Wahhab has just quarreled with the leading lady, Laylā Murād. As he sings, the perspective shifts from a shot of a roomful of beautiful women to the perspective of what the singer "sees" (or imagines): an empty room.

33 The actual story for *White Rose* was written by committee: Muḥammad Mitwallī, Muhammad Karim, Taufiq al-Mardanli, Sulaymān Nagīb, and Abd

al-Wahhab. The film credits say: "An Egyptian story devised by Muhammad Mitwalli, adapted to the screen by Muhammad Karim, dialogue by Taufīq al-Mardanli and Sulayman Nagib."

34 Both *Lāshīn* (directed by Fritz Kramp, 1938), and *al-ʿAzīma* (Resolution, 1939) featured harmonic scores written by an Egyptian, ʿAbd al-Ḥamīd ʿAbd al-Raḥmān. Racy also mentions that well-tempered European instruments, particularly the piano and the accordion, were commonly used by the turn of the century, and that military bands since the mid-nineteenth century had transposed indigenous music into the well-tempered scale (Racy 1977, 62–64). Although Racy notes that such instruments were not necessarily used harmonically, their presence and the increasing familiarity of Egyptian composers with them certainly helped set the stage for forays into harmony.

35 The idea that Abd al-Wahhab was seeking to make the ensemble into an integrated unit rather than a background for a singer (or other soloist) tallies with Abd al-Wahhab's own statements in 1938 (*al-Ithnayn* 209 [1938]).

36 See, for example, Racy's discussion of heterophony in recorded Egyptian music of 1904 to 1932. In the early recordings accompanists responded to the soloist's musical line by replicating the line, but the structure of traditional music left them considerable freedom to introduce variations in melodic and rhythmic detail. In later recordings the texture of the music was characterized by exact unisons among the accompanists, and octave doubling that gave a thicker musical texture, at the expense of the traditional varied nuance in the accompanist's response to the melody (Racy 1977, 286–90).

37 Later composers sometimes arranged Abd al-Wahhab pieces with harmony. For example, some of the songs in the 1962 film *Almaz and Abduh al-Hamuli* (based on the life of the singer Abduh al-Hamuli, who was part of Abd al-Wahhab's self-constructed musical *isnād*) were harmonic arrangements of songs Abd al-Wahhab was credited with having composed. ʿAlī Ismāʿīl was the arranger. Ismail had begun harmonic composing and arranging in the 1950s, and worked on the film scores of a number of productions in the 1960s.

38 However, Danielson (1991b) gives a useful description of Egyptian musical culture from the turn of the century to the 1970s in the context of writing about Abd al-Wahhab's female rival Umm Kulthum.

5 Classic, clunker, national narrative

1 Salim's filmography includes: *Warā' al-sitār* (Behind the curtain, 1937); *al-ʿAzīma* (Resolution, 1939); *Ilā al-abad* (Forever, 1941); *Aḥlām al-shabāb* (Dreams of youth, 1942); *al-Bu'asā'* (*Les Misérables*, an adaptation of the Victor Hugo novel, 1943); *Qaḍīyat al-yaum* (A contemporary issue, 1943); *Ḥanān* (Compassion, 1944); *Shuhadā' al-ghurām* (Martyrs of love, an adaptation of *Romeo and Juliet*, 1944); *al-Maẓāhir* (Manifestations, 1945); *Laylat al-Gumʿa* (Friday night, 1945). Muḥammad al-Sayyid Shūsha (introduction to K. Salīm 1975, 11) also credits Salim with having directed *Qiṣṣat ghurām* (Love story, 1945, with Muḥammad ʿAbd al-Gawwād).

2 The key to the scene for a nonaristocratic audience was probably that the cat was obviously purebred. If attitudes in the 1930s were anything like those of contemporary Egypt, non-purebred *baladī* cats would be viewed as just above

vermin, tolerated, if at all, only out of recognition of their value in suppressing more serious vermin such as rats. But people who greet the sight of *baladī* cats with disgust are often happy to hold and even sleep in the same room with Siamese or other purebred cats.

3 Samira Khalusi was Karim's second choice for the part of Raga. His first choice, Naglā' ʻAbduh, fell ill with typhoid during the early stages of shooting outdoor scenes in Egypt. After a well-publicized search for a replacement a friend of Daulat Abyaḍ (the actress who played Raga's mother and a professional of relatively long standing) suggested Khalusi, who was only sixteen years old at the time. Khalusi's mother, a Frenchwoman (her father was Egyptian), stipulated that her fee must include the cost of clothing, since her daughter would be playing the part of a wealthy girl. Karim agreed, but then his leading lady appeared on the set with cheap unsuitable clothes. The girl's mother had used the money on clothes for Samira's brother. Karim was, therefore, forced to spend still more on Khalusi's wardrobe (Karīm 1972, 167–69).

4 In addition to *White Rose* (1933) Abd al-Wahhab starred in *Dumūʻ al-ḥubb* (Tears of love, 1935); *Yaḥyā al-ḥubb* (Long live love, 1938); *Yaum saʻīd* (Happy day, 1940); *Mamnūʻ al-ḥubb* (No love allowed, 1942); *Raṣāṣa fī-l-qalb* (Bullet in the heart, 1944); and *Anā lastu malākan* (I am no angel, 1946). He also appeared as a singer (but not as an actor) in two films: *Ghazal al-banāt* (The love of girls, 1949, directed by Anwar Wagdī) and *Muntahā al-faraḥ* (The ultimate in happiness, 1963, directed by Muḥammad Sālim).

5 Egyptian society between 1920 and 1950, Hawwas says, was divided between elite and popular culture, related to each other only by the filmmakers' need to market their product in a cultural milieu radically different from their own. Elite culture, in turn, was divided between those completely opposed to films in principle (the traditional religious establishment) and those "who wanted reform, and to escape the old reformist movements in order to attain more modern forms in the various spheres of culture" (Ḥawwās 1986, 164). This meant that they had to turn to the West for inspiration. Throughout the article Hawwas assumes that the early films utilized at best a "phony blending" (*ibid.*, 166) of local and foreign elements, rendering even the most authentic film of the period, *Resolution*, more "romantic" than "folkloric."

6 In his other films Abd al-Wahhab always has an air of the self-made man, even when he plays the part of an aristocrat. In *Long Live Love* he is an aristocrat working as a bank teller just so that he can be appreciated on his own merits. In *No Love Allowed*, a comic adaptation of the Romeo and Juliet story, he and the girl he loves commit "social suicide" by marrying in opposition to their feuding families and forsaking the family fortune in order to live a middle-class existence. The point is driven home in a scene in which he and leading lady Ragā' ʻAbduh sing a lovely duet (featuring short harmonic sections) in the kitchen while he, wearing an apron, cooks dinner. He is a clerk who marries an aristocratic girl in *Bullet in the Heart*. In *Happy Day* he is neither a clerk nor an aristocrat, but a professional singer who marries (as usual) an aristocratic girl.

7 Probably the office of justice, since Ismail Bey was supposed to be a judge, and could be expected to have the most influence in this area. Nonetheless, *dīwān* in this context is a generic term, and could refer to any government office.

8 *Mahr* is money paid by a groom's family to the bride's as a contribution to her trousseau.

9 Usually portrayals of the *awlād al-balad* were restricted to comedy. Nagib al-Rihani's "Kishkish Bey" and Ali al-Kassar's "barbarian" (see chapter 4) were typical. More often than not the *awlād al-balad* were the butt of the jokes. The humor came not from "life in the popular quarters," but from subjecting *ibn al-balad* figures to modern situations. For instance, in al-Kassar's *Sallifnī thalātha ginayh* (Loan me three pounds, 1939, directed by Tōgō Mizrāḥī) al-Kassar's bumbling "barbarian," a doorman at a school in this case, manages to get himself hired as a dentist's assistant. The dentist is having an affair with his secretary, and leaves his office for a midday tryst. The "barbarian" proceeds to assume the dentist's role and terrorize his hapless customers, one of whom is a salesman who faints from pain as the "barbarian" removes twenty-six of his teeth with a pair of pliers.

10 Rushdi started her career in the Ramsīs Troupe, a theatrical company formed by Yusuf Wahbi. In 1927 Rushdi and Aziz Id, her husband at the time, split from Ramsīs to found their own company (Rushdī 1970, 62–79). *Resolution* was her fourth film, and she had also directed a film – *al-Zawāj* (The marriage, 1933).

11 The dialogue of *Resolution* translated here comes mostly from the published text of the screenplay. Differences between the screenplay and the film are noted. Descriptions of the scenes connecting the dialogue are based on the screenplay, but are not literal. These first two scenes come on pages 53–55 of Salim's original screenplay (K. Salīm 1975 [1939]).

12 The "pastry vendor" is *bā'iʿ faṭīr* – seller of *faṭāyir*, pancake-like loaves of bread, usually eaten with honey or something sweet. His call, *ghayyar rīʕ-ak*, means literally "change your saliva."

13 *Fūl nābit* are dried fava beans soaked until they sprout. Calling them "white" is typical of the hyperbole used in vendors' cries. It simply means "excellent quality."

14 "*Si*" is an informal lower-class term of address to a man. The term implies respect when an uneducated man uses it to address a superior.

15 Ironically Nazih Pasha is played by Zakī Rustam, the actor who played Shafiq in *White Rose*.

16 The following scene is taken from Salim (1975, 68–70). Minor differences between the screenplay and the film are noted. As before, the connecting scenes are translated less literally than the dialogue.

17 "At a table . . .": In the screenplay this is *li-mashrab al-bār*: "at the bar." In the film Adli's friends sit at a table. Adli and Muhammad go to the bar.

18 "Mad as hell . . .": *muḥḍira-lak mayyit nār. Ma-timshī-sh bi-wishsh-ak ʿaryān*, lit. "she's ready for you with acid," i.e. extremely angry – "she's coming after you with a gun." "Watch out for her," lit. "don't walk with your face bare" (she will "throw acid" in it). Also, in the text the name of the girl is "Charlotte" the first time, and then "Regina" a few lines later.

19 Adli uses "*Si*" here patronizingly, pointing up what a "square" Muhammad is among the fast crowd he runs with. In the 1960s *Si* acquired an additional resonance from a film adaptation of Naguib Mahfouz's Cairo trilogy. The main character, Aḥmad ʿAbd al-Gawwād, became known as the prototype for a "*Si*

Sayyid," specifically a very conservative man who allows the women in his family no freedom.

20 "Let's . . . drink": *nihanni anfus-na*, literally "congratulate ourselves." This is a variant of a formulaic response to *bil-hanā wi-shifā*, "God give you health," when someone begins a meal or *haniyyan*, when someone has a haircut. Normally Adli's friends should be congratulating Muhammad, not themselves.

21 "That hick": *garābīʿ il-balad*, "country trash." *Garābīʿ* (pl. of *garbūʿ*) means "trashy," "good-for-nothing." Their condescension becomes more open.

22 "Check it out": *ʕayyid ʿandak*, lit. "write that down" (in your register etc.). He is being sarcastic.

23 "That says it all": *ʾahi tammit*, lit. "and there it is, finished." Possibly they mean his degree, but the sense of the phrase is "that really puts the dot on the 'i'!"

24 Several other early Egyptian films imply the same type of relationship between traditional society and modernity without, however, coming anywhere near *Resolution*'s naturalistic technique. For example: *Laylā* (Layla, 1927, directed by Widād ʿUrfī); *Salāma fī khayr* (Salama is fine, 1937, directed by Niyāzī Muṣṭafā); *Long Live Love* (1938, directed by Muhammad Karim); *Al-Duktūr* (The doctor, 1939, directed by Niyazi Mustafa); *Layla bint al-rīf* (Layla daughter of the countryside, 1941, directed by Togo Mizrahi); *Kidb fī kidb* (lies upon lies, 1944, directed by Togo Mizrahi).

25 "When you're married": *nahār ʿadal-ik*. An ideal thing can be described as *ʿadal*, such as "*il-gawāz il-ʿadal*" – "an ideal marriage."

26 "Made for each other": *il-nās bi-l-nās*, lit. "people for people." This is a compliment for the two families. Both are *ibn (bint) il-nās* – son (and daughter) of the people, "regular guys," "alright people," as well as birds of a feather.

27 "Strangers . . . other." In the text this is *il-ghurb bi-yigāmlu baʿḍ*: "strangers flatter each other." In the film it is *il-ghurb bi-yisāʿdu baʿḍ*, "strangers help each other." The two variants of the line give slightly different senses. "Strangers flatter" evokes the notion that the best marriage is between families that are well known to each other – less alienating for the bride because she will be moving to a household already on good terms with her father's household. The film variant, however, is more consistent with the lines that follow. Umm Firdus calls attention to her daughter and herself – relative strangers compared to Fatima's family, which lives just upstairs from Muhammad's family.

28 "Auntie . . .": *khāltī*, lit. "maternal aunt." Kinship terms are often used by people on familiar terms.

29 "Demon in a bottle": *ʿafrīt il-ʿilba*, lit. "demon of the can (or other container)."

30 "Look . . . them!" *shāyfa il-maʕārīṣ wi-baḥlaʕit-hum fīhum*, "Look how tight they are and how they stare at them." *Maqārīṣ*, pl. of *maqrūṣ*, the participial form of *qaraṣ*. Therefore "tight" in the sense of "pulled tight," or "firm," e.g. *uʕruṣ il-ḥizām*, "tighten the girth."

The women are, half seriously, expressing their jealousy at Fatima's good fortune. The exchange between Firdus and her mother has the sense of "so what am I, chopped liver?" Later in the film this jealous vein becomes more serious, when the women discover that Muhammad has lost his job and is working as a clerk, unbeknown to Fatima. They conspire to reveal this fact to her, and the marriage is temporarily ruined.

31 "Thank you . . .": *in shā' Allāh mā niʿdam-ik*, lit. "God willing, you won't be deprived." This is a formula said by traditional women when receiving food or drink.

32 "Won't ... washing": *natashit 'īd-i min ṭisht il-ghasīl*, lit. "she snatched my hands from the wash basin." The sentence refers either to Firdus's hardworking nature, or to her hurry to get over to Umm Muhammad's house. In either case, the women continue the half-serious joking, advertising their daughters' suitability as partners for the very desirable Muhammad.

33 In the script the woman is supposed to be ululating, which she does not do in the film. In the film she doesn't actually enter, but comes down the stairs of the apartment building and stands on the landing.

34 "God forbid": *ʿadawīn-ik*, lit. "may it happen to your enemy." This is said when someone mentions something unpleasant.

35 "What . . . toadying": the Turkish woman, who wears a headscarf very similar to the *ḥijāb* worn by neo-Islamicists today, speaks accented, but oddly classical, Arabic, as well as using a Turkish word. In the first of these lines she says *'īfīt kalām*, "yes [Turkish *evet*] this is [loose] talk." What follows is in *sajʿ* – rhymed prose of the sort used in classical Arabic writing: *ṣarāḥāt min ghayr 'īmānāt min ghayr ḥilfānāt al-ḥamdu li-llah . . . ana māfish ʿandi banāt . . . māfish ʿandi miḥmalisāt* (utterances without belief, without oaths, God be praised, I don't have girls, [so] I don't have [all this] toadying).

36 She uses the boy to make an excuse to exit so that she can meet Muhammad.

37 "Good . . . you": *Kashḥa*, slang, "shove off" or "beat it." *Allāh mā yiwarrī-ki ṭarīq il-salāma*, "May God not show you the path of safety." Later in the film Firdus, encouraged by the butcher Itir, who is jealous at Muhammad's marriage to Fatima, plays a prominent role in the plot to expose Muhammad's misfortunes to his wife.

38 *Resolution* is a particularly fine example of a common trope in Egyptian cinema: the tension between modern romance and traditional conservatism, which features in countless films. Although modernist ideology would have it that tradition makes concessions to change without, however, compromising authenticity, the social complexity of a love match remains a potent issue around which to construct a story. *Indhār bil-ṭāʿa* (Warning of obedience, 1993, directed by ʿĀṭif al-Ṭayyib), for example, depicts a young man engaged in a far more bitter struggle to marry the woman he loves (and who loves him) in the 1990s than *Resolution* described in the 1930s.

39 Abd al-Wahhab sings a song during the scene – "*Jafnuhu 'allama al-ghazal*" ([Her] eye showed love). The song is slightly disjointed because it was superimposed on the original film through a primitive postdubbing process (Karīm 1972, 192–94). Karim describes the difficulties of synchronizing sound with lip movements at length, leading to the startling (and naive) conclusion that he was the first to tackle the problem. René Claire, who worked in the same technical milieu as Karim in the early 1930s, gives a more realistic description of the problems of integrating sound and image in early talkies (Dale 1986, 138).

40 "*Al-muṭrib al-nābigh*" (the gifted singer) was a moniker frequently applied to Abd al-Wahhab in later biographical treatments (in the 1930s, however, it was applied to many singers).

41 The song is identified in "'*Abd al-Wahhāb al-mumaththil*" (1991, 64).

42 The process of authenticating Arab artists is starkly different from the way Western artists present themselves to the public. Elvis Presley is an excellent example of how differently we present artistic authenticity. His first film, *Jailhouse Rock*, portrays the singer as a rebel, and artistically as a unique phenomenon. He tries to *deny* his links to other musicians. At one point in the film he gives an old jailhouse comrade a chance to appear on his television show. His friend pressured Presley into giving him a chance by saying that he had been his teacher, implying that Presley owed some of his success to him. But when the ex-con friend appears on the show the falsity of his claim becomes obvious: he looks and sounds utterly different from Presley. He is a flop. There can be no question of an artistic genealogy leading from this ex-con to the self-styled king of rock and roll.

Thus while scholars might point out Presley's debt to the blues and various slighted black artists that he essentially plagiarized, the manner of presenting Presley to the public was invariably as a "unique event." The public presentation of Arab artists is always as "the next link in the chain."

43 Foreigners tend to echo the Egyptian critics: Taufiq notes that French critic George Sadoul praised *Resolution* in his 1962 *History of the Cinema* (Taufīq 1969, 80). Malkmus (Malkmus and Armes 1991, 30) makes much the same point about *Resolution* (which she translates as *The Will*): "The Egyptian cinema of pre-1945 was more a cinema of genres than of auteurs, though it did possess one individual film-maker of widely acknowledged exceptional status in Kamal Selim who, after making his debut as a scriptwriter, went on to make one of Egypt's most important and innovatory realist films, *The Will [al-Azima*, in 1939."

44 Of the pre-1950s films film historians sometimes put *al-Sūq al-sodā'* (Black market, released in 1945 and directed by Kāmil al-Telmisānī) in the same class as *Resolution* (e.g. Abū Shādī 1994 [53–69], which contains a chapter on *Black Market* and *White Rose* but, surprisingly, not on *Resolution*). The period in which *Black Market* was made was a transition phase in Egyptian cinema, in which filmmaking expanded into a well-established industry (Malkmus and Armes 1991, 31).

45 Possibly the only other Egyptian film from the 1930s that rivals *Resolution* in terms of technique is *Lāshīn*, a medieval spectacle directed by Fritz Kramp, a German. *Lāshīn*, however, has none of the social immediacy of *Resolution* or even *White Rose*. Salim never again approached the level of *Resolution*. For example, his penultimate film, *Friday Night* (1945), was a relatively pathetic comedy farce in which a number of stars played themselves. The film does, however, indicate that by the mid-1940s the tradition of film consumption was already so deeply rooted that Egyptian films could be marketed solely on the basis of their stars. Other such films, such as *The Flirtation of Girls* (1949) were well made and are still fondly remembered and avidly watched.

46 For example, the Cairo trilogy novels *Bayn al-qaṣrayn*, *Qaṣr al-shauq*, and *al-Sukkariyya*. The first two novels especially resemble *Resolution*: the younger generation becomes differentiated from its forebears through its contact with modern institutions, particularly the educational system.

47 One of the items in "'*Ishmiʿnā*" was about Abd al-Wahhab. Q: "'*Ishmiʿnā Abd al-Wahhab yimīl lil-nawāḥ?*" A: "ʿ*Alashān il-ʕulūb tiriʕʕ luh*" (Why does Abd al-Wahhab like to sob? So that hearts [of pretty girls] will feel tender for him). This is probably a light-hearted rejoinder to the sort of heavy-handed criticism of Arabic singing leveled by highbrow magazines such as *al-Hilāl*.

The form of the joke – "why especially this [and not some other thing]" – is a kind of traditional "knock-knock" joke in which the object is witty repartee. Such jokes are called *qafya*, and often rely on punning. Through such a device the article appeals to the assumed *baladī* sympathies of the reader (at least in the context of being cheated out of advancement by well-connected competitors) in much the same way as Abd al-Wahhab's language-dependent humor in the rent-collecting scene of *White Rose*.

48 Books and articles on the Egyptian cinema do, however, give high marks to Karim as a technical pioneer, and at least a nod to Abd al-Wahhab for adapting Egyptian song to the screen. Even Farīd (1986, 208) allows that the production of early films was a national triumph over colonialist occupiers who had every intention of keeping Egypt in a position of dependency. But attempts to find merit in early Egyptian cinema are generally halfhearted.

49 According to Karim, politicians had the film moved during the second week to the Metropole, which was also owned by foreigners. The idea was to spread the "protection" around. Then the film was moved to the Fu'ād Cinema, which had been founded by a group of business-school students forming the Cinematograph Company. The group included Abd Allah Fikri Abaza, who first introduced Karim to Abd al-Wahhab. The Fu'ād had been the Gōzī Palace, but it was soon abandoned by the group in favor of the Cosmo, which was also temporarily renamed the Fu'ād. *White Rose* moved to the new theater on January 10, 1934, but the theater still closed in May of the same year with a loss of LE 12,000 (Karīm 1972, 199).

50 Taufīq (1969, 72) reports that *Resolution* was a commercial record breaker, earning something in excess of a quarter of a million pounds – a phenomenal sum for the time. However, similar numbers are occasionally bandied about for Abd al-Wahhab films. In the end, the reliability of estimates of a film's earnings is questionable, as is certainly the case today. I was warned by Egyptian filmmakers not to trust any published figures on film profits.

6 Popular commentary, real lives

1 *Zuzu*'s author and director was Ḥasan al-Imām, a veteran known for melodrama who had produced popular (but critically condemned) adaptations of several Naguib Mahfouz novels. The scenario and dialogue for *Zuzu* was written by colloquial artist Salah Jahin, the "poet of Nasser" (see chapter 3).

2 Zuzu's mother was played by Taḥīya Kāriyōkā who was, in fact, a famous dancer and film star of the 1940s and 1950s. The part of Zuzu was played by Suʿād Ḥusnī, a dancing (and singing) film star of the 1960s and 1970s.

3 The practice of forming "families" among students began after 1968, when students joined with workers in protesting against what they perceived as a corrupt state of social institutions in the wake of the crushing defeat in the Six Day War of 1967. They replaced a discredited government-sponsored student

institution called the Student Youth Organization. Still, government pressure on students never ceased, and student leaders were periodically arrested. The period between 1968 and 1972 – just before *Zuzu* was made – was a particularly turbulent period of student unrest (Abdalla 1985, 176).

4 A central student newspaper at Cairo University was only permitted in 1968, after rebellious students won limited concessions from the government (Abdalla 1985, 158). Currently there is no student newspaper at Cairo University.

5 Another of the concessions gained by students in the 1968 riots was to remove censorship of the wall magazines. They were described at the time as "the freest press in Egypt" (Abdalla 1985, 158). Wall magazines were frequently the target of official ire. At about the time *Zuzu* came out Sadat himself had condemned the posters, and accused a renegade student organization, called the Higher National Committee of Cairo University Students, of treason (*ibid.*).

6 The early 1970s marked the first upsurge of Islamist ideology on the campuses of Egyptian universities. As Gilles Kepel notes: "At that time [1972] the Islamist students were opposing the Nasserists and Communists, to the great satisfaction of the regime" (Kepel 1984, 138). It is important to remember, in this connection, that Salah Jahin, a thoroughly Nasserist artist, was involved in the making of *Zuzu*. The confrontation between Zuzu's group and Umran's group is meant to recapitulate the ideological battle raging between Nasserists and the newly invigorated Islamists.

7 Women's fashions of 1972 were both more Western and more revealing than today. As one middle-class woman of that generation put it, "We all wore miniskirts then." The woman who said this now wears a neo-Islamic *ḥijāb*. She had pictures of herself from the early 1970s which support her claim that skirts were indeed shorter.

8 According to Nieuwkerk (n.d., 66), the rise of the Pyramids Road nightclubs began during World War II and was associated with prostitution catering to British soldiers. Muḥammad ʿAlī Street was the home of the traditional entertainment trade, which was somewhat more respectable, was dominated by established families, and which separated female performers from men, each performing for their respective sex (*ibid.*, 68–72).

9 Farida Fahmi was the prima ballerina of the Riḍā Troupe for the Folkloric Arts, founded by Maḥmūd Riḍā in 1960. The Riḍā Troupe is considered to have been among the first successful attempts to adapt elements of folk art to high culture (see Riḍā 1968).

10 If recent films deal directly with Islamists they tend to oppose them vehemently. For example, Īnās al-Daghaydī's *Dīskū dīskū* (Disco disco, 1994) and Nādir Galāl's *al-Irhābī* (The terrorist, 1994) depict Islamists as lacking even rudimentary modern education and coming entirely from outside state institutions. A notable exception to this anti-Islamist tendency in Egyptian cinema is Atif al-Tayyib's *Abnā' wa-qatala* (Sons and murderers, 1987), in which an Islamist character is both positively depicted and university educated. Samir Farid also describes Saʿd ʿArafa's *al-Ḥubb qabla al-khubz aḥyānan* (Love before bread sometimes, 1977) as a film that "consecrates" religious extremism and calls for women to wear the *ḥijāb* (Farīd 1988, 21).

11 All of the names of these individuals, as well as some other details, have been changed to preserve their anonymity. This is also true of the family mentioned in a later section of this chapter ("1990: the wasteland").

12 Two years after my fieldwork the café was sold to the American franchise Pizza Hut, which is extremely expensive by local standards. The crowd is still mixed in terms of gender, but no longer affordable for junior-high-school teachers such as Farid.

13 The words to the original were: "*ahwāk, wi-atmanna lau ansāk, wi-ansā rūḥī wayyāk, wi-in ḍā'it yibqā fadāk wi-arga' tānī*" (I love you, I hope if I forget you, and my love with you, if [my love] is lost may I die, and come back again).

14 Just how far an annual income of LE 500 would have gone in 1974 (the time of the survey) would depend on one's circumstances – how many dependants one had, whether one lived in a rent-controlled apartment (or indeed, had an apartment). By 1979 a popular film, *Shaban below Zero* (see chapter 7), depicted a rural bureaucrat making a salary of LE 28.50. The point was that such a salary was absurdly low even for a single man living in the relatively inexpensive countryside. Thus it is safe to say that LE 41 per month (the monthly rate of LE 500) was at best a very modest salary for Cairo in the early 1970s.

15 Over 20 percent of the sample were illiterate, while more than 70 percent fell somewhere between "able to read and write" and "college educated" (Ibrahim 1982, 425).

16 By "neither desperately poor nor extravagantly rich" I mean between LE 300 per year and LE 2,000 (Ibrahim 1982, 425). Again, how far LE 300 might go would depend on one's circumstances. It is safe to say that at the time of the survey (1979) one could conceivably be quite poor on LE 300 per year, but one could not be extremely well off even on LE 2,000 per year. But while 15 percent of the group were college graduates, being a college graduate did not guarantee making even a moderate income. Only 0.6 percent of the sample falls into the next-to-highest income category (between LE 3,000 and LE 5,000) and even fewer in the above LE 5,000 category.

17 This is not to say that all pre-1970s Egyptian films make an easy connection between education and wealth. Even old classics such as *White Rose*, *Resolution*, and *Black Market* portrayed embattled graduates. However, such films generally also portrayed an optimistic resolution of the problems facing educated protagonists. From the 1970s on this optimism has faded from many Egyptian films.

18 In terms of educational (as opposed to occupational) mobility, the tendency is toward greater diversity from one generation to the next. Illiteracy in the generation of respondents tended to be inherited, but was not passed on to the next generation.

19 The film was released in the summer of 1990. It was directed by Khayrī Bishāra and starred Ahmad Zaki as a boxer. Critics thought the film a misstep by Bishara, who is considered one of the best directors in Egypt. The public, however, loved it, and made it the most popular film of the year. The hairstyle came ultimately from that of the American heavyweight Mike Tyson, who was champion when Bishara started making the film.

20 The line is *ana fi-lābōriyā*. "*Lābōriyā*," according to lyricist Husayn al-Imam, is slang for "liberty" (personal conversation, July 1994).

21 "*Wi-mā tbī'sh illī inshabaklak*" refers to the girl in the old neighborhood whom the boxer wants to marry.

22 "*Ash-shinganinga nau mā kulsh[i] samakmak.*" Husayn al-Imam says that *ash-shinganinga nau* is what Alexandrian fishermen say in the course of their folkloric dance.

23 "*Ḥāga fīgā*," according to al-Imam, is a hashish-laced cigarette. As for "*Il-bīga fīga mātisnidsh*" (previous line), al-Imam said that *bīgā fīgā* is a variant of *bagā fīgā*, which are small birds, also called '*asfūr al-nīl* (sparrows of the Nile), eaten in low-class bars and at *mulid*s.

24 *Al-bunīya kilitsh* – the punch misses. *Kilitsh*, al-Imam said, is slang for slightly off target.

25 Danielson (1991b, 213–21) describes the circumstances of Abd al-Wahhab's collaboration with Umm Kulthum. "*Inta 'umrī*" was the first of ten songs the two did together (Abd al-Wahhab composing and Umm Kulthum singing). Gamal Abdel Nasser was said to have promoted the idea of collaboration between the two (*ibid.*, 216), and the song remains among the most popular of Umm Kulthum's recordings. Purists, however, including many composers, found the song too modern for their tastes (*ibid.*, 219–20).

26 She says, "Who told you to play for money?" (*yil'ab li-fulūs*). Throughout the film the characters use the phrase "to play with money" in the sense of "to gamble." The distinction in the context of the film is ambiguous, but the important thing is a general sense of people with so much money that they neither know nor care what to do with it as long as they are entertained.

27 Husayn al-Imam, the lyricist, was also the film's producer. He told me that his preference was to have Hudhud keep the money at the end of the film, but that he was overruled by director Khayri Bishara (personal conversation, July 1994).

28 Husayn al-Imam is the son of Hasan al-Imam, who was the director of *Pay Attention to Zuzu*. Primarily a musician, Husayn spent several years teaching the guitar in Chicago, played guitar on the soundtrack of *Crabs*, produced the film, played Sulayman Bey (the rich man in the film), and (in real life) is the husband of Saḥar Rāmī, the actress who played Nur, the secretary in the film.

29 Even director Khayri Bishara admitted at a public meeting held after his film was shown during a local film festival (held in the summer of 1991) that the practice of setting up boxing rings in the street – a critical component of Hudhud's neighborhood in the film – was pure invention.

30 The cassette version of the film's songs was not, however, sung by Ahmad Zaki, the actor who played Hudhud, but by Husayn al-Imam, who is a member of *niqābat al-mūsīqiyīn* (the musicians' association).

31 In 1993 the Ezbekīya market was dismantled to make room for subway construction. Many of the cassette merchants now operate from a street behind the nearby al-'Ataba bus station, but the old ambience is gone, probably for good.

32 Even if one can buy out of military service (I have never met anyone who did this), in practice few would exercise such an option, as it would constitute a black mark on one's record that would complicate everything from starting a business to foreign travel. Family connections can, however, be used to assure more comfortable circumstances for the well-off army recruit.

33 Salmawi was actually the new managing editor when I began working for the paper. The project of producing an English-language weekly had been germinating for many months, initially under someone else's management.

34 This is not to say that Egyptians do not attempt to learn English. Indeed, there is an obvious hunger for learning English manifested in the spread of "language schools" (in which the primary language of instruction is European), ubiquitous advertisements for language courses, and high salaries commanded by English teachers. The impetus for learning English, however, is mainly economic – one can more easily obtain high-paying technical jobs, and can more easily interact with the world economy. The status of the English press in Egypt, assumptions of its local appeal, and *al-Ahrām*'s attempt to elevate its quality are symptomatic of a worldwide tendency to promote English-language expression. In Egypt as in other places (India for example) the value of cultural expression in English is hotly debated.

Ahmad (1992, 95–122; 159–219) argues that postcolonial writing in English has contributed to a homogenizing canon of "Third World" literature that serves bourgeois metropolitan interests. In particular he criticizes Jameson (*ibid.*, 95–122, in response to Jameson 1986) and Said (Ahmad 1992, 159–219, dealing with Said 1978 and 1990 among others). Said, for his part, disparages the tendency of Arab and Egyptian educational institutions to teach English as a "technical language almost totally stripped not only of expressive and aesthetic characteristics but also denuded of any critical or self-conscious dimension . . . English, such as it was [in Arab societies], existed in what seemed to be a seething cauldron of Islamic revivalism" (Said 1990, 3–4). For Said the publication of *al-Ahram Weekly* was a welcome development. He publishes in it regularly.

35 His publications include *Fī al-Nāṣiriyya* (On Nasserism), Cairo: Dār Alif, 1984; *Fūt ʿalayna bukra* (Drop by tomorrow), Cairo: Dār al-Wafā', 1983; *Maṣraḥiyat Salūmī: usṭūra tārīkhīya fī juz'ayn* (Salome: a tragic fable in two acts) al-Maʿādī al-Jadīda: Dār Alif, 1986; *Muḥarrir al-shu'ūn al-khārijiyya* (The foreign-affairs editor), s.n. 1976; *al-Qātil khārij al-sijn* (The murderer is out of prison), Cairo (al-Maʿādī al-Jadīda): Dār Alif, 1985; *al-Rajul alladhī ʿādat ilayhi dhākiratuhu, wa-qiṣaṣ ukhrā* (The man whose memory returned to him and other stories), Cairo: Dār al-Wafā', 1983; *al-Ṣūra al-jamāhīriyya li-Jamāl ʿAbd al-Nāṣir* (The public image of Gamal Abdel Nasser), Cairo: Dār al-Mauqif al-ʿArabī, 1983; *Uṣūl al-ishtirākiyya al-Biriṭāniyya: al-Fābiyya* (Principles of British socialism: Fabianism), Cairo: GEBO, 1978.

36 Shortly before the first issue was published (February 28, 1990) I returned briefly to sports (in addition to my editorial-page translations) because Sophie could find no other assistant, and would be absent for some time at the World Swimming Championships in Australia.

37 The old Opera House, which had been built as part of the celebrations for the inauguration of the Suez Canal, had burned down in 1970 in suspicious circumstances. The old location is now occupied by a parking structure, and the new Opera House is on Gezira Island.

38 Tickets for many events are indeed far too expensive for most Egyptians, at anywhere from LE 10 to LE 50 or more, depending on the event.

39 When I returned to Egypt in 1993 I found that Salmawi was working on a different project (*al-Ahrām* in French) and Shebl had rejoined the *Weekly*. This time, however, he seemed only interested in writing about high culture, particularly the filmmaker Yusuf Shahin (whose autobiographical work in the 1980s and 1990s was popular with intellectuals and metropolitan critics [e.g. Armes 1987, 243–54], but not with the Egyptian masses), about whom he was making a documentary.

40 A summary of Mursi Saad al-Din's professional life can be found in *Who's Who in the Arab World* (1990–91, 481). Dr. Mursi's accomplishments include: censor of foreign books and publications; assistant secretary general and public relations officer for the Afro-Asian People's Solidarity Conference (subsequently Organization) (1958); cultural attaché, Embassy to East Germany (1969–72); controller general, Egyptian Higher Council for the Arts (1973); director general, Ministry of Information and Culture (1975–78); chairman of the State Information Service (1977–79); editor in chief, *Cairo Today*. His publications include *An Approach to English Philology* (in English), *The Rise of Political Parties*, and *Communication and the Future* (both in Arabic).

41 For a description of the tumultuous politics – allegedly a thing of the past according to Mursi Saad al-Din – surrounding the sculpture *Nahḍat Miṣr* (al-Ashari's *Egypt Awakening*, translated also as "the revival of Egypt" and "Egyptian awakening") in the 1920s and 1930s see Gershoni and Jankowski (1986, 186–90). For more on Mukhtar's career as a sculptor see Karnouk (1988, 11–18).

42 Just before publication of mass-circulated editions, the paper began a digest page, which was exclusively translations of material published in other *al-Ahrām* publications: the daily *al-Ahrām*, the economics and women's magazines, and a newly developed evening edition of *al-Ahrām*. The other side of the new page was a travel section. The goal of trying to have most of the *Weekly*'s articles written by the paper's own staff had been largely realized by 1994 when I returned to Cairo.

7 "Vulgarity"

1 Bahā' Ṭāhir claimed that, as early as the late 1960s, "the serious theatre has been on the wane and the commercial theatre has taken over" (Allen 1979, 126). Casting commercial theater as the villain in this equation obviously implies that the hero is public-sector theater. As Allen notes, the period between 1952 and the late 1960s (when Gamal Abdel Nasser ruled Egypt) was considered outstanding in Egyptian theatrical history. The period also saw a sharp rise in the state's interest in subsidizing the arts. The result, as Allen puts it, was the creation of "a dramatic language which can bridge the gap between the written language and the colloquial" (*ibid.*, 122). A similar nostalgia for the synthesizing character of 1960s cultural production (particularly state-funded art) pertains to the cinema and to popular music. After the 1960s public-sector financing in all the arts (except, perhaps, television) declined, and private financing increased.

2 The writer, Ali Salim, was and is considered a "serious" playwright (see Allen

1979, 106–7). Most of the others involved in the production tend to be ignored by academic analysts on the grounds that they are overly commercial.

3 Word reached me that during Ramadan of 1992 the entire play was aired. The airing of *School of Troublemakers* in its entirety was somewhat unusual, although old theatrical and cinematic favorites are typically aired throughout the month of Ramadan, along with much-ballyhooed new programs, many of which are continuations of old series.

4 The character Ahmad was played by Ahmad Zaki, who also played Hudhud the boxer in *Crabs*. Ahmad the "troublemaker" was Zaki's first notable role.

5 The cast consisted of Adil Imam, Said Salih, Yūnis Shalabī, Ahmad Zaki, Hādī al-Ghayār, Sohayr al-Bāblī, ʿAbd al-Munʿim Madbūlī, Ḥasan Muṣṭafā, Naẓīm Shaʿrāwī, and ʿAbd Allāh Farghālī.

Mustafa and Madbuli both played the principal of the school (Mustafa replaced Madbuli sometime after the first season). Sharawi played the father of the most troublesome of the students. Mustafa and Farghali both played the role of an incompetent teacher in the school (Mustafa first, and when he moved to the role of the principal, Farghali). All of these actors were well established by the time of the play, but all were cast in what proved, at least in popular memory, to be secondary roles in *School of Troublemakers*. Al-Babli, who played the new teacher, was (and is) a popular stage actress, but never a big star in the cinema or television. Imam, Salih, Shalabi, Zaki, and al-Ghayar (respectively students at the school named Bahgat, Mursī, Manṣūr, Aḥmad, and Luṭfī) were all young actors at the time of *School*. Later Adil Imam, who acts in the cinema and on stage, and has done television work, became the biggest star in Egypt. He plays both comedy and drama, but is considered most effective in comic roles. Ahmad Zaki is presently not far behind, although it took him longer to get to the top. Zaki also plays both comedy and drama, but leans more to the dramatic roles. Said Salih and Yunis Shalabi are successful comedians, but not as popular as Adil Imam. Hadi al-Ghayar plays mainly dramatic roles, but was never quite as popular as the others.

6 This is largely the attitude toward commercial theater transmitted by Western commentators (e.g. Allen 1976, 228–30; Allen 1979, 125–29).

7 It is likely that *School* was part of a broad movement toward a new formula of popular-culture themes in which the mediating influence of state institutions was absent or endangered. In 1969, for example, the film *al-Bōsṭagī* (The postman, directed by Ḥusayn Kamāl) was produced. The story is about a bureaucrat sent to an Upper Egyptian town to work as a postman. He considers himself the vanguard of change in the backward village to which he is sent, but ultimately he fails in his self-imposed mission to bring modernity to the countryside. Similarly, *Yaumiyyāt nā'ib fī-l-aryāf* (Diary of a country magistrate, directed by Taufīq Ṣāliḥ, 1969) and *al-Ḥarām* (The sin, directed by Henri Barakat, 1965) were quite negative about the prospects for modernizing the definitively unmodern sectors of society. But while these films were doubtful about the reality of a modernized society, none of them comes anywhere near making the kind of frontal assault on a key institution that was carried out in the performance (although not the text) of *School of Troublemakers*.

8 Imam was also the only member of the filmmaking establishment to attend the

funeral of assassinated anti-Islamist writer Farag Fōda. In 1994 he also starred in the anti-Islamist film *al-Irhābī* (The terrorist, directed by Nadir Galal), which was received by the establishment with unprecedented warmth.

9 I was told by the person who wrote out the lyrics to this song that this line refers to a pair of contemporary pop dance tunes, "*Nigmat saharnā*" (Star of our soirée) and "*Qamar yigmaʿnā*" (The moon that brings us together). He could not, however, remember who sang these songs.

10 The phrase for "worn-out nose" is *ʿanfⁱ dāyib*. I was told that it was a synonym for an old man.

11 The "noise he's making" is *ḥissⁱ biss*, which is directed at the girl as he tries to get her attention in a rude manner.

12 For a longer treatment of *Supermarket* see Armbrust 1995.

13 The private-sector cinema magazine *Fann* carries regular music reviews that typify conservative attitudes toward modern music. In most cases musicians who emulate the recognized masters of Arabic music (especially Abd al-Wahhab, Umm Kulthum, and Abd al-Halim Hafiz), or who make extensive reference to classical conventions, are praised. Musicians and singers who make extensive use of Western instruments or styles are dismissed as part of *al-mauja al-hābiṭa* (the vulgar wave), or sometimes simply *al-mauja al-jadīda* (the new wave), or simply "the wave."

14 Another scheme for classifying post-1970s (and therefore post-Abd al-Wahhab, Umm Kulthum and Abd al-Halim Hafiz) Egyptian music is to divide it between *mūsīqā al-gīl* (lit. "music of the generation," i.e. the younger generation) and *al-mūsīqā al-shaʿbiyya* ("folk music," but with the usual ambiguities conjured by the word *shaʿbī*). The former is allegedly more tinged with Western conventions, the latter influenced by "folklore." In practice the line between the two is often indistinct, rather like saying that "What's the Story," presumably a *shaʿbī* song due to its conventional instrumentation, is more folkloric than the electronically juiced-up "*al-Ustāz*." Such a distinction obscures the fact that the two songs occupy very nearly the same position in the musical spectrum *vis-à-vis* the establishment.

15 Perhaps the most prominent of these is Muhammad Munir, a popular singer who uses folkloric themes, but is much closer to the mainstream than Adawiya. In recent years many fans complain that Munir has strayed very far from his Upper Egyptian roots.

16 In the late 1980s record numbers came, mostly from the countryside, to the two largest *mūlid*s in Cairo, those of Ḥusayn (the Prophet Muhammad's grandson) and Sayyida Zaynab (Muhammad's granddaughter). Crowds (over a period of several days) numbered in the millions. Lately these events have become nearly out of control. The young men in general use the excitement and anonymity of the *mūlid* to create an atmosphere of near-complete abandon. Groups of men form phalanxes and push through the massive crowds, sometimes creating panics. Games of chance and skill abound. Any women not protected by male contingents are likely to be molested during the peak hours and near the most crowded areas.

17 In another version of this particular song recorded on compact disc by EMI in Greece and issued under the title "ʿ*Adawiyāt*," the word was *baladī*, not *waladi*

as it sometimes sounded to my scribe on the Cairo version of the song. The foreign release of the song was recorded in a deliberately retro style compared to the Egyptian version (also issued by EMI). The "fusion" band of guitar and synthesizer playing harmonically was replaced with an impeccably traditional band – *ṭabla* (drum), *ʿūd* (lute), *kamanga* (violin), and *nay* (reed flute), sometimes cornet or accordion – neither quite "folkloric" nor "classical," and playing monophonically. Several of the songs on "*ʿAdawiyāt*" overlapped with "ʿAdawiya 91," but the pace on the foreign release was much slower and the songs were distinct rather than thrust into a madcap mosaic as in the local Egyptian tape.

Adawiya's retro Greek compact disc belied the fact that the singer lives in the bourgeois suburb of Maʿādī, and drives a red Fiat. Adawiya's public image, assiduously cultivated in such songs as "O My Country/Boy," is one of deprivation, specifically the deprivation of middle-class youth, and not of a mythical untouched "folkloric" quarter. The ambiguity between Adawiya's "folksiness" and "classicism" on his Greek compact disc did not provoke as much suspicion as the East–West fusion in his Cairo tape. All the great singers incorporated a touch of "folklore" in their music. This may explain the foreign version of Adawiya: he was "cleaned up" for foreign consumption by being made more securely "folkloric." At the same time the suggestive parallelism brought about in the local tape by the juxtaposition of styles and the ambiguity of the subject matter were removed.

18 *Al-Sīnimā wa-l-nās* (244 [June 15–21, 1991], 5) claimed that "ʿAdawiya 91" was the best-selling tape of the year. However, as with film statistics, there are no reliable figures. The ease with which people recalled titles of songs on the tape left no doubt that "ʿAdawiya 91" was successful, if not necessarily the number one money-maker of the year.

19 Muhammad Munir is a Nubian singer who, like Shenuda, helped popularize the "rock and roll"-oriented East–West fusion style of music.

20 Shenuda also asserted that "Crowded World" 's line "*mūlid wi-ṣaḥb-u ghāyib*" (a saint's festival with the saint absent, i.e. chaos) made the authorities nervous because it conjured images of a society not thoroughly dominated by the state. He also characterizes "Crowded World" as Adawiya's first "respectable" hit – the first Adawiya song with appeal beyond either the private party circuit (Adawiya, like many *shaʿbī* singers, often sang at weddings, especially in his early years) or the nightclub scene.

21 "Without Asking Why" created something of a stir when a *shaykh* at al-Azhar issued a *fatwā* (legal opinion) condemning the song as idolatrous. See "*Ākhir maʿārik*" 1991, 56–58.

22 "May the Spirit Live" was a song in *Ghazal al-banāt* (The flirtation of girls, directed by Anwar Wagdi in 1949), a film in which Abd al-Wahhab sang but did not act.

23 Nasir's point was that a simple listing of common place names can be evocative of a complex and detailed history for the listeners (or readers) of the poem.

24 *A Hundred Years of Enlightenment* was a mass-produced copy of a painting by contemporary artist Ṣalāḥ ʿInānī. Inani is the director of a government-sponsored gallery called the *Wikālat al-Ghūrī*, which is located in a beautifully

restored caravanserai in medieval Cairo. Although the Ministry of Culture reproduced his work, and despite the fact that Inani is the director of a government-sponsored institution, others have discerned a satiric, almost subversive spirit in his caricature paintings (see Golding 1985, 101–92).

25 They include Naguib Mahfouz, Yahya Haqqi, Yusuf Idris, ʿAbbās al-ʿAqqād, Taufiq al-Hakim, and Taha Husayn. Members of the group did not march in lockstep regarding their attitude toward classicism in language (Haqqi and Idris, for example, are known for a more lenient attitude toward colloquialisms than, say, Mahfouz or Husayn). But they differed from the true colloquialists in that they drew inspiration more from either classicist "high art" or from foreign sources than from the folk tradition.

26 There is just such a statue of Muhammad Ali in Alexandria. A very similar statue sits in Opera Square in Cairo, but is the likeness of Muhammad Ali's son Ibrāhīm Pasha.

27 I have been told that all of the faces in the picture represent specific people, including the *shaykh*s, the scientists, and even those of the peasants and workers. I have not, however, been able to confirm this claim.

28 This is not to say that all intellectuals in Egypt take this position. As in Western modernism, there is a wide range of opinion and practice in Egyptian modernism. What I describe here, however, is the modernist position invariably taken by any person or agency attempting to represent modernism to the public in either the educational system (below the university level) or in popular culture. The "conservative radical," and the political and social agenda promoted by such figures, is the ideal contested in any popular culture that attempts to subvert the state-sanctioned concept of modernism.

29 Anderson (1991, 22) illustrates the idea of a simultaneous time sense by a medieval Flemish painting showing a town burgher kneeling in adoration of the Virgin Mary beside biblical shepherds. Anderson's example is more extreme (i.e. the burgher and shepherds are separated by far more years than any of the figures shown in *A Hundred Years*), but the principle of showing an inevitable link between past, present, and future events is the same.

30 For more on ironic detachment in the reception of popular culture see Ien Ang (1989, 96–104). Ang's point is that some people profess to consume "bad" television shows, films, and music, so that they can feel superior to it, while others simply condemn such "vulgarity," or at least condemn it in formal public situations.

31 The series, called "*Ra'fat al-Haggān*," was an adaptation of a true story about an Egyptian spy in Israel. The series lasted through several parts, which were shown annually during Ramadan. The first installment was extremely popular, although many felt that the quality fell off in the later parts. For more on "*Ra'fat*" see Abu-Lughod (1993b).

32 *Awlād al-zawāt* and *Awlād al-fuqarā'* (Sons of aristocracy and Sons of the poor respectively) were plays written by Wahbi and performed by Wahbi's theatrical company. Wahbi of course played the lead in both plays. *Sons of Aristocracy* was adapted to the screen in 1932, and was the first Egyptian talkie, directed by Muhammad Karim and produced by Wahbi, who was also the star of the film version of the story.

33 Although Wahbi may have been slighted by this particular event, he is by no means systematically excluded from the cultural canon. Salah Inani's *Hundred Years of Enlightenment*, for example, featured him most prominently of all the three actors (the other two, as previously mentioned, were Zaki Tulaymat and Nagib al-Rihani).

34 Wahbi lists the founding members of the troupe in his autobiography (Wahbi 1973 vol. I, 73). Many of them later became famous in other theatrical troupes and in the cinema.

35 Early editions of *Rūz al-Yūsuf* reported assiduously on the activities of the Ramsīs Troupe, sometimes to the point of malicious gossip. Fatima Rushdi was a favorite target of such attacks. In 1927 the magazine reported how the young Rushdi, then married to the theater director Aziz Id, dominated her husband. In the article the couple was alleged to have been in the company of "*al-khawāga*" (the foreigner) Elie al-Darʿī. Id asked his wife for a cigarette and she turned to al-Dari and borrowed a pound, then handed it to Id, telling him that she was "off to have lunch with Elie" without her husband. Id is then alleged to have burst into tears (*Rūz al-Yūsuf* 105 [November 10, 1927], 16). Rushdi's version of her relationship to a Monsieur Elie, who she claims financed the establishment of her own theatrical troupe in 1927 (and took her shopping at the most chic store in town) differs from *Rūz al-Yūsuf*'s scandalmongering in no essential detail except that her husband's attitude toward lavish gifts (over LE 10,000 according to Rushdi) from a male admirer is not mentioned (Rushdī 1970, 69–75). She does refer to the problems caused by her relationship with Elie in another autobiographical book in which she mentions that Id divorced her, although Rushdi still claimed that her relationship with Elie was platonic (*ibid.*, 62–71).

36 The directorial credit for *Layla* is disputed. Bindārī et al. (1994, 305) lists Stephan Rustī (of Italian and Turkish descent) and Widad Urfi as the directors. There is also some sentiment for the idea that Aḥmad Galāl, the actor who played the hero in the film, contributed to the direction (Marī Kawīnī [Galal's widow], personal conversation, July 15, 1994). While the film was being made *Rūz al-Yūsuf* attacked Stephan Rusti's morals in much the same way it went after Fatima Rushdi, insinuating, in this case, that he was homosexual ("*Akhbār al-masāriḥ wa-l-malāhī*," *Rūz al-Yūsuf* 103 [October 27, 1927], 17).
For a synopsis of *Layla*'s plot see *Rūz al-Yūsuf* (106 [November 17, 1927], 24–25) and *Rūz al-Yūsuf* (107 [November 24, 1927], 16).

37 Kazim, whose wit is as sharp as her pen, is one of the few female public figures to have put on the neo-Islamic *ḥijāb*, which a majority of urban Egyptian women now wear. During my brief stay at *al-Ahrām* I was introduced to her in the staff dining room. I was happy to learn that she had attended the University of Kansas, not far from Nebraska where I grew up. Her stay in Kansas seems to have strengthened her resolve to live what she saw as a fully Islamic life, for she refused to shake my hand on the grounds that this would be improper behavior between the sexes.

38 Whereas Abd al-Wahhab's biographies all assiduously connect him to the major figures of his time, Wahbi's autobiography lists his first theatrical contact as being with an obscure traveling Lebanese troupe led by Salīm al-Qardāḥī

during his childhood in the Upper Egyptian town of Sohāg (Wahbī 1973 vol. I, 13–22). When he does begin describing his experience with known figures, he tends to dwell on the seedier aspects of ʿImād al-Dīn Street (Cairo's Broadway in the first half of the century).

39 Wahbi swears that the amulet story is true (1973 vol. I, 70). He obtained the amulet through an older man who attended a reform school Wahbi was put in because he was doing so poorly in his regular studies.

40 He continued to act in films throughout *School*'s run, but it was only in 1974, the last year the play showed, that he got the lead in a film, *Shayāṭīn ilā al-abad* (Devils forever), directed by Maḥmūd Farīd. Before Imam's breakthrough in *School* he was known for his portrayal of a relatively minor character called Disūqī Effendi in the 1963 play *Anā wa-huwa wa-hiya* (I and he and she). The play was a vehicle for comedian Fu'ād al-Muhandis, but Imam's performance as an uneducated "simple man" who uttered the line "*balad shahādāt, ṣaḥīḥ*!" (it's a country of [school] diplomas, for sure) earned the young actor some attention (Sālim 1991, 67–68).

41 This was an unofficial figure mentioned to me in 1990 by several industry insiders. Very probably his fee is even higher now, although true figures are hard to obtain. The claim that Fatin Hamama commands similar fees may be nothing more than a sentimental nod to a legend of Egyptian cinema. Certainly her presence in a film is not as sure a guarantee of commercial success as Adil Imam's. A recent Fatin Hamama vehicle *Arḍ al-aḥlām* (Land of dreams, 1993), directed by Dāūd ʿAbd al-Sayyid, was much praised, but a commercial flop.

42 *Ragab* and *Shaban* were actually part of a trilogy, the final installment of which was *Ramaḍān fōq al-burkān* (Ramadan on the volcano, 1985, directed by Aḥmad al-Sabʿāwī). My friends did not explicitly present the films to me as a trilogy, but there is ample evidence that the films were intentionally linked. One reviewer noted when the first film, *Ragab*, came to the theaters, that there were plans for "two or three Ragab films" ("*Ragab fōq ṣafīḥ sākhin*" 1979). There were, in fact, no more Ragab films, but there were two more films in which the main character was named after an Islamic month, and in which this character was described as "over" or "under" something. All three characters were similar – naively believing in the system at first, corrupted by the end. The months after which the characters are named, Ragab, Shaʿbān, and Ramaḍān, fall consecutively in the Islamic calendar (as they do in the films) and are considered the best months to perform an ʿ*umra* – a minor pilgrimage to Mecca. The three films also describe a kind of pilgrimage from the margins of modern society to its putative center represented in the third film by a well-known and heartily loathed government building called *al-Mugammaʿ* (the combine).

43 The third film of the "vulgar trilogy" is both closest to the heart of modern institutional life (an enormous government building) and gives the most self-conscious image of corruption. In *Ramadan on the Volcano* Imam plays a payroll officer who finally succumbs to the temptation to steal the monthly disbursement of some LE 400,000.

44 I know of only two Egyptian films that extensively address homosexuality. The first is Salah Abu Sayf's *Ḥammām al-Malāṭīlī* (The bathhouse of Malāṭīlī,

1973), which does not condone homosexuality, but portrays it as part of a general moral decline that Abu Sayf suggests was the reason for Egypt's defeat in 1967. The second was *Mercedes* (Mercedes – the car), directed by Yusrī Naṣr Allāh in 1993. *Mercedes* takes the view that one's sexual orientation is an inborn trait and not a moral issue. Moral issues addressed by the film had more to do with the rampant corruption of *infitāḥī* Egyptian society than with sexual behavior. The film was not commercially successful.

45 The way the Friday prayer is incorporated into the story is typical of the way the film took a pastiche of elements from the American original and adapted them to the local setting. *Midnight Cowboy* also featured a "prayer" which was intended to consecrate a task about to be undertaken. The "task" in *Cowboy* is for Joe Buck to begin working as a male prostitute, and the "prayer" is initiated by a dangerously addled old pimp (who appears to be planning on being Joe Buck's first customer). Aside from the general outline of the two stories, many of the elements of *Cowboy* appear scrambled throughout *Ragab*, some changed greatly, and some very little. Not all the elements match perfectly, and there are some differences (although not in the alienated tone of the films) but there are enough similarities for *Ragab*'s pedigree not to be in doubt. At least one critic also noted in an article that *Ragab* was based on *Midnight Cowboy* (*Ragab* file in the Catholic Egyptian Office for the Cinema Library).

46 Some of the outstanding pre-1970s films depicting peasants are: Salah Abu Sayf's *al-Waḥsh* (The beast, 1954); Henri Barakat's *Duʿā' al-karawān* (Call of the curlew, 1959); Barakat's *al-Ḥarām* (The sin, 1965); Abu Sayf's *al-Zauga al-thāniyya* (The second wife, 1967); Husayn Kamal's *al-Bōsṭagī* (The postman, 1968); Taufiq Salih's *Yaumiyyāt nā'ib fi-l-aryāf* (Diary of a country magistrate, 1969); Yusuf Shahin's *al-Arḍ* (The earth, 1970). For more on the image of the peasant in Egyptian cinema see al-Ṭayyār (1980; 1981, 45–46). The image of the ignorant peasant who needs to be uplifted by the progressive city is deeply rooted in modern Egyptian culture (see Brown 1990, 59–82). The rhetoric of Egyptian elites about peasant reform bore a great deal of resemblance to the attitude toward "sons of the country," who, from the perspective of journalists and administrators, were considered little more than "urban peasants."

47 Very probably some of these musical references were understood by the audience. For example, sections of *Fantasia*, the Disney cartoon featuring *The Sorcerer's Apprentice*, are played often on the television (although nobody I knew remembered if it was played when *Ragab* was first run). The *Psycho* tune was very likely also familiar to many viewers; I found that Hitchcock was well known and liked by many of my friends and acquaintances. The same was true of James Bond.

48 Both of the names are slightly odd, although not to the degree that they are remarkable in and of themselves. The corrupt Iglāl's name means "honor," "respect," or "reverence." Inshirāḥ means "joy," "delight," or "gaiety." Each woman's name actually denotes the attributes of her alter ego: Inshirah, the good girl, was in fact respectful, living humbly and caring for her ailing father; Iglal, the corrupted woman of nightclubs and thievery, overindulges in gaiety. Iglal was played by Nāhid Sharīf, and Inshirah by Nāhid Gabr.

49 *Midnight Cowboy* depicts Joe Buck's fantasies of how he will describe his

exploits in the Big City to the people back home in Texas. The Texans only appear in Joe Buck's recollections of how they brutalized him.

50 *Among the Ruins* featured numerous scenes of a tree on the edge of the desert where the lovers would meet. When they became separated he would pine for her at sunset by the tree. By the end of the film he dies, leaving her to raise his child by another woman. *Shaban* parodies the tree scenes by showing Zaynab standing by a tree at sunset, followed by scenes of Shaban living it up with prostitutes.

51 In the third film of the series, *Ramadan on the Volcano*, prison plays a more prominent role. This time Imam's oppressed *ibn al-balad* is a fully urbanized and partially educated (halfway through law school) bureaucrat responsible for disbursing a LE 400,000 payroll. As in *Shaban*, he wants to get married, but cannot because his bureaucrat's salary is barely enough to support him in a tiny rooftop apartment, let alone a family in housing considered respectable for the middle class. The story turns on Imam having learned of a loophole in the law that would give him a maximum sentence of seven years for theft. He steals the payroll and finds that he gets far more respect as an admitted thief with money than as an honest bureaucrat. Although the plot goes through a number of machinations that take him in and out of prison, the end of the film finds him, once again, behind bars. The difference is that this time being behind bars appears better than being on the outside. Thus over the course of three films Adil Imam has gone from being a naive peasant in the fields to being a worldly wise (and wise-cracking) convict – hardly the transformation that *A Hundred Years of Enlightenment* had in mind.

References

ʿAbd al-Gawwād, Ṣalāḥ al-ʿArab and Anwar ʿĀmir. 1988. *al-Uslūb al-ʿilmī fī taṭawwur al-mujtamaʿ al-Miṣrī*. Cairo: Ministry of Education.

ʿAbd al-Qādir, Ramaḍān. 1991. "Public Talk: 'Imamism': Legend or Big Lie?" *Egyptian Gazette* (June 18): 3.

ʿAbd al-Wahhāb, Muḥammad. 1938. "*Mudhakkirāt ʿAbd al-Wahhāb*." *al-Ithnayn* 195 (March 7): 16–17, 49; 196 (March 14): 18–20; 197 (March 21): 20–21, 50; 198 (March 28): 14–15, 50; 199 (April 4): 22–24; 200 (April 11): 18–20; 201 (April 18): 20–21, 47; 202 (April 25): 16–17, 48; 203 (May 2): 22–24; 206 (May 23): 20–21; 207 (May 30): 18–20; 208 (June 6):18–19; 209 (June 13): 18–20.

ʿAbd al-Wahhāb, Muḥammad and Saʿd al-Dīn Wahba. 1992. *al-Nahr al-khālid: Muḥammad ʿAbd al-Wahhāb fī ḥiwār maʿ Saʿd al-Dīn Wahba*. Cairo: Dār Suʿād al-Ṣabāḥ.

"*ʿAbd al-Wahhāb ʿalā ṭarīqat Kāmil al-Shināwī*." 1991. A summary of a book by Kāmil al-Shināwī entitled *ʿAraftu Muḥammad ʿAbd al-Wahhāb*. *Rūz al-Yūsuf* 3283 (May 13): 12–15.

"*ʿAbd al-Wahhāb al-mumaththil*." 1991. *Ṣabāḥ al-khayr* 1844 (May 9): 62–65.

Abdalla, Ahmad. 1985. *The Student Movement and National Politics in Egypt*. London: al-Saqi.

Abdel-Fadil, Mahmoud. 1982. "Educational Expansion and Income Distribution in Egypt, 1952–1977." In Gouda Abdel-Khalek and Robert Tignor, eds., *The Political Economy of Income Distribution in Egypt*. New York: Holmes & Meier.

Abdel-Malek, Kamal. 1990. *A Study of the Vernacular Poetry of Aḥmad Fu'ād Nigm*. Leiden: E. J. Brill.

Abu-Absi, Samir. 1991. "The 'Simplified Arabic' of *Iftaḥ Yaa Simsim*: Pedagogical and Sociolinguistic Implications." *al-ʿArabiyya* 24: 111–21.

Abū Buthayna. 1934. "*Yā afandī, il-maẓhar mā-yihimm-ish*." *al-Ithnayn* 3 (July 2): 31.

Abu-Lughod, Lila. 1989. "Bedouins, Cassettes and Technologies of Public Culture." *Middle East Report: Popular Culture* 159 (July/August): 7–11.

1993a. "Islam and Public Culture: The Politics of Egyptian Television Serials." *Middle East Report* (January/February): 25–30.

1993b. "Finding a Place for Islam: Egyptian Television Serials and the National Interest." *Public Culture* 5, 3 (Spring): 493–514.

Abū Shādī, ʿAlī. 1994. *Klāsīkiyyāt al-sīnimā al-ʿArabiyya*. Cairo: al-Hay'a al-ʿĀmma li-Quṣūr al-Thaqāfa.

Adonis. 1992. *An Introduction to Arab Poetics*. Cairo: The American University in Cairo.

Ahmad, Aijaz. 1992. *In Theory: Classes, Nations, Literatures*. New York: Verso.

"*Ākhir maʿārik ʿAbd al-Wahhāb: al-taṭarruf.*" 1991. *Ṣabāḥ al-khayr* 1844 (May 9): 56–58.

Allen, Roger. 1974. *A Study of Ḥadīth ʿĪsā ibn Hishām, Muḥammad al-Muwayliḥī's View of Egyptian Society during the British Occupation, with an English Translation of the Third Edition*. Albany: State University of New York Press.

1976. "Egyptian Drama and Fiction in the 1970s." *Edebiyat* 1, 2: 219–234.

1979. "Egyptian Drama after the Revolution." *Edebiyat* 4, 1: 97–134.

Altoma, Salih J. 1969. *The Problem of Diglossia in Arabic: A Comparative Study of Classical and Iraqi Arabic*. Harvard Middle Eastern Monograph Series, no. 21. Cambridge, Mass.: Harvard University Press.

Amīn, Muṣṭafā. 1987. "*al-Amīr alladhī kāna yaḥlumu bi-ratabat al-bāshawiyya.*" In Muṣṭafā Amīn, *Asmā' lā tamūt*. Beirut: al-ʿAṣr al-Ḥadīth.

1991. "*Asrār ʿAbd al-Wahhāb al-khāṣṣa.*" *Ākhir sāʿa* 2951 (May 15): 23–26, 41.

Anderson, Benedict. 1991. *Imagined Communities: Reflections on the Origin and Spread of Nationalism*. London: Verso.

Ang, Ien. 1989. *Watching Dallas: Soap Opera and the Melodramatic Imagination*. New York: Routledge.

Appadurai, Arjun and Carol A. Breckenridge. 1988. "Why Public Culture?" *Public Culture* 1 (Fall): 5–9.

Armbrust, Walter. 1992. "The Nationalist Vernacular: Folklore and Egyptian Popular Culture." *Michigan Quarterly Review* 31 (Fall): 525–42.

1995. "New Cinema, Commercial Cinema, and the Modernist Tradition." *Alif: Journal of Comparative Poetics* 15:81–129.

Armes, Roy. 1987. *Third World Film Making and the West*. Berkeley: University of California Press.

Asad, Talal. *Genealogies of Religion: Discipline and Reasons of Power in Christianity and Islam*. Baltimore: Johns Hopkins University Press.

ʿAsharī, Galāl al-. 1971. "*Najaḥa al-mushāghibīn, wa-saqaṭa al-masraḥ al-kūmīdī.*" *Rūz al-Yūsuf* 2257 (September 13): 44–45.

ʿAsharī, Nagwa al-. 1991. "Mokhtar, An Artist with Vision." *al-Ahram Weekly* 1 (February 28): 9.

ʿAwaḍ, Luīs. 1969a. "*al-Arājūz fī al-Yūniskū.*" *al-Ahrām* (November 14): 6.

1969b. "*Mulāḥaẓāt ʿalā al-nāy wa-al-qānūn.*" *al-Ahrām* (December 19): 6.

1974. "*al-Lugha wa-madāris al-taʿbīr.*" In Luīs ʿAwaḍ, *Thaqāfatunā fī-muftaraq al-ṭuruq*. Beirut: Dār al-Ādāb.

ʿAwaḍ, Maḥmūd. 1991. *Muḥammad ʿAbd al-Wahhāb alladhī lā yaʿrifuhu aḥad*. Cairo: Dār al-Maʿārif.

ʿAyyād, Ra'ūf. 1986. "*Yā ḥaṣṣād . . . al-thaura, yā ḥilm . . . wa-ʿilm.*" *Ṣabāḥ al-khayr* 1582 (May 1): 44–45.

ʿAzab, Yusrī al-. 1986. "*Ibn al-balad kamā shāhadahu Bayram.*" *Ṣabāḥ al-khayr* 1580 (April 17): 36–37.

Badawī, E. M. 1973. *Mustawayāt al-ʿArabiyya al-muʿāṣira*. Cairo: Dār al-Maʿārif.

Badawi, E. M. and Martin Hinds. 1986. *A Dictionary of Egyptian Arabic*. Beirut: Librairie du Liban.

Badawi, M. M. 1984. "*Mushkilat al-ḥadātha wa-l-taghayyur al-ḥaḍarī fī al-adab al-ʿArabī al-ḥadīth.*" *Fuṣūl* (April/June): 98–106.

1992. "Introduction." In M. M. Badawi, ed., *Modern Arabic Literature*. Cambridge: Cambridge University Press.

Baer, Gabriel. 1982. *Fallah and Townsman in the Middle East: Studies in Social History*. London: F. Cass.

Baṭrāwī, ʿĀdil al-. 1986. "*Ḥikāyatī maʿ al-fahhāma.*" *Ṣabāḥ al-khayr* 1582 (May 1): 30–32.

Beeston, A. F. L. 1971. "The Genesis of the *Maqāmāt* Genre." *Journal of Arabic Literature* 2: 1–12.

1983. "The Evolution of the Arabic Language." In A. F. L. Beeston et al., eds., *Cambridge History of Arabic Literature: Arabic Literature to the End of the Umayyad Period*. New York: Cambridge University Press.

Bhabha, Homi, ed. 1990. *Nation and Narration*. New York: Routledge.

Bindārī, Monā al-, Maḥmūd Qāsim, and Yaʿqūb Wahbī, eds. 1994. *Mausūʿat al-aflām al-ʿArabiyya*. Cairo: Bayt al-Maʿrifa.

Blanc, Haim. 1960. "Style Variations in Spoken Arabic: A Sample of Interdialectical Educated Conversation." Harvard Middle Eastern Monographs, no. 3. Cambridge, Mass.: Harvard University Press.

Booth, Marilyn. 1990. *Bayram al-Tunisi's Egypt: Social Criticism and Narrative Strategies*. Oxford: Ithaca Press.

1992. "Poetry in the Vernacular." In M. M. Badawi, ed., *The Cambridge History of Arabic Literature:* vol. IV, *Modern Arabic Literature*. New York: Cambridge University Press.

Bosworth, C. E. 1976. *The Medieval Islamic Underworld: The Banū Sāsān in Arabic Society and Literature*. Leiden: E. J. Brill.

Bourdieu, Pierre. 1991. *Language and Symbolic Power*. Cambridge, Mass.: Harvard University Press.

Brooks, Peter. 1976. *The Melodramatic Imagination*. New Haven: Yale University Press.

Brown, Nathan. 1990. *Peasant Politics in Egypt*. New Haven: Yale University Press.

"*Buldōzir Faḍḍa al-Maʿdāwī yiẓhar fī al-Darrāsa.*" 1990. *Akhbār al-yaum* (March 17): 14.

Buṭrus, Fikrī. 1964. *Fannānū Iskandariyya*. Cairo: al-Dār al-Qaumiyya li-l-Ṭibāʿa wa-l-Nashr.

Cachia, Pierre. 1967. "The Use of Colloquial in Modern Arabic Literature." *Journal of Oriental and African Studies* 87, 1 (January/March): 12–22.

Clifford, James and George Marcus, eds. 1986. *Writing Culture: The Poetics and Politics of Ethnography*. Berkeley: University of Clifornia Press.

Dale, R. C. 1986. *The Films of René Clair:* vol. I, *Exposition and Analysis*. New Jersey: Scarecrow Press, Inc.

Danielson, Virginia. 1991. *Shaping Tradition in Arabic Song: The Career and Repertory of Umm Kulthūm.* Unpublished Ph.D. dissertation, University of Illinois.

de Certeau, Michel. 1988. *The Practice of Everyday Life.* Berkeley: University of California Press.

Dickey, Sara. 1993. *Cinema and the Urban Poor in South India.* Cambridge: Cambridge University Press.

Douglas, Alan and Fedwa Malti-Douglas. 1994. *Arab Comic Strips: Politics of an Emerging Mass Culture.* Bloomington: University of Indiana Press.

Downing, John. 1987. *Film and Politics in the Third World.* New York: Autonomedia.

Early, Evelyn. 1993. *Baladi Women of Cairo: Playing with an Egg and a Stone.* Cairo: American University in Cairo.

Eliot, T. S. 1952 [1922]. "The Waste Land." In T. S. Eliot, *The Complete Poems and Plays.* New York: Harcourt, Brace & Company.

Ezzat, Ali. 1974. *Intelligibility among Arabic Dialects.* Beirut: Beirut Arab University.

Farīd, Samīr. 1986. "*Ṣūrat al-insān al-Miṣrī ʿalā al-shāsha bayn al-aflām al-istihlākiyya wa-l-aflām al-fanniyya.*" In Hāshim al-Naḥḥās, ed., *al-Insān al-Miṣrī ʿalā al-shāsha.* Cairo: General Egyptian Book Organization.

1988. *Huwiyyat al-sinīmā al-ʿArabiyya.* Cairo: Dār al-Farābī. Originally published in *al-Sinīmā al-ʿArabiyya*, issued for the 1980 Carthage Film Festival.

Fauzī, Mufīd. 1991. "*Shahāda lil-tārikh.*" *Ṣabāḥ al-khayr* 1844 (May 9): 9–12.

Ferguson, Charles. 1971 [1959]. "Diglossia." In Charles Ferguson, *Language Structure and Language Use: Essays by Charles Ferguson* (selected and introduced by Anwar S. Dil). Stanford: Stanford University Press.

"*Firānsā turīdu Sanāʾ Gamīl.*" 1976. *Uktōbir* 31: 71.

Fishman, Joshua. 1972. *Language and Nationalism: Two Integrative Essays.* Rowley, Mass.: Newbury House.

"*Futūwāyat sūq al-khuḍār.*" 1929. *al-Dunyā al-muṣawwara* 16 (September 4): 9.

Gamal, Samīr al-. 1991. *Fann al-adab al-tilifizyōnī.* Cairo: Dār al-Shaʿb al-ʿArabī.

Gershoni, Israel and James Jankowski. 1986. *Egypt, Islam, and the Arabs: The Search for Egyptian Nationhood, 1900–1930.* New York: Oxford University Press.

Ghabn, ʿAbd al-Fattāḥ. 1975. "*Bayram wa-l-fuṣḥā.*" Supplement to *al-Idhāʿa wa-al-tilifizyōn* 2078 (January 11). Introduction by Ṣalāḥ Jāhīn.

Ghānim, Fatḥī. 1991. "*Ṣirāʿ al-fann wa-l-siyāsa wa-l-thaqāfa min thaurat 1919 ilā thaurat 1952.*" *Rūz al-Yūsuf* 3283 (May 13): 8–9.

Golding, William. 1985. *An Egyptian Journal.* London: Faber & Faber.

Grendzier, Irene. 1966. *The Practical Visions of Ya'qub Sanu'.* Cambridge, Mass.: Harvard University Press.

Gumperz, John. 1982. *Discourse Strategies.* London: Cambridge University Press.

Hakim, Taufiq al-. 1964. *The Prison of Life.* Tr. Pierre Cachia. Cairo: American University in Cairo Press.

1973. *Ahl al-kahf.* Cairo: Maktabat Taufīq al-Ḥakīm al-Shaʿbiyya.

Harvey, David. 1989. *The Condition of Postmodernity.* Oxford: Basil Blackwell.

Ḥasanayn, ʿĀdil. 1991. "*Mugāmalāt ʿAbd al-Wahhāb allatī lam yuwāfiq ʿalayhā sha'b Miṣr.*" In 'Ādil Ḥasanayn, *Muḥammad 'Abd al-Wahhāb*. Cairo: Sharikat Traykrūmī.

Hassan, S. A. el-. 1979. "Educated Spoken Arabic in Egypt and the Levant: A Critical Review of Diglossia and Related Concepts." *Archivum Linguisticum* 10: 112–25.

Ḥawwās, 'Abd al-Ḥamīd. 1986. "*al-Sīnimā 'al-Miṣriyya' wa-l-thaqāfa al-sha'biyya.*" In Hāshim al-Naḥḥās, ed., *al-Insān al-Miṣrī 'alā al-shāsha*. Cairo: General Egyptian Book Organization.

Heath, Jeffrey. 1989. *From Code-Switching to Borrowing: Foreign and Diglossic Mixing in Moroccan Arabic*. London, New York: Kegan Paul International.

Ḥifnī, Ratība al-. 1991. *Muḥammad 'Abd al-Wahhāb*. Cairo: Dār al-Shurūq.

Ḥusayn, Ṭāhā. 1935. *al-Ayyām*. Cairo: Dār al-Ma'ārif.

1954. *The Future of Culture in Egypt*. Tr. Sidney Glazer. Washington, D.C.: American Council of Learned Societies. Originally *Mustaqbal al-thaqāfa fī Miṣr*. Cairo: Dār al-Ma'ārif, 1944.

Ḥusnī, Fārūq. 1992. "*Anā wazīr sha'bī.*" *al-Rāfi'ī* 19 (February): 90–92.

Ibrahim, Saad Eddin. 1982. "Social Mobility and Income Distribution in Egypt, 1952–1977." In Gouda Abdel-Khalek and Robert Tignor, eds., *The Political Economy of Income Distribution in Egypt*. New York: Holmes & Meier.

Ikram, Khalid. 1980. *Egypt: Economic Management in a Period of Transition*. Baltimore: Johns Hopkins University Press.

"*Ishmi'nā.*" 1934. *al-Ithnayn* 10 (August 20): 36.

"*Isma' yā bēh . . . isma'ī yā hānim.*" 1934. *al-Ithnayn* 1 (June 18): 38.

Jameson, Fredric. 1986. "Third-World Literature in the Era of Multinational Capitalism." *Social Text* 15 (Fall): 65–88.

Juynboll, T. W. 1927. "*Ḥadīth.*" *Encyclopaedia of Islam*. Leiden: E. J. Brill.

Kamāl, 'Abd Allāh. 1991. "*Muṭrib kull al-'uṣūr.*" *Rūz al-Yūsuf* 3283 (May 13): 74–75.

Kāmil, Maḥmūd. 1971. *'Abduh al-Ḥamūlī: za'īm al-ṭarab wa-l-fann*. Cairo: Muḥammad al-Amīn.

Karnouk, Liliane. 1988. *Modern Egyptian Art*. Cairo: American University Press.

Kaye, Alan. 1972. "Remarks on Diglossia in Arabic: Well-Defined versus Ill-Defined." *Linguistics* 81: 32–48.

"*Kayfa ya'īshūna al-futūwāt fī Miṣr.*" 1929. *al-Dunyā al-muṣawwara* 14 (August 21): 5.

Kāẓim, Ṣāfīnāz. 1991. "*Wahāt yā 'ayāṭ 'alā Yūsuf Wahbī!*" *al-Muṣawwar* 3478 (June 7): 41.

Kepel, Gilles. 1984. *Muslim Extremism in Egypt: The Prophet and Pharaoh*. Tr. Jon Rothschild. Berkeley: University of California Press.

Khalidi, Tarif. 1994. *Arabic Historical Thought in the Classical Period*. Cambridge: Cambridge University Press.

Landau, Jacob. 1958. *Studies in the Arab Theatre and Cinema*. Philadelphia: University of Pennsylvania Press.

Leila, Ali, Monte Palmer, and El-Sayed Yassin. 1988. *The Egyptian Bureaucracy*. New York: Syracuse University Press.

Lofgren, Hans. 1993. "Economic Policy in Egypt: A Breakdown in Reform Resistance?" *International Journal of Middle East Studies* 25: 407–21.

"*Lōlākī. . . ughniya lā arfuḍuhā!!*" 1991. *al-Idhā'a wa-l-tilifizyōn* 2930 (May 11): 16–19.

"*Mā alladhī aḍāfahu 'Abd al-Wahhāb li-l-mūsīqā ba'da Sayyid Darwīsh.*" 1991. *al-Muṣawwar* 3478 (May 10): 26–27.

Macleod, Arlene. 1991. *Accommodating Protest: Working Women, the New Veiling, and Change in Cairo*. New York: Columbia.

Madame Sosostris. 1991. "Pack of Cards." *al-Ahram Weekly* 1 (February 28): 14.

Madkūr, Ibrāhīm. 1990. "*Ṭabīb al-lugha yaktubu rushitta.*" *al-Idhā'a wa-l-tilifizyōn* 2877 (May 5): 46–47.

Maḥfūẓ, Najīb [Naguib Mahfouz]. 1956. *Bayn al-qaṣrayn*. Cairo: Maktabat Miṣr.

1957a. *Qaṣr al-shauq*. Cairo: Maktabat Miṣr.

1957b. *al-Sukkariyya*. Cairo: Maktabat Miṣr.

Mahmoud, Yousseff. 1986. "Arabic after Diglossia." In J. A. Fishman et al., eds., *The Fergusonian Impact*, vol. I. New York: Mouton de Gruyter.

Makdisi, George. 1990. *The Rise of Humanism in Classical Islam and the Christian West: With Special Reference to Scholasticism*. Edinburgh: Edinburgh University Press.

Malkmus, Lizbeth and Roy Armes. 1991. *Arab and African Film Making*. London: Zed.

"*al-Mashhad al-ghinā'ī fī Miṣr.*" 1991. *al-Idhā'a wa-l-tilifizyōn* 2930 (May 11): 26.

Meiseles, G. 1980. "Educated Spoken Arabic and the Arabic Language Continuum." *Archivum Linguisticum*. n.s. 1.

Messick, Brinkley. 1993. *The Calligraphic State: Textual Domination and History in a Muslim Society*. Berkeley: University of California Press.

Messiri, Sawsan el-. 1978a. Ibn al-Balad: *A Concept of Egyptian Identity*. Leiden: E. J. Brill.

1978b. "Self Images of Traditional Urban Women in Cairo." In Lois Beck and Nikki Keddie, eds., *Women in the Muslim World*. Cambridge, Mass.: Harvard University Press.

Mitchell, T. F. 1986. "What is Spoken Educated Arabic?" *International Journal of the Sociology of Language* 61: 7–32.

Mitchell, Timothy. 1988. *Colonising Egypt*. New York: Cambridge University Press.

"*al-Mu'allima Faḍḍa fī Gabal Muqaṭṭam.*" 1990. *Akhbār al-yaum* (March 3): 14.

Mumtāz, I'tidāl. 1985. *Mudhakkirāt raqībat al-sīnimā*. Cairo: General Egyptian Book Organization.

Murād, Maḥmūd. 1991. "Arab Security Arrangements for Post-War Era." *al-Ahram Weekly*, zero issue 5 (February 14): 1.

Najmī, Kamāl al-. 1991. "*Muṭrib wa-mulaḥḥin al-mi'at 'ām.*" *al-Muṣawwar* 3474 (May 10): 20–22.

Naṣṣār, Fāyiz. 1975. *Mudhakkirāt Muḥammad 'Abd al-Wahhāb*. Beirut: Dār al-Nahḍa al-Ḥadītha.

Naẓmī, Irīs. 1991. "*al-Ṭarīq al-ṣa'b: min Bāb al-Sha'riyya ilā-l-qimma.*" *Ākhir sā'a* 2951 (May 15): 27–29.

Nelson, Kristina. 1985. *The Art of Reciting the Qur'an*. Austin: University of Texas Press.

Nieuwkerk, Karin van. n.d. *A Trade Like Any Other: Female Singers and Dancers in Egypt. An Anthropological Study of the Relation between Gender and*

Respectability in the Entertainment Trade. Ph.D. dissertation, University of Amsterdam.

Ortner, Sherry. 1984. "Theory in Anthropology since the Sixties." *Comparative Studies in Society and History* 1 (January): 126–66.

Paglia, Camille. 1992. "Madonna I: Animality and Artifice," and "Madonna II: Venus of the Airwaves." In Camille Paglia, *Sex, Art and American Culture*. New York: Vintage Books.

Parkinson, Dilworth. 1991. "Searching for Modern Fuṣḥa: Real-life Formal Arabic." *al-ʿArabiyya* 24: 31–64.

Pedersen, Johannes. 1984. *The Arabic Book*. Princeton: Princeton University Press.

Pritchett, V. S. 1970 [1942]. *In My Good Books*. Port Washington, N.Y.: Kennikat Press.

"*Qānūn al-istiḥmām*." 1934. *al-Ithnayn* 8 (August 6): 26–27.

Racy, Ali Jihad. 1977. *Musical Change and Commercial Recording in Egypt, 1904–1932*. Unpublished Ph.D. dissertation, University of Illinois.

Radwan, Lutfi. 1991. *Muḥammad ʿAbd al-Wahhāb: sīra dhātiyya*. Cairo: Dār al-Hilāl.

"*Ragab fōq ṣafīḥ sākhin*." 1979. File of reviews on the film *Ragab on a Hot Tin Roof* at the Catholic Egyptian Office for the Cinema Library: reviews from the year the film was released.

Ramaḍān, ʿAbd al-ʿAẓīm. 1991. "*ʿAbd al-Wahhāb wa-l-ṭabaqa al-wusṭā*." *Uktōbir* 759 (May 12): 16–17.

Ramaḍān, Birkasām. 1990. "*al-Lugha al-ʿArabiyya wa-l-ightirāb*." *al-Akhbār* (July 11): 14.

Rāwī, Ṣalāḥ al-. 1986. "*Bayram al-Tūnsī laysa shāʿiran shaʿbiyyan*." *Ṣabāḥ al-khayr* 1580 (April 17): 42–43.

Reid, Donald Malcolm. 1990. *Cairo University and the Making of Modern Egypt*. New York: Cambridge University Press.

Renan, Ernest. 1990 [1882]. "What is a Nation?" In Homi Bhabha, ed., *Nation and Narration*. New York: Routledge.

Richards, Alan and John Waterbury. 1990. *A Political Economy of the Middle East: State, Class, and Economic Development*. Boulder: Westview Press.

Riḍā, Maḥmūd. 1968. *Fī maʿbad al-raqṣ*. Cairo: Dār al-Maʿārif.

Rosen, Charles. 1971. *The Classical Style: Haydn, Mozart, Beethoven*. New York: Norton.

Rushdī, Fāṭima. 1970. *Kifāḥī fī al-masraḥ wa-l-sīnimā*. Cairo: Dār al-Maʿārif.

1971. *Fāṭima Rushdī bayn al-ḥubb wa-l-fann*. Cairo: Maṭbaʿat Saʿdī wa-Shandī (Fāṭima Rushdī).

Saʿd al-Dīn, Mursī. 1989. *Dhikrayāt thaqāfiyya*. Cairo: al-Maktab al-Miṣrī al-Ḥadīth.

1991. "Plain Talk." *al-Ahram Weekly* 1 (February 28): 9.

Said, Edward. 1978. *Orientalism*. New York: Pantheon.

1990. "Figures, Configurations, Transfigurations." *Race and Class* 32:1.

Saʿīd, Nafūsa Zakariyyā. 1964. *Tārīkh al-daʿwa ilā al-ʿāmmiyya wa-āthārihā fī Miṣr*. Alexandria: Dār al-Thaqāfa.

Sālim, ʿAlī. 1979. *Madrasat al-mushāghibīn*. Adapted from the play *Les J3: Comédie en Quatre Actes* by Roger Ferdinand. Cairo: Madbūlī.

Sālim, Ḥilmī. 1991. *al-Ṣaʿlūk: ʿĀdil Imām*. Cairo: Midlight.

Salīm, Kamāl. 1975 [1939]. *al-Naṣṣ al-kāmil li-sīnāryū film al-ʿAzīma*. With an introduction by Muḥammad al-Sayyid Shūsha. Cairo: General Egyptian Book Organization.

Salmawi, Muhammad. 1991. "Entre Nous." *al-Ahram Weekly* 1 (February 28): 14.

Scotton, Carol. 1986. "Diglossia and Code Switching." In J. A. Fishman et al., eds., *The Fergusonian Impact*, vol. II. New York: Mouton de Gruyter.

Sharabi, Hisham al-. 1988. *Neopatriarchy: A Theory of Distorted Change in Arab Society*. Oxford: Oxford University Press.

Shauqī, Aḥmad. 1925–36. *Shauqiyāt*, vol. III. Cairo: Maṭbaʿat Miṣr.

Shauqī, Farīd. 1977. *Malik al-tirsū*. With Īrīs Naẓmī. Cairo: Rūz al-Yūsuf.

Shināwī, Ṭāriq al-. 1991. "*ʿAbd al-Wahhāb: al-mawāqif wa-l-mutanāqiḍāt*." *Rūz al-Yūsuf* 3283 (May 13): 3–7.

Shūsha, Muḥammad al-Sayyid. 1978. *Ruwwād wa-rā'idāt al-sīnimā al-Miṣriyya*. Cairo: Rūz al-Yūsuf.

Siddiq, Muhammad. 1992. "Partial Theory: A Review of Sasson Somekh's *Genre and Language in Modern Arabic Literature*." *al-ʿArabiyya* 25: 97–105.

Somekh, Sasson. 1991. *Genre and Language in Modern Arabic Literature*. Wiesbaden: Otto Harrassowitz.

Spitulnik, Debra. 1993. "Anthropology and Mass Media." *Annual Review of Anthropology*: 293–315.

Springborg, Robert. 1989. *Mubarak's Egypt: Fragmentation of the Political Order*. Boulder: Westview Press.

Starrett, Gregory. 1995. "The Political Economy of Religious Commodities in Cairo." *American Anthropologist* 97, 1 (March): 51–68.

Stetkevych, Jaroslav. 1970. *The Modern Arabic Literary Language: Lexical and Stylistic Developments*. Chicago: University of Chicago Press.

Strachey, Lytton. n.d. [1918]. *Eminent Victorians: Cardinal Manning, Florence Nightingale, Dr. Arnold, General Gordon*. New York: Harcourt, Brace and World, Inc.

Swedenburg, Ted. 1994. "Multiple Struggles and Multiple Sites: New Social Movements in Egypt." Paper presented at the American Anthropological Association Annual Meetings, Atlanta.

Tabārak, Muḥammad. 1991. *Laghz ʿAbd al-Wahhāb*. Cairo: Akhbār al-Yaum.

Ṭamāwī, Aḥmad Ḥusayn al-. 1992. *al-Hilāl: mi'at ʿāmm min al-taḥdīth wa-l-tanwīr*. Cairo: Dār al-Hilāl.

Ṭanāḥī, Aḥmad Ṭāhir al-. 1933. "*Lughat al-ṭarab ka-wasīla li-l-tarbiyya*." *al-Hilāl* (December 1): 217.

Taufīq, Saʿd al-Dīn. 1969. *Qiṣṣat al-sīnimā fī Miṣr*. Cairo: Dār al-Hilāl.

Ṭayyār, Riḍā al-. 1980. *al-Fallāḥ fī al-sīnimā al-ʿArabiyya*. Beirut: al-Mu'assasa al-ʿArabiyya li-l-Dirāsāt wa-al-Nashr.

1981. *al-Madīna fī al-sīnimā al-ʿArabiyya*. Beirut: al-Mu'assasa al-ʿArabiyya li-l-Dirāsāt wa-al-Nashr.

Thompson, John B. 1990. *Ideology and Modern Culture*. Cambridge: Polity Press.

"*al-Tilifizyōn al-Miṣrī*." 1961. *Ākhir sāʿa* 1396 (July 26): 28–29.

Tresilian, David. 1991. "A Crow among Beautiful Birds." *al-Ahram Weekly* 4 (March 21): 14.

Tūnsī, Bayram al-. 1974. *Maqāmāt Bayram al-Tūnsī*. Cairo: Maktabat Madbūlī.

1978. "*Maṣr ḥitta min Urōbba*." *al-Aʿmāl al-kāmila li-Bayram al-Tūnsī*, vol. VI. Cairo: General Egyptian Book Organization.

UNESCO. 1984. *Statistical Yearbook, 1983*. Paris.

Vatikiotis, P. J. 1969. *The Modern History of Egypt*. New York: Praeger.

Wahbī, Yūsuf. n.d. *Awlād al-fuqarā'*. Cairo: Rūz al-Yūsuf.

1973. *ʿIshtu alf ʿām*. Cairo: Dār al-Maʿārif.

Waterbury, John. 1982. "Patterns of Urban Growth and Income Distribution in Egypt." In Gouda Abdel-Khalek and Robert Tignor, eds., *The Political Economy of Income Distribution in Egypt*. New York: Holmes & Meier.

Who's Who in the Arab World. 1990–91. Beirut: Publitec.

Wilmore, John Selden. 1905. *The Spoken Arabic of Egypt: Grammar, Exercises, Vocabularies*. London: D. Nutt.

World Bank. 1978. *Arab Republic of Egypt: Economic Management in a Period of Transition*. 6 vols. Washington, D.C.: International Bank for Reconstruction and Development.

Yūnis, ʿAbd al-Ḥamīd. 1973. "*al-Difāʿ ʿan al-fūlklūr*." In ʿAbd al-Ḥamīd Yūnis, *Difāʿ ʿan al-Fūlklūr*. Cairo: GEBO: 21–28.

Yūsuf, Rōza (Fāṭima al-Yūsuf). 1972. *Dhikrayāt*. Cairo: Rūz al-Yūsuf.

Zakarīyā, ʿIṣām. 1991. "*Aʿdā' ʿAbd al-Wahhāb*." *Rūz al-Yūsuf* 3283 (May 13): 79.

Zughoul, Muhammed Raji. 1980. "Diglossia in Arabic: Investigating Solutions." *Anthropological Linguistics* 22: 201–17.

Select nonprint materials

ʿAbd al-Wahhāb, Muḥammad. 1990. *Sahra muṭawwala maʿ al-mūsīqār Muḥammad ʿAbd al-Wahhāb: al-Gundūl, al-Nahr al-Khālid*. Compact disc. Beirut: Cairophon.

Abī fōʕ ash-shagara (My father is up the tree). 1969. A film directed by Ḥusayn Kamāl, starring ʿAbd al-Ḥalīm Ḥāfiẓ, Mervet Amīn, Nādiyā Luṭfī, and ʿImād Ḥamdī. Cairo: Heliopolis Video Film.

ʿAdawīya, Aḥmad. 1991. "*ʿAdawīya 91*." Cassette tape. Cairo: EMI and Ṣaut al-Ḥubb.

1991. "*ʿAdawiyāt*." Vol. I. Compact disc. Athens, Greece: EMI.

al-ʿAzīma (Resolution). 1939. A film directed by Kamāl Salīm, starring Ḥusayn Sidqī and Fāṭima Rushdī. Cairo: Gamāl al-Laythī.

Batshān, Ḥamdī. 1988. "*'Ēh il-ḥikāya*" (What's the story?). Cassette tape. Cairo: Ṣaut al-Hudā.

Bayn al-aṭlāl (Among the ruins). 1959. A film directed by ʿIzz al-Dīn Dhū al-Faqār, starring Fātin Ḥamāma, ʿImād Ḥamdī, and Ṣāfīya Tharwat. Cairo: Gamāl al-Laythī.

Ḥamayda, ʿAlī. 1988. "*Lōlākī*." Cassette tape. Cairo: Sharikat al-Sharq.

Imam, Husayn al-. 1991. *Kābūryā*. Cassette of songs from the film *Kābūryā*. Cairo: Americana.

ʿInānī, Ṣalāḥ. 1990. *Mi'at ʿām min al-tanwīr* (A hundred years of enlightenment). A poster of his painting issued by the Egyptian Ministry of Culture.

Kābūryā (Crabs). 1990. A film directed by Khayrī Bishāra, starring Aḥmad Zakī and Raghda. Cairo: Hōrus li-l-Vidyō wa-l-Sīnimā.

Khallī bālak min Zūzū (Pay attention to Zuzu). 1972. A film directed by Ḥasan al-Imām, starring Suʿād Ḥusnī and Ḥusayn Fahmī. Cairo: Gamāl al-Laythī.

Lau kunt[i] ghanī (If I were rich). 1942. A film directed by Henrī Barakāt, starring Bishāra Wākīm, Iḥsān al-Gazāyirlī, and ʿAbd al-Fattāḥ al-Qaṣarī. Cairo: Gamāl al-Laythī.

Madrasat al-mushāghibīn (School of troublemakers). Video of a play directed by Galāl al-Sharqāwī, starring ʿĀdil Imām and Saʿīd Ṣāliḥ. Cairo: Heliopolis Video.

Mohamed Abdelwahab: Archives de la Musique Arabe, vol. I, 1920–1925. 1989. Program notes by A. Hachlef. Les Artistes Arabes Associés AAA 011/Club du Disque Arabe CDA 401.

Ragab fōʕ ṣafīḥ sākhin (Ragab on a hot tin roof). 1979. A film directed by Aḥmad Fu'ād, starring ʿĀdil Imām and Saʿīd Ṣāliḥ. Cairo: Gamāl al-Laythī.

Ramaḍān fōʕ al-burkān (Ramadan on the volcano). 1985. A film directed by Aḥmad al-Sabʿāwī, starring ʿĀdil Imām. Cairo: Duqqi Video Film.

"*al-Rāya al-bayḍā*" (The white flag). 1989. A fifteen-part serial broadcast on Egyptian television, directed by Muḥammad Fāḍil, starring Sanā' Gamīl and Gamīl Rātib. Riyāḍ: al-Sharika al-ʿArabiyya li-l-Intāg al-Iʿlāmī.

Shaʿbān taḥt al-ṣifr (Shaban below zero). 1980. A film directed by Henrī Barakāt, starring ʿĀdil Imām and Gamīl Rātib. Cairo: Gamāl al-Laythī.

Sūbirmārkit (Supermarket). 1990. A film directed by Muḥammad Khān, starring Naglā' Fatḥī and Mamdūḥ ʿAbd al-ʿAlīm. Cairo: Film Beach.

"*al-Ustāz*" (The master). 1990. A song on the cassette tape "*Ṣayf sākhin giddan.*" Cairo: al-Gīl Sāūnd.

al-Warda al-bayḍa (The white rose). 1933. A film directed by Muḥammad Karīm, starring Muḥammad ʿAbd al-Wahhāb and Samīra al-Khalūṣī. Cairo: Heliopolis Video Film.

Index

Cambridge Studies in Social and Cultural Anthropology

11 Rethinking Symbolism*
DAN SPERBER. Translated by Alice L. Morton

15 World Conqueror and World Renouncer: A Study of Buddhism and Polity in Thailand against a Historical Background*
S.J. TAMBIAH

16 Outline of a Theory of Practice*
PIERRE BOURDIEU. Translated by Richard Nice

17 Production and Reproduction: A Comparative Study of the Domestic Domain*
JACK GOODY

28 Hunters, Pastoralists and Ranchers: Reindeer Economies and their Transformations*
TIM INGOLD

32 Muslim Society*
ERNEST GELLNER

39 The Fish-People: Linguistic Exogamy and Tukanoan Identity in Northwest Amazonia*
JEAN E. JACKSON

51 Individual and Society in Guiana: A Comparative Study of Amerindian Social Organizations*
PETER RIVIERE

53 Inequality among Brothers: Class and Kinship in South China
RUBIE S. WATSON

54 On Anthropological Knowledge*
DAN SPERBER

55 Tales of the Yanomami: Daily Life in the Venezuelan Forest*
JACQUES LIZOT. Translated by Ernest Simon

56 The Making of Great Men: Male Domination and Power among the New Guinea Baruya*
MAURICE GODELIER. Translated by Ruper Swyer

59 Native Lords of Quito in the Age of the Incas: The

Political Economy of North-Andean Chiefdoms
FRANK SALOMON

60 Culture and Class in Anthropology and History: A Newfoundland Illustration*
GERALD SIDER

61 From Blessing to Violence: History and Ideology in the Circumcision Ritual of the Merina of Madagascar*
MAURICE BLOCH

62 The Huli Response to Illness
STEPHEN FRANKEL

63 Social Inequality in a Northern Portugese Hamlet: Land, Late Marriage, and Bastardy, 1870-1978
BRIAN JUAN O'NEILL

64 Cosmologies in the Making: A Generative Approach to Cultural Variation in Inner New Guinea*
FREDRIK BARTH

65 Kinship and Class in the West Indies: A Genealogical Study of Jamaica and Guyana*
RAYMOND T. SMITH

68 Tradition as Truth and Communication
PASCAL BOYER

70 The Anthropology of Numbers*
THOMAS CRUMP

71 Stealing People's Names: History and Politics in a Sepik River Cosmology
SIMON J. HARRISON

72 The Bedouin of Cyrenaica: Studies in Personal and Corporate Power
EMRYS L. PETERS. Edited by Jack Goody and Emanuel Marx

73 Bartered Brides: Politics, Gender and Marriage in an Afghan Tribal Society
NANCY TAPPER

74 Property, Production and Family in Neckerhausen*
DAVID WARREN SABEAN

75 Fifteen Generations of Bretons: Kinship and Society in Lower Brittany, 1720–1980
MARTINE SEGALEN. Translated by J.A. Underwood

76 Honor and Grace in Anthropology
Edited by J.G. PERISTIANY and JULIAN PITT-RIVERS

77 The Making of the Modern Greek Family: Marriage and Exchange in Nineteenth-Century Athens
PAUL SANT CASSIA with CONSTANTINA BADA

78 Religion and Custom in a Muslim Society: The Berti of Sudan
LADISLAV HOLY

79 Quiet Days in Burgundy: A Study of Local Politics
MARC ABÉLÈS. Translated by Annella McDermott

80 Sacred Void: Spatial Images of Work and Ritual among the Giriama of Kenya
DAVID PARKIN

* *available in paperback*

9 780521 484923